GETTYSBURG'S UNKNOWN SOLDIER

Amos Humiston. This sixth-plate ambrotype by an unknown photographer is his only known portrait from life. *Courtesy of David Humiston Kelley.*

GETTYSBURG'S UNKNOWN SOLDIER

The Life, Death, and Celebrity of Amos Humiston

MARK H. DUNKELMAN

Westport, Connecticut
London

MAR 0 4 '00

Library of Congress Cataloging-in-Publication Data

Dunkelman, Mark H.
  Gettysburg's unknown soldier : the life, death, and celebrity of
Amos Humiston / Mark H. Dunkelman.
    p. cm.
  Includes bibliographical references and index.
  ISBN 0–275–96294–6 (alk. paper)
  1. Humiston, Amos, 1830–1863. 2. Gettysburg (Pa.), Battle of,
1863. 3. United States–History–Civil War, 1861–1865–Unknown
military personnel. 4. Pennsylvania–History–Civil War, 1861–1865–
Unknown military personnel. 5. New York (State)–History–Civil
War, 1861–1865–Unknown military personnel. 6. Soldiers–New York
(State)–Biography. 7. Portville (N.Y.)–Biography. I. Title.
E475.53.D86 1999
973.7'349–dc21   98–40342

British Library Cataloguing in Publication Data is available.

Copyright © 1999 by Mark H. Dunkelman

Library of Congress Catalog Card Number: 98–40342
ISBN: 0–275–96294–6

First published in 1999

Praeger Publishers, 88 Post Road West, Westport, CT 06881
An imprint of Greenwood Publishing Group, Inc.
www.praeger.com

Printed in the United States of America

∞

The paper used in this book complies with the
Permanent Paper Standard issued by the National
Information Standards Organization (Z39.48–1984).

10 9 8 7 6 5 4 3 2 1

For Annette and Karl

Contents

Contents

Contents

Photographic essay follows page 126.

Introduction

HIS HAS BEEN one of the most frequently told tales of one of the most chronicled events in our history, the Battle of Gettysburg. Publicity in the press—savvy editors knew a good story when they read one—broadcast the account across the North a few months after the armies marched out of Pennsylvania. Soon folks throughout the land were wondering about the unknown Union soldier who had been found dead on the battlefield clutching a photograph of his three small children. The melodramatic aspects of the tale played perfect tones on the heartstrings of readers. They could picture the pathetic scene: the lifeless body, the stiffened grip, the unseeing eyes of the father staring at the cherubic faces of his children—his last sight on earth. He was only one of thousands of dead men strewn about Gettysburg's fields, but he was special. Of all the blackened, bloated, contorted corpses on the battleground, his death pose spoke of devotion. In the silence of death, he spoke of love.

With a great wave of empathy, as the powerful wheels of the press spun the story in ever wider circles throughout the North, the nation wondered: Who was he? Whose father was he? Would the children and their mother ever learn of his fate? A month after the first article appeared in the newspapers, the mother and children were traced to their western New York State home, and the fallen soldier was identified as a sergeant of the 154th New York Volunteers. This ending proved to be the beginning of a larger story. A charitable drive to aid the fatherless family inspired a broad appeal, resulting in the establishment of a home for soldiers' orphans in Gettysburg. For several postwar years, the orphanage thrived. Among the residents were the sergeant's widow and children, living just a short walk from their beloved's final resting place in the great Soldiers' National Cemetery.

That in brief is the story of Amos Humiston, as it has been told and retold over the decades. Virtually without exception, from the earliest tellings to those of recent years, the tale begins on the battlefield, with Amos Humiston a corpse. "After the Battle of Gettysburg" is the typical opening line of more than one account. He was probably the best-known common soldier and most heralded enlisted man to emerge in the lore of the battle, but his fame centered on the heart-rending circumstances of his death. Once he was identified, the public seemed content; they knew then who Amos Humiston was. His death had made him famous, but it had rendered his life an afterthought. And so, in the vast annals of the Civil War, Amos Humiston has reappeared again and again as a dead man, fixed by time and rigor mortis on the Gettysburg battleground, his children's picture in his hand. Like his contemporaries, well might we wonder: Who was he?

Fate allotted Amos Humiston thirty-three years, two months, and five days of life before concealing him briefly in death and then resurrecting him as a celebrity. Most of those years are clouded by obscurity, like the lives of so many of our common folk ancestors. Because his fame focused on his death, accounts of Amos's life were seldom included when his story was first told. Most writers were content merely to identify him by name, and only a couple of them bothered to sum up his years in a few sentences. From those scant sources, we know the landmarks of his days and times, but the details have long since been dimmed by the passing decades. Much of Amos Humiston's life remains shadowed by conjecture and blurred by presumption.

In bright contrast, the several years of Amos's two great adventures—his lengthy whaling voyage and his Civil War service—have been documented in detail, offering luminous pictures of those tumultuous periods of his life. Most significant, surviving letters he wrote during the war enable us to hear him for the first time. During the publicity surrounding his discovery, Amos was mute. Only one newspaper published a single quote of a solitary sentence he once supposedly said. But in his letters, we can eavesdrop on his voice, hear him express his cares and concerns, and hearken to the tenor of his personality. We learn about the young family he loved so much but left behind; their voices echo in the background of his written responses and admonitions.

We find that Amos was a determined, duty-bound soldier, ready and willing to fight for the Union, while at the same time wishing in the worst way that he was at home instead of in the army in Virginia. We find a dedicated, steady friend, a favorite of his regimental comrades. We find a lucky escapee from a devastating battle, spared by an accident of velocity and geometry to live and fight another time. But above all, we find a soldier who first and foremost was a devoted, loving husband and father, a man who seems fitted to his fate. Thus a portrait emerges of the life preceding the death that made Amos Humiston famous. It is right to remember the man, as generations have remembered him, for his tender, dying gesture. It is right, too, to remember the man not only as he expired but as he lived and loved.

Amos Humiston was transfigured by his dying act of affection into an emblem of devotion. His tale is timeless. Civil War America, with a great outpouring of sympathy, was inspired by its pathos to create a great good. Ensuing generations regularly recalled it, as moved by its sentiment as their ancestors had been. We too find it touches our hearts. We find it to be a fable of the power of love.

CHAPTER 1

Amos

HUMBERSTON IS AN old surname in England, derived from the river Humber, which meets the North Sea at Spurn Head. In America, the name underwent changes; the early spelling "Humberston" or "Humerson" gradually transmuted to "Humaston," and by the nineteenth century was usually recorded as "Humiston." The Humberstons lived in Norfolk and Hertfordshire, and it was from there that Henry Humiston, the progenitor of the family in America, emigrated circa 1644. He settled in the fledgling community of New Haven, married Joane Walker in 1651, fathered four boys and a girl, and died in 1663. So the first Humiston in America passed away leaving young children, a circumstance that would afflict the family in several later generations before Amos Humiston became the most celebrated instance.[1]

Three of Henry Humiston's sons are known to have had sons of their own, but through which line the next few generations are to be traced is unknown. Bisley Humiston was the next certain forefather of Amos, according to a note in a family Bible. Little is known about Bisley or his son, James. Around 1800 James Humiston and his wife, Rachel Boice, were living in her home town of Hillsdale, New York, in the Taconic Mountains near the Massachusetts border.[2] Five children had blessed their union when James died. (He was said to have died while serving in the army, although no evidence has been found to support that claim.)[3] On the death of James, his youngest child, Ambrose, was adopted by the neighboring Willoughby family. The boy, who was born about 1804, was raised as Ambrose Willoughby, but eventually retook his ancestral name, reportedly at the urging of his two older Humiston brothers.[4]

Ambrose Humiston continued the family's westward migration, moving as a young man to Tioga County in central New York State. By 1830 he had a family and was living in the town of Owego, at the confluence of the Susquehanna River and Owego Creek. His wife, the former Mary Bronson, was about the same age as Ambrose.[5] The couple had four children, each apparently born about a year apart: Lois Ann, Morris, Maria, and Amos, who was born in Owego on April 26, 1830, and probably named after his maternal grandfather.[6]

Amos Humiston grew up in modest circumstances. A state census taker surveyed Owego in 1835 and recorded the family's wealth: one cow, one hog, and sixteen yards of flannel and other woolen cloth, spun and woven by Mary.[7]

Death twice devastated the Humistons during Amos's boyhood. First, at age six or seven, he lost his father. Ambrose Humiston died in 1837, in his thirties, and was buried in Owego. His four children then underwent a dislocation when their widowed mother wed Philander Boice, a first cousin of her late husband and close friend of the bereaved family. (The couple eventually had a son, William Almanso Boice, but it is supposed this half-brother of Amos Humiston died young. None of the Humiston descendants remembered him.) A fatal tragedy next took one of Amos's sisters. At an unknown date, young Maria Humiston drowned while crossing a mill pond, an accident apparently witnessed by her stepfather, who was working at the mill.[8]

Mary Bronson Humiston Boice died on November 26, 1851; her headstone in the Tioga County town of Candor, about a dozen miles north of Owego, states she was aged forty-seven years, seven months, and twenty-four days. Amos Humiston was not able to visit his mother during her last days. By then, he was half a world away, at a place she had probably never heard of.[9]

Owego must have seemed like a big place to Amos as he grew up there, and it grew apace with the boy. The township's population was about three thousand when he was born in 1830; by the time he turned fifteen, it had more than doubled. Many of those people were centered in the village of Owego, on the north bank of the Susquehanna. During Amos's boyhood, Owego became the permanent seat of Tioga County, and home to an abolition society and a temperance movement. A railroad linking the village to Ithaca was completed in 1833; its tracks ran through the center of Owego, passed the county courthouse, and terminated at the riverbank. If Amos climbed a nearby hill, his entire home town was visible in a splendid panorama: a patchwork of fields and woods on the distant hazy hills; the broad, glistening ribbon of the Susquehanna, spanned by a lengthy toll bridge; and the wide, flat plain north of the river, crisscrossed by the streets of the village and row after row of buildings, stitched by the tracks of the railroad, and punctuated by the spires of seven churches and the courthouse.

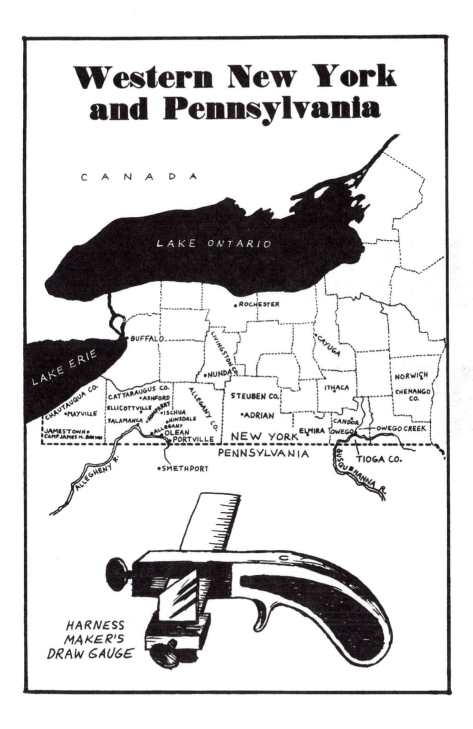

Western New York and Pennsylvania

CANADA

LAKE ONTARIO

LAKE ERIE

ROCHESTER

BUFFALO

LIVINGSTON CO.

CAYUGA

NUNDA

NORWICH

CHAUTAUQUA CO.

CATTARAUGUS CO.

ASHFORD

ALLEGANY CO.

STEUBEN CO.

ITHACA

CHENANGO CO.

MAYVILLE

ELLICOTTVILLE

HUMPHREY

ISCHUA

ADRIAN

SALAMANCA

HINSDALE

ALLEGANY

CANDOR

JAMESTOWN

OLEAN

ELMIRA

OWEGO

OWEGO CREEK

CAMP JAMES M. BROWN

PORTVILLE

NEW YORK

PENNSYLVANIA

TIOGA CO.

ALLEGHENY R.

SMETHPORT

SUSQUEHANNA R.

HARNESS
MAKER'S
DRAW GAUGE

That panorama was dramatically and drastically altered early on a September morning in 1849, when a fire broke out in the Sons of Temperance hall and swept through the business district. The conflagration destroyed more than a hundred buildings and part of the toll bridge, leaving most of the village's commercial property in ashes. Only three stores were left standing. Despite the enormity of the disaster, Owego was rapidly rebuilt. Its recovery was hastened by another milestone in its history, which occurred within months of the fire: the Erie Railroad was completed to the village, linking it to New York City and, as construction continued, to points west.[10]

Years before the great fire, Amos attended the common school in his neighborhood and learned the rudiments of arithmetic, reading, and writing, although his spelling remained somewhat erratic for the rest of his life.[11] Those several terms were the sum total of his formal learning; he did not attend the Owego Academy, the educational pathway to one of the professions. Instead, he and his older brother, Morris, learned a trade. A Tioga County harness shop, redolent of leather and harness oil, was the Humiston brothers' school for several years.[12]

It seems likely that the Humiston brothers apprenticed to a harness maker around the time they turned fifteen, which for Amos occurred in 1845. It also seems likely that Amos remained an apprentice in a Tioga County harness shop until he reached his twentieth birthday, in 1850. Amos and Morris perhaps were apprenticed to the same harness maker, and it is possible that they were joined by a neighbor boy, three years older than Amos, an Owego native named George W. Lillie.[13]

It took years of patient study and practice for an apprentice to master the complexities of harness making. A relatively simple buggy harness consisted of about a dozen main components, and each of those components included a number of individual parts: straps, bands, saddle, collar, and hardware. What Amos and Morris had seen before as a mere bridle, they came to see as a sum of its parts: brow band and nose band, cheek straps and blinds, bit and head stall, throat latch and winker. The brothers learned to differentiate the various types of harnesses, bridles, and bits, and the seemingly endless variations of each. They studied the several styles of halters and learned about harnesses used to break horses: the bitting harness, used to accustom a horse to the bit, and the dumb jockey, used to acquaint a horse with the position of a rider's hands. Riding saddles were a separate field of study, with wooden saddle trees and fabric girths and surcingles to be mastered, in addition to the skirts and other leather parts, and another complex assortment of hardware. Like harnesses, saddles were made in extensive varieties of many basic kinds.

Not all of the products of a harness shop were horse equipment, the

Humiston brothers learned. A harness maker occasionally was called on to assemble a harness for a pony or a goat, and traditionally produced miscellaneous items as a sideline: trunks, suitcases, dog collars and muzzles, holsters, and other leather goods.

Three main steps—cutting, finishing, and stitching the leather—were involved in making harnesses or saddles. Cutting leather demanded great care: the ability to get the most useable material from a tanned cowhide with the least amount of waste could mean the difference between profit and loss for a harness maker. Amos and Morris learned to use a draw gauge to cut straps and other straight-edged pieces from the hide. Round or head knives, with half-circle blades, were used to cut curved pieces in exact arcs. Square point knives and cap knives saw occasional use. Various punches were used to round off strap ends and cut slots and perforations. Wielding pinking irons or scalloping carriages of various shapes, Amos and Morris edged pieces with a sawtooth pattern. The brothers quickly learned the importance of keeping their knives and cutters sharp, and they could frequently be found at the whetstone. They also soon became aware of dangers inherent in the trade. Slips were inevitable when applying pressure to sharp tools; harness makers were prone to punctures and lacerations, and their hands were commonly scarred.

Finishing required another set of implements and tools. The Humistons smoothed leather surfaces with slickers made of glass or lignum vitae, a tropical hardwood. They wet edges, beveled them with edge tools, and dyed them to match the face of the leather. They indented decorative creases on straps and bands with metal or wood creasers. They folded and stitched one strap around another, trimmed off any excess with an edger or knife, wet it thoroughly, and pulled it through a rounder—an iron form perforated with different sizes of circles—to make perfectly round lengths of leather. They used baton-like steel stuffers to pack cruppers with flax seed or hair. They embossed wet leather with punches, hand wheels, and brass stamps for fancy work. They carefully moved pricking wheels over pieces about to be stitched, puncturing the leather with a series of evenly spaced indentations to mark where stitches were to be made.

While Morris continued cutting or finishing, Amos often left the cluttered workbench for the stitching horse. At the front of that four-legged wooden stool protruded two curved wooden jaws, capable of clamping pieces of leather like a vise, at a comfortable height for the harness maker to work while seated on the back of the bench. Amos positioned the leather in the tightened jaws, pierced each pricking-wheel mark with an awl, waxed a length of linen thread with beeswax, threaded two needles, and began to stitch. He worked the needles back and forth, from side to side, usually making about eight stitches per inch—more for finer work, fewer for heavy harnesses. When he had traversed the width of the stitching horse's jaws, he unlatched them, pulled the leather to its next segment, refastened the jaws, and repeated the process. And so, piece by piece, harness was stitched together: strap to strap, strap to hardware, strap to breeching, band, and saddle. Hesitant at first, ever more confident with practice, Amos and Morris eventually worked rapidly and proficiently at the stitching horse. In time, they developed enough dexterity to hold an awl while they stitched, ready to pierce more holes and continue to stitch without having to put down or pick up the tool or needles.

A harness maker signed his completed work by using a punch or stamp to emboss his name in the leather. The final step was to oil the harness, coating the leather with a protective finish. Oiling was usually done by hand or with a paintbrush, but some harness makers used a special device—a galvanized barrel of oil into which a wire basket holding the leather was dipped.

An accomplished harness maker was capable of turning out a hand-stitched light harness for a single horse in about a hundred hours of work, but producing one harness from start to finish without interruption never happened. Usually several new harnesses and saddles were in progress at once, and there was always repair work to be done, an indispensable part of a harness maker's business.

Although mass production by big city firms was gaining an increasing share of the industry when the Humiston brothers learned the trade, independent harness shops remained dominant in small town America, and the small town harness maker primarily worked by hand. Large saddle and harness tool manufacturers offered a few hand-cranked machines—skivers, creasers, hole punchers—to ease some tasks, but hand tools were the mainstay of the shop. The finished products of skilled independent harness makers were examples of precise and painstaking handicraft, things of both utility and beauty. With its gleaming leather, shining hardware, elaborate stitching, and exact fit, a new harness was proof of the consummate craftsmanship of its maker.[14]

After years of work and study, the Humiston brothers were ready to strike off on their own, to open their own shop, to stamp the harnesses they made with their own names. The two reacted to that prospect in entirely different ways. On completing his apprenticeship at age twenty, Morris Humiston established a harness and saddle shop in Candor. He opened for business in 1848, and within a few years was training an apprentice of his own, a boy named Jerome Richardson.[15]

Amos Humiston pondered his future when he finished his apprenticeship. Ahead of him stretched a harness maker's lifetime: day after day of cutting, finishing, and stitching leather, year after year of intricate labor at the workbench and stitching horse. Apparently that vision of the future was not entirely agreeable to him. He decided to do something else—something totally unrelated to the trade he had spent years learning. He turned his back on the harness shop, left Tioga County for the seacoast, and embarked on a new career.

NOTES

1. Wallace Dwight Humiston, "Henry Humiston—Emigrated from England in 1644," *Connecticut Magazine* 11 (1907): 161–162.

2. David Humiston Kelley (hereafter DHK), "Notes on One Branch of the HUMISTON Family," typescript, 1986. The name Boice is variously spelled Boyce, Boise, or Boyes.

3. DHK, "Notes on the HUMISTON Family"; DHK to Laura Jopling, May 29, 1989, Portville Historical and Preservation Society (hereafter PHPS); H. S Humiston to Dear cousin, January 30, 1897, courtesy of DHK; Lois Ann (Humiston) Goodwin to My Dear neice [*sic*] Alice, September 8, 1896, courtesy of DHK; New York (State) Bureau of Military Statistics, *First Annual Report of the Chief of the Bureau of Military Statistics* (n.p., 1864), p. 32. The latter declared Amos inherited "the blood of his grandfather, who was killed in the service of his country during the war of 1812." Humiston family records indicate, however, that James Humiston died before then, one source suggesting 1801, another 1806. Lois Ann Humiston, in the letter cited above, said of her paternal grandfather, James, "He must have been a soldier in the revolution, but did not die there. I never thought him any thing but a common soldier." There is no evidence that Amos's maternal grandfather, Amos Bronson, fought in the War of 1812, and he certainly did not die then. DHK speculates the dead grandfather was Elisha Willoughby, who was possibly the person who adopted Amos's father, Ambrose Humiston. Willoughby was serving in the army when he died in camp in June 1813. DHK, letters to the author of March 15, 1990 and February 8, 1996.

4. Alice E. Humiston to Dear Cousin, August 15, 1896, courtesy of DHK.

5. DHK, "Notes on the HUMISTON Family." The name Bronson sometimes appears as Brunson.

6. Ibid. Family records state Amos Humiston's sister Lois Ann was born at Apalachin, Tioga County, in 1828; Maria's date and place of birth are unknown. Amos's brother, Morris, was born in Onondaga County, New York, in 1829. New York State censuses for the town of Candor, Tioga County Historical Society, 1855, 1865.

7. New York State Census, town of Owego, 1835. The Humiston household included three unmarried females under age sixteen; who the third girl was is unknown.

8. Lois Ann (Humiston) Goodwin to My Dear neice [*sic*] Alice, September 8, 1896. Alice E. Humiston to Dear Cousin, August 27, 1896, courtesy of DHK; DHK, "Notes on the HUMISTON Family."

9. DHK, "Notes on the HUMISTON Family."

10. Henry B. Pierce and D. Hamilton Hurd, *History of Tioga, Chemung, Tompkins, and Schuyler Counties, New York* (Philadelphia: Everts & Ensign, 1879), pp. 72, 82, 87, 156, 171–183.

11. New York (State) Bureau of Military Statistics, *First Annual Report*, p. 32. Amos's Civil War letters offer examples of his spelling peculiarities. He also usually ignored the rules of punctuation and capitalization when he wrote, like many others of his generation.

12. Ibid.; U.S. Census for the town of Candor, Tioga County Historical Society, 1850; DHK, "Notes on the HUMISTON Family."

13. New York State Census, town of Owego, 1835; obituary, George Washington Lillie, *Owego Gazette*, September 12, 1918, 2.

14. This account of harness making and saddlery is based on an undated catalog of the Smith-Worthington Company, New York; C. S. Osborne & Company's 1897 catalog of saddle and harness tools; John C. Simonds, *The Leather Crafter's Bible* (Columbiana, Ohio: Sitler The Printer, 1983), passim; and interviews with David S. LaSalle of the LaSalle Harness Company, North Scituate, R.I., December 5, 1995 and March 5, 1996.

15. 1850 U.S. and 1855 New York State censuses, town of Candor.

CHAPTER 2

A Green Hand Sails from New Bedford

ON NOVEMBER 28, 1850, Amos Humiston signed a whaleman's shipping paper in New Bedford, Massachusetts, committing himself to sail as a crewman aboard the whaleship *Harrison*, soon to leave home port on a voyage to the Pacific Ocean. He was now part of one of the most colorful, dangerous, adventurous, and notorious enterprises in the United States.[1]

American whaling was in the midst of its golden era when Amos entered the industry, and New Bedford was its capital. More than six hundred whaleships from American ports roamed the seas in an average year at midcentury, harvesting whale products worth eight million dollars, and almost half of the fleet was outfitted in New Bedford. In 1850, when Amos Humiston went to sea, New Bedford was home port to 237 whaleships. That year, 117 whaleships, carrying 2,814 men, sailed from New Bedford; most of the others were already roving the world's oceans. With the production of other Massachusetts ports added to New Bedford's prodigious output, whaling ranked as the Bay State's third largest industry, behind the manufacture of shoes and cotton.[2]

Three species were the main prey of the New Bedford whalemen. Sperm whales—high-spirited and pugnacious, with a long lower jaw equipped with about fifty teeth to tear apart their favorite food, squid—were hunted in the tropical and subtropical waters of the Pacific, Indian, and Atlantic oceans. Right whales—generally sluggish and noncombative—were found in vast areas of the temperate zones of the world's seas. Bowhead whales—the most timid of the trio, and consequently hardest to capture—swam in the frigid North: the Bering Sea, the Sea of Okhotsk, and the Arctic Ocean—waters the New Bedford whalemen had only recently begun to hunt.[3]

Five important products were wrested by the whalemen from the carcasses of their victims. Two types of oil were widely used as illuminants and lubricants. Found in its purest state in the head of sperm whales, sperm oil was the best standard illuminant available. Whale oil, rendered from the thicker blubber of right and bowhead whales, was a heavier, cruder, and cheaper oil. Spermaceti, a spongy substance extracted from the head of sperm whales, was used in the manufacture of the highest-grade candles. *Whalebone* was the commercial term for baleen. Light, strong, and flexible, whalebone could be bent to any shape when heated; it was used in making corsets, hoops, whips, umbrellas, and numerous other articles. Ambergris, the most valuable whale product, was also the rarest. A waxy gray matter infrequently found in sperm whales, ambergris was used in making perfume and was said to possess medicinal (and aphrodisiacal) qualities.[4]

Whaling's economic benefits to New Bedford extended far beyond the city's waterfront. Many of the city's twenty thousand inhabitants depended on support industries for their livelihood. They built and repaired whaleships; manufactured the iron weapons (collectively called whalecraft) and other gear used in whaleboats; refined whale oil and made candles; crafted and sold nautical instruments, charts, and books; and worked in ropewalks, sail lofts, and cooperages. They baked biscuits, salted beef, and prepared other provisions for whaling voyages. They made clothing to stock the ship's store, or "slop chest," aboard whalers. They outfitted whalemen, provided them with room and board, and catered to crewmen in barrooms and brothels.[5]

The mix of people in the world's greatest whaling port was unlike anything Amos had ever seen. Bearded and tattooed old salts reeled in and out of grog shops and whorehouses under the disapproving glare of somberly clad Quakers and stern-faced puritans. There were Americans from every port in the land, country bumpkins from distant farms, Gay Head Indians from Martha's Vineyard, Portuguese and mulattoes from the Azores and Cape Verde Islands, Maoris from New Zealand, Kanakas from the Sandwich Islands, and blacks from the United States, Africa, and the West Indies. Adventurous young men like Amos, fresh from inland farms or workshops, mingled in boardinghouses with all sorts of human flotsam—drunks, vagrants, crooks, and convicts.[6]

How did Amos Humiston come to find himself in New Bedford, about to board a whaleship for a voyage of several years? As they had since the beginning of the industry, New Englanders dominated whaling crews in 1850. But "runners" for shipping agents were traversing the United States to recruit additional whalemen, and they met with the most success in the northeastern states. Men from that part of the country were an increasingly larger presence aboard whaleships. Amos was probably convinced to become a whaleman by a runner passing through Owego. He could have

A Green Hand Sails from New Bedford

been easily swayed by a runner's practiced and persuasive lies and exaggerations about the constant thrills and ample rewards of whaling. A future consisting of dreary years in a harness shop would have made a sorry comparison to the possibilities promised by a get-rich-quick whaling voyage. He could continue to sit at a stitching horse, Amos pondered—or he could sail 'round the Horn, and see the world![7]

He was now in the clutches of that segment of the whaling industry known collectively as "landsharks"—the shipping agents, boardinghouse keepers, and outfitters who procured and provided for the recruits headed onto whaleships, and the grog sellers, brothel keepers, pimps, and prostitutes who preyed on them. The shipping agent who recruited Amos, N. S. Ellis of New Bedford, was most likely paid between eight and ten dollars for providing the new man to the *Harrison*. In New Bedford, Ellis sent Amos to a sailors' boardinghouse, where he lodged until the *Harrison* sailed. Next to get his hands on Amos was an outfitter, a merchant whose store was crammed with supplies regularly sold to whalemen before sailing. The outfitter provided Amos with a cheap pine sea chest stocked with shoddy clothing, foul weather gear, bedding, eating utensils, and other necessities. Amos was probably charged about seventy-five dollars for his outfit, but chances are the inferior goods were worth as little as a third of that amount. The outfitter's bill would be delivered to the ship's agent after the *Harrison* sailed, to be charged to Amos's account—and to accrue interest.[8]

The *Harrison*'s ship's agent was Gilbert Hatheway, a New Bedford merchant who was administering preparations to sail and would keep accounts of the voyage at his Commercial Wharf counting house. Hatheway's 6/32 share in the ship, purchased at auction in October 1850 after the *Harrison* returned to New Bedford after an unsuccessful voyage, made him the managing owner of the *Harrison*. The remaining shares were divided among a dozen other co-owners, most of them New Bedford tradesmen. The *Harrison* would continue in the whaling business, Hatheway assured the *Whalemen's Shipping List and Merchants' Transcript*, the New Bedford trade newspaper, and he immediately began to prepare the ship for a voyage. Only eight days after purchasing his shares, on November 5, Hatheway signed his name at the head of the same whalemen's shipping paper Amos Humiston would sign later that month. He then began to assemble officers and crew to man the ship. The same day that Gilbert Hatheway signed the shipping paper, the man who would command the *Harrison* as master also signed. He was Captain John Keen Hatheway, Gilbert's brother.[9]

Amos Humiston and the rest of the crew of the *Harrison* were fortunate to have the experienced John Hatheway as master. He first went to sea in 1828 at age thirteen, as cook aboard a sloop. His first voyage aboard a whaleship was as a boatsteerer, his second as a mate, and his third—from 1840 to 1842, on the New Bedford ship *Fenelon*—as master. Hatheway made a second voyage as captain of the *Fenelon*, from 1842 to 1844; both times he returned to New Bedford with a ship full of oil. As master of the New Bedford bark *Cowper*, Hatheway filled his ship yet again, this time on a voyage to the Indian Ocean and Northwest Coast whaling grounds from 1845 to 1848. "As a shipmaster," the *New Bedford Daily Mercury* later observed of Captain Hatheway, "he was a man of great prudence, energy and ability." He certainly had the confidence of the *Harrison*'s owners, four of whom had profited, as co-owners of the *Fenelon* and *Cowper*, from his previous successful voyages.[10]

Like about half of the masters of New Bedford whaling vessels, Captain Hatheway was an employee, not a part owner. His reward, like the rest of the crew's, would come in the form of a share of the final profits of the voyage—an allotment called a "lay." In the traditional method of paying whaling crews, officers and skilled artisans took "short lays," or the largest shares; other crewmen took smaller shares in "long lays." By the great age of American whaling, a fairly standard range of lays had evolved, and the lays of the officers and crew of the *Harrison* fell within the typical scope. As master, Captain Hatheway took the shortest lay of all, 1/14.[11]

During the rest of November and early December, the Hatheway brothers signed up a full crew for the upcoming voyage. Among them were four mates, four boatsteerers, three ordinary seamen, a cooper, a steward, and a cook, with lays ranging from 1/24 for the first mate to 1/175 for the ordinary seamen. Thirteen men in addition to Amos Humiston signed on as green hands—men who had never been to sea—at a lay of 1/185. Two more green hands were also categorized as "boys"; they would serve a sort of whaling apprenticeship and were assigned the longest lays of all, 1/225.[12]

The crew assembled to man the *Harrison* was in all regards typical for the era: white, literate, young Americans almost exclusively from the northeastern states, about half of them inexperienced. All were white men but one—an Indian, Fourth Mate William H. Duffee. Only three of the thirty-one were illiterate, fewer than the 20 to 25 percent usually found on whaleships in 1850. Sixteen of the men had never been to sea. The average age of the foremast hands—the green hands and seamen—was twenty-two years. About two-fifths of the men were from coastal New England towns; the rest, like Amos, came from inland communities of seven states.[13]

Amos spent at least two weeks in New Bedford before the *Harrison* sailed, plenty of time for him to explore the city and absorb the atmosphere. In the maze of narrow streets climbing the hill, away from the commercial bustle of the waterfront, he found quiet and respectable residential neighborhoods, with neat and well-built houses. Opportunities to indulge in debauchery also were to be found. One notorious street near the waterfront was crowded with houses of ill repute, and liquor was widely available in numerous taverns. At the crest of the hill stood an outpost of godliness, the Seamen's Bethel, founded in 1830 by some of the city's leading citizens to fight for the virtues and rights of whalemen. Not far from the chapel stood the imposing granite U.S. Custom House. Amos and five of his soon-to-be shipmates visited the office of the collector of customs there on December 5 to obtain their protection papers: a printed form, stamped and signed by the collector, that certified they were American citizens and therefore entitled to "sufficient subsistence" and passage home at government expense if they became destitute or were discharged in a foreign port when their ship was sold. Amos's protection paper included a physical description. He was five feet six and three-quarter inches tall, with a dark complexion, dark hair, and black eyes. Although his age was recorded as twenty-one, he actually was twenty.[14]

During their wait to sail, Amos and his fellow green hands must have been drawn repeatedly to the waterfront, where a forest of masts spiked the sky and endless rows of casks cluttered the wharves. Everywhere on the waterfront there was activity: men loading, unloading, and repairing ships, coopering and rolling casks, and carting bundles of whalebone. Amid the commotion, Amos and the others found the *Harrison*, their future home.

A typical whaleship, the *Harrison*'s heavy construction stressed strength and seaworthiness over speed and graceful lines. Built in 1841 at Rochester, Massachusetts (the Hatheway brothers' home town), the *Harrison* was approximately 107 feet in length, 28 feet in breadth, and 14 feet in depth, and was registered at 371 tons. She had two decks, three masts, and a square stern. Jutting from the bow was a bust figurehead of her namesake, William Henry Harrison, whose death from pneumonia after only one month in office as president of the United States occurred during the building of the ship. From a mast waved the flag of Gilbert Hatheway, Agent—a white banner with bands of red on top and bottom, and a big, blue "H" in the center.[15]

Ever since the ship's purchase by Gilbert Hatheway and his partners in October, the *Harrison* had been in the care of a shipkeeper, who had complete control of the vessel until she was ready to return to sea. She had been "hoved down"—tilted to one side—so her bottom could be caulked, tarred, sheathed, and covered in copper if necessary. After putting her back on an even keel, the work crew had tended to the topsides and rigging. A mason had built a brick furnace on deck—the tryworks, Amos was told it was called. When the repairing and refurbishing were completed, stevedores began the task of loading the ship. Cask after cask after cask—hundreds of sturdy white oak casks—were brought aboard and stowed in the hold. There were empty casks and casks full of supplies, which when emptied would be filled (everyone hoped) with oil. Practically everything needed aboard the *Harrison*—provisions, water, sails, whalecraft, and slop chest supplies—came onto the ship in casks. Materials for making more casks— staves, heads, and iron hoops—were carried aboard in casks.[16]

Manifests signed on December 10 by Agent Gilbert Hatheway and Captain John K. Hatheway noted $20,000 worth of provisions and stores had been loaded aboard the ship. With a full crew ready to board her, the *Harrison* was ready to make a whaling voyage.[17]

Thursday, December 12, 1850, dawned in New Bedford with light breezes and good weather. Early that morning, Amos Humiston and his fellow crewmen were herded aboard the *Harrison*, some of them no doubt miserable with hangovers, and Captain Hatheway and the mates began issuing orders. The green hands were entirely ignorant of how to respond to those orders, so the master and his officers and the veteran seamen had to show them what to do.

At 8 A.M. the ship weighed anchor; a tugboat towed her away from the wharf and down the Acushnet River, and at 10 A.M. the *Harrison* made sail for the sea. For the first time, Amos and his fellow green hands felt the pitch and sway of a wind-propelled vessel beneath their feet. The rocking became more pronounced around noon, when the ship encountered some squalls. Nauseated by the unfamiliar motion, many of the miserable green hands were soon retching. Others experienced the sheer terror of vertigo when they made their first trip aloft into the high rigging on the rolling ship, or were posted as lookouts in iron hoops atop the lofty, waving foremast and mainmast. And if they faltered when ordered to perform a task, they quite possibly were cursed or swatted by a mate. Altogether, their first experiences aboard ship were enough to make the wretched, dejected, and seasick green hands think they had made a horrible mistake in becoming whalemen.

During the first day or two out, Captain Hatheway called the entire crew aft and made a short speech, after which the men were divided into two watches. First Mate Joseph A. Slocum and Second Mate Daniel L. F. Swift, who would act as watch headers, made alternate choices until all the crewmen were picked. For the rest of the voyage, one watch would always be on deck while the other was off duty—unless the sails had to be trimmed in rough weather, or there were whales to chase, in which cases all hands would be called to work. Cooper James Sadler, cook James L. Jenison, and steward Daniel Turner were exempt from the watches; their work was basically confined to the daytime hours. Those three would be left on board

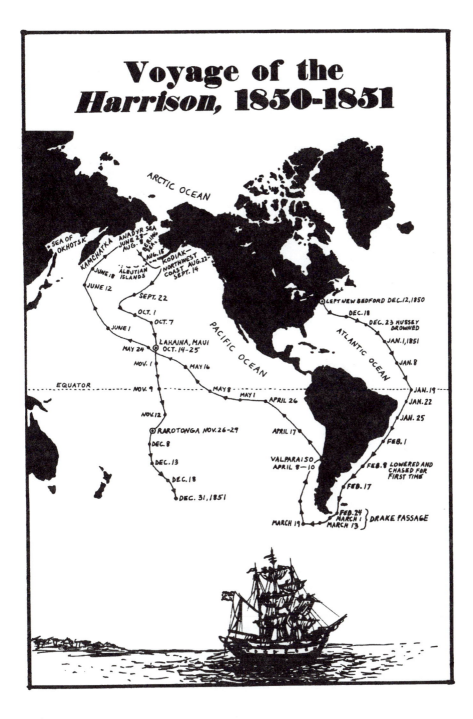

Voyage of the
Harrison, 1850-1851

ARCTIC OCEAN

SEA OF OKHOTSK

KAMCHATKA

ANADYR SEA
JUNE 29
AUG. 8

BERING

AUG. 15

KODIAK–
NORTHWEST
COAST AUG.22–
SEPT. 14

JUNE 18
ALEUTIAN
ISLANDS

JUNE 12

SEPT. 22

LEFT NEW BEDFORD DEC. 12, 1850

DEC. 18

DEC. 23 HUSSEY
DROWNED

OCT. 1

OCT. 7

JUNE 1

PACIFIC OCEAN

ATLANTIC OCEAN

JAN. 1, 1851

LAHAINA, MAUI
OCT. 14-25

MAY 24

NOV. 1

MAY 16

JAN. 8

EQUATOR

NOV. 9

MAY 8

MAY 1

APRIL 26

JAN. 19

JAN. 22

NOV. 12

JAN. 25

RAROTONGA NOV. 26-29

APRIL 17

FEB. 1

DEC. 8

VALPARAISO
APRIL 8–10

FEB. 8 LOWERED AND
CHASED FOR
FIRST TIME

DEC. 13

DEC. 18

FEB. 17

DEC. 31, 1851

FEB. 24
MARCH 1 } DRAKE PASSAGE
MARCH 13

MARCH 19

the *Harrison* as "shipkeepers" when the whaleboats were lowered for the chase, assisted quite possibly by seaman and second cooper David Hussey and the two boys, Frederick Burnham and Abner F. Barstow. Choosing in order of rank, the officers divided the rest of the men into crews for the four whaleboats (the starboard, larboard, waist, and bow boats). Each officer chose one of the four boatsteerers and four hands to fill his boat crew.[18]

Some time that first day or night, when his watch was off duty, Amos made his way to a hatch on the main deck and climbed down a ladder to the forecastle. He must have been dismayed when he first saw the place he would call home for the next few years. A double tier of bunks, crudely built of rough planks, bent along both curves of the ship's bow. The ceiling formed by the main deck was low, and the air in the damp, cramped space was foul with a vile, mingled stench of tobacco smoke, bad food, and vomit. The only source of ventilation and natural light, the hatch, was kept closed against the cold night. The place was black with filth and slime, and crawling with vermin. The men's sea chests took up most of the deck space, and in the narrow places where Amos was able to walk between them, he slipped on a thick scum of vomit, food scraps, spilled coffee, and spit tobacco juice.

For several weeks, as the *Harrison* marked a southeasterly course toward the mid-Atlantic, Amos and his fellow green hands received an intensive education in seamanship and the techniques of whaling, under the supervision of Captain Hatheway and the mates. They absorbed nautical lingo, learning the names of myriad lines, sails, parts of the ship, pieces of equipment, and shipboard routines and procedures. They became familiar with elements of navigation, and learned the points of the compass. They regularly practiced the constant tasks of working the ship: reefing, furling, and shaking out sails; posting lookouts at the mastheads; manning the wheel; and scrubbing the decks after hauling the washwater up in large canvas buckets lowered over the side. The crew prepared intensively for the day when they would first lower the boats and chase whales. They broke gear out of casks and sharpened the iron weapons of their war against whales: harpoons, lances, spades, and knives. The whaleboats were readied for action. The men overhauled the boats' sails, oars and paddles, and precisely coiled great lengths of whaleline in tubs. On calm days, the four boats were lowered from their davits into the sea, and the green hands were taught the procedures of chasing and capturing whales. Every night, the impatient foremast hands wondered if the morrow would bring their first real chase.[19]

Less than two weeks after leaving New Bedford, the crew of the *Harrison* learned a sobering lesson in the importance of constant vigilance aboard ship. At 5:30 in the afternoon of December 23, David Hussey fell overboard, and before his shipmates could lower a boat and reach him, he disappeared beneath the waves. That night the green hands were introduced to a somber custom when the contents of Hussey's sea chest were auctioned off to the crew. The men paid high prices for the stuff, knowing that Captain Hatheway would present the proceeds to the deceased's family.[20]

Christmas came two days after Hussey drowned. Some masters allowed a ration of whiskey or rum to be issued to the crew on holidays, but in the 1840s alcohol use aboard whaleships had steadily declined as a result of the temperance movement, and a majority of ships were dry. During the voyage of the *Harrison*, Captain Hatheway tended to anchor in ports where the availability of liquor was limited, indicating his too was a dry ship. Even if a ration of grog was denied them, a special meal would have been welcome to Amos and the rest of the crew. If the food prepared by cook Jenison was typical of whaleship fare, it was shockingly bad: monotonous, poorly cooked, and often scanty. Staples included salt beef, salt pork, salt cod, potatoes, beans, and hardtack—sweetened with molasses, garnished with cockroaches, and washed down with tea, coffee, or bad water. Jenison dumped meat into one wooden container and whatever else he was serving into another, poured tea or coffee into a large bucket, and ordered some hands to deliver it to the deck or the stuffy forecastle, depending on the weather. Then Amos and the other foremast hands scooped some food onto their tin plates and pots and ate using their knives, spoons, and fingers.[21]

After supper and during leisure time off duty, whalemen enjoyed smoking their pipes. The rest of the time, many of the men kept a wad of tobacco in their mouths. It was not unusual for a whaleman to consume between one hundred and two hundred pounds of tobacco during a three-year voyage, and charges for tobacco often amounted to a good portion of a man's slop chest account. A decade after his whaling voyage, Amos was a habitual tobacco user. If he had not already been addicted to nicotine before he sailed, it seems likely that it happened aboard the *Harrison*.[22]

After crossing the equator on January 19, 1851, First Mate Slocum recorded a southwesterly course for the *Harrison* in the logbook, and during late January and all of February, the ship made steady progress, sailing roughly parallel to the east coast of South America and anywhere from a hundred to six hundred miles offshore. On the afternoon of February 8, for the first time, the cry "There she blows!" rang from one of the masthead lookouts: he had spotted the distant spouting of whales. Instantly, the crew was galvanized with wide-eyed, pulse-racing excitement. "Where away?" shouted Captain Hatheway from the deck, and on learning the location of the pod of sperm whales, he issued a flurry of orders, putting the crew into rapid motion. Hands scrambled aloft and trimmed the sails to bring the ship closer, and when within reasonable range of their prey, the master ordered the boats lowered. Mates and boatsteerers took position in the four boats, tackle whirred, the boats splashed into the water; Amos and the other crewmen scurried down ropes, jumped nimbly to their places, and quickly were off.

After weeks of practice, every man in each boat was thoroughly familiar with his duty. At the forward thwart was the boatsteerer, who would pull an oar until the boat was close enough for him to stand in the bow and strike the whale with a harpoon. In the stern was the mate, or boat header, who manned the steering oar, commanded the crew, and directed the chase. Between the two were four foremast hands, each with special tasks in addition to their work rowing. The bowman, the most experienced crewman in the boat, helped the boatsteerer set a small mast and sail if the breeze was favorable. The midship oarsman handled the longest and heaviest oar. The tub oarsman was responsible for the whaleline, coiled about three hundred fathoms long in its two tubs, with one end snaking to the harpoon. The stroke oarsman bailed the boat if necessary and helped with the mast if needed.

The boatsteerer and foremast hands rowed with their backs to their prey, facing the mate. As Amos pulled his oar, the *Harrison* receded in view, the other boats were hidden by swells, and the rhythm of rowing grew more rapid as the boat header urged on the crew with exclamations, exhortations, and expletives. But the whales outraced the boats. Soon the mate was looking back to the *Harrison* for signal flags aloft to direct his pursuit, and then that too was useless. The whales had escaped, as they would so often.[23]

After his unsuccessful first chase, Amos settled back into a familiar routine: taking his turn manning the helm or as masthead lookout, spreading sails, shortening sails, scrubbing decks, eating, sleeping, chewing tobacco, passing the time, watch after watch and day after day. The monotony was interrupted early in the morning of February 23, when land was spotted for the first time since the Massachusetts coast had disappeared from sight. Peering through his telescope, Captain Hatheway could see the rugged, evergreen-clad, snow-topped mountains of Staten Island, stretching into the sea off the tip of Tierra del Fuego. Skirting the eastern end of the island the next day, the *Harrison* came in sight of several ships, all bound around Cape Horn. On February 25, the ship hove to in a gale under double-reefed topsails and began her hazardous journey southwest through the pounding storms and powerful currents of the Drake Passage. For the next two weeks, First Mate Slocum recorded the ship's longitudinal progress in minutes rather than degrees; on some days he noted the *Harrison* had been pushed backward by the gales. Rain and hail lashed Amos and his shipmates as they worked the ship to fight the storm and reach the Pacific Ocean. Finally, in mid-March, westward progress began to come easier, and on March 20 the *Harrison* steered a northerly course on the boundless Pacific, as the southern summer waned.[24]

Smooth sailing carried the *Harrison* steadily northward, and on April 5 she again came within sight of land. Two days later, the lighthouse at Valparaiso was visible, and at 10 P.M. on April 8, the *Harrison* came to anchor in the harbor of the Chilean port. One of the principal commercial cities on the west coast of South America, Valparaiso was a prime landing place for American whaleships and vessels bound for the California gold fields, drawn by the fresh water, beef, vegetables, and other stores available there at reasonable prices. "Vallipo" and "Wallop-my-ass-with-a-razor," Yankee whalemen called the place. Valparaiso was built on a small, triangular plain fronted by a crescent-shaped shoreline. Imposing architecture was found throughout the city: a custom house, an exchange, a castle, a fort and barracks, plazas, theaters, clubs, hotels, cathedrals, and monasteries. Behind it rose three hilly districts, known as Fore-top, Main-top, and Mizzen-top, separated from each other and the city below by ravines. In those hills were bars, brothels, and dance halls—an anything-goes sailor town, seldom visited by the constabulary. When Amos's watch was granted liberty in its turn, he set foot on land for the first time in four months. The first foreign port he ever visited, Valparaiso was unlike any other Amos would encounter during the voyage of the *Harrison*—a cosmopolitan, rapidly growing city, burnished with the patina of three centuries of colonial history, home to an exotic population of Indians, mestizos, and foreigners.[25]

After a day and a half at Valparaiso, the *Harrison* weighed anchor on the afternoon of April 10 and again set sail for sea. Weeks of uneventful cruising ensued as the ship followed a generally northwestern course. Amos passed his twenty-first birthday on April 26, and in the next few days two faraway ships were spotted. On May 7 a lookout sighted a school of blackfish (or pilot whales), and the boat crews got some more practice in another chase. Oil from the foreheads of blackfish was one of the finest lubricants known, so the chase was in earnest. It was, however, another failure.[26]

On the afternoon of May 9, about the time she recrossed the equator into the northern hemisphere, the *Harrison* approached close enough to another ship for Captain Hatheway to hail his counterpart aboard the other vessel, the bark *Superior* of New Bedford—the first of many such times Captain Hatheway would "speak" another ship and exchange news. All such communications were recorded in the logbook, and in that manner news of the whaling fleet eventually made its way on ships inbound to New Bedford, and into the pages of the *Whalemen's Shipping List and Mer-*

chants' Transcript—usually about two months after the visit. On a couple of occasions when Captain Hatheway spoke another whaleship, a full-fledged "gam" took place: the officers exchanged visits to each others' ships, ferried back and forth in whaleboats. Work ceased, and a celebration of sorts took place. Sometimes the visiting ships sailed in company for a while and hunted whales in common. Gams also afforded whalemen an opportunity to send mail home with an inbound ship and to forward mail it had received from other vessels during other gams. Although the practice was common within the tightly bound New Bedford whaling fraternity, evidence indicates that Captain Hatheway seldom gammed.[27]

An immense stretch of the North Pacific was traversed during the remainder of May and the early part of June. On May 22 the *Harrison* passed within sight of the distant island of Hawaii; on June 2 the men made their first kill: two blackfish. Finally, on June 12, the lookouts spotted several right whales, but bad weather prevented the crew from lowering the boats to give chase. The *Harrison* was now far to the north, on the Coast of Kamchatka whaling grounds in the Bering Sea, and as the ship crossed those grounds in a northeasterly direction over the next two weeks, the crew lowered boats and chased whales on five occasions, each time without success.

By June 28 the *Harrison* had reached the Anadyr Sea whaling grounds, off the far northeastern coast of Russia. The first hours of the day passed quietly, with fine breezes, good weather, and the calm, cold Bering Sea sparkling in the arctic summer's sunlit nighttime. Suddenly, at 3 A.M., a lookout's cry hurried the ship's crew into action. A solitary right whale had been spied. During a two-hour pursuit by the ship, the whale's pace slowed noticeably. At 5 A.M. the four boats were lowered and after a quick chase, First Mate Slocum's larboard boat approached the fatigued whale. When near enough, Slocum ordered the boatsteerer to stand up and prepare to strike. So the man did, bracing himself in the bow and aiming his harpoon. Then he struck, plunging the harpoon deep into the blubber of the whale.

"Stern all! For your lives!" shouted Slocum, as a frenzy of commotion erupted. The whale churned the water with wild, convulsive thrashings; the whaleboat tossed in the frothing waves; the oarsmen strained mightily to pull away from the maddened creature; Slocum and the boatsteerer scrambled to exchange places, the mate taking a lance and the harpooner taking the steering oar; the tub oarsman dumped water over the whaleline as it sped around a loggerhead in the stern, so it would not burst into flames from the friction; and all of the men concentrated on avoiding the rope as it tore from tub to loggerhead, down the entire length of the boat, and through a special slit in the bow into the water, pulled by the frantic whale—for if a man's arm or leg got tangled in the whizzing rope, he could lose the limb or be yanked to his death in the water.

The whale's attempt to escape was short-lived. The doomed creature soon lay listless in the water, the line was hauled in, and the boat drew near to the whale's glistening, iridescent black side. Mate Slocum wielded his razor-sharp lance and thrust it deep into the huge body; he "churned" the lance, stabbing it deeper into his victim, until its spouting was tinted a grotesque pink with its blood, and the spray turned a deeper, thicker red with each spewing. The whale "went into its flurry," as the whalemen described its death throes—flailing spasmodically, whirling in tight circles, spouting great gouts of blood. Then the sea stilled around the massive body, and the exhausted boatmen rested quietly beside their prize.

By 6 A.M., an hour after lowering the boat, Mate Slocum and his weary crew returned to the *Harrison* with their whale in tow after a long, hard row. Then, for the first time, Amos Humiston and the other green hands helped to process a whale. The carcass was chained to the starboard side of the ship, with its head astern. Attaching the whale to the ship took two hours, and at 8 A.M. the cutting-in began.

As the waters reddened while sharks ripped at the valuable blubber, the cutting stage—a narrow plank platform outfitted with a railing—was rigged a few feet above and just beyond the whale. Captain Hatheway, First Mate Slocum, and Second Mate Swift, armed with long-handled cutting spades, mounted the stage. They decapitated the creature, secured the head astern, and began "scarfing" the blubber—scoring cuts into it about twelve to eighteen inches apart. Meanwhile, one of the boatsteerers knotted a rope around his chest and was carefully lowered onto the slippery, swaying carcass to insert a hook into a hole cut in the blubber for the purpose, while a hand above made sure the man's safety line was secure and poked sharks away from the whale with a pole. Then, overseen by Fourth Mate Duffee, the foremast hands heaved at the windlass on deck, hoisting the scarfed strip of blubber high into the air with a block and tackle hanging from the main yard. Below, the whale slowly rotated in the water, and the blubber was peeled away from it like spirals of rind from an orange. When the strip neared the block, a second hook was inserted at its bottom, and just above the new hook the boatsteerer—carefully balancing on the bloody, slick carcass—cut through the blubber with a knife, freeing the first length from the whale.

In the waist of the *Harrison*, Third Mate James Monroe supervised the hoisting of the strip of blubber—a "blanket piece," the whalemen called it—and under his direction, it was lowered through a hatchway into the blubber room, below the main deck. There a few foremast hands, slimy with blood and grease, cut the blanket pieces into smaller "horse pieces."

Gettysburg's Unknown Soldier

Meanwhile, a man was assigned to turn the cooper's grindstone, while James Sadler constantly sharpened cutting spades, and another wielded the long-handled "scoop net" to retrieve small scraps of floating blubber. Blanket pieces were peeled from the whale and hoisted aboard until the carcass was stripped of all its blubber. After the head was hoisted to the deck, what was left of the mutilated body was unchained and drifted away, sharks and seabirds tugging at its flesh. After three hours of intense work, at 11 A.M., the crew of the *Harrison* finished cutting-in its first whale.

When First Mate Slocum finally got a chance to enter the day's events in the *Harrison's* log, he stamped a woodcut image of a whale in the margin of the book. By the end of the voyage, if the *Harrison* was lucky, clusters of whale stamps on certain pages of the log would reveal the days spent on the most bountiful whaling grounds.[28]

Unfortunately, after two consecutive productive seasons, the Anadyr Sea grounds were a disaster in 1851. That summer, the American fleet found much more ice and far fewer whales than usual, and the catch dropped off dramatically. By the end of July some ships began to leave the grounds; by mid-August the exodus became general, and the *Harrison* joined it. By November, the disappointing news reached New Bedford. The *Whalemen's Shipping List and Merchants' Transcript* glumly reported "almost a total failure of the fleet" in the northern waters and quoted the despondent summary of a New Bedford master: "I have done nothing but get my ship stove most to pieces by ice. The Anadir sea has been a dead failure. Ships have not averaged a whale."[29]

The *Harrison* shared in the fleet's failure. On the evening of June 28, just hours after the crew had finished cutting-in its first kill, two of the *Harrison's* boats struck a whale, but after a struggle of two hours, one boat's line broke, the other's harpoon shattered, and the whale escaped. Later that night, Third Mate Monroe's bow boat struck and killed a whale; the boat crew spent the overnight hours tied fast to the whale and towed it to the ship the following afternoon. Four hours were spent cutting-in. It was the last whale the *Harrison's* crew would cut-in on the Anadyr Sea grounds.[30]

Now the *Harrison's* green hands learned the third essential task of whalemen: rendering the blubber into oil by the process known as trying-out. They began as soon as they could; the wet blubber stowed in the blubber room would begin to rot before a day had passed. From below, the horse pieces were delivered to a mincing block on deck, where hands using special two-handled knives cut them into thin slices without penetrating entirely through the blubber. The resulting slices, splayed from their backing like the pages of a book, were traditionally called "bible-leaves" by the whalemen. Other hands readied the trypots, two huge iron cauldrons set into

A Green Hand Sails from New Bedford

the brick tryworks on deck. Fires were stoked, and men began tossing bible-leaves into the trypots. Boiling eventually separated the oil from the blub-ber's fibrous matter, and hands bailed the bubbling oil into copper coolers. When it had cooled sufficiently, the oil was transferred into casks, which were lashed on deck for several days to ensure complete coolness before being stowed in the hold. In the meantime, the fibrous residue was retrieved from the trypots. When dried, those "cracklings" were used as fuel for the tryworks' fires.

Day and night, trying-out was kept up by watch after watch until it was completed. Under the vigilant eyes of the mates and boatsteerers, Amos and the other green hands, coated with oil, blood, and grease, moved around the slippery deck through wafts of thick, black smoke, one side of them toasted by the blazing tryworks, the other chilled by the arctic cold. Trying-out permeated Amos's senses with potent sensations: the irrational, hellish sight of flames on the deck of a ship; a cacophony of voices, accom-panied by the dull roar of the tryworks; the sickening stench of boiling oil and burning cracklings; the deep ache of overworked muscles and a thor-oughly fatigued body.

A final task awaited the whalemen: processing the thousands of pounds of whalebone from the severed heads of their prey. They had already carved the huge, oil-rich tongues and lips from the creatures to be tried-out. Now Amos and the others extracted the long lengths of baleen from the huge jaws, split it into its individual slabs, scraped it clean of flesh, washed it, polished it, and dried it. If it was not carefully cleaned, the whalebone would stink; if it was not adequately dried, it tended to shrink. When it was satisfactorily cured, the men tied it in bundles of about sixty slabs apiece and lashed it to the rigging or stowed it in the hold, where it had to be guarded against dampness and vermin. A ton of whalebone, in lengths of about fifteen feet, could be extracted from a single whalebone whale—enough for ten or so bundles.[31]

The *Harrison* spent all of July and the first few days of August on the Anadyr Sea grounds, much of the time groping through dense fog and treacherous floes of pack ice. Sometimes, when the fog diminished, Amos could see the distant, desolate shore—the towering, black rocky mass of Cape Navarin, rising almost perpendicular from the sea, and the high bluffs of Cape St. Thaddeus. At times the fog-shrouded ship neared the unseen land, close enough for the men to hear the breakers crashing and the rau-cous cries of millions of roosting seabirds. When the fog was at its thickest, Amos heard eerie echoes of bellowing foghorns and cracking pistol shots, sounded by anxious masters seeking to avoid collisions.

In more than a month of hunting on the Anadyr Sea after her first suc-cesses, the *Harrison*'s boats were lowered only seven times. All of the chases were in vain. Finally, tiring of the futility, Captain Hatheway decided to abandon the grounds, and the *Harrison* put away to the south on August 4. But the frigid waters would not let the ship escape before a final misadventure. When the fog lifted that afternoon, the men found themselves in the midst of an ice field. Only after several hours of carefully beating to the windward was the *Harrison* able to withdraw from the ice and escape the disastrous Anadyr Sea.[32]

She sailed to the southwest, cut through the Aleutian Islands, and entered the waters where the Northwest Coast and the Kodiak whaling grounds met. During late August and early September, the ship cruised south of the Aleutians, often in sight of the land and sometimes as close as ten miles to the shoreline. A dramatic landscape linked the prominent landmarks of Cape Kronotskoi and Cape Shipunskoi—a thirty-mile chain of snow-capped mountains, behind which loomed an immense, cone-shaped volcano, visible for more than a hundred miles at sea. Unfortunately for the crew of the *Harrison*, the seas proved to be as barren as the Anadyr grounds. Only four times did they lower boats and chase whales, and just once did they cut-in and try-out a kill.[33]

By mid-September, Captain Hatheway decided to curtail the dismal hunt, and the *Harrison* sailed south. For a while, it appeared the master might change his mind, and the ship headed west as though it might return to the Kamchatka Coast grounds; but by October 1 the course was again southerly. For the *Harrison*, the disappointing northern season was over. Now, following the typical pattern of a New Bedford whaleship on a North Pacific voyage, she would put in at the Sandwich Islands for a week or so to recruit supplies and allow the crew some long-sought liberty ashore. Then the *Harrison* would sail for southern whaling grounds and spend the winter months in the Southern Hemisphere's summer weather; in the spring she would return to the Sandwich Islands to recruit again, and then she would begin the cycle again by sailing back to the northern waters for the summer season's hunting.[34]

All thirty men aboard ship, from Captain Hatheway to green hand Humiston, knew that the success of the voyage depended on a productive outcome to those future hunts. The ultimate measure of that outcome would be weighed by the whaling industry's standard gauge: barrels of oil. A barrel consisted of 31 1/2 gallons; about six barrels filled an average cask. Deep in the swaying hold of the *Harrison*, only 280 barrels of oil sloshed in fewer than fifty casks, a relatively low yield from the summer season's paltry three kills. (Up to two hundred barrels could be produced from a large right whale.) So far, the voyage of the *Harrison* had been an utter disaster. If future seasons proved to be equally hopeless, Amos Humiston might return to New Bedford after years of hard, dangerous work and find his reward to be a pair of empty pockets.[35]

NOTES

1. Whalemen's Shipping Paper, Ship *Harrison*, New Bedford Free Public Library (hereafter NBFPL).

2. Elmo Paul Hohman, *The American Whaleman: A Study of Life and Labor in the Whaling Industry* (New York: Longmans, Green, 1928), 5–6, 9, 42, 305; Clifford W. Ashley, *The Yankee Whaler* (New York: Dover, 1991), 41–42; Briton Cooper Busch, *"Whaling Will Never Do for Me": The American Whaleman in the Nineteenth Century* (Lexington: University Press of Kentucky, 1994), 2–4; New Bedford Port Society, *List of Ships Sailed from New Bedford in the Year 1850*, Old Dartmouth Historical Society Whaling Museum, New Bedford (hereafter ODHSWM).

3. Hohman, *American Whaleman*, 144–145, 147–149; Ashley, *Yankee Whaler*, 65–67; Richard Ellis, *Men and Whales* (New York: Knopf, 1991), 4–32. A fourth species, the humpback whale, described by Hohman as "unimportant," was hunted only in the absence of the three named species.

4. Hohman, *American Whaleman*, 4, 148; Ashley, *Yankee Whaler*, 74–75, 82–83; Busch, *"Whaling Will Never Do for Me,"* 3; Ellis, *Men and Whales*, 131–145.

5. Hohman, *American Whaleman*, 5; Ashley, *Yankee Whaler*, 34, 38–39; Ellis, *Men and Whales*, 174; *The New Bedford Directory* (New Bedford: C. & A. Taylor, 1849), passim.

6. Hohman, *American Whaleman*, 42, 46, 51–52; Busch, *"Whaling Will Never Do for Me,"* 9; Ellis, *Men and Whales*, 169.

7. Busch, *"Whaling Will Never Do for Me,"* 8–9; Ashley, *Yankee Whaler*, 100; Hohman, *American Whaleman*, 48, 88–91; Margaret S. Creighton, *Rites and Passages: The Experience of American Whaling, 1830–1870* (Cambridge: Cambridge University Press, 1995), 9, 43, 47–57.

8. Hohman, *American Whaleman*, 88–93, 96–100; Ashley, *Yankee Whaler*, 107–108; Busch, *"Whaling Will Never Do for Me,"* 10; Creighton, *Rites and Passages*, 45.

9. *Whalemen's Shipping List and Merchants' Transcript*, November 5, 1850. Survey of Federal Archives, Division of Professional and Service Projects, Works Projects Administration, comp., *Ship Registers of New Bedford Massachusetts* (Boston: National Archives Projects, 1940), 136; Whalemen's Shipping Paper, Ship *Harrison*, NBFPL.

10. Elizabeth Starr Versailles, *Hathaways of America* (Northampton, Mass.: Gazette Printing Company, 1970), 330, 497, 647; "Obituary, Capt. John Keen Hatheway," *New Bedford Daily Mercury*, January 15, 1879, 2; Survey of Federal Archives, *Ship Registers of New Bedford, Massachusetts*, 68, 105, 136; Federal Writers' Project, Works Progress Administration of Massachusetts, *Whaling Masters* (New Bedford: Old Dartmouth Historical Society, 1938); shipping agreements,

ships *Fenelon* and *Cowper*, NBFPL; Alexander Starbuck, *History of the American Whale Fishery* (reprint, Secaucus, N.J.: Castle Books, 1989), 364–365, 386–387, 420–421.

11. Creighton, *Rites and Passages*, 89; Hohman, *American Whaleman*, 217–218; Busch, *"Whaling Will Never Do for Me,"* 5–6; Ashley, *Yankee Whaler*, 109; whalemen's shipping paper, Ship *Harrison*, NBFPL.

12. Whalemen's shipping paper, Ship *Harrison*, NBFPL; New Bedford Port Society, *List of Ships Sailed from New Bedford in the Year 1850*; crew list card files, NBFPL; American Seamen's Protection Papers, NBFPL.

13. On typical whalemen of the era, see Busch, *"Whaling Will Never Do for Me,"* 7–8; Creighton, *Rites and Passages*, 9, 42; Hohman, *American Whaleman*, 58.

14. *The New Bedford Directory* (1849), 9; American seamen's protection papers, NBFPL; Stuart C. Sherman, *The Voice of the Whaleman, with an Account of the Nicholson Whaling Collection* (Providence: Providence Public Library, 1965), 62–63.

15. Survey of Federal Archives, *Ship Registers of New Bedford, Massachusetts*, 136; *New Bedford and Fairhaven Signal Book, 1850* (New Bedford: Abraham Taber, 1850), 23; Hohman, *American Whaleman*, 12; Ashley, *Yankee Whaler*, 48; William B. Whitecar, Jr., *Four Years Aboard the Whaleship* (Philadelphia: J. B. Lippincott & Co., 1864), 16–17.

16. John R. Bockstoce, *Whales, Ice and Men: The History of Whaling in the Western Arctic* (Seattle: University of Washington Press, 1986), 30–33; Ashley, *Yankee Whaler*, 97.

17. Captain's and shipper's manifest, ship *Harrison*, December 10, 1850, NBFPL.

18. Logbook, Ship *Harrison*, Nicholson Whaling Collection, Providence Public Library; Hohman, *The American Whaleman*, 114–115, 128, 156; Bockstoce, *Whales, Ice and Men*, 37, 39; Creighton, *Rites and Passages*, 116–117. A second logbook of the *Harrison*'s voyage, covering the period from October 1, 1852 to April 13, 1854, was sold at auction by the Richard A. Bourne Company of Hyannis, Massachusetts, on August 23, 1969. Its current whereabouts are unknown. See lot 213 in the catalog, *Important Marine Auction: An Exceptional Collection of Marine Paintings, Scrimshaw, Journal Whaling Log Books, and Related Marine Items*, courtesy ODHSWM; and Mark H. Dunkelman, "Whaleship *Harrison*?" *Nautical World* (October 1997): 8, 10.

19. Hohman, *American Whaleman*, 118; Creighton, *Rites and Passages*, 60, 62–63; Bockstoce, *Whales, Ice and Men*, 40.

20. Logbook, Ship *Harrison*; Creighton, *Rites and Passages*, 136–138; Hohman, *American Whaleman*, 139.

21. Hohman, *American Whaleman*, 120, 130–136; Busch, *"Whaling Will Never Do for Me,"* 14–15, 160–163; Creighton, *Rites and Passages*, 101–102; Ellis, *Men and Whales*, 178–179.

22. Hohman, *American Whaleman*, 135; Busch, *"Whaling Will Never Do for*

A Green Hand Sails from New Bedford

Me," 11; Ellis, *Men and Whales*, 172–173. Amos mentions his tobacco use in his wartime letters of December 2 and 8, 1862, and January 2 and February 1, 1863.

23. Logbook, Ship *Harrison*; Hohman, *American Whaleman*, 156–159; Ellis, *Men and Whales*, 183–185; Ashley, *The Yankee Whaler*, 10–12; Henry T. Cheever, *The Whale and His Captors; or, the Whaleman's Adventures, and the Whale's Biography* (New York: Harper & Brothers, 1849), 89–90.

24. Logbook, Ship *Harrison*; Alexander G. Findlay, *A Directory for the Navigation of the South Pacific Ocean* (London: Richard Holmes Laurie, 1863), 44–45. Staten Island is today's Isla de los Estados, Argentina.

25. Logbook, Ship *Harrison*; Findlay, *A Directory of the South Pacific Ocean*, 116–118; Busch, *"Whaling Will Never Do for Me,"* 175; Recaredo S. Tornero, *Chile Ilustrado: Guia Descriptivo del Territotio de Chile* (Valparaiso: Librerias i Ajencias del Mercurio, 1872), 118–125, 150–153, 182–185.

26. Logbook, Ship *Harrison*; Ashley, *Yankee Whaler*, 29, 124; Ellis, *Men and Whales*, 3, 529.

27. Logbook, Ship *Harrison*; Hohman, *American Whaleman*, 87, 141; Ashley, *Yankee Whaler*, 103–104. The *Harrison*'s logbook recorded forty-four occasions when Captain Hatheway spoke other ships. In an effort to establish whether Hatheway ever gammed with his counterparts, I examined the logbooks of nineteen of the ships the *Harrison* spoke. Four logbooks were inconclusive. Of the fifteen other entries, only two mention gamming with the *Harrison*: the New Bedford Bark *Fortune*, on July 9, 1851 (Nicholson Whaling Collection, Providence Public Library), and the Sag Harbor Ship *Timor*, on December 18, 1851 (East Hampton Free Library, East Hampton, New York).

28. Logbook, Ship *Harrison*; Hohman, *American Whaleman*, 159–162, 165–171, 178; Ashley, *Yankee Whaler*, 12–18; Cheever, *The Whale and His Captors*, 57–60, 84–85, 93–94; Ellis, *Men and Whales*, 185–186, 196–197.

29. Bockstoce, *Whales, Ice and Men*, 29, 44, 95; *Whalemen's Shipping List and Merchants' Transcript*, November 25, 1851.

30. Logbook, Ship *Harrison*.

31. Hohman, *American Whaleman*, 172–175, 181; Ashley, *Yankee Whaler*, 19, 74–75; Cheever, *The Whale and His Captors*, 85–89; Creighton, *Rites and Passages*, 72; Ellis, *Men and Whales*, 198–199.

32. Logbook, Ship *Harrison*; Bockstoce, *Whales, Ice and Men*, 45–48, 52–53; Alexander G. Findlay, *A Directory for the Navigation of the North Pacific Ocean* (London: Richard Holmes Laurie, 1870), 546.

33. Logbook, Ship *Harrison*; Findlay, *A Directory of the North Pacific Ocean*, 554.

34. Logbook, Ship *Harrison*; Hohman, *American Whaleman*, 152.

35. *Whalemen's Shipping List and Merchants' Transcript*, December 23, 1851; Ashley, *Yankee Whaler*, 96; Hohman, *American Whaleman*, 181.

CHAPTER 3

Roving the Pacific

STRONG WINDS WERE blowing at sea, but inside the well-sheltered anchorage at Lahaina, light breezes gently rocked the assembled whaleships. At noon on October 14, 1851, the *Harrison* closed in with the shipping, and at 2 P.M. came to anchor in the roadstead. As soon as his watch was granted liberty, Amos Humiston and a group of his shipmates rowed one of the whaleboats to the beach and stepped ashore for the first time in six months, a full half-year since the last stop, in Valparaiso. It was the first of several visits Amos would make to the Sandwich Islands during the voyage of the *Harrison*, and he was enchanted by the place. The Hawaiian archipelago cast a spell over him, and for the rest of his years, he dreamed of returning to the beautiful islands.[1]

The Sandwich Islands had long been an important base of operations for the American whaling fleet, and in the years Amos visited aboard the *Harrison*, with the recent opening of the arctic whaling grounds, Hawaiian ports were at their peak as whaleship stopovers. They were an excellent place to recruit provisions, water, and men; to refit ships battered by long voyages; and to warehouse or transship oil and bone. And with their balmy climate and friendly natives, the Sandwich Islands were an ideal spot to rest weary crews, to satisfy men hungry for a return to dry land. Supplying the needs of the whaling fleet drove the islands' economy. Shipyards, chandlers, warehouses, farms, ranches, markets, bawdyhouses, grogshops—all depended on the clockwork spring and fall visits of the whaleships for their profits. Three ports dominated the trade. Honolulu, on the island of Oahu, capital of the kingdom and largest city in the islands, drew the most ships. Lahaina, at the western end of the island of Maui, ranked a solid second. Hilo, on the eastern shore of the big island of Hawaii, was a distinct third, with considerably less traffic and a shorter history of serving whaleships. To whalemen, the names of Honolulu and Lahaina and their respective islands were interchangeable, as the *Whalemen's Shipping List and Mer-*

chants' Transcript emphasized during the voyage of the *Harrison*: "Our readers will please bear in mind that *Oahu* and *Honolulu* is one and the same place. This is true also of *Maui* and *Lahaina*."[2]

Viewed from the rail of the *Harrison*, or in glances over his shoulder as Amos rowed ashore, Lahaina looked lovely. Breakers foamed over the coral reef bounding the shore; sunlight sparkled on the water and the luxuriant greenery of breadfruit and coconut trees; the buildings of the town nestled in garden groves along and beyond the long stretch of beach; and a steep, verdant ridge rose behind the town, reaching into puffy clouds lazily crossing the bright blue sky. Exploring, Amos found stores and dwellings of foreign residents scattered along the shore, and the more numerous grass houses of the natives shaded by landward groves. Among the larger structures were the coral-block fort, used to confine unruly sailors; the palace, unused by King Kamehameha III and covered with graffiti and drawings made by the natives, but still housing the police and circuit courts; and the whitewashed stone native church.

If Lahaina seemed a bit sunbaked, dirty, and flea-bitten up close there was nevertheless much to observe and enjoy for a green hand on his first visit to the islands. Species of birds Amos had never seen before landed in equally unfamiliar varieties of trees. Day and night, the temperature hovered near perfection for human comfort. At the beach, Amos could enjoy bathing and swimming, and watch with delight as native men, women, boys, and girls demonstrated their skill in riding surfboards. If he sought vice, he was not hard-pressed to find it. Liquor had recently been prohibited, and one visitor to Lahaina, who had been shocked by the behavior of drunken whalemen there in the past, was relieved to note, "This port and Hilo are now probably the only two places in all the Pacific Ocean frequented by ships, where a sailor cannot get drunk." But that assessment overlooked the beer halls, where a potent brew of tobacco, potatoes, and awa root (a narcotic and natural anesthetic) was sold as "spruce beer." Prostitution was outlawed, but the ban was ineffectively policed. Although not as commonplace as in the past, it was still possible to see drunken whalemen reeling down the main street in Lahaina with native prostitutes in their embrace and young native boys scampering in their wake, mimicking their stumbling gait and repeating their lewd language.[3]

Eleven days after arriving at Lahaina, early on the morning of October 25, the *Harrison* weighed anchor, made sail for sea, and cleared the shipping in the roadstead. By 5 P.M. the following day, First Mate Slocum reported, the ship "commenced busting out of Mowhee," riding the trade winds westward through the passage between the islands of Molokai and Lanai, and, a day later, losing sight of the land. Steering almost due south, the *Harrison* headed off to her winter season.

Roving the Pacific

A month of sailing ensued, during which the crew captured its first sperm whale and passed within six miles of the high breakers crashing on small, thickly wooded Flint Island. Early in the morning of November 25 the island of Rarotonga came into view about thirty miles distant, and the *Harrison* steered for it and closed in with it the next afternoon. On November 26, as Amos Humiston did his part to help maneuver the ship near the island, more than seven thousand miles to the northeast, back home in Tioga County, Mary Bronson Humiston Boice died. Months would pass—perhaps years, and maybe not until he returned to the United States—before Amos would learn of the loss of his mother.

About thirty miles in circumference and surrounded by a reef, a beautiful mass of high, craggy mountains rising above a fringe of waving palms, Rarotonga was the largest of the Hervey Island group, home to perhaps four thousand people. At the island, the *Harrison* "lay off and on," that is, stood unanchored and sent whaleboats through small openings in the reef to recruit ashore. Although the ship had resupplied just a month before, Captain Hatheway wanted to take advantage of the plenty that the fertile island offered, and to add some of the pigs, turkeys, chickens, ducks, yams, sweet potatoes, and pineapples to his stores. Amos and his crewmates consequently were able to view one of the grandest landscapes the South Pacific had to offer.[4]

Until noon of November 27, the *Harrison* lay off and on getting recruits from the Rarotonga shore. Then, ready to sail, the crew experienced a frustrating delay when two of its members, enticed by the island's splendors, failed to return to the ship. Finally, on the afternoon of November 29, natives brought the deserters aboard (probably receiving a reward from Captain Hatheway for the captures), and the *Harrison* left the island.[5]

The winter season passed with long stretches of boring inactivity interrupted by intense periods of hunting. The day after leaving Rarotonga, in a heavy rain, one of the boatsteerers struck a sperm whale, and the enraged creature attacked and "stove" the boat—smashed it up; the harpoon pulled out as the whale escaped. In another failed effort two days later, a crew struck a large sperm whale and held onto it for a few hours until darkness fell, when the men surrendered to the creature and cut the line. Days of uneventful sailing ensued as the *Harrison* followed a southerly course through the South Pacific. Late in December 1851 and early in January 1852, the ship cruised waters far to the south of any recognized mid-Pacific whaling grounds. Nevertheless, whales were spotted every two or three days; boats were lowered and chases made on nine occasions, but only once did Mate Slocum press his stamp onto a page of the logbook to signify a killed and cut-in whale. The *Harrison's* unlucky boat crews lost whales in every possible way: a boatsteerer missed with his harpoon; the

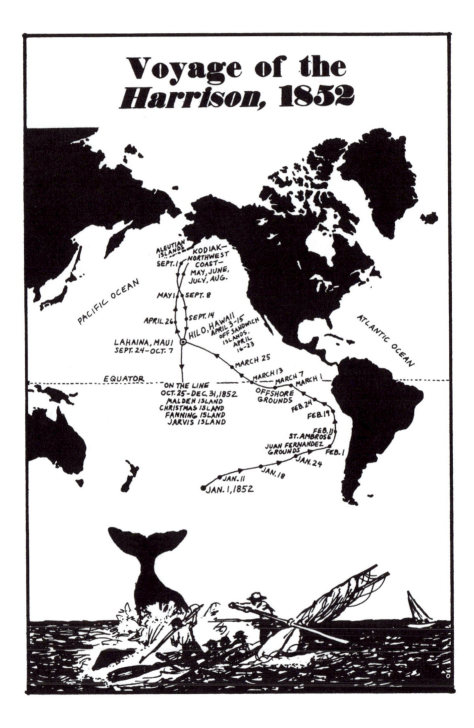

Voyage of the Harrison, 1852

ALEUTIAN ISLANDS SEPT. I

KODIAK—NORTHWEST COAST—MAY, JUNE, JULY, AUG.

PACIFIC OCEAN

MAY I · SEPT. 8

APRIL 26 · SEPT. 14

HILO, HAWAII APRIL 3-15

OFF SANDWICH ISLANDS, APRIL 16-23

LAHAINA, MAUI SEPT. 24-OCT. 7

ATLANTIC OCEAN

MARCH 25

EQUATOR

MARCH 13

MARCH 7

MARCH 1

ON THE LINE OCT. 25-DEC. 31, 1852
MALDEN ISLAND
CHRISTMAS ISLAND
FANNING ISLAND
JARVIS ISLAND

OFFSHORE GROUNDS

FEB. 24

FEB. 19

FEB. 11 ST. AMBROSE

JUAN FERNANDEZ GROUNDS

FEB. 1

JAN. 24

JAN. 18

JAN. 11

JAN. 1, 1852

Roving the Pacific

line to a struck whale was accidentally cut; a boatsteerer unsuccessfully "darted" his harpoon (that is, tossed it instead of thrusting it); a harpoon in a struck whale broke. Another boat was stove, and when a member of its crew was injured, the line was cut to free the furious whale. On the evening of January 11, the crew of the *Harrison* saw a whale "lobtailing"— standing on its head with its body vertically erect out of the water, waving its giant tail back and forth, violently slapping the surface with each stroke, churning the water into a fountain of white froth. The beast seemed to be taunting them, but the men could not be goaded into lowering the boats and giving chase. The next day a mighty wave washed over the *Harrison* and broke the waist boat down from the davits.[6]

After that accident, another period of quiet commenced as Captain Hatheway directed the ship to the east. By the first days of February, the *Harrison* was cruising the Juan Fernandez whaling grounds, named after a group of islands off the coast of Chile. The island of Mas-a-fuera, swarming with seals, came in sight on the morning of February 2, and within hours a boat crew had struck and killed a sperm whale. The following afternoon, the boat towed its prize to the ship, and cutting-in began. There were extra steps to be taken in cutting-in a sperm whale, Amos learned, most of them involving the severed head. Hoisted halfway on deck, it was cut into three parts: the lower jaw, the junk, and the case. The jaw had no commercial value, but provided the bone and teeth that the whalemen used to make scrimshaw. The junk, the wedge-shaped lower half of the sperm whale's forehead, was the source of spermaceti. The case, the upper part of the forehead, was a reservoir of pulp that yielded the purest oil to be had. When all of the oil and spermaceti was obtained, the shredded remains of the case and junk were shoved overboard. Finally, before the crew cast the body of the cut-in sperm whale adrift, it was disemboweled and searched for ambergris.[7]

On the afternoon of February 11, the *Harrison* approached the tiny island of St. Ambrose. Only four miles in circumference, topped with a freshwater pond, the place was home to a large population of seabirds. Two of the whaleboats put off from the ship on a fishing trip, and probably landed at a snug little cove on the north side of the island. The fishermen returned a few hours later; the results of their efforts went unrecorded. Perhaps curiosity drove Amos Humiston to join the expedition to St. Ambrose, to inspect a place that shared his father's name.

The *Harrison* was steering to the north now, and in mid-February Captain Hatheway altered the course to the northwest, in order to reach the Sandwich Islands for the spring recruiting stop. The ship crossed the large Offshore grounds in early March, and a chase of sperm whales ended at dusk of March 6 with another stove boat and a line attached to a maddened whale cut in an act of surrender. As March ended, First Mate Slocum recorded some disturbing news in the logbook: "the Capt Sick." Fortunately for Captain Hatheway, he would shortly have good circumstances in which to recuperate. Two days after he fell ill, the *Harrison* came within sight of the island of Hawaii, and night fell that April 2, Mate Slocum reported, with good weather, fine breezes, and the *Harrison* "running down for the Harbor of Hilo."[8]

Visitors were always favorably impressed as they neared Hilo from the sea. A safe, spacious anchorage in a beautiful bay, protected by a lava reef; a crescent beach of fine, volcanic sand, divided by three streams of pure water and ringed with coconut palms, their fronds gently rustling in the breeze; the neat buildings of the town itself, barely visible in a dense grove of breadfruit, candlenut, plantain, ohia, and pandanus trees; the broad lands rising in gentle sweeps of lush forests, verdant valleys, sparkling streams, and plunging waterfalls; higher, rougher country of hilly lava fields and pastures and plains where wild goats, cattle, hogs, and geese grazed; and the entire landscape surmounted by the bold, towering, distant domes of the snow-capped volcanoes, extinct Mauna Kea and active Mauna Loa— altogether, the panorama offered a stunning prospect to approaching crewmen.

On the afternoon of April 3, 1852, in response to the *Harrison*'s signal flags, a harbor pilot came aboard and guided the ship to an anchorage. Then Amos Humiston and his crewmates explored "the paradise of Hawaii," as an American whaleman described Hilo.

The town was one continuous grove, with exotic shrubs, flowers, and trees flourishing in gardens enclosed by stone walls. The fertile soil, moistened by almost daily showers, produced rich crops of fruit and vegetables. But although fresh recruits of livestock and produce were available, they were less plentiful than at Lahaina or Honolulu, a situation one American visitor attributed to "the lack of enterprise and industry on the part of the inhabitants." But Hilo was just emerging as a popular retreat for whaleships, and food supplies were adequate for the score or so of ships making their spring stopover. Pure, fresh water was abundant and easily obtained. All the *Harrison*'s crewmen had to do was raft their casks to a nearby waterfall and fill them.

A single road running parallel to the beach bisected the town. Several of the native houses were uncommonly neat and attractive to American eyes, with verandas on opposite sides and borders of neatly trimmed hedges. There were the usual stores, warehouses, and chandleries run by Americans and other foreigners, including many Chinese. In a well-groomed garden stood the thatched-roof cottage of the American collector of the port. On the neighboring property stood a dwelling that must have sent a wave of homesickness washing over the men when they saw it: another visiting whaleman declared it looked just like "a snug little New-England homestead." It was the home of the Reverend Titus Coan, since 1835 a Presbyterian missionary at Hilo—a man who sought the souls of whalemen as zealously as whalemen sought the oil and bone of whales.[9]

Most, if not all, of the *Harrison*'s crew probably had some sort of encounter with Reverend Coan or his associates, and surely some of the men attended services on April 4 and 11, the two Sundays they were in Hilo. No doubt the men were harangued by the preacher to forgo whaling on the Sabbath. "No man can serve two masters," the Reverend Coan was fond of declaring. *"Ye can not serve God and mammon."* If Captain Hatheway was urged by Coan to forgo Sunday whaling, he chose to ignore the admonishment, as did most of his fellow masters. In the coming months, the *Harrison*'s boats would splash into the water on many a Sabbath.[10]

Prohibition made Pastor Coan's duty considerably easier when whaleships anchored in Hilo Bay. The ban on liquor eliminated much of the behavior whalemen were infamous for in other ports, as Coan explained in a letter to the American Seamen's Friend Society:

Whale ships are now in, and our streets are alive with sailors. Hundreds are having liberty on shore, and our town is like a bee-hive. Still all are quiet. No man staggers, no man fights, none are noisy or boisterous. We have nothing here to inflame the blood, nothing to muddle the brain. Our verdant landscape, our peaceful streets, our pure cold water, and the absence of those inebriating vials of wrath which consume all good, induce wise commanders to visit this port, in order to refresh and give liberty to their crews.[11]

For a dozen delightful days, Amos Humiston and his shipmates enjoyed their liberty at Hilo, basking in its warmth, admiring its lush beauty, and appreciating its pleasant society. The whalemen walked to the nearby waterfall, viewed ancient craters, strolled under the palms along the mile-long beach, paddled canoes to Coconut Island to swim and hunt shells, wandered groves of breadfruit trees, sailed on peaceful lakes, and hired horses for the thirty-five-mile ride to the active volcano of Kilauea. They also inspected the scars, only ten miles from Hilo, left by burning rivers of lava during two eruptions of Mauna Loa just two months before their visit. Destroyed forests, filled valleys, and leveled mounds marked the track of the lava flow for forty miles, from the mountainside to the sea. The violence of the eruption, as evidenced by the destruction it wrought, was in curious contrast to the peaceful Hawaii the whalemen experienced. At night, from the deck of the *Harrison*, Amos gazed at an enchanting sight: a bright crescent of light marking the shoreline and town, the glimmering lights of scattered mountainside homes, and, above an expanse of black mountaintop, the sky full of stars.[12]

It was hard to leave such an exotic paradise for the perils and hardships of whaling in cold northern waters, and an unknown number of the *Harrison*'s foremast hands deserted at Hilo. The ship herself, as if also reluctant to leave the balmy waters, experienced difficulty leaving Hilo Bay. The crew weighed anchor at 4 A.M. of April 15, and a half-hour later the *Harrison* was stuck on the reef. But another half-hour raised the tide enough to free the ship, and, undamaged, she stood out to sea. For the next four days, the *Harrison* lay off the Hawaiian coast, waiting in vain for the deserters to return. Finally, losing patience, Captain Hatheway ordered the ship to close in with the land on April 20 and sent a boat's crew ashore to hunt for the missing men. They returned the following afternoon with three of the deserters, and the *Harrison* sailed for Oahu on a special mission. Green hand Frederick Hubbard was sick, and Captain Hatheway wanted to deliver him to Honolulu, where he could best be treated. Steering through the passage between Maui and Molokai, the *Harrison* reached Honolulu on the morning of April 22. That day a boat carried Hubbard ashore, and the crew arranged for his care. The next day the ship left the Sandwich Islands for the summer season on the Northwest Coast and Kodiak whaling grounds.[13]

The run north was not without its problems; the jibboom was carried away when a hook broke, and Amos and his mates endured several consecutive days of heavy gales and rain. But by the third week of May, the *Harrison* had reached the southern edge of the Northwest Coast grounds, about five hundred miles south of the Aleutians, and for the next two months the ship hunted within the bounds of a few degrees of latitude and longitude. During that time, usually no more than a day or two passed between chases, and on several days the whaleboats were lowered more than once. The usual failures occurred: lines were cut, accidentally and on purpose; fog cut short chases; boatsteerers missed strikes; irons broke; boats were stove; and twice dead whales sank, carrying to the bottom between them a dozen harpoons and hundreds of fathoms of line—but Mate Slocum nevertheless stamped seven kills into the logbook. A shackle gave way in cutting-in one of those kills, and the accident cost the crew the whale's head and both lips.

In August the *Harrison* sailed north into the Gulf of Alaska and the Kodiak grounds, but the men made only a few chases in those waters and had only one kill. Nevertheless, the 1852 summer season had been a marked improvement over the previous year's Anadyr Sea disaster, and certainly qualified as a success. When the ship anchored at Lahaina for autumn recruiting on September 24, she was carrying seventy barrels of sperm oil, twelve hundred barrels of whale oil, and more than eighty-five hundred pounds of whalebone. The crew had tried-out more than nine hundred barrels of oil during the season.[14]

The ship lost an officer during the *Harrison*'s 1852 autumn layover at Lahaina. First Mate Joseph Slocum, ailing with an unknown illness, went ashore on October 5 to recuperate for an indefinite period. Three months later, the *Whalemen's Shipping List* reported the *Harrison* "would sail . . . on a cruise of one month, and return for her mate, who was on shore, sick." But the ensuing cruise lasted longer than a month.

In addition to the usual recruiting at Maui, Captain Hatheway took advantage of an opportunity to transship the *Harrison*'s accumulated whalebone on the New Bedford bark *Isabella*, bound for home carrying 800,000 pounds of bone from different ships. The *Isabella* turned over 8,630 pounds of whalebone from the *Harrison* to Gilbert Hatheway on its return to New Bedford.[15]

At Lahaina the *Harrison*'s crew joyfully received mail that had been accumulating since their spring stop at Hilo. The Honolulu temperance newspaper the *Friend*—a Sandwich Islands version of the *Whalemen's Shipping List*, full of whaling news—reported that when the *Harrison* sailed later, there were no letters for its crew remaining in Hawaiian post offices. Their mail was at least five months old, but the lucky crewmen who received letters no doubt relished the news from home despite its being outdated.[16]

Two weeks of pleasurable rest at Lahaina passed rapidly, and on October 7 the *Harrison* weighed anchor and began its winter season. An uneventful southward sail brought the ship to Malden Island, a few degrees south of the equator, on October 30. That afternoon the men lowered boats and rowed through shark-infested waters to an easy landing on the island, a low coral formation about a dozen miles long, with some clusters of trees, a few brackish ponds, a marsh, and an immense deposit of guano. In the next several days, the *Harrison* approached other equatorial islands. On November 4 she closed in to the western end of Christmas Island, a belt of low land covered with stunted bushes and a few coconut palms surrounding a shallow lagoon, teeming with seabirds and fish but bereft of fresh water. The ship lay off and on at Fanning Island from November 7 to 10, sending boat crews to procure wood ashore and fish in the lagoon. Unlike Christmas Island, Fanning was a rich place. An Englishman had settled there with some natives of other islands to engage in the production of coconut oil, and they also grew bananas, pumpkins, taro, figs, melons, cabbages, and other garden vegetables. Fresh water was abundant near "Whaleman Anchorage," a deep-water harbor, and fish were plentiful in the lagoon. The settlers were most accommodating in providing recruits to whalemen, and Fanning Island was frequently visited by whalers. On November 14 the *Harrison* closed in with Jarvis Island, a small, triangular jumble of coral against which the sea broke violently. It looked simply like a low white sand beach with a few patches of grass and the usual flock of seabirds, but it was considered a dangerous place, and the men did not lower boats to explore it.[17]

The *Harrison* spent the 1852–1853 winter season hunting the On the Line whaling grounds, rarely straying more than four degrees in latitude from the equator. It was not a very productive period; in four months the men killed only three blackfish and three sperm whales, and caught a couple of porpoises for food. While she cruised the lonely equatorial ocean, the *Harrison* lost another of her officers. Fourth Mate William Duffee was reported to be very sick on November 21, 1852, and the next morning, "the 4th mate at 8 A.M. breathed his last." A simple burial service took place the following afternoon, and as Amos and the rest of the crew watched solemnly, the Indian's body, with a weight attached to his feet, was slipped over the side into the sea.[18]

As the winter whaling season waned, the men of the *Harrison* spent three days in February 1853 coopering oil. After they were filled with oil, the huge, iron-hooped casks were lowered through hatches into the hold, a process that required considerable skill, and stowed on their sides in two tiers, wedged into place by pieces of cordwood. After the oil was stowed down, Amos and the other foremast hands had to pour water over the casks every other day or so to keep them tight and prevent leakage.[19]

Crossing twenty degrees of latitude from the equator to the Sandwich Islands took the *Harrison* a mere dozen days, and she anchored at Hilo for spring recruiting on March 7, 1853. The crew enjoyed a lengthy stay, until March 30, when the *Harrison* weighed anchor and sailed for Maui. After crossing the passage between Maui and Molokai, the ship lay off and on at Lahaina for two days, during which First Mate Joseph Slocum returned to the *Harrison* after his long absence, and Captain Hatheway shipped a new fourth mate, a Mr. Comstock, to replace the deceased Duffee. Then the *Harrison* passed through the channel between Molokai and Lanai, and after spending two days laying off and on at Oahu, sailed for Kauai. For four days the ship lay off and on at Kauai, waiting for good weather and getting off recruits, and on the afternoon of April 9, once all hands were again on board, the *Harrison* left the islands for the summer season.

Scarcely a week had passed when the men of the *Harrison* received a shock, recorded in the logbook entries for April 17 and 18: "at 8 P.M. Mr. Slocum 1st mate was taken Sick with pain in the breast, at 11 more comfortable, at 5 A.M. found dead in his berth . . . at 4 P.M. committed the

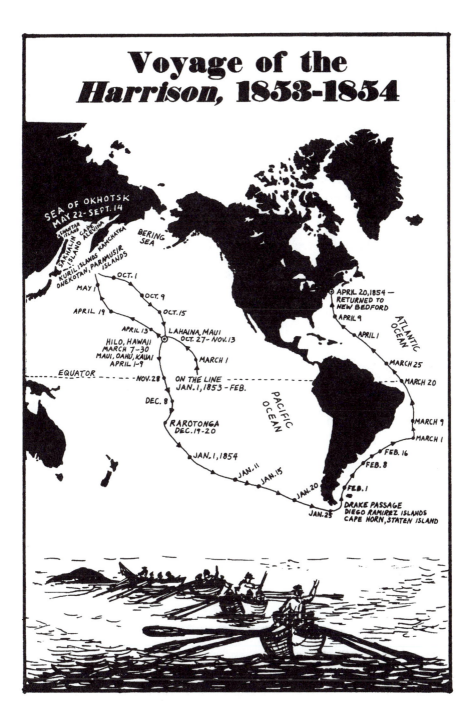

Voyage of the Harrison, 1853-1854

SEA OF OKHOTSK
MAY 22-SEPT. 14

SHANTAR ISLAND
CAPE ALEVINA
SAKHALIN ISLAND
KAMCHATKA
KURIL ISLANDS PARAMUSIR
ONEKOTAN, ISLANDS

BERING SEA

MAY 1

OCT. 1

OCT. 9

APRIL 19

OCT. 15

APRIL 13

LAHAINA, MAUI
OCT. 27- NOV. 13

HILO, HAWAII
MARCH 7-30
MAUI, OAHU, KAUAI
APRIL 1-9

MARCH 1

EQUATOR

ON THE LINE
JAN. 1, 1853 - FEB.

NOV. 28

PACIFIC OCEAN

DEC. 8

RAROTONGA
DEC. 19-20

JAN. 1, 1854

JAN. 11

JAN. 15

JAN. 20

JAN. 25

APRIL 20, 1854 —
RETURNED TO
NEW BEDFORD

APRIL 9

ATLANTIC OCEAN

APRIL 1

MARCH 25

MARCH 20

MARCH 9

MARCH 1

FEB. 16

FEB. 8

FEB. 1

DRAKE PASSAGE
DIEGO RAMIREZ ISLANDS
CAPE HORN, STATEN ISLAND

Body of Joseph A. Slocum to the waterry deep." Second Mate Swift again assumed Slocum's duties, and Captain Hatheway was once more short an officer.

Far to the northwest the *Harrison* sailed, into bone-chilling cold and a solid week of snow and hailstorms, until May 17, when land once again came within sight. It was Onekotan Island, one of the Kuril Islands, and the next afternoon the ship passed through the chain into the Sea of Okhotsk. Immediately, Captain Hatheway spoke two New England whaleships. The men of the *Harrison* would encounter more whaleships in the Sea of Okhotsk than on any other grounds they ever cruised, but the competition would not prove to be detrimental to their success. The crew would kill more whales on the Okhotsk grounds than on any other waters they hunted.[20]

Remote, frequently fog bound and stormy, its shoreline waters clotted with ice, the vast cold expanse of the Okhotsk Sea seemed to offer one purpose only: to yield its rich supply of right and bowhead whales to hardy American whalemen. Shallow at its center, not more than two hundred fathoms deep, the sea was bounded on the southeast by the Kurils, on the east by the Kamchatka Peninsula, on the southwest by lengthy Sakhalin Island, and on the northwest and north by the Asian continent. The shores—when they could be seen through blankets of fog and fields of ice—were closely surrounded by brooding, bleak mountains. It seemed a forbidding, if not foreboding, seascape, but to the men of the *Harrison*, the Sea of Okhotsk turned out to be what they had been searching for since they left New Bedford.[21]

A week after the *Harrison* entered the sea, after sailing through thick snowstorms and hugging immense ice fields as closely as possible, the slaughter began. Eighteen ships were in sight on May 25 when the crew of the bow boat made the first kill, a bowhead, and in the next four days, while a heavy snowstorm raged, the men resharpened their skills at cutting-in and trying-out. Almost a month passed before the next time the whale stamp was pressed on the pages of the logbook, but then the kills came in clusters. In all, the crew cut-in eighteen whales between late May and early September. Four of them were found floating dead, killed but lost and unclaimed by other ships.

It was a summer unlike any other Amos Humiston ever experienced—a summer of constant fog, ice, blood, and oil. Every few days Captain Hatheway spoke ships; on one occasion a score of whaleships could be sighted from the deck. Early in June the *Harrison*'s boats unsuccessfully chased whales in tandem with those from the Fairhaven ship *Columbus*, the first and only time the men engaged in a cooperative effort. The *Harrison* frequently hovered close to the ice, and Amos and the others often rowed boats among the floes on the hunt. The usual unsuccessful chases occurred, but only twice did struck whales escape. Only once was cutting-in partially unsuccessful, when a whale's head was lost to rugged seas. Otherwise, the hunt was carried out skillfully and successfully. Amos and his fellow green hands were green in name only; experience had transformed them into able whalemen.

At times the thick Okhotsk fog lifted to reveal distant views of desolate landmarks such as Cape Alevina and Great Shantar Island, and on occasion the ship closed in with the ice-choked land. From August 30 to September 1, the *Harrison* anchored at Feklistova Island, and boat crews rowed ashore to stock up on wood and fresh water. The season ended with a rash of kills. Within hours after leaving the island on the night of September 1, the waist boat struck, killed, and towed a whale to the ship. The next day, the final three whales of the season were killed—one of them a calf—and two were cut-in. With its last carcass in tow, the *Harrison* returned to Feklistova Island on September 3, anchored in six fathoms of water, and finished cutting-in.

For the next three days, the ship sat in a smudge of smoke as the *Harrison*'s tryworks blazed and the men boiled oil. Two succeeding days were spent stowing down the casks. On September 9 the men ferried back and forth to Feklistova, getting off wood and water, and the next day they waited for the wind to pick up. Finally, at 5 A.M. on the morning of September 11, the crew of the *Harrison* weighed anchor and sailed for the Sandwich Islands, with a ship full of oil and bone.

Passing within sight of Cape Elizabeth's barren, rocky hills, on the northern end of Sakhalin Island, the *Harrison* sailed eastward through the southern Okhotsk waters and reached the Kuril Islands on the night of September 21. Navigating the passage between Onekotan and Paramusir islands the following morning, the ship emerged from the Sea of Okhotsk at noon and began its Pacific run in a heavy rain. After an uneventful voyage, the *Harrison* anchored at Lahaina on the afternoon of October 27, and the men enjoyed liberty on Maui for the last time.[22]

A letter Captain Hatheway wrote at Lahaina on November 6 carried word of the *Harrison*'s success to New Bedford. Recruited for its homeward journey, her crew well rested, the ship weighed anchor at Lahaina on November 13 and sailed for Oahu, reaching Honolulu the following morning. While the *Harrison* lay off and on outside the harbor, a boat crew went ashore, and two green hands took advantage of the opportunity to slip away. A search for the deserters was futile, and rather than waste time waiting for them to return or be apprehended, Captain Hatheway left them behind. By succumbing to the temptations of Hawaiian paradise, the two forfeited whatever gains they had coming after three years of work. Captain Hatheway was perfectly content to leave them and their lays behind, consequently increasing the profits for Gilbert Hatheway and the other owners of the *Harrison*.[23]

Half an hour after noon on November 15, 1853, the ship left Oahu bound to the south, and Amos Humiston bid a fond aloha to the Sandwich Islands for the last time. Gradually the lush green islands disappeared from his sight; they would never fade from his memory. The *Harrison* crossed the equator late in November, and on the morning of December 3, a sperm whale was the ship's final kill. From December 19 to 21, laying off and on in rugged seas at Rarotonga, the *Harrison* got off its last recruits for the trip home, and the crew took a final look at Polynesia. Two men found that last look irresistible and deserted. Captain Hatheway readily left them behind.

New Year's Day found the *Harrison* in the middle of the South Pacific. After a routine voyage, the ship crossed the Drake Passage from January 25 to 28, 1854, sailing within sight of the Diego Ramirez Islands, viewing Cape Horn through a snowstorm, and passing within ten miles of Staten Island. On the afternoon of February 4, in response to the familiar cry from the masthead lookouts, the *Harrison*'s boats splashed into the water for the last time. The men rowed after a pod of sperm whales until sunset, but their final chase ended as so many others had: with the whales running away from the boats, spouting and sounding in freedom.[24]

Three years, four months, and eight days after leaving New Bedford, on April 20, 1854, in light westward winds and good weather, the *Harrison* reached home. No sooner was the gangplank in place than a swarm of land sharks boarded the ship to welcome the returning whalemen with open and greedy arms. Runners badgered Amos and the others to lodge at certain boardinghouses, to have a bath, haircut, or shave, to buy a new set of shore clothes, or to borrow some spending money—all to be paid for when the whalemen received their lays. Amos really did not have a choice. For the next day or two, before he was paid, he was just as much at the mercy of the infitters in 1854 as he had been with the outfitters in 1850.[25]

In the meantime, Gilbert Hatheway figured out how much he owed Amos and the rest of the crew. Stevedores unloaded 19,000 pounds of whalebone and casks containing 180 barrels of sperm oil and 2,700 barrels of whale oil from the *Harrison*. According to the *Whalemen's Shipping List* of April 25, 1854, the New Bedford market for sperm oil had been quiet for the previous week; a gallon of sperm oil was selling for $1.50. The whale oil market, on the other hand, had been active, with considerable sales at an average of 55 cents a gallon. Whalebone was selling at 35 cents per pound. Using those figures, Gilbert Hatheway determined the *Harrison* had produced sperm oil worth $8,505, whale oil worth $46,777.50, and whalebone (including that transshipped from Lahaina in 1852) worth $9,670.50, for a total gross profit of $64,953. Hatheway next subtracted various fees the *Harrison* had incurred (charges for pilotage, wharfage, and transshipment), reducing the net profit to approximately $64,300.[26]

When Amos Humiston was summoned to Gilbert Hatheway's counting room to receive his pay, he learned that his 1/185 lay as a green hand amounted to about $350. That equaled wages of $8.70 per month, or 29 cents a day. But Amos would not receive even that meager sum. From that amount, Hatheway deducted charges for Amos's outfit, cash advances, slop chest charges, and various other incidental fees, totaling perhaps $100 to $200. Estimating Amos's debits at $150, his final payment would have been reduced to about $200—less than $5 a month, and only 17 cents a day.[27]

About $200 dollars was all he had to show for more than three years of hardship, danger, boredom, grime, and toil. Seventeen cents per day was about the average wage for a green hand during the great age of American whaling, but it was five or six times less, Amos knew, than he would have made had he stayed home as a harness maker. Suddenly life in a harness shop did not look all that bad to Amos Humiston. Land sharks pestered him to sign aboard other whaleships for other voyages, but like most other green hands, one voyage had been enough for Amos. He made his way to the railroad depot on Pearl Street or to one of the steamship lines, bought himself a ticket, and left New Bedford for home.

NOTES

1. Logbook, Ship *Harrison*, Nicholson Whaling Collection, Providence Public Library; Marian Reynolds, "Letter Ties the Centuries," *Olean Times Herald*, April 23, 1962, 18.

2. Briton Cooper Busch, *"Whaling Will Never Do for Me": The American Whaleman in the Nineteenth Century* (Lexington: University Press of Kentucky, 1994), 177, 185; Elmo Paul Hohman, *The American Whaleman: A Study of Life and Labor in the Whaling Industry* (New York: Longmans, Green, 1928), 111–113; MacKinnon Simpson, *Whale Song: A Pictorial History of Whaling and Hawaii* (Honolulu: Beyond Words Publishing Co., 1986), 33–34, 94; *Whalemen's Shipping List and Merchants' Transcript*, March 8, 1853.

3. Henry T. Cheever, *Life in the Sandwich Islands: or, The Heart of the Pacific, As It Was and Is* (New York: A. S. Barnes & Co., 1851), 62–78; Edward T. Perkins, *Na Motu: or, Reef-Rovings in the South Seas* (New York: Pudney & Russell, 1854), 93–97; Alexander G. Findlay, *A Directory for the Navigation of the North Pacific Ocean* (London: Richard Holmes Laurie, 1870), 842–843; Simpson, *Whale Song*, 95.

4. Logbook, Ship *Harrison*; Alexander G. Findlay, *A Directory for the Navi-*

gation of the South Pacific Ocean (London: Richard Holmes Laurie, 1863), 389, 484; Busch, *"Whaling Will Never Do for Me,"* 70, 97; William Wyatt Gill, *Life in the Southern Isles; or, Scenes and Incidents in the South Pacific and New Guinea* (London: Religious Tract Society, 1876), 5, 8, 11, 15–16. Today Rarotonga is one of the Cook Islands.

5. Logbook, Ship *Harrison.*

6. Ibid.; *Whalemen's Shipping List and Merchants' Transcript,* April 6, 1852; Clifford W. Ashley, *The Yankee Whaler* (New York: Dover, 1991), 81.

7. Logbook, Ship *Harrison*; Findlay, *A Directory of the South Pacific Ocean,* 381; Hohman, *American Whaleman,* 169; Ashley, *Yankee Whaler,* 17–18.

8. Logbook, Ship *Harrison*; Findlay, *A Directory of the South Pacific Ocean,* 381–382.

9. Henry T. Cheever, *The Island World of the Pacific* (New York: Harper & Brothers, 1851), 313, 322, 340, 352, 379; Perkins, *Na Motu,* 198–200; Findlay, *A Directory of the North Pacific Ocean,* 828–829; Titus Coan, *Life in Hawaii: An Autobiographic Sketch of Mission Life and Labors (1835–1881)* (New York: Anson D. F. Randolph & Company, 1882), 24–25, 29, 40; James F. Munger, *Two Years in the Pacific and Arctic Oceans and China* (Fairfield, Wash.: Ye Galleon Press, 1967), 21–22, 62–63, 70.

10. Logbook, Ship *Harrison*; Busch, *"Whaling Will Never Do for Me,"* 121–123; Coan quoted in Henry T. Cheever, *The Whale and His Captors; or, the Whaleman's Adventures, and the Whale's Biography* (New York: Harper & Brothers, 1849), 248.

11. Cheever, *Island World of the Pacific,* 355, quoting Coan's letter of October 16, 1849.

12. Ibid., 339–340; Perkins, *Na Motu,* 199–200; Coan, *Life in Hawaii,* 279–281.

13. Logbook, Ship *Harrison.* Hubbard's fate is unknown.

14. Ibid.; *Whalemen's Shipping List and Merchants' Transcript,* December 7, 1852; *Friend* [Honolulu], October 8, 1852.

15. Logbook, Ship *Harrison; Whalemen's Shipping List and Merchants' Transcript,* January 11, 25, 1853.

16. Logbook, Ship *Harrison*; *Friend,* October 8, 1852; Hohman, *American Whaleman,* 87–88.

17. Logbook, Ship *Harrison*; Findlay, *A Directory of the South Pacific Ocean,* 592–594; Findlay, *A Directory of the North Pacific Ocean,* 697–701; Munger, *Two Years in the Pacific,* 41.

18. Logbook, Ship *Harrison*; Hohman, *American Whaleman,* 139; Busch, *"Whaling Will Never Do for Me,"* 169–170.

19. Logbook, Ship *Harrison*; Ashley, *Yankee Whaler,* 97–98.

20. Logbook, Ship *Harrison.*

21. Findlay, *A Directory of the North Pacific Ocean,* 567–568.

22. Logbook, Ship *Harrison*; Findlay, *A Directory of the North Pacific Ocean,* 572, 574. According to the spelling in the logbook, it is *Fiklistov* Island; Findlay spells it *Feklistoff*; the accepted current English spelling is *Feklistova.*

23. *Whalemen's Shipping List and Merchants' Transcript*, January 17, 1854; Logbook, Ship *Harrison*; Busch, *"Whaling Will Never Do for Me,"* 91; Hohman, *American Whaleman*, 66–67.

24. Logbook, Ship *Harrison*.

25. Hohman, *American Whaleman*, 104.

26. *Whalemen's Shipping List and Merchants' Transcript*, April 25, 1864; Hohman, *American Whaleman*, 218. The *Whalemen's Shipping List and Merchants' Transcript* of June 20, 1854, published the following total amounts of the voyage, as corrected by gaugers' and weighers' returns: 177 barrels of sperm oil and 2,543 barrels of whale oil.

27. Hohman, *American Whaleman*, 220, 246–264; Busch, *"Whaling Will Never Do for Me,"* 6–7, 10, 12. Total lays, less those uncollected, equaled $16,340.93, or 25 percent of the net profit, leaving 75 percent to be divided among the owners. That amounted to about 5 percent more to the owners than usual, according to Hohman (223, 285–286).

CHAPTER 4

Philinda

It was a whirlwind courtship. Amos was fresh back in Tioga County, well seasoned with spindrift and full of exciting, exotic, and romantic tales of the balmy Sandwich Islands, the perilous Okhotsk ice fields, and the wild pursuit of the great leviathan. Philinda was a young widow, buffeted by life's vicissitudes to an uncertain future in Candor. Eleven weeks after they met, they were married. It was a classic example of love at first sight—a love that endured unabated for nine years, until the two were parted by death.

Philinda Betsy Ensworth Smith, like Amos, had wandered in recent years, albeit on a much narrower scale. While his voyage on the *Harrison* had carried him halfway around the globe, her travels had taken her from central and western New York State and nearby Pennsylvania to Michigan and back. Their reasons for being in Tioga County were likewise dissimilar. Amos's return to Candor was a homecoming; Philinda's presence there was an unhappy happenstance.

Born on February 1, 1831, in Norwich, Chenango County, New York, she was the fourth of eleven children of Tracy and Harriet (Williams) Ensworth. Many years later, Philinda told her grandchildren about girlhood trips in her native state, to Cayuga on the Finger Lake of the same name, and far to the west to Olean, on the Allegheny River in Cattaraugus County, territory she would return to in coming years.[1]

At the age of nineteen, Philinda Ensworth married eighteen-year-old Justin H. Smith on April 15, 1850. Nothing is known of Smith's background or where they wed, but Philinda later recorded that the young couple lived in Michigan. Less than a year after the marriage, Philinda was made a widow when Smith died of unknown causes on January 10, 1851. There is evidence Philinda lived in Hunt's Hollow, Livingston County, New York, and Smethport, McKean County, Pennsylvania, during the years before and after the time of her marriage to Smith. She had an uncle (her mother's brother, William A. Williams) in Smethport, a town situated on a tributary of the Allegheny River about twenty miles south of Olean. But eventually Philinda made her way back to New York State.

She did not go Cattaraugus County, where her parents and family had moved and were living in the town of Ashford, but journeyed instead to Tioga County. Harriet Williams Ensworth was from Candor, and no doubt it was the presence of many of her mother's relatives in that town that drew the Widow Smith there during the early 1850s. One of those relatives, her first cousin, the former Sarah Cowles, must have been the link that brought Philinda Smith and Amos Humiston together. Since 1848, Sarah had been Mrs. Morris Humiston, married to Amos's older brother.[2]

And so the two met in Candor, where Morris Humiston had his saddle and harness shop. Perhaps they were introduced at a welcome-home gathering for Amos hosted by Morris and Sarah. It is even possible that Amos arrived in Candor in time to celebrate his twenty-fourth birthday on April 26, 1854, and he and Philinda might have met on that occasion. However it began, their romance quickly blossomed, and the couple was soon betrothed. With élan—and a certain amount of irony—they picked Independence Day as their wedding date. The Reverend Asa Brooks, Methodist Episcopal preacher, married Amos Humiston and Philinda Betsy Ensworth Smith on the Fourth of July 1854, at the home of the groom's brother in Candor, with Morris and Sarah Humiston and a group of family and friends witnessing the ceremony.[3]

The newlyweds were quick to start a family. Their first child, a boy they named Franklin, was born at Candor on April 10, 1855, nine months and six days after the wedding. Daughter Alice Eliza was born two years after Franklin, on March 30, 1857. Her birthplace, as recorded in a family Bible, was Adrian, Steuben County, New York, approximately sixty miles west of Candor. Whether Amos and Philinda had moved there, or she was there solely for her confinement, is unknown. The middle name Eliza was no doubt given to the baby girl in honor of Philinda's sister, Eliza Ensworth, four years younger than Philinda, who lived with her sister and brother-in-law for several years around the time of the births of Franklin and Alice, and was nurse to both babies.[4]

The Humiston brothers apparently worked together in Morris's harness shop after Amos returned and married Philinda. One source states positively that Amos worked as a harness maker in Candor, and it seems reasonable to assume that he worked in partnership with his brother.[5]

Morris Humiston had established himself as a well-regarded citizen of Candor by the time Amos returned; in 1855, 1857, and 1858 his townsmen elected him town clerk. Candor was smaller than Owego, with fewer than half of the inhabitants; its population in 1855 was fewer than four thousand. The township's forested uplands were divided into ridges by streams flowing south toward the Susquehanna; the fertile valleys yielded fine crops of grain. The village of Candor, situated on Catatonk Creek near the center of the township, included a gristmill, an ironworks, a tannery, and four churches. It was also a station on the Cayuga and Susquehanna Railroad (the former Ithaca-Owego Railroad), which connected with the Erie line at Owego.[6]

Although it appears they spent their early married life in Candor, Amos and Philinda at some point made a trip to Michigan together, according to one of their grandchildren. That was a round trip of more than a thousand miles from Tioga County, and consequently not to be undertaken lightly— except perhaps to the widely traveled Amos and his young wife, who herself was not unfamiliar with wandering.

According to the family story, Amos took Philinda to Grand Rapids at the time trees were being felled for the state capitol at Lansing. But the timber for Michigan's state house was cut in 1847, seven years before Amos met Philinda (and three years before she was in Michigan during her first marriage), so that part of the tale must be a mistake. Two apparent reasons might have drawn the Humistons to make the journey west. Philinda already had connections in Michigan from her previous residence with Justin Smith, and Amos had family there.

Amos's older sister, Lois Ann, had married as a thirteen-year-old girl, and she and her husband, Phineas Goodwin, moved in 1855 to Michigan, where they settled in the town of Ionia, in the central part of the lower peninsula. Ionia is situated about halfway between Lansing and Grand Rapids, on the north bank of the Grand River, which links all three places. It is quite likely that the Humistons would have seen the sights in both Lansing and Grand Rapids (as mentioned in the family story) if they visited Ionia. The death of Phineas Goodwin at Ionia on August 8, 1859, suggests another possible motive for the trip to Michigan. Perhaps Amos and Philinda went there that summer to comfort and assist his widowed sister and her brood of five children. In considering that possibility, however, another circumstance must be taken into account. Philinda was nursing her third child, a seven-month-old son, when her Michigan brother-in-law died. If she did journey west with Amos at that time, she either took the baby with her or left him with a wet nurse in the east.

What is certain is that by 1859, Amos and Philinda had established a new home in western New York; it was there that their third child was born and the family spent its remaining few years together.[7]

Portville is a rectangular township anchoring the southeastern corner of Cattaraugus County, New York. The Allegheny River, running northward from its Pennsylvania source, enters New York State in Portville and carves an oxbow through southern Cattaraugus County before returning to the Keystone State and its rendezvous with the Monongahela at Pittsburgh. Formed from the township of Olean in 1837, Portville took its name from its prominence as a place of embarkation for shipments of goods down the Allegheny to Pittsburgh and places beyond via the Ohio River.

Prior to its formation, Portville was sparsely settled by pioneer homesteaders from central New York and New England. Only 462 souls were recorded in the town in the national census of 1840. By the state census of 1855, Portville's population had more than doubled, to 1,164, and during the next five years, it added another 461 people, including the 5 Humistons. Although the place was much smaller than Owego and less than a third of the size of Candor, its steady growth offered particularly good prospects to a young harness maker and his family.

Cattaraugus County's countryside was rumpled by the foothills of the Allegheny Mountains, and Portville's uplands were covered with forests of pine and hemlock. Making use of that abundance, the early settlers were mostly lumbermen and shingle makers. During autumn and winter, men milled and stockpiled their lumber and shingles; when the spring floods came, they were ready to raft their product down the Allegheny and Ohio to markets in Pittsburgh, Cincinnati, and Louisville. By June they were back in Portville, flush with their earnings and able to pay off debts accumulated over the past year. Lumbering and shingle making were still the major industries when the Humistons arrived in town in the late 1850s, and it was rare for Amos or Philinda to meet a man who had not rafted the rivers—and most of them had made the return trip to Portville from their distant destinations at least once on foot, the mark of a proud veteran raftsman. There were times when the Humistons could not see the surface of the Allegheny because of the river's bristling mat of jumbled logs.

Certain of the lumber mills had grown dramatically by the time the Humistons arrived in Portville, shipping millions of feet of board and shingles each year and greatly enriching their owners. Portville's most prominent and prosperous families—the Wheelers, the Westons, the Mersereaus, and the Dusenburys—owned the largest lumber firms. More than a hundred men were employed by each of the big companies, and some of them lived in company houses near the mills. Logs and lumber and the people who worked with them drove much of Portville's economy and colored much of the town's landscape.

A second prominent Portville industry connected logging to harness making. Hemlock bark was an important ingredient in tanning leather; bark was a by-product of lumbering. In 1849 Mark Comstock, for the previous decade a jobber sawing lumber for Dusenbury, Wheeler and Company, opened a tannery in the village of Portville. After years of indifferent success, he sold the business to Charles K. Wright, who enlarged the tannery, converted from water to steam power, and greatly increased production. Amos Humiston was assured of an abundant supply of leather in Portville. Mark Comstock, meanwhile, turned to farming, keeping a grocery store, and dealing in real estate—in which capacity he would do business with the Humistons.

Lumbering and tanning were the dominant businesses in Portville, but by the late 1850s agriculture had made significant gains, and about 15 percent of the township's acreage was cleared and productive. Farmsteads in the flat, fertile valleys of several creeks produced thousands of bushels of wheat, oats, corn, potatoes, and apples and thousands of pounds of butter and cheese. Sheep were the predominant livestock, far outnumbering cows or hogs, and farm wives spun and wove hundreds of yards of wool each year. Farmers relied on more than three hundred oxen to work their fields. Of significance to Amos, the horse population in Portville stood at about two hundred.

About a fifth of the township's population—almost three hundred people—lived in the village of Portville when the Humistons arrived. In addition to lumbermen, tannery workers, and farmers, residents included blacksmiths, grocers, general merchants, physicians, druggists, mechanics, carpenters, and other tradesmen. On Main Street were two churches—the Methodist Episcopal, built in 1845, and the Presbyterian, erected in 1852. A new minister, the Reverend Isaac G. Ogden, arrived to tend the flock of the latter church in October 1858. Pastor Ogden probably did not know the Humiston family very well during his first few years in the village—they were not members of his church—but their fates were destined to intertwine at a future date.

One Portville peculiarity is worthy of mention. During its growth as a lumber town, the place had a large share of rough young men who ignored the Sabbath day, drank copious amounts of whiskey, and were generally proficient at raising hell. The proprietors of Dusenbury, Wheeler and Company recognized a need to elevate the moral standard in Portville, and around 1850 they managed to have the town pass a law prohibiting the sale of intoxicating liquors. So Portville was a temperance town when the Humistons arrived. Whether the absence of grog was important to Amos or not, we do not know.[8]

Two main reasons seem likely to explain why the Humistons chose Portville. Amos no doubt saw a good business opportunity in the place. According to the 1860 census, his was the only harness shop in the township. And Portville's location brought Philinda into fair proximity to her family.

Her parents in Ashford were about thirty-five miles away over the most direct Cattaraugus County roads, and her Smethport relatives were about twenty-five miles south in Pennsylvania. Philinda was familiar with the area from her childhood visits to neighboring Olean, and it is possible the Humistons discovered Portville while passing through it on their way to visit her relatives.[9]

However it came about, the Humistons were living in Portville as the 1850s closed. Five or six years before their arrival, the new bride of lumber company owner William F. Wheeler had been dismayed at her first sight of the place. "I never saw a rougher, more primitive country," Marilla Clarke Wheeler recollected in 1852. "There were very few houses, and those poor, little ones. There were stumps and logs and heaps of rubbish everywhere." By the time the Humistons arrived in 1857 or 1858, a half-decade of progress had smoothed some of Portville's roughness, but the town nevertheless retained a frontier air.[10]

In Portville the Humiston family circle was completed when baby Frederick was born on January 17, 1859. Within a few months, Alice turned two and Franklin four. For the next few years, bonds of intimacy embraced the Humistons, and the family charted its course through life guided by joys, hopes, and dreams. They gave each other pet nicknames: Ame, Philind, Frankie, Allie, and Freddy.[11] Frank and Alice watched baby brother Fred learn to walk and talk as two years swiftly passed. They grew quickly, but all three children remained his babies to Amos. He loved to hold them on his knees and listen to their cheerful babble.[12]

Content as he was surrounded by the love of his family, Amos nevertheless let his fantasies fly on occasion to a far corner of the world. When autumn leaves swirled in chill gusts of wind, or snow blanketed Portville on frigid winter nights, he regaled Philinda with tales of the eternally warm Sandwich Islands, and told her how much he wanted to take her to that Pacific paradise.[13]

It seems that Amos had a coworker in his Portville harness shop, at least for a couple of years: his boyhood Owego neighbor, George Lillie. When the two began to work together is unknown, but by 1860 Lillie was living as part of the Humiston household in Portville. Whether they were full partners or Lillie was just an assistant is also unknown. In any case, harnesses made or repaired by Humiston and Lillie could doubtless be spotted throughout Portville, on horses pulling the plow of a farmer, the logs of a teamster, or the best buggy of a lumber baron's wife.

Much of harness making was solitary work, and Amos and George often toiled together in seclusion at the workbench or stitching horse. But interruptions to deal with customers were frequent, and a wide spectrum of

Portville's population passed through the harness shop and met Amos Humiston.[14]

As time passed, the town took the measure of its new citizen. Although the only known estimation of Amos by a Portville resident dated from after his death, it had the frank ring of honesty. The Reverend Isaac Ogden described Amos as "a man of noble, generous impulses, a quiet citizen, a kind neighbor and devotedly attached to his family. His sailor-like generosity will account largely for the fact that he never accumulated property." It is certain that the Humistons lived in humble circumstances in Portville. According to the census of 1860, Amos had no personal estate or property of any value. As best can be determined, the Humistons and George Lillie were then living on Main Street, in the heart of the village, in close proximity to the stores and the two churches. Nearby neighbors included lumberman Smith Parish, merchant Henry C. Scofield, and carpenter and builder Guy T. Lowery.[15]

Evidence indicates that the Humistons moved to a cottage a mile or two outside the village between 1860 and 1862. This place was in unfinished condition and not entirely weatherproof, subject to leaks and drafts. Amos was never able to afford to fix it up, one reason being the "sailor-like generosity" mentioned by Isaac Ogden. Amos admittedly was an easy mark for a sad story, impulsively lending money to friends and acquaintances on the slightest pretext. This was a trait he was coming to regret as he realized the impact it had on his family's living conditions.[16]

Amos was not a familiar figure in either of Portville's two houses of worship. "Mr. H. made a profession of religion some eight or ten years ago," Pastor Ogden observed, "but like many others, did not walk as a Christian should." The comment would seem to criticize Amos for a lack of religious orthodoxy and steady attendance at church rather than a life of unmitigated wrongdoing. Determining exactly when Amos was converted is clouded by Ogden's imprecise estimation of "some eight or ten years" before 1863, when he penned his description. Perhaps it was in 1853, at Hilo, with Amos renouncing a whaleman's life of sin for the godliness exhorted by the Reverend Titus Coan. Maybe it was in 1855, about the time when Frank was born, and Amos and Philinda were living in Owego. In any case, his faith apparently had lapsed by the time he brought his family to Portville. The extensive series of letters he sent to Philinda a few years later are entirely devoid of religious content.[17]

If the spiritual man is an enigma, the physical man can be scrutinized. The only photographic portrait of Amos Humiston made from life was likely taken during his Portville years. He wore a coat and vest—probably his best clothes—and tied his necktie with a bowknot to pose for an unknown photographer. A single exposure captured Amos's likeness as a negative on a chemically sensitized sheet of glass, which when backed by a dark surface resulted in a positive image called an ambrotype. The camera revealed a strong face—dark hair neatly combed back from a broad forehead; dark eyes staring beneath low, straight brows; high cheekbones; clean-shaven, ruddy cheeks (rouged a bit by the photographer's paintbrush); a long nose; and a thin-lipped mouth barely hinting at a smile over a large, square chin. Amos's features in his portrait were seen as in a mirror, reversed by the photographic process. The ambrotype was a sixth plate, a standard size for portraiture about two and three-quarters by three and a quarter inches in dimension. It was mounted under a gilt matte embossed with a floral motif, opposite a crimson velvet cushion, in a hinged, clasped, booklike case.[18]

It was a family treasure. How many times did Philinda unclasp the ambrotype and stare at it with longing after Amos left for the war? How many times did she open it to give little Frank, Alice, and Fred a treasured glance at their absent father? Or did she leave the case open, sitting on a mantel or a table, so she and the children could meet the ambrotype's gaze whenever they wanted? Maybe it was just such a look that inspired Philinda to dress up the children and have them sit for another ambrotype, a gift to send to her distant husband as a token of his family's love.

Embracing his wife or cuddling his children, Amos forgot the worries of the world. But he and Philinda knew all too well that their babies were growing up during perilous times. North and South, sectional discord sprouted like weeds in a garden during the 1850s, and animosities increased with each passing year. When Frank was born, pro- and anti-slavery forces were struggling for control of a new western territory, a smoldering portent of violence in "Bleeding Kansas." Weeks before Alice was born, the Supreme Court ruling in the *Dred Scott* case denied citizenship to blacks, declared the Missouri Compromise unconstitutional, and fanned the flames of the debate over slavery. Ten months after Fred was born, those flames burst into a flash fire at the hands of the incendiary John Brown, flaring from Harpers Ferry to every corner of the land.

After years of sliding steadily toward disunion, the country plunged into the abyss in 1860. The November election of Abraham Lincoln triggered the secession crisis; within three months several southern states withdrew from the Union and met to declare a new nation. Portville voters favored Lincoln by a margin of more than two to one over his three opponents combined, 235 to 109. The town had a decidedly Republican slant. The lumber magnates—Henry Dusenbury, John G. Mersereau, William W. Weston, and William Wheeler—and tannery owner Charles Wright were

Philinda

all former Whigs and early and ardent converts to the Republican party, ready to exert their considerable influence to sway the views of their townsmen. Who Amos Humiston voted for, or indeed if he voted at all, is unknown. He was apparently as apolitical as he was irreligious. None of the writings about Amos make any mention of his political leanings, and his wartime letters lack any commentary on political issues.[19]

Amos was not lacking in patriotism, however, and when the North was electrified by the fall of Fort Sumter, he too was shocked by the spark. But as eager as he was to volunteer, concern for his family gave him pause. When the first recruits left Cattaraugus County in response to President Lincoln's call for troops in the wake of Fort Sumter's surrender, Amos stayed at home. "When the rebellion first took the form of open war upon the country, he was anxious to enlist," testified the Reverend Ogden, "but his duty to his family seemed then to be paramount to his duty to his country." Struggling with mixed emotions, Amos was a restless observer rather than an active participant as his adopted home town and county reacted to the crisis.[20]

He wrestled with his conscience as he watched his friends and neighbors volunteer to fight to uphold the Union in 1861. He followed their exploits at the front as reported in the two local newspapers, the *Olean Advertiser* and the *Olean Times*, and evaluated the latest war news in discussions with customers at the harness shop. A whirlwind of events swept by with the passing months. In Virginia in the spring of 1862, the Union Army of the Potomac under Major General George B. McClellan cautiously crept up the peninsula between the York and James rivers to within a few miles of Richmond, capital of the Confederate States of America. On May 31 and June 1, 1862, the rebel army brought McClellan to an abrupt halt at the Battle of Fair Oaks. For the first time, many of the home folk in Cattaraugus County felt the sickening sensation of scanning newspaper casualty lists for the names of loved ones. The 37th, 64th, and 85th New York Volunteer Infantry Regiments, each containing Cattaraugus County men, all participated in the battle, and all suffered substantial losses.[21]

A crucial development of the Battle of Fair Oaks was the ascent of General Robert E. Lee to the command of the Army of Northern Virginia. At the end of June, Lee's Confederates drove McClellan's army away from Richmond in the Seven Days fighting, culminating in the Battle of Malvern Hill. The Peninsula Campaign was over; the Union army was defeated. Casualties in the three regiments containing Cattaraugus County men were relatively light, but total Federal losses in the Seven Days amounted to almost 16,000 soldiers. Northerners were stunned by the staggering cost and dismayed by the retreat of their army.

On the day fighting raged at Malvern Hill, July 1, 1862, President Lincoln issued a call for 300,000 volunteers to serve the Union cause for three years. Within a week after the president's summons, the War Department in Washington imposed a quota of twenty-eight regiments on New York State. That same day, July 7, the state ordered one of those regiments to be raised in Cattaraugus County and its western neighbor, Chautauqua County. At a meeting on July 12 at Mayville, the Chautauqua County seat, representatives of the two counties resolved to recruit the apportioned regiment—six companies to be raised in Chautauqua, four in Cattaraugus. On July 17, delegates from Cattaraugus convened at the county courthouse in Ellicottville. At the meeting, committees of three men from each town in the county were appointed to oversee recruiting in their communities. Chosen to represent Portville were lumber company owner William Wheeler and two of Amos's neighbors, Guy Lowery and Henry Scofield.[22]

Less than three weeks after the appointment of the committee, the *Olean Times* reported, "The town of Portville has done her duty nobly in the present emergency." Citizens had gathered at several war meetings and responded with enthusiastic cheers and applause to stirring orations and patriotic music. "Prominent citizens have taken hold of the work in good earnest, and complete success has been the result," the newspaper observed, citing in particular the support of lumber barons John Mersereau, Smith Parish, and committeeman William Wheeler. Portville's highly esteemed town supervisor, Lewis D. Warner, a raftsman, carpenter, and joiner, was the first to sign the enlistment roll. "This example of course had its effect," noted the *Times*, "and the result was his neighbors and friends followed, and the roll was soon completed." Portville's quota was rapidly filled. "All honor to Mr. Warner," declared the *Times*. "Three cheers for Portville!"

At the Portville war meetings, more than a thousand dollars was subscribed by generous and sympathetic townspeople "towards supporting the families of volunteers and helping along in the good work," noted the *Times*. That endowment was the key factor in Amos Humiston's decision to enlist. He had long wanted to go, but resisted the urge out of concern for his family. Now, Pastor Ogden observed, "when he received assurance from responsible citizens that his family should be cared for during his absence," Amos could volunteer in good conscience. He enlisted at the first opportunity.[23]

Years later, a close friend of Philinda Humiston wrote a poem describing Amos's decision to enlist. Because Philinda provided intimate details to the author, the verses no doubt revealed the essence of the dialogue between husband and wife. According to the poem, Amos returned one evening from the harness shop and told Philinda he was going to enlist. Despite his love for her and the children, he felt it was wrong to stay at home in the light of the recent call. Philinda admonished him to remember his promise to repair their run-down home, and pleaded with him to think of the children. She made him look at little Frank, Alice, and Fred, sweetly asleep. Her pleading wounded his heart, Amos admitted, and he confessed his faults—the wild ways he learned as a whaleman, his careless generosity with money. But he assured Philinda that their Portville neighbors would fix the little house and care for her and the children. Pastor Ogden had counseled him to enlist, and promised to watch over the family. Amos was not to be dissuaded, and he left Philinda sobbing in silence. His final request (perhaps a bit of poetic license) was that she send him a picture of the children.[24]

Twelve days before Amos enlisted, an act of Congress increased the pension rates for widows and orphans of deceased soldiers. Amos was always candidly realistic about the possibility he would not return from the war, and it is possible news of the bill was another mitigating factor in his decision to enlist, albeit a macabre one.[25]

Saturday, July 26, 1862, was a busy day for Arthur Hotchkiss. That day, the Olean carpenter and joiner appeared at war meetings in his home town and at Portville and Allegany, inaugurating the drive to recruit the new regiment in those communities. At the Portville meeting, the town's first volunteers to answer President Lincoln's latest call came forward. With the cheers of the crowd ringing in their ears, Amos Humiston and ten other men signed Hotchkiss's roll, enlisting to serve three years. Amos himself encouraged one of the enlistments. A young man on the verge of volunteering held back because he doubted he had the stamina to endure the army's long, tiring marches. "Come on," said Amos, "I will carry your musket for you." The gentle offer was illustrative of Amos's character, Isaac Ogden thought.[26]

Lewis Warner joined Arthur Hotchkiss in enrolling volunteers in the southeastern corner of Cattaraugus County, canvassing the towns of Portville, Hinsdale, Ischua, Humphrey, Allegany, and Olean. Warner signed up sixteen men in Portville during August. In the meantime, the original plan to recruit a single regiment in Cattaraugus and Chautauqua counties was amended. Chautauqua had raised its six required companies, and Cattaraugus had recruited its quota of four, including the company enrolled by Warner and Hotchkiss. On August 19, Addison G. Rice, an Ellicottville lawyer and state assemblyman, was appointed colonel with authority to recruit a second regiment. As things turned out, Chautauqua County sent a full regiment of ten companies to the front as the 112th New York Volunteer Infantry. Two surplus Chautauqua companies were added to eight eventual Cattaraugus companies to form Colonel Rice's regiment, soon to be designated the 154th New York. One of the last Cattaraugus companies, enrolled primarily in southeastern quadrant of the county, included eleven more men who enlisted in Portville.[27]

About a month after Amos volunteered, Portville's harness shop closed for good when George Lillie followed his partner's lead and enlisted. Lillie enrolled in Olean on August 30 as a member of the 9th New York Cavalry, a regiment with sizable numbers of Chautauqua and Cattaraugus county men. He was destined to put his skills to use in the service, eventually becoming the saddler of his company.[28]

By the time Lillie joined the cavalry, Amos and the other volunteers Warner and Hotchkiss recruited had left home and proceeded to their regimental rendezvous. Amos's parting with Philinda and the children can only be imagined. Did they exchange tender hugs, sweet kisses, and heartfelt words of endearment, and try to subdue their fears? Or did Amos depart when the children were asleep, unable to stand the oppression of leaving them, gently kissing his slumbering little ones before taking his leave? According to Pastor Ogden—and apparently related to him by Philinda—Amos engaged in some solemn introspection on his departure from Portville. "He said to his wife as he was leaving," the minister later wrote, "that he wished he was a better man, and hoped he might be."[29]

NOTES

1. Ensworth Family Record, courtesy David Humiston Kelley (hereafter DHK); Marian Reynolds, "Letter Ties the Centuries," *Olean Times Herald*, April 23, 1962, 18. A younger sister of Philinda died in infancy; a younger brother died in early childhood.

2. DHK, "Notes on Philinda Betsy Ensworth," typescript, 1993; Warren Humiston memoir, August 1870, Vol. 1, p. 268, courtesy David B. Morgan.

3. Affidavits of Morris Humiston, John R. Chidsey, and Sarah A. Humiston, April 27, 1866, and of Asa Brooks, June 7, 1866, Amos Humiston pension records, National Archives; *Owego Gazette*, August 10, 1854; *Binghamton Daily Republican*, August 3, 1855; DHK, "Notes on Philinda Betsy Ensworth."

4. *Owego Gazette*, April 19, 1855; "Ensworth Family Record"; affidavit of Eliza Lake, February 15, 1869, Amos Humiston pension records.

5. New York (State) Bureau of Military Statistics, *First Annual Report of the Chief of the Bureau of Military Statistics* (n.p., 1864), 32.

6. Henry B. Pierce and D. Hamilton H·ird, *History of Tioga, Chemung, Tompkins, and Schuyler Counties, New York* (Philadelphia, Everts & Ensign, 1879), 129, 133, 137–138.

7. Letter of Ruth Tarbell Humiston, quoted in Marian Reynolds, "Letter Ties the Centuries," 18; James Junius Goodwin, *The Goodwins of Hartford, Connecticut, Descendants of William and Ozias Goodwin* (Hartford: Brown and Gross, 1891), 410–411.

8. William Adams, ed., *Historical Gazetteer and Biographical Memorial of Cattaraugus County, N.Y.* (Syracuse: Lyman, Horton & Co., 1893), 170–171, 1000–1027; Franklin Ellis, ed., *History of Cattaraugus County, New York* (Philadelphia: L. H. Everts, 1879), 51–55, 80, 408–413, 463; J. H. French, *Gazetteer of the State of New York* (Syracuse: R. Pearsall Smith, 1860), 194; W. Reginald Wheeler, *Pine Knots and Bark Peelers: The Story of Five Generations of American Lumbermen* (LaJolla, Calif.: Wheeler, 1960), 18–36; Thomas C. Pollock and Ronda S. Pollock, *A History of the Town of Portville, 1805–1920* (Portville: Portville Historical and Preservation Society, 1986), passim.

9. 1860 U.S. Census, Portville.

10. Marilla Clarke Wheeler, autobiographical notes, 21, Portville Historical and Preservation Society.

11. Amos uses the various nicknames in his letters of September 26, December 22, 1862, February 1, 1863, and his poem of March 25, 1863, courtesy of Allan L. Cox, as are all the Humiston letters.

12. Amos Humiston to Dear wife, December 2, 1862.

13. Reynolds, "Letter Ties the Centuries," 18.

14. 1860 U. S. Census, Portville.

15. Rev. Isaac G. Ogden, "Sergeant Hummiston and His Family. Letter from Rev. Isaac G. Ogden," *American Presbyterian*, December 17, 1863, 201; 1860 U. S. Census, Portville; map of the village of Portville in *Atlas of Cattaraugus County, New York* (New York: D. G. Beers & Co., 1869).

16. Miss E. Latimer, *The Unknown* (Philadelphia: Bryson & Son, 1867), 5; Miss E. Latimer, *Idyls of Gettysburg* (Philadelphia: George Maclean, 1872), 59.

17. Ogden, "Sergeant Hummiston and His Family," *American Presbyterian*, December 17, 1863, 201.

18. The original ambrotype is in the possession of David Humiston Kelley.

19. Adams, *Historical Gazetteer and Biographical Memorial*, pp. 1009, 1014, 1021, 1024, 1027.

20. Ogden, "Sergeant Hummiston and His Family," 201.

21. Frederick Phisterer, *New York in the War of the Rebellion* (Albany: Weed, Parsons and Company, 1890), 171.

22. Mark H. Dunkelman and Michael J. Winey, *The Hardtack Regiment: An Illustrated History of the 154th Regiment, New York State Infantry Volunteers* (East Brunswick, N.J.: Fairleigh Dickinson University Press, 1981), 21–22; Mark H. Dunkelman, *Camp James M. Brown: Jamestown's Civil War Rendezvous* (Jamestown, N.Y.: Fenton Historical Society, 1996), 1–6, 34–36; Ellis, *History of Cattaraugus County*, 107.

23. "A Good Example," *Cattaraugus Freeman*, August 7, 1862, quoting the *Olean Times*; Ogden, "Sergeant Hummiston and His Family," 201.

24. Latimer, *The Unknown*, 3–6; Latimer, *Idyls of Gettysburg*, 54–62.

25. Megan J. McClintock, "Civil War Pensions and the Reconstruction of Union Families," *Journal of American History* 83, no. 2 (September 1996): 456–480, argues that the liberalization of pension rates boosted recruiting and cites Amos Humiston specifically, adding (457–458): "Humiston's story cautioned Union supporters

that the success of the North's war effort required not only temporary support of enlistees' wives and children but extended maintenance of bereaved families as well."

26. Descriptive books and muster-in roll of Company C, 154th New York, National Archives; Ogden, "Sergeant Hummiston and His Family," 201.

27. Dunkelman and Winey, *The Hardtack Regiment*, 22–23; Dunkelman, *Camp James M. Brown*, 5–6, 33–36; muster-in rolls of Companies C and I, 154th New York, National Archives.

28. Obituary, George Washington Lillie, *Owego Gazette*, September 12, 1918, 2; Newell Cheney, *History of the Ninth Regiment, New York Volunteer Cavalry* (Jamestown: Martin Merz & Son, 1901), 419.

29. Latimer, *Idyls of Gettysburg*, 62; Ogden, "Sergeant Hummiston and His Family," 201.

CHAPTER 5

To the Front

BY AUGUST 22, 1862, Amos Humiston and the rest of the company recruited by Lewis D. Warner and Arthur Hotchkiss had traveled to Jamestown, the regimental rendezvous in Chautauqua County, where the local fairgrounds, on a rise in the outskirts of town, had been converted into a military depot. Camp James M. Brown, named after a Jamestown officer killed at the Battle of Fair Oaks, was Amos's new address. Set in a grove of pines adjacent to a racetrack, the former fair buildings, transformed into barracks, dining hall, and kitchen, were his new home.[1]

To head the company, the men elected officers. In voting in late August, the two recruiters were chosen to hold the two highest ranks. Lewis Warner was elected captain; Arthur Hotchkiss was voted first lieutenant. An Allegany farmer-turned-lumberman, Warren Onan, became second lieutenant. Next the noncommissioned officers were chosen. Amos Humiston was the fifth corporal selected—a sign of the esteem in which Amos was held by his neighbors and an acknowledgment that his experiences—he was probably the most widely traveled man in the company, and whaling was no job for those lacking bravery—would hold him in good stead during their coming adventures.[2]

Life at Camp Brown often formed an awkward transition from the civilian to the military spheres. Most of the men in the newly formed regiment had no military experience whatsoever and absolutely no idea of what to do. Politician and attorney Addison Rice had wisely accepted his appointment as colonel with the understanding that after he raised the regiment and delivered it to the front, he would be relieved by a veteran officer from Cattaraugus County. That officer turned out to be Patrick Henry Jones of Ellicottville, a native Irishman and Rice's former law partner, who as one of the county's first volunteers in the 37th New York had risen steadily in rank from second lieutenant to major, earning the accolades of his commander for his services during the Peninsula Campaign. In the meantime, Rice relied on the expertise of his lieutenant colonel, Henry C. Loomis, a former lieutenant in the 64th New York who had recovered from a wound received at Fair Oaks.[3]

Because of the general lack of experience, military duties were light: the men answered roll calls, stood guard, and drilled without arms. They had much free time, which they whiled away gabbing, singing, playing baseball, getting up card games, and (surreptitiously) drinking. They got used to sleeping on straw-covered hemlock planks in the barracks, and took on some of the trappings of soldiers when they were issued uniforms, knapsacks, haversacks, and canteens. In general they had few complaints, but many chafed at the restrictions military discipline placed on their freedom. A high fence surrounded the fairgrounds, but it proved to be a surmountable barrier to those determined to run the guard. Guard running in fact became epidemic, and culminated one night in a minor riot during which the guard house was burned to the ground.[4]

In fact, passes and furloughs were granted liberally, and men were constantly passing back and forth between camp and home. Visits from the home folk to Jamestown were common too. Philinda Humiston had recently visited her "old man" at Camp Brown when Amos wrote his first letter to her on September 5. "Thare has ben quite a rush here from Portville since you left," Amos wrote; a visiting Portville citizen would convey his letter home. He had not been very well since Philinda left, having caught a cold during her visit and since aggravated it by getting wet (probably while standing guard in the rain). Most of his comments were about a subject that was the cause of universal dissatisfaction among the men: the quality and quantity of the food. "Thare is some hard talking in the camp," Amos wrote. "The boys think that they cannot get anough to eat but I can get along very well." He noted a Portville man had promised to deliver a box of food donated by families and friends of the town's soldiers. "If you are [of] a mind to send some thing along It will be very axceptable," he told Philinda. But if it was not convenient for her to send anything, Amos assured his wife, "do not trouble your self about it for I shal do very well on what I get here," despite the fact that "the food is hard here now."

In his first letter, Amos touched on themes that would characterize his entire wartime correspondence with Philinda: his love for her and the children, how much he missed them, his concern for their welfare. "It will not do for me to say that I would like to see you," he wrote. "They would say that I was home sick." He had a message for Frank, Alice, and Fred: "Tel the babies that I want to see them very mutch." Anxious to do what he could to provide for his family's support, Amos told Philinda he was supposed to receive some money during the following week, and he would send it to her then.[5]

To the Front

Three weeks passed before Amos was able to send that money. By that time, he had become a full-fledged soldier. He had been examined by a medical inspector; signed the state and federal payrolls; received a quarter of the United States bounty ($25), a $2 premium, the $50 state bounty, and one month's pay in advance ($13); and signed an allotment roll, whereby a designated portion of his future monthly pay would be sent by check to Philinda. On September 24, 1862, he was mustered in the service of the United States, to serve three years, as a corporal of Company C, 154th Regiment, New York State Volunteer Infantry.[6]

Two days after he was mustered in, "old Ame" sent $40 to Philinda and explained how he had allotted $10 of his monthly pay to her, "so that if I am taken prisoner or aney thing eltse should happen," she would have a steady source of income. The Humistons were in debt to Portville real estate agent and grocer Mark Comstock. Comstock expected the money to be sent directly to him, Amos told Philinda, "but I made up my mind that I would send it to you then you can do with it as you like." At the close of his letter he reiterated, "You must use your own judgement about this money that I have sent to you," and suggested that maybe she should not pay Comstock all that was owed him at once.[7]

Amos and a number of other Portville men sent their bounty and advance money home with Franklin Witherell, a townsman returning home after a visit to Camp Brown. A day laborer whose son Burnett was a private in Company C, Witherell obviously was an upstanding member of the Portville community to be thus entrusted with his neighbors' money. Among the other soldiers who sent money home with him were Privates Seymour Sikes and William H. Keyes (who was keeping a secret from the company: he was a deserter from the 78th New York). Writing to his father, Keyes expressed a bit of bravado. "We are all well & expect to leave for Dixie & then the rebels will catch H_l under the flag. I guess the general opinion is that the war will be closed up this Fall & winter." The newly minted soldiers of Company C were brimming with confidence in their ability to help put down the rebellion.[8]

At Camp Brown, an entry was made in a company descriptive book for each enlisted man. The listing for Amos Humiston in Company C's book recorded the same dark complexion and black hair and eyes that had been noted on his seaman's protection paper in New Bedford in 1850, but he had added another quarter-inch to his stature since he sailed as a whaleman; he now measured five feet, seven inches tall. There was one distinctive change in his appearance since he had posed several years before for his ambrotype: he had grown a beard.[9]

As September waned, the time finally came for the regiment's departure for the front. Corporal Humiston and the rest of the 154th New York were roused at an early hour on September 29, and the camp was soon astir with men packing knapsacks, eating breakfast, and receiving one day's rations. That afternoon the regiment was assembled to witness a local dignitary present a stand of colors. Colonel Rice made a brief acceptance speech and ordered Corporal Lewis Bishop of Company C to receive the national flag as the regiment's first color bearer. Then the Chautauqua County Bible Society presented each soldier with a Bible. Thus armed, the regiment marched through the gates of Camp Brown and down the hill to the railroad depot. All along the way, crowds of citizens cheered the marchers, and while a cornet band played patriotic tunes, the men and their families, friends, and lovers on the platform made their fervent goodbyes. As the soldiers boarded the train, a local man presented more than a hundred dollars worth of fruit and other delicacies to them as a parting gift.

At dusk the train steamed away from the ovation at the Jamestown depot, and the cars rolled eastward through Chautauqua County and into Cattaraugus. At brief stops at each station in the regiment's home counties, soldiers leaned out the open windows, scanning the cheering crowds for relatives and friends. The men deboarded at Salamanca, where they were served supper, and a few stops later, the train braked to a halt at the Olean depot.[10]

Amos and Philinda's final parting might have occurred that night in Olean. Certainly Portville folk were there to see their men off—it was the nearest stop to their town that the train made—and Philinda could have been with them; perhaps she brought Frank, Alice, and Fred along to bid their father farewell. Whatever the case, as the train pulled away from Olean, rattled over the tracks to the Hinsdale station, made its final stop in Cattaraugus County, and continued to sway along through the nighttime, Amos and the rest of the men of the 154th New York left home for good.

At 6 A.M. the next morning the train arrived at Elmira, New York, where the men marched to a cow pasture on the outskirts of town and were issued belts, cartridge boxes, cap pouches, and bayonet sheaths. On returning to the depot, each received a British-made Enfield rifled musket, a bayonet, and forty rounds of ammunition. They then discovered a change in their travel arrangements. Private Charles McKay of Company C, an Allegany fifteen-year-old who had fibbed about his age to enlist, later recalled: "Instead of the comfortable upholstered coaches in which we had come thus far, we were loaded onto ordinary boxcars of the Northern Central Railroad; cars that had been hastily fitted up for carrying troops. Nothing seemed to daunt the enthusiasm of the boys who good naturedly piled into the freight cars and were again underway."[11]

From Elmira the tracks ran south into Pennsylvania, winding around mountains and through tunnels, and excitement built as the men viewed the unfamiliar landscapes. Stops were made at Williamsport and York, and Williamsport's patriotic citizens treated the soldiers to supper. Crossing the Mason-Dixon Line, the train entered the slave state of Maryland. "I do not suppose there were a dozen men in our regiment who had ever been as far south as this before," Private McKay noted. "The quaint villages and old buildings looked strange to our unaccustomed eyes." At Baltimore the men were fed dinner at a soldiers' relief agency and changed trains. After a slow overnight trip, they arrived in Washington on the morning of October 2. Fog obscured the city, but the unfinished dome of the Capitol could be seen rising above the mist. It was an unworldly sight, the men thought, like the projection of a giant stereopticon against the sky.

That afternoon, after a tedious wait alongside the tracks, the regiment marched through the city and across the Potomac River on the Long Bridge into Virginia. It was a relatively short march—about seven miles—and their knapsacks were hauled by wagons, but nevertheless, under the burden of the rest of their load, the tramp wore the men out. "By the time we reached Fort Richardson," Private McKay remembered, "we thought we had endured hardship enough to put down the rebellion." The weary soldiers came to a halt just below Fort Richardson's hilltop, wrapped themselves in blankets, and fell asleep on the bare ground.[12]

From their camp on Arlington Heights, the men discovered the next morning, a magnificent panorama was in view: the broad Potomac, busy with shipping; the lengthy stretch of the Long Bridge, with its segment of drawbridge to allow vessels to pass; the city of Washington, prominently marked by the Capitol, the Executive Mansion, and the unfinished Washington monument; and on the Virginia side of the river, tents and fortifications as far as the eye could see, part of the vast ring of defensive works encircling the capital, with a surrounding countryside made desolate by war, denuded of trees, fences, and inhabitants. The 154th New York named its new home Camp Seward, in honor of former New York State governor and current secretary of state, William H. Seward, who returned the compliment by paying the regiment a visit.

For ten days, the men became acquainted with camp life and acclimated to the Virginia weather. They received their tents and pitched them in rows by companies. They were issued their mess equipment, and performed their first shaky experiments in cooking for themselves. They drank poor water, and some of them began to fall sick. Much of their time was spent drilling: they struggled awkwardly with squad drill, officer drill, company drill, and battalion drill. In their spare time, they requested passes and went sightseeing, bought treats from sutlers and local blacks, wrote letters home, and pondered their future.[13]

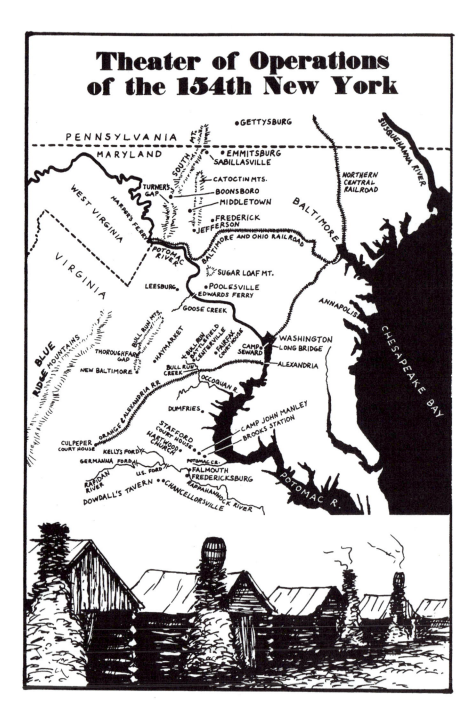

Theater of Operations of the 154th New York

To the Front

Smith Parish, the prominent Portville lumberman who had strongly supported the recruiting of Captain Warner's company, visited Camp Seward and afforded the Portville boys a chance to forward letters home. Amos took advantage of the opportunity, scrawling a short letter to Philinda on the rainy morning of October 11 before he had to "knock off" abruptly to go on duty. "I do not call this a letter," he apologized, "onley a line." The regiment had received orders to march the following morning to Fairfax Court House, where it was to join the corps commanded by Major General Franz Sigel. That he was about to move closer to the front did not daunt him, Amos indicated. "Thare is a prospect of our having some fun before long," he declared: "The prospects is that we shal have a fight before long the sooner the better."

Mingled with his carefree predictions of battle were expressions of longing. "I would like to see you all very mutch," he told Philinda, "and you in peticular." He had not as yet heard from home—"I am looking for a letter from you evry day," he wrote—and he urged her to write as often as she could. If she addressed her letters to him via Washington, Amos declared, "I shal get it let me be whare I may."[14]

A gap of six weeks exists between the dates of Amos's Camp Seward note and his next surviving letter. During that time he received five letters from Philinda, and no doubt sent some himself, which either were lost in transit or disappeared in subsequent years. Their loss is regrettable, because some significant events occurred during those six weeks, both in his regiment and for Amos personally.[15]

As ordered, the 154th New York marched for Fairfax Court House on October 12, arriving the following day. There the regiment joined the 1st Brigade, 2d Division, 11th Corps, of the Army of the Potomac. The brigade's other three regiments—the 29th New York and 27th and 73d Pennsylvania—were battle-tested outfits, largely composed of German Americans; the brigade commander was Colonel Adolphus Buschbeck of the 27th Pennsylvania. As indicated by Buschbeck's name and those of the commanders of the 2d Division and the 11th Corps—Brigadier General Adolph von Steinwehr and Major General Franz Sigel, respectively—Germans were to be found throughout the corps. Indeed, German immigrants made up about half of the personnel of the 11th Corps, and that simple fact created some complex problems. Widespread prejudice and scorn were directed at the Germans, not only from the rest of the army in general, but also from the native-born men of their own corps, who resented being associated with them—a situation that had a deleterious effect on 11th Corps morale.[16]

In a letter from Fairfax to a Portville friend, Captain Warner declared, "We have as yet no reason to complain of the disposition that has been made of us; indeed we are all highly gratified and thank our lucky stars that, to use the Dutchman's phrase, we are to fight 'mit Sigel' [referring to a song popular among the Germans, "I Goes to Fight Mit Sigel"]." But if Captain Warner was not being subtly sarcastic (he went on to relate an anecdote characterizing the Germans as "trinkers"), he was putting a good face on the situation, because in truth the men of the 154th New York were not immune to the prejudice poisoning the atmosphere in the 11th Corps. Overwhelmingly native born, they were quick to denigrate the "damned Dutchmen" and make snide comments about the "sauerkrauts"—insulting the very men they were most closely associated with in the army and with whom they would some day form in line of battle, under the most desperate circumstances.[17]

Having delivered his regiment to the front as arranged, Colonel Rice relinquished command of the 154th New York at Fairfax Court House and returned to his Cattaraugus County home. His replacement, Colonel Patrick H. Jones, was sick and unable to join the regiment immediately, however, so command of the 154th devolved on Lieutenant Colonel Loomis. Several other members of the regiment, like their new colonel, were absent at various hospitals. When Captain Warner signed Company C's first muster roll in the field, on October 31, two privates were absent hospitalized with unknown ailments, and another had already died. Private Evander Evans, a Portville farmer who left a wife and young children, succumbed to pneumonia on October 17 at a hospital in Alexandria, the first of many members of the regiment to die in Virginia.[18]

The day Evans died, Private Martin Van Buren Champlin of Company C, a Portville laborer, addressed a letter to a friend at home, notifying him that the Portville boys in camp were doing well. "We half to drill most of the time now," Champlin wrote, "for we expect to go into a battle before long." The men also did picket duty, marched in reviews, and fought sham battles. Some were assigned to an assortment of other duties: as teamsters, pioneers, orderlies, guards, clerks, stewards, cooks, and nurses, in hospitals, ambulance details, headquarters, commissaries, and ordnance and supply trains at the regimental, brigade, division, and corps levels. Most of them, however, including Amos, remained on duty with their companies.

Camp life grew routine at Fairfax Court House, although preparing their food remained somewhat of an adventure for many of the men. "We have a good deel of fun here cooking," Private Champlin informed his friend. "We eat drink and be merry Some of the boys is home sick here but it hant me if they will give me enough to eat I am O peachy." Rations of hardtack, salt pork, rice, beans, and fresh beef were plentiful. "The officers of this Department," Captain Warner declared, "seem determined that the troops shall lack for nothing to make them comfortable and to place them on a war footing at the earliest possible moment." Amos could not complain, as he and others had at Camp Brown, of insufficient food.

"This is a hard looking Country here," Martin Champlin informed his Portville correspondent. The village's buildings were dilapidated; the court-house was used as a guard house, and the sole church was serving as a hospital. Much of the hilly countryside was wooded, but the most conspicuous feature of the Fairfax landscape was the vast encampment of the 11th Corps. White tents dotted the terrain in all directions. Other than soldiers, the only people to be seen were former slaves.[19]

During thoughtful moments, the men of Company C solemnly pondered the transformations war had wrought in the veteran regiments of their corps. On the morning of October 20, the 154th New York and a half-dozen other new regiments of the 11th Corps were reviewed by General Sigel and then marched along a road lined with Sigel's veteran troops. Captain Warner recorded the questions he asked himself as Company C passed the cheering veterans:

Many of the regiments we saw are reduced from two to three hundred soldiers. Their regimental colors were torn and tattered in every imaginable form, and many a scarred face greeted our inquiring eyes as we marched along. How long ere the 154th Regiment will be reduced to the same condition? Of the 950 men who left Cattaraugus will not more than one in four be on hand to answer to their names when we are mustered out of the service?[20]

Those were questions only future events would answer, Warner knew. At some unknown date, the regiment would embark on its first campaign and fight its first battle. The men must have thought that day was fast approaching on November 2, when Colonel Buschbeck's brigade left Fair-fax Court House and marched in a westerly direction, presumably headed toward the enemy. As things turned out, the 154th New York did not encounter any Confederates during the subsequent movement, but its ranks were thinned nonetheless. Amos Humiston was one who was laid low.

From Fairfax, the route of the regiment led, during several days of marching, through the deserted village of Centerville, where the earth was scarred in all directions by massive fortifications; over the Bull Run battle-field, where the appalled men witnessed the grisly residue of combat: scat-tered cannonballs, torn trees, rotting horses, and human arms, legs, and skulls protruding from shallow graves; to the village of Haymarket, which they looted and burned in retaliation for some shots fired at them during their passage. After a few days of rest, the march continued across hills, valleys, and ravines, on a roundabout route via New Baltimore to Thoroughfare Gap, a crossing in the Bull Run Mountains about thirty miles west of their starting point, which they reached on November 8. Picket duty and foraging were their primary activities during the ensuing occupation of the gap.[21]

"The regions around here, and particularly to the westward of the mountains," Captain Warner wrote from Thoroughfare Gap in a letter to the *Olean Times*, "is the finest I have seen in Virginia." Before the war began, he noted, the local farmers had been wealthy and contented. "But situated as they are in a region, which has several times alternately been possessed by Federal and Rebel armies, they have been prey to both, and little now remains to show the former fatness of the land." However, the countryside remained richer than the well-scavenged sections of Virginia the 154th had seen so far, and the men grew quite proficient at looting sheep, hogs, poultry, apples, and potatoes from nearby farms.

Noteworthy news regarding the army's leadership reached camp during the stay. The replacement of Major General George B. McClellan as commander of the Army of the Potomac by Major General Ambrose E. Burnside caused comment throughout the company streets. Apart from the interest stirred by that announcement and the novelty of foraging, the men chafed at the inactivity at Thoroughfare Gap. They knew that they were acting as reserves, guarding a position unthreatened by the enemy, "as completely isolated as if in the center of the Atlantic," commented Captain Warner. After a stay of nine uneventful days, welcome orders to march were received. The regiment left the gap on November 17 and retraced its route in rainy weather to the vicinity of Fairfax Court House, which it reached on November 19.

A number of sick soldiers were all the 154th New York had to show for the movement to Thoroughfare Gap. In his letter from the gap, Captain Warner noted, "Our recent marches, and consequent exposure and fatigue, tells somewhat upon our soldiers who are not yet inured to these hardships, and quite a number are unfit for duty. The most prevalent complaint is hard colds and bowel complaints which latter have been caused in a measure by the irregular diet to which we have been for several days subjected."[22]

At least a dozen sick members of Company C were sent to Washington hospitals directly from Thoroughfare Gap or from Fairfax in the weeks after the regiment's return, and another half-dozen or so were hospitalized in the Fairfax camp. An unknown number of men remained with the company despite their illnesses. Among them was Amos.[23]

A few flakes of snow were falling on the cold night of November 21, when Amos received a welcome letter from Philinda. He responded the next day, a raw, cold Sunday, and used his last stamp to send his reply. Inform-

To the Front

ing Philinda of his illness, Amos credited his comrades of Company C for their steady support, which enabled him to remain with the company:

I have had a hard time of it for the last two weeks I took a hard cold and it settled on my lungs and that threw me into the camp fever and having nothing to shelter me from the cold and storm but our shelter tents which are not as good as a last years birds nest it went hard with me but I have bin on the gain for the last two or three days if I do not have any pull backs I think that I shal get along I am very weak yet the boys have stuck to me like brothers if they had not I do not know whare I should have ben now.

After some insightful philosophising about his current situation, Amos commented favorably on the recent change in army command, echoing Abraham Lincoln's celebrated remark about the deposed McClellan ("He has got the 'slows'," said the president of the general):

I am sick cold but I am not home sick I am hoping for better times when we shal all be together in our little home enjoying our selves again you may think by the run of my letters that I am down harted but that is not so I have not for one moment been sorry that I enlisted all I ask is my health I can die in battle like a man but I hate the idea of dieing here like a hog not that I think thare is any danger of it for the pressent for I am quite well [compared] to what I have ben but if thare is a place on gods earth that I hate that place is virginia wel I have growled anough here goes for some thing more plessent if I can think of any thing thare is one thing that pleasses us here that is the removle of McLelland he is to slow for these fast times we think that Burnside is the man.

Regarding domestic matters, Amos was glad to hear that Philinda and the children were getting along well. Her latest letter was the fifth he had received during his time in Virginia—he apparently had preserved them all—and she had also sent him some stamps and two issues of the *Flag*, a weekly publication (perhaps the *Flag of Our Union*, a popular periodical published in Boston). "I wish you would send me the flag evry week after you have read it," Amos told Philinda. "It goes the rounds all the company look for it as mutch as I." As usual, he voiced concern about financial matters. He had signed a payroll two weeks earlier; she should be receiving twenty dollars, but "how soon you will get it I can not tel I hope before long." It seems a relative was staying with Philinda. Perhaps it was her sister Eliza Ensworth or her brother George's wife, Lydia (White) Ensworth, whom Amos referred to when he closed his letter, "Kiss lide and the babies for me and if I was thare I would kiss you."[24]

About a week later, Amos received another letter and a couple of newspapers from his wife, and on December 2 he replied. He and the rest of the regiment had been rudely awakened at one o'clock that morning with orders to pack knapsacks and be ready to march at a minute's notice, but the day had dragged by without further orders. "What it all means none of us know," Amos admitted. "Thare is some thing in the wind that we can not tell But we are going to leave this camping ground that is shure." As it happened, however, the 154th New York did not leave its Fairfax camp that day, and Amos spent the afternoon writing to Philinda.

A month had now passed since Company C signed the payroll, but the men still had not received their money. "We are all out of money and out of tobacco and every thing else," Amos complained, "but I would not care for that so mutch if I could send you some money." He encouraged Philinda to "keep up good courage," and expressed a hope he would be paid within the week, but also mentioned that he would have to stop sending her letters if she did not send him some stamps, "for I have not seene money anough to by a stamp since I can remember."

In response to a comment Philinda had made about her gaining weight, he revealed he was feeling better after his recent bout with illness, although his appearance belied the fact: "Now you say that you are getting fleshy put in and get as fat as you can you cannot gain as much as I have lost I am nothing but an old frame my fingers looks like birds claws but I feal quite well."

Amos told his wife about one of the men who had cared for him with brotherly compassion while he was sick. Corporal Joel M. Bouton of Company C was a printer from Olean who worked in the office of the *Olean Times* before he enlisted. Bouton was one of Amos's messmates, and Amos judged Joel "a first rate fellow." (The other members of their mess Amos did not mention.)

A good portion of Amos's December 2 letter was an earnest expression of longing:

Now I want you to write to me and let me [know] all the news how Mr Bingham gets along [Allen W. Bingham, a Portville tanner, his wife, Elvira, and their four children were apparently family friends] and how your house looks on the outside and how you feel on the in side of it and how you like to sleep alone these cold nights and how you enjoy your selfe [in] jeneral I wil tel you how [I] feal if I can in the first [place] I would give all most any thing if I could make you a good long visit and be back here again but that can not be but when I do come those red cheeks will get kissed more [than] once I can tel you how I would like to be with you christmas and new years and [enjoy] one of your diners again and have the babies on my knee to hear them prattle as they used to this war can not last for ever it does seeme to me.

To the Front

Joel Bouton was cooking supper for the mess while those lines were being written, and Amos guessed the regiment would be staying in camp for the night after all, so he closed his letter with a final endearment. "Rest asured thare is no being on earth that wants to se you half as mutch as I do," he guaranteed Philinda. "Be a good girl and do the best that you can and think of him that is always thinking of you."[25]

By the end of December, Philinda and the children had moved to a different dwelling in Portville. Amos's curiosity about Philinda's house in his December 2 letter indicated she had possibly already moved. On December 8, however, Amos wrote again, obviously in response to another letter from her, and discussed a visit she was contemplating. "You want to know what I think about going down to georges," he wrote, probably referring to Philinda's older brother, George W. Ensworth, who was living with his wife, Lydia, and three small children near Nunda, in Livingston County, New York. Amos wanted her to go if she could "leave things safe at home," and cover her potatoes to keep them warm, but he foresaw one nagging problem: "The devvle of it is when you will get any money I have tired of looking for the pay master my selfe I hope that he [will] be here before long so that you can go." But the paymaster did not arrive, and Philinda did not immediately make her visit.

Amos began his letter of December 8 during the night, while he and his messmates huddled in blankets by a fire in the woods, where they had fled the cold and a lack of wood in camp. A couple of inches of snow covered the ground. Sleepy after a tour of picket duty the previous night, Amos had trouble seeing clearly as he wrote by the flickering firelight. "I hope that you can read this," he told Philinda. "If you cannot send it back to old virginia." When he finished the letter the next morning, he used other excuses to apologize for his handwriting: "If I had a good chew of tobacco I think that I could write a grate deal better than I do. . . . you must over look mistakes for I have wrote this in a hurey."

Cautiously—"I do not want to get up aney excitement," he wrote— Amos reported that rumors of peace were sweeping the camps, but he admitted, "What grounds thare is for it I cannot tel." Nonetheless, he engaged in a bit of optimism. "Now you would be surprised to see me coming home about the first of May with an honerable discharge," he told Philinda. "That may or may not be we can not tel." With home on his mind, his thoughts turned to Frank, Alice, and Fred. "Tel them babies that pa wants to see them very mutch," Amos directed, and he cautioned his wife about exposing their oldest boy to an outbreak of smallpox in Portville: "I think that you had not better send Frank to school til the smal pock has pased over."

Gettysburg's Unknown Soldier

The period of inactivity at Fairfax was apparently coming to a close, Amos told Philinda on December 9; the 154th New York had received marching orders that afternoon. But he conceded, "As usual I cannot tel where we are going." Ever-present rumors were all he could base his guesses on. Wherever the regiment was headed, it would be Amos's first march since he returned sick from Thoroughfare Gap, and he wondered how he would hold up. "I am not very strong yet," he told Philinda, "but I think that I can go it."[26]

He got the chance to test his mettle the next day.

NOTES

1. "The New Recruits," *Cattaraugus Union*, August 22, 1862; Mark H. Dunkelman, *Camp James M. Brown: Jamestown's Civil War Rendezvous* (Jamestown, N.Y.: Fenton Historical Society, 1996), 6–9.

2. Muster-in roll, September 24, 1862, and descriptive book, Company C, 154th New York, September 24, 1862, National Archives; "The New Recruits," *Cattaraugus Union*, August 22, 1862; L. D. Warner to Ed[itor]. Freeman, September 13, 1862, in "From Camp James M. Brown," *Cattaraugus Freeman*, September 18, 1862.

3. Dunkelman, *Camp James M. Brown*, 25–26; Mark H. Dunkelman and Michael J. Winey, *The Hardtack Regiment: An Illustrated History of the 154th Regiment, New York State Infantry Volunteers* (East Brunswick, N.J.: Fairleigh Dickinson University Press, 1981), 25, 174–176, 184.

4. Dunkelman, *Camp James M. Brown*, 6, 8, 10–21.

5. Amos Humiston to Dear Wife, September 5, 1862, courtesy of Allan L. Cox, as are all the Humiston letters.

6. Dunkelman and Winey, *The Hardtack Regiment*, 25; Dunkelman, *Camp James M. Brown*, 26; muster-in roll, Company C, 154th New York, September 24, 1862, National Archives.

7. Amos Humiston to Dear Wife, September 26, 1862.

8. William H. Keyes to Old Gent [Thomas Keyes], September 26, 1862, William H. Keyes pension file, National Archives; 1860 U.S. Census, Portville.

9. Descriptive book, Company C, 154th New York, National Archives; carte de visite, "Sergt. Amos Humiston, Of the 154th N.Y. Vols." by F. Gutekunst, Philadelphia, author's collection.

10. Dunkelman and Winey, *The Hardtack Regiment*, 25–26; Dunkelman, *Camp James M. Brown*, 28–29.

11. Dunkelman and Winey, *The Hardtack Regiment*, 26; Charles W. McKay, "Three Years or During the War, with the Crescent and Star," in *The National Tribune Scrap Book* (Washington, D.C., n.d.), 122.

12. Dunkelman and Winey, *The Hardtack Regiment*, 26–27; McKay, "Three Years or During the War," 122–123.

13. Mark H. Dunkelman, "Camp Seward on Arlington Heights: A Yankee Reg-

iment's First Stop in Dixie," *Arlington Historical Magazine* 10, no. 2 (October 1994): 6–21.

14. Amos Humiston to dear wife, October 11, 1862. Amos mistakenly wrote the 154th was to join "Seagels divission," instead of corps.

15. Ibid., November 22, 1862.

16. Dunkelman and Winey, *The Hardtack Regiment*, 28–31.

17. Lewis D. Warner to Friend, Nelson P. [Wheeler], October 21, 1862, in W. Reginald Wheeler, *Pine Knots and Bark Peelers: The Story of Five Generations of American Lumbermen* (New York: Ganis and Harris, 1960), 64; Dunkelman and Winey, *The Hardtack Regiment*, 31.

18. Dunkelman and Winey, *The Hardtack Regiment*, 31; muster roll, Company C, 154th New York, October 31, 1862, National Archives.

19. Martin V. B. Champlin to Friend Joel [Crandall], October 17, 1862, courtesy of Donald K. Ryberg, Jr.; Lewis D. Warner to Friend, Nelson P. [Wheeler], October 21, 1862, in Wheeler, *Pine Knots and Bark Peelers*, 64; Dunkelman and Winey, *The Hardtack Regiment*, 32–33.

20. Lewis D. Warner to Friend, Nelson P. [Wheeler], October 21, 1862, in Wheeler, *Pine Knots and Bark Peelers*, 65.

21. Dunkelman and Winey, *The Hardtack Regiment*, 34–35.

22. Lewis D. Warner to the *Olean Times*, undated letter reprinted in the *Fredonia Censor*, November 26, 1862; Dunkelman and Winey, *The Hardtack Regiment*, 36.

23. Muster roll, Company C, 154th New York, December 31, 1862, National Archives.

24. Amos Humiston to Dear wife, November 22, 1862; Frank Luther Mott, *A History of American Magazines 1850–1865* (Cambridge: Belknap Press of Harvard University Press, 1957), 35; Ensworth Family Record, courtesy of David Humiston Kelley.

25. Amos Humiston to Dear wife, December 2, 1862; descriptive book, Company C, 154th New York, National Archives; 1860 U. S. Census, Portville; Dunkelman and Winey, *The Hardtack Regiment*, 36–37.

26. Amos Humiston to Dear wife, December 8, 1862; Dunkelman and Winey, *The Hardtack Regiment*, 37.

CHAPTER 6

Camp Misery

A WEEK'S MARCH, from December 10 to 17, 1862, carried the 154th New York south from its Fairfax camp to the banks of the Rappahannock River near Falmouth, Virginia. The regiment's route ran to Fairfax Station, across the Occoquan River, and through the villages of Dumfries and Stafford Court House, over approximately fifty miles of alternately frozen and muddy roads. Nighttimes the men scraped away the snow or vainly sought dry spots on which to pitch their tents, and mornings they awoke on frozen ground. Despite his recent bout with fever, Amos Humiston stood the exposures and rigors of the march well, perhaps was even strengthened by them. Five days after reaching Falmouth, on December 22, he informed Philinda, "My health is better than it has ben in some time I am getting fat again as usual."

During several days of the march, Amos and his comrades of the 154th heard the distant rumble of artillery, and when they reached the Rappahannock, they learned of the disastrous repulse of the Army of the Potomac across the river at Fredericksburg. Fortunately for them, by the time they arrived in the vicinity the great battle was over and the Union forces had retreated to the Falmouth side of the river. All that separated the contending armies was the cold Rappahannock. As they picketed the riverbank near Dam Number Four, the men of the 154th New York soon got to know their Confederate counterparts, swapping newspapers, coffee, tobacco, and friendly banter with the members of an Alabama brigade stationed on the opposite shore.

Only general details of the recent fighting and the staggering losses suffered by the army had reached the 154th when Amos first wrote to Philinda from Falmouth. "It was a hard battle," was all he could tell her about the Fredericksburg carnage. As he had at Arlington Heights, he again voiced a hope that the regiment would soon meet the enemy and the war would somehow be settled. "We do not know [how] soon we shal have to go in on them," he wrote. "The sooner the better we want to see this thing closed [in] some way."

Although Amos was feeling better at Falmouth than he had for some time, other members of the regiment were suffering from ill health. Among them was his Portville townsman and fellow corporal in Company C, Amos F. Keyes, who had typhoid fever. "I have just ben up to the hospital to se Frank Keyes," Amos notified Philinda. Speaking from experience he added, "This is a hard place for a sick man."

Philinda's news was good, Amos was pleased to note. His family had moved, and knowing they were comfortably situated and cheerful in a new home "helps me along a great deal," he informed his wife. "I surpose that you will hardley know the old soldier when he gets back," he quipped, "you will be so grand in your new house and other fixings." Philinda and the children were still residing in the township of Portville. Seven-year-old Frank was attending school and making good progress, Amos was pleased to learn. "I am glad to hear that Franky is getting along so well in his studdies," the proud father wrote. "Tel him that pa will be home to hear him read some time tel Ally and Freddy that pa has not forgot them how I would like to see them and you to." If he could give Philinda "a smack on the cheak" he would be all right, Amos declared.

Money matters continued to rankle. The paymaster still had not arrived, and "it is hard times with us here as far as money is conserned," Amos declared. He hoped to draw four months' pay in January, so Philinda could receive a check for forty dollars. "Then you can go whare you pleas," he told her. She could find out when Company C was paid by checking with Captain Warner's family, Amos suggested. Engaging in some macabre speculation, he revealed a distrust of Mark Comstock and suggested that Philinda consult with lumber baron William Wheeler to avoid trouble with their creditor. "If I get kiled you had better take 30 dollars of this money that you get now and pay mark," Amos wrote. "Get mr Whelur or some one eltse to attend to it for you for I feal a [bit] uneasey about the way that Mark acts about it or if he is honest if he should die the hole thing should be lost." Exactly what "the whole thing" was is uncertain, but the debt obviously weighed heavily on Amos.[1]

When he wrote again ten days later, on January 2, 1863, the financial prospects appeared to have improved. The 154th had been mustered for pay on the last day of December, and the men hoped to receive some money before long. In the meantime, Amos could only counsel Philinda to be patient: "If you get hard up you must run your pace," he advised his wife. "That is the onley [way] that I know of I can not hurrey them up if I could I would rais the D with them the onley way is to take it cool." Frustration over the lack of pay was giving way to resignation.

Camp Misery

A summer-like day in January had the men of Company C feeling "chereful if not happy," Amos noted, and he interrupted the composition of his letter to go on battalion drill and watch one of Professor Thaddeus S. C. Lowe's balloons ascend to observe the Confederate defensive works. As usual, the common soldiers were in the dark regarding plans for the army, although they had plenty of rumors to choose from. "We have not had any engagement with the rebs yet we do not know the moves that are to be made here as well as you do at home," Amos told Philinda, "and I think it is best that it should be so thare is so maney rumors in camp that I shal not write aney of them I have made up my mind to take things as they come and pay no attention to the rumors."

His health was good, Amos reported, but there were a great many sick in the regiment, and he estimated there were not five hundred able to do duty of the near thousand men who had left Jamestown three months before. And he had sad news to report. "We buried Frank Keyes the 27 of last monthe [December] he died of the inflamation of the lungs and the typhoid fever," Amos wrote. "It cast a gloom over the hole company he was liked by us all." Keyes, who died on December 26, 1862, left a wife and two children to mourn him in their Portville home. For Philinda and the children, the war struck closer to home when they learned of Keyes's passing, and offered sympathy to his grieving widow and orphans.[2]

The recent devastating defeat at Fredericksburg cast a pall of depression over the entire Army of the Potomac. Amos noted the mood when he received a visit from a friend and veteran of the battle, Sergeant William Spraker, Jr., of the 64th New York, who had lived in Portville and Allegany while working as a clerk and merchant in the prewar years.[3] Spraker was healthy and feeling well, Amos reported, "but curses this war with all the rest of us." Voicing the demoralization prevalent in the army and the widespread discontent with Burnside's generalship at Fredericksburg, he continued: "We do not like the way things are managed we are ready to fight when it will amount to some thing but the battle at this place had done a great deal to cool the patriotism of the troops as a jeneral thing the Irish briggade call it Burnsides slawtter yard."

Another visitor named Jake Stanley spent the night of New Year's Day 1863 with Amos and his tent mates. Amos described Stanley as "tough as a buck and as od as ever," and added, "He gave me a large peace of tobacco that made me happy as a lamb." The night of Stanley's visit, Amos received a letter from Philinda, and as he answered it the next day, his thoughts as usual turned to her and the children. "Now thare is no use of trying to tel you how mutch I want to see you or how often I think of you," he wrote. "thare is no use to talk about it thare is no prospects of peace at pressent." A humorous reference to his recent holiday menus led to a fantasy of home and an intimate promise, and he closed his letter with a thought for the three little ones:

What do you surpose that we had for Christmas wel we had hard bread and salt pork and for New years we had pork and hard bread So you see that we had a change I would like to go into your pantry a little while it would astonish you to see me eat If I ever live to get home you will not complain of being lonesome again or of sleeping cold for I will lay as close to you as the bark to a tree that is so do you not feel afraid to stay alone nights keep up good courage this is like every thing eltse it must have an end Now kiss the children for me tel them they must be good children.[4]

A little more than a week later, the receipt of two letters from Philinda prompted Amos to write again. On the night of January 11, writing by candlelight, he expressed his pleasure at hearing from home and learning that his family was well and enjoying themselves. "A letter from you," Amos assured Philinda, "does me more good than you can imagine."

He was situated more comfortably than when he had written last, Amos informed his wife. On January 3, Colonel Jones had ordered the regiment to clear their Falmouth campground and construct log huts. For the next several days, the men worked on their shanties. Amos described the process to Philinda. He and his tent mates erected walls of pine logs, four logs high, and stretched their shelter tents over poles to make a roof. Inside, they built beds of poles, pine boughs, and dried grass at one end of the hut, and a stone, stick, and mud-daubed fireplace and chimney at the other end. The center of the structure was used as a kitchen. The end result "rivles all modern architecture," Amos quipped. He thought Philinda "would laugh to see us do our house work." The hut was an improvement over living outdoors, he noted, but "how long we shall be permitted to enjoy it I can not say." He hoped to be able to inhabit it until warm weather arrived, but guessed that would not be the case, considering the uncertainty of army life. "We are liable to be caled on to take up our line of march eny moment," he wrote.

Perhaps in response to a comment in Philinda's letters, Amos urged his wife to make herself comfortable—if she ever got any money to do so. The paymaster had yet to appear, but Amos hoped to be paid before too long. "I do not want you to stent your selfe to one or two desses if you nead them," he told her, "or aney thing eltse that you want." Several weeks before, Amos had told Philinda to pay their debt to Mark Comstock; now he contradicted that advice and told her perhaps she should not make the payment at present. "If they are going to be so long about paying me," he wrote, "you may ned all the money that you can get." Then, with the stub of his candle sputtering out, he turned in for the night.

Amos recommenced his letter the next morning on a sad note: "Daniel Keyes is here to mark the place whare we buried Frank." (The relationship between Daniel and Frank Keyes is unknown.) The extent of sickness among the soldiers had abated somewhat recently, Amos noted, and he declared himself to be in very good health. Distractions then caused him to finish his letter with a quick passage:

Thare [is] no chance to write our tent is full this morning [with men] talking about home and the close of the war for my part I have give the idea up of settleing this thing up I think that we shal have to serve our time out here wel I can stand it but I do not want to if you were here I would not care but thare is no use talking that cannot be we will hope for the best and let it go at that you must not burry any trouble on my acount it wil do no good use your judgement in regard to matters at home and do the best that you can rest asured that my mind [is] on you and home continualy take good care of the babies and kiss them for me and throw one in for [your]selfe write soon.[5]

Amos decided he would not write home again until he received his pay, but after two eventful weeks passed—and he began to fear that Philinda would worry about him—he wrote again on January 29, starting his letter with some good news: The 154th New York had received word that the paymaster would arrive in a few days. The men were somewhat disappointed to learn the regiment would draw only two months' pay, but in Amos's case, that intelligence was balanced by the fact that he had been promoted from corporal to sergeant on January 25. From that date, his pay would be raised four dollars, to seventeen dollars per month.

Despite the impending visit of the paymaster, his tardiness still annoyed the soldiers, and Amos noted that displeasure while venting his own feelings on the subject:

If uncle sam has got so poor that he can not pay his men he had better close the war thare is a grate menney men in this regiment that say that if they cannot get their pay they will desert and go whare they can surport there families it is not right to promise pay every 2 months and then not pay atall but do not blame me for I feel worse about it than you do.[6]

Amos was promoted to sergeant over several corporals ahead of him on the rolls of Company C, a sign of the esteem he was held in by Captain Warner. Two Portville men were promoted to corporal on the same day Amos was elevated to sergeant—Seymour Sikes and William Keyes, whose secret of desertion was so far still safe.[7]

"We have ben on the move ever since I wrote you last," Amos told Philinda, and he summarized the regiment's recent futile campaign succinctly: "We started to attact the rebs but the mud was so deep that we got stuck so we had to give it up and wait till the weather is better." Along with the rest of Colonel Adolphus Buschbeck's brigade, the 154th New York had twice moved upstream to build roads to the banks of the Rappahannock, and after the second occasion, on January 20, the regiment marched to the pontoon train and prepared to escort it to the river. But the ensuing campaign—Burnside's attempt to redeem the reputation he lost at Fredericksburg and reverse the army's fortune after the terrible defeat there—was an ignominious failure: a brief, forlorn, humiliating, and thoroughly sodden effort known as the Mud March. As Amos later noted, Virginia mud was a formidable enemy. "The mud is not like the mud in our country," he informed Philinda. "It is like glue."[8]

Years later, Private Charles McKay of Company C recalled the Mud March:

For three days and as many nights the rain fell. The roads became impassable, the fields were miniature lakes, and the streams roaring torrents. Pontoon trains were axle deep in the red Virginia mud, cannon, caisson, and limber chest were scattered and mired, and when at last the wearied and mud-bespattered troops reached the ford, the rebel pickets yelled at us in derision, "Burnside stuck in the mud," and that sentence embraces all the results of the campaign.[9]

The dismal Mud March yielded one important result: the hapless General Burnside was replaced as commander of the Army of the Potomac by Major General Joseph Hooker, a cocksure, boastful, ambitious intriguer with a reputation as a fighter. The entire Army of the Potomac languished after the Mud March. Huddled in its wind-blown tents in the snow and mud, defeated, demoralized, and denigrated, the army plunged to its nadir. General Hooker faced a formidable challenge to restore esprit de corps in his battered and buffeted command.

Slogging and straggling through the mire, the 154th New York returned to the vicinity of Falmouth and pitched their tents in the muck about a mile from their old camp. Rain continued to fall for the next several days, and then more than a half-foot of snow fell. "We have had a hard time of it in our small tents," Amos informed Philinda, and he dubbed his new home "Camp Misery." Virginia's blanket of white would make snowy old Cattaraugus County blush, Amos declared, and he added, "This storm makes me think [of] you at home how are you getting along?" He closed his letter with more thoughts of home. "How I would like to call in this morning and se how you are getting along and then I should not like to leave you again," he wrote. "Remember me to the children and be a good girl."[10]

After an inordinate wait, Amos was able to write on the night of February 1 to his "Dear Philind" and enclose a check for twenty dollars. The paymaster had finally arrived. Amos instructed Philinda to cash the check at any of Portville's stores. "I want you to take and make your selves as cumfortable as you can," he urged her. "By the children some thing that will pleas them and tel them that pa sent it." His pay disappeared rapidly. After deducting the allotment and paying his debts to his comrades, Amos was left with one dollar to buy tobacco.

Amos was one of many members of the 154th New York who sent his letter with its enclosed check in care of the regimental surgeon, Henry Van Aernam, who was shortly to return to his Cattaraugus County home on a leave of absence. Among others of Company C who entrusted their allotments to Surgeon Van Aernam were Corporal William Keyes, Private James W. Washburn, a farmer from Hinsdale, and Sergeant Stephen Welch, an Allegany farmer. Van Aernam, a highly respected physician and former state assemblyman, must have carried checks worth hundreds of dollars to Cattaraugus County for members of his regiment. He told the Company C boys he would mail their letters at the Olean post office.[11]

Amos voiced concern at not having heard from Philinda in a long time. "I am looking very anciously for a letter from you," he wrote. "I want to hear from you very mutch." He noted the last letter he had received from her had been mailed from Smethport, where she had been visiting, and he wondered if she had written since or if her letters had been lost. While he was writing, a mail arrived for the regiment, but there was nothing for him. "That is to bad," Amos wrote, "but it cant be helped." He would not write again, he declared, until he heard from her. "I want to see you very mutch," he added. "I wuld talk faster than I can write."

Taps were sounded and lights extinguished before Amos could add much news to his letter. According to Corporal Keyes's letter of the same day, Company C had again built comfortable winter huts, with fireplaces and chimneys. Squads were drawing pork, beef, potatoes, dried apples, beans, and hardtack, and the men were enjoying cooking for themselves. General Hooker had improved the quality and quantity of rations, an important first step in his successful restoration of the army's morale.[12]

No sooner had the 154th New York settled in its new winter quarters near Falmouth than orders were received to break camp and march. On February 4 and 5, the regiment marched through mud, snow, and rain to the northeast, across Potomac Creek to the vicinity of Stafford Court House, where they encamped on a hilltop in a forest of pines. Over the next few days, the men built the neatest village of log huts they had yet occupied, and they began to enjoy a great level of comfort by army standards. Snug in their warm huts, they relished soft bread for the first time in months, had their initial taste of desiccated vegetables, and bought pies and other treats from sutlers. Duties were light—drills, inspections, and standing picket—and the men filled their spare time visiting and writing letters. Even the weather seemed to improve: a day in mid-February seemed "as nice as any hay day in Cattaraugus," Sergeant Welch observed. Overhead, wild geese were flying north, and bluebirds and robins twittered cheerful songs around the camp.[13]

On February 16, the regiment got its first close look at the army's new commander when General Hooker reviewed the 11th Corps, an event that inspired the martial spirit of the men. From the ranks of Company C, Private Washburn described the spectacle:

Gen Hooker was mounted on a beautiful Silver Grey and Gen Seigel was on a dark bay and trimmed their horses were you cannot imagine [how] finely. they rode around us twise on a full gallop the last time they came around in front the whole Division cheered him. they came in front and stopped then we wheeled in companies and marched past him and came into camp our officers told us that we done the best that day that we ever did and I think so my self for we had good music and we were pleased to see our commander it was as fine a time as we have had since we came in Old Virginia.[14]

If spirits rose during the pomp of Hooker's review, they soared when boxes from Cattaraugus County began to arrive for members of Company C. Filled with pies and dried fruit, butter and cakes, new socks and mittens, and useful little sundries—all neatly packed with tender touches by loving hands at home—the boxes made life in camp more comfortable and reminded the soldiers they were not forgotten. An innovation of Hooker—ten-day furloughs for selected enlisted men—lifted spirits. In Company C, the recipient of the first furlough was chosen by a "one-sided cast-lot game," according to Sergeant Welch. Private Harris Lamb, a Portville farmer, was the lucky winner. Like Surgeon Van Aernam before him, Lamb no doubt returned to Cattaraugus County carrying letters written hastily by his comrades. (Knowing Philinda was on a visit to her brother George Ensworth and his family in Nunda, New York, Amos did not send a letter to Portville with Lamb.) On Lamb's return, another Company C man was chosen, and so the procedure continued.[15]

Superstitious members of Company C were heartened when an old German fortune teller in a nearby regiment predicted that the 154th New York would never see a fight and that the men would be home within three months. Luck ran out for one member of the company, however, on Feb-

Camp Misery

ruary 27. That day Corporal Keyes was revealed as a deserter from the 78th New York Volunteers and arrested by provost marshals of the 12th Corps.[16]

After about two weeks of camp life near Stafford Court House, luck also ran out for Amos Humiston. "My health [is] as good as it has ben in a long time," he wrote on February 1, but late that month, it took a turn for the worse. By March 9, the date of his next surviving letter, sent to Philinda in Nunda, he had bad news. He was suffering from chronic diarrhea:

You will pardon me for not writing sooner when I tel you that I have ben very sick for the last two weeks it has went pretty hard with me this pull but I am better now my complaint is the durty hurey or in other words the virginia quick step the doctor would not let me write before I have not sufferd for the want of suitable food for a good menney of the boys have got boxes lately and they have ben very kind to me. . . . How the days and hours have pased with me since I have ben sick you may judge It has ben very lonely here without you but thare is no use of talking about it let us hope for the best.[17]

A few days after Amos wrote, Private Edwin R. Osgood of Company C, a farmer from Ischua, noted in a letter home that an army camp in Virginia was "the worst place that a man Can be sick in." Osgood, who had two brothers serving with him in Company C, added, "The less relation a [sick] man has hear the worse he is off."[18] With no relatives to look after him in his sickness, Amos depended on the kindness of his comrades of Company C. They rallied to his support and did their best to keep him comfortable. Captain Warner and Surgeon Van Aernam made efforts on his behalf, albeit unsuccessfully. With the help of his friends, Amos avoided being sent to the division hospital, which many soldiers viewed as the equivalent of a death sentence, thinking the mortality rate there inordinately high. On the summer-like day of March 25, Amos summed up his situation for Philinda:

My health is very poor but I am some better than it was when I wrote you last the Captain and the regamentle sergeon have ben trying to get me a sick furlow for 30 days but they cannot do it the medical director will not grant aney well never mind I can stay here do not worey about me for I am getting better all the time but it is slow I would like to come home and see you first rate but we cannot do as we are a mind to here. . . . I have done no duty for more than 3 weeks I did not go to the hospital for I had a good shanty and the boys said that they [would] rather do my work than to have me go thare is so mutch dissease thare that a man stands a poor chance of getting out again.

Gettysburg's Unknown Soldier

Hoping to receive a furlough, Amos had not planned to write home. But the failure of Captain Warner and Surgeon Van Aernam to procure a leave for him, and the receipt of a letter from Philinda, prompted his letter of March 25. His family was well and back home in Portville, Amos was pleased to note. Apparently Philinda had made some self-deprecating comments about her writing, and Amos, aware of his own spelling shortfalls, gently asked her to overlook their respective mistakes: "Thare is one thing I want you to stop that is finding so mutch fault with your letters if they please me it nead not trouble you if you do not I shal think that you are making fun of mine we will call it an even thing and make no apologies." With her letter, Philinda had enclosed notes from the children. After seeing Frank's schoolboy script, Alice's more childish scrawl, and maybe even some scribbles from Fred, Amos wrote, "Tel the children that I was very mutch pleased with their letters and think they done well." In closing, he offered Philinda some encouragement, and made a wish. "You must keep up good courage for this rebellion must go down," he wrote. "I would like to kiss bouth of those cheeks of yours to night that is so."

In a postscript, Amos added, "I thought that I would send along some of the crasy productions of my brain in the shape of poetry." He had put into verse the dream he had dreamed ever since he had left Portville—his dream of wife, children, and home:

To my wife

You have put the little ones to bed dear wife
And coverd them ore with care
My Frankey Alley and Fred
And they have said their evening prair

Perhaps they breathed the name of one
Who is far in southern land
And wished he to were thare
To join their little band

I am very sad to night dear wife
My thoughts are dwelling on home and thee
As I keep the lone night watch
Beneath the holley tree

The winds are sighing through the trees
And as they onward roam
They whisper hopes of happyness
Within our cottage home

And as they onward pased
Ore hill and vale and bubling stream

Camp Misery

They wake up thoughts within my soul
Like music in a dream

Oh when will this rebellion cease
This cursed war be ore
And we our dear ones meat
To part from them no more?[19]

NOTES

1. Mark H. Dunkelman and Michael J. Winey, *The Hardtack Regiment: An Illustrated History of the 154th Regiment, New York State Infantry Volunteers* (East Brunswick, N.J.: Fairleigh Dickinson University Press, 1981), 39–40; Amos Humiston to Dear wife, December 22, 1862.

2. Amos Humiston to Dear wife, January 2, 1863; descriptive book, Company C, 154th New York, National Archives; Listing for Amos F. Keyes under Portville, Records of Soldiers by Towns, Cattaraugus County Memorial and Historical Museum, Little Valley, New York.

3. Amos Humiston to Dear wife, January 2, 1863; 1860 U.S. Census, Portville; *Presidents, Soldiers, Statesmen* (New York: H. H. Hardesty, Publisher, 1899), Vol. 2, 1589–1590; New York State Adjutant General, *Annual Report of the Adjutant General of the State of New York* (Albany: J. B. Lyon Company, State Printers, 1902, Serial No. 27), 386.

4. Amos Humiston to Dear wife, January 2, 1863.

5. Ibid., January 11, 1863; Dunkelman and Winey, *The Hardtack Regiment*, 42, 47.

6. Amos Humiston to Dear Wife, January 29, 1863.

7. Muster rolls, Company C, 154th New York, December 31, 1862, February 28, 1863, National Archives.

8. Amos Humiston to Dear Wife, January 29, March 25, 1863; Dunkelman and Winey, *The Hardtack Regiment*, 43–44.

9. Charles W. McKay, "Three Years or During the War, with the Crescent and Star," in *The National Tribune Scrap Book* (Washington, n.d.), 125.

10. Amos Humiston to Dear Wife, January 29, 1863; Dunkelman and Winey, *The Hardtack Regiment*, 44.

11. Amos Humiston to Dear Philind, February 1, 1863; William H. Keyes to Old Gent, February 1, 1863, National Archives; James W. Washburn to Dear Parents, February 1, 1863, National Archives; Stephen Welch diary, February 4, 1863, courtesy of Carolyn Stoltz.

12. Amos Humiston to Dear Philind, February 1, 1863; William H. Keyes to Old Gent, February 1, 1863.

13. Stephen Welch diary, February 4–15, 1863; Dunkelman and Winey, *The Hardtack Regiment*, 44–45.

14. James W. Washburn to Dear Parents, February 24, 1863, National Archives.

15. Dunkelman and Winey, *The Hardtack Regiment*, 45; Stephen Welch diary,

February 18, March 5, 11, 22, 23, April 6, 1863; John J. Hennessy, "We Shall Make Richmond Howl: The Army of the Potomac on the Eve of Chancellorsville," in Gary W. Gallagher, ed., *Chancellorsville: The Battle and Its Aftermath* (Chapel Hill: University of North Carolina Press, 1996), 10–11; Amos Humiston to Dear wife, March 9, 1863, and cover of letter, postmarked Washington, D.C., March 13, 1863; Amos Humiston to Dear wife, March 25, 1863.

16. Stephen Welch diary, February 20, 28, 1863; Dunkelman and Winey, *The Hardtack Regiment*, 45; muster roll, Company C, 154th New York, February 28, 1863, National Archives; New York State Adjutant General, *Annual Report of the Adjutant General of the State of New York* (Albany: J. B. Lyon Company, State Printers, 1902, Serial No. 29), 716. Returned to the ranks of the 78th New York, Keyes was wounded at Gettysburg on July 3, 1863, and died of his wounds at the 12th Corps Hospital in Gettysburg on July 15.

17. Amos Humiston to Dear wife, March 9, 1863.

18. Edwin R. Osgood to deer brother, March 12, 1863, National Archives. Osgood was captured at Gettysburg on July 1, 1863, and died of chronic diarrhea on December 19, 1863, as a prisoner of war at Belle Island, Richmond, Virginia.

19. Amos Humiston to Dear wife, March 25, 1863; poem, "To my wife," March 25, 1863.

CHAPTER 7

A Close Call at Chancellorsville

WHILE SERGEANT AMOS Humiston was prostrated with illness in his hut—or at a nearby shallow trench, the company sink—the pace of life quickened for his comrades of Company C as the spring campaign season approached. On several occasions in March 1863, large numbers from the 154th New York were detailed for three-day tours of picket duty. "I dont like that," Private Martin Champlin complained in a letter to his sister, "for I dont get much sleep." When the men were not on post, they had to turn out the guard, Champlin noted, and just as they were about to get to sleep, the officer of the day was sure to come around.[1]

On a couple of occasions, Company C had target practice. In the first session, Private Orton Rounds, who had recently returned from a furlough to his Allegany farm, was the only man to hit the mark. On the second try, Sergeant Stephen Welch observed, "Some good shots [were] made."[2]

Members of the company were assigned to fatigue duty. Private Champlin was one of 180 men of the 154th ordered to build roads in late March. The remainder of the work detail was composed of men from German regiments. "I tooked my shovel and went to work with the rest of the dutchmen," Champlin noted. "They keep us to work all the time when we hant out on picket."[3]

An order read at the regimental dress parade on March 18 resulted in dissatisfaction. Messes would no longer do their own cooking, and company cooks were to be assigned. Privates Charles A. McIntosh of Portville and George Bishop (brother of colorbearer Lewis Bishop) were detailed as Company C's cooks the next day. After two weeks of the experiment, Sergeant Welch observed, "Company cooks don't go very well." On finishing a dinner of burned beans, he added, "We don't live half as well as we did when we cooked in squads or everyone for himself." On the last day of

March, a special treat was issued to the men, and perhaps it briefly took their minds off their poor food—or maybe it caused even more grumbling about the cooks. "A whiskey ration was served out to the men," Sergeant Welch recorded, "and some of them got as drunk as fools."[4]

Whiskey also saturated the camp of the 154th New York when a civilian named John Manley came to visit. A resident of the Cattaraugus County town of Little Valley, Manley was a clerk in the Interior Department in Washington when the war broke out, and ever since had taken an active interest in promoting the well-being of his home county's soldiers. In visiting camps, writing letters on behalf of the men, sending their pay home, cutting through red tape at the War Department on their behalf, and helping to organize the New York Soldiers' Relief Association in the capital, Manley well deserved his sobriquet, "the Soldier's Friend." During the war he received more than four thousand letters from Cattaraugus County soldiers and their relatives seeking his assistance in a wide range of matters. Manley also kept the home folk apprised of news of their boys in regular correspondence to the county press.

On his March 16 visit to the 154th New York, Manley brought with him a huge load of boxes and packages sent from the regiment's home folk, filled with foodstuffs and other comforts for the soldiers, along with a barrel of whiskey. At dress parade, an order naming the regiment's camp in his honor was greeted with great enthusiasm by the soldiers, and a brief responding speech by Manley inspired a rousing ovation. "The Regiment gave him 3 cheers," Sergeant Welch wrote, "and he paid the whiskey and then they cheered him again."[5]

It was at Camp John Manley in the spring of 1863 that the 154th New York was tagged with a nickname that stuck with the regiment until the end of the war and beyond. Coffee was a favorite of the German members of the 27th and 73rd Pennsylvania Volunteers, and they did not draw enough of it to suit their needs, while they drew an excess of hardtack. The situation was just the opposite in the 154th New York. An extensive trade grew among the three regiments, with the 154th swapping its surplus coffee to the Germans for their extra hardtack. Before long, some of the New York boys hatched an unscrupulous scheme. They saved their used coffee grounds, dried them, packaged them in sacks, and traded them for good hardtack. "Of course it did not take long for the Teutons to discover that their much loved beverage had lost most of its flavor," Private Charles McKay recalled, "and they were not slow in discovering the cause. They immediately named us the 'hardtacks.' When we passed their camp either singly or in a body they would turn out and yell, 'Hardtacks!' as loud as their lungs would allow. . . . Our boys always took it in good part and invariably answered their cry with the one word, 'Coffee.' "[6] According to

A Close Call at Chancellorsville

Private George W. Newcomb of Company K, the bantering was not as lighthearted as McKay indicated, but instead revealed the prejudice festering in the two groups. "The Dutch Regts in our Brigade call our Regt the hard tack Regt and we call them the sour crout Regts," Newcomb notified his wife. "They are all dutch in our Brigade except our Regt and they do not like us verry well. We can hardly get any water to use but what some Dutchman has washed his ass in it."[7]

Changes occurred in commanders from the company to corps level during the spring. The stalwart Captain Lewis D. Warner remained in command of Company C, but in March and April, five of the 154th New York's original ten company captains resigned and were discharged. In filling the vacancies, First Lieutenant Arthur Hotchkiss of Company C was promoted to captain and assigned to Company K. Second Lieutenant Warren Onan, away from Company C on detached duty as head of the brigade ambulance corps since the previous autumn, was not promoted to take Hotchkiss's place. Instead, Second Lieutenant Henry Martin of Company G, an Olean farmer who began his service as a private in Company I, was commissioned first lieutenant and assigned to duty with Company C on April 4. Colonel Jones justified Martin's rapid rise on his good qualifications: he was the only man in the regiment who had attended the U.S. Military Academy at West Point (although he did not graduate with his class of 1857, having resigned after his first year).[8]

Sergeant Welch recorded in his diary on March 7, "There is a rumor that Sigel has resigned." General Sigel, dissatisfied with the size of his command, had indeed resigned on February 22, and in the following weeks, General von Steinwehr and 3d Division commander Major General Carl Schurz served as interim commanders of the 11th Corps. On April 2, Major General Oliver Otis Howard, a Maine native known for his piety, a former division commander in the 2d Corps who had lost his right arm at the Battle of Fair Oaks, was assigned to command the corps. Reaction in the 154th New York to Howard's appointment was neutral and muted, but the replacement of their beloved Sigel caused widespread dissatisfaction among the German troops, exacerbated when Howard replaced some long-term high-ranking officers with outsiders in an apparent effort to reduce German influence in the corps. Edgy ethnic tensions, already a divisive factor in 11th Corps morale, were heightened by Howard's appointment, and that increase in bad feelings could not have come at a worse time.[9]

Corporal Joel Bouton was arrested on the night of March 17 for having a candle lit after taps. Perhaps he was writing a letter describing the events of the previous day, when the camp had been christened in honor of John Manley. Or maybe he was nursing his sick mess mate, Sergeant Amos

Humiston. But despite the desire of Bouton and other friends to keep Amos in camp—and Amos's own determination to avoid the place—he was admitted to the 2d Division hospital at Stafford Court House on March 27. Either his condition had changed drastically in response to treatment by the regimental medical staff, or a clerk made a mistake, because the hospital register listed his complaint as constipation.[10]

Not having heard from Philinda for a while, and worried that she or the children might be sick or having some other difficulty, Amos wrote from the hospital on April 3. His health was very poor, he informed his wife, but he encouraged her not to worry about him. "I think that I shal get up again before long," he declared, and he mentioned once more the support he received from his companions. "I am very cumfortable here," he wrote. "It is oneley a little ways from the regament and some of the boys are here every day to see me so that I do not get very lonesome."

Amos decided to send his letter home with Captain Warner, who was starting for Portville in a few days on a furlough. Amos urged Philinda to visit Warner during his return to Portville, and to "make him promise" to grant her husband a furlough, if only for ten days—but not to let the captain know that Amos had made the suggestion. Fatigued, Amos added a few lines before closing his letter:

I want to come home once more you may cal me home sick I do not know but I am thare is one thing surtain I want to see you all I am getting tired so you will have to make a short letter do for this time write to me often and believe me that you are ever in my mind tel the children pa wants to see them.[11]

Captain Warner left for home on April 7. If Philinda did indeed visit him and plead for a furlough for Amos, it was to no avail. By the time Warner returned to Virginia on April 18, he found Camp John Manley vacated. The 154th New York and the rest of Buschbeck's brigade had left several days before, bound for the upper Rappahannock River. And Amos was out of the hospital, and off with the regiment.[12]

During Warner's absence, he missed a momentous event when the 154th New York and the rest of the 11th Corps were reviewed by President Lincoln on April 10. Their first view of Old Abe (and the only time they saw him, as it turned out) inspired a small flood of letters by members of the Hardtack Regiment, describing to loved ones at home the gaunt and gangly Lincoln, the enormous presidential entourage, the music of the brass bands, the newspaper artists busily sketching the scene, the booming artillery salute, and the precise movements of the immense mass of troops.[13]

Amos was listed as absent in the division hospital on a special muster roll made out on April 10, but later in the day he was released from the hospital and returned to duty. Whether he was present at the review and saw the president is unknown.[14]

Lincoln's visit to the Army of the Potomac was the prelude to Hooker's spring campaign. Days later, Buschbeck's brigade was sent up the Rappahannock in support of the army's cavalry corps, which was to cross the river and make a raid in the rear of the Confederate forces. The march to Kelly's Ford, via Hartwood Church, was made on April 13 and 14 in clement weather, over firm, dry roads, through a fine countryside. But on April 15 it rained all day, and Sergeant Welch grumbled, "This is the 2nd stick-in-the-mud expedition and [we] are just one day too late for a fight. It seems as though the god of battles was against us." But the weather cleared, the mud dried, and the 154th New York spent the next two weeks fixing up a camp near Mount Holly Church, guarding a battery, drilling, picketing the riverbank, peering at the ragged rebels on the opposite shore, playing baseball and cards, and wondering what the next move would be.

Nearby farms lost a considerable number of hogs and chickens during the Hardtack Regiment's stay at Kelly's Ford. Some of the men were apprehended and tried for the thefts, including Private Albert E. Hall of Company C, who was sentenced to forfeit one month's pay and to wear a signboard reading "Marauder" on his back. While Amos enjoyed an occasional piece of roast pork or chicken, he apparently made do without another pleasure. "Most of the tobacco chewers are suffering for the want of it," Sergeant Welch noted (the men had left their knapsacks at Camp John Manley), and he added hopefully, "Let them get some before marching."[15]

A hearty welcome greeted Captain Warner on the afternoon of April 27, when he rejoined the 154th accompanied by a number of convalescents and wagons filled with the regimental baggage, including the men's knapsacks and mail. A scramble ensued, and soon the soldiers were eagerly reading letters, changing their dirty, lice-ridden underclothes, and savoring a wad or pipeful of tobacco. For Company C, and particularly for Amos and the other Portville boys, there was the added satisfaction of news direct from home, as related by their captain. "Found the Regt well and in good spirits," Warner recorded in his diary, "preparing for a moove to some place."[16]

It was not long in coming. Late in the afternoon of April 28, Colonel Jones called together the company officers and gave them orders. Shortly before sunset, the regiment left camp, marched to Marsh Run, a tributary of the Rappahannock, and boarded pontoon boats. Around dusk, the regiment pushed off into the stream and rowed into the river, heading for the opposite shore. From the shadowy riverbank looming ahead came flashes of light and the crackle of gunfire, and for the first time, Amos and his comrades experienced the sensation of being under fire. But the hasty round fired by the Confederate videttes splashed harmlessly into the water around the surging pontoons, and by the time the first boat beached on the southern shore, the enemy had fled. The men quickly scrambled out of the boats, deployed in a skirmish line, and cautiously advanced across the river bottom. Behind them, members of the 15th New York Engineers, helped by men of the 11th Corps and superintended by General Hooker himself, began to lay a pontoon bridge. Several hours later, when the bridge was completed, a force of Brigadier General Francis C. Barlow's 2d Brigade of von Steinwehr's division crossed and took position in advance of the 154th, and the regiment was ordered back to the river. For two hours the men waited until the bridge was clear, and then they crossed to the northern bank and marched back to their camp, reaching their tents at 1 A.M. on April 29. All night, a steady stream of infantry, cavalry, and artillery rattled and rumbled over the bridge.[17]

After a few brief hours of sleep, the 154th was roused at 6 A.M., broke camp, crossed the bridge, marched about a half-mile, and halted and stacked arms. Throughout the day, the flow of troops over the bridge and past the regiment's position, coursing down roads to the south, never ceased. The mighty river of men and materiel made a tremendous impression on the Hardtack Regiment. "We have laid near the crossing all day," remarked Sergeant Welch, "and have had a chance to see more than we ever have before."

Three entire corps—the 5th, 11th, and 12th—crossed the pontoon bridge at Kelly's Ford. Captain Warner and Sergeant Welch estimated the number of men at between 65,000 and 70,000; returns for the three corps recorded a smaller but still substantial 42,250. Where the immense force was headed was unknown to the men in the ranks, but it seemed to bode an encounter with the enemy, as Captain Warner confided to his diary. "What the destination of this vast boddy is is of course only conjecture with us who are not of the councill. That it means work is certain and God speed the Ball. The long looked for moove has at length commenced, and now the onward to Richmond I hope & trust is not to be a meaningless boast but a living reality."[18]

What had happened was this: Hooker had divided his army, leaving a portion of it—designated the left wing—to confront Lee's army at Fredericksburg, while the remainder—composing the right wing and accompanied by Hooker himself—marched upriver to Kelly's Ford and other crossings, to approach Lee from the rear. Hooker intended to press Lee front and rear, cut off any avenue of escape, and rout the Confederates.

Ignorant of their destination and fate, Amos and the other Hardtacks were nevertheless enjoying themselves as they rested near Kelly's Ford on

A Close Call at Chancellorsville

April 29 and watched the three corps pass by. In the vicinity was the rich farm of the wealthy namesake of the ford, and during the day Mr. Kelly's large mill was emptied of flour and meal, his big smokehouse was relieved of its hams and bacon, his several wheat fields became fodder for horses and mules, and his dwelling and store were thoroughly looted, with members of the 154th getting their fair share of the spoils. "What was a thriving Farm and appurtenances in the morning was a desert waste in the Evening," Captain Warner wrote. "So much for Cecession." Kellysville, as the place was called, would long remember the passage of the Union army, Sergeant Welch thought.

After a wet night, Captain Warner was ordered to wake Company C at 4 A.M. on April 30 and prepare to march. Before the men could finish their coffee, they were ordered into line, and the 154th marched as rear guard to the immense supply train of pack mules and mule-driven wagons. Slipping in mud and manure on a road heading in the direction of Fredericksburg and the rear of Lee's army, they moved at a plodding pace through a fine countryside. About 9 A.M. the regiment halted to rest and was mustered by Colonel Jones. Six hundred and ten officers and enlisted men were counted in the tally; Company C recorded an even sixty. A number of men were on extra or detached duty, including three of Company C, leaving a total of 57 present with the company, and 590 present with the regiment.[19]

Underway again after the stop, the 154th crossed the Rapidan River on a pontoon bridge at Germanna Ford and halted for dinner and a rest on the southern shore. While Amos and the others ate and loafed, they were greatly amused by the antics of the mules as the train forded the swiftly running river, with the wagon boxes half submerged in the swirling water. Private Timothy Glines of Company C, a laborer from Potter County, Pennsylvania, who had enlisted at Portville, wrote, "The water would take the mules off their feet, they would flounce around, get tangled in the harness and then they would make the water foam." Captain Warner noted, "In one or two cases it was supposed that his muleship had crossed over Jordan, but on their emerging on the other side they flapped their ears shook themselves and were all right, and ready for the next adventure of the sort." When the train completed its crossing, the 154th again fell in as rear guard and added another dozen miles to the ten it had marched in the morning, wearily shuffling along into the night. About midnight the column halted. The Company C boys were "pretty considerably tired," Captain Warner recorded, "and lay down without putting up tents."[20]

It was chilly when the men awoke at sunrise on May Day, but a heavy fog indicated a warm, pleasant day was in store. For a force supposedly driving onto the rear of the enemy, Hooker's right wing now proceeded with surprising leisure. "No hurry about starting this morning," Captain

Warner noted in his diary, and the forenoon passed without the regiment's making a move. Amos and the rest cleaned their rifles, readied them for use, and lined up for an inspection of arms. Finally, around noon, the regiment was ordered into line and marched out the road toward Fredericksburg. But after proceeding approximately a half-mile, the men did an about-face and tramped back to their campsite of the previous night, where they lolled away the afternoon.[21]

Unbeknown to the rank and file of the 154th New York, the campaign's initiative had shifted dramatically from General Hooker to General Lee— and the result was to have a profound impact on the fortunes of the Hardtack Regiment. Hooker's right wing was strung out along roads cutting through the dense thickets and tangled forests of a region aptly named the Wilderness. Instead of pushing into the open country to the east and driving the Confederates as he had planned, Hooker pulled his troops back into a defensive posture after his advance met opposition from the enemy. Lee had divided his army, leaving a portion of it in his Fredericksburg defenses to face the Union forces there, and turning the remainder westward to confront Hooker's right wing. Now, with his opponent stymied, Lee made one of the most brilliant tactical strokes of the war: he decided to divide his army yet again and send Lieutenant General Thomas J. "Stonewall" Jackson on a wide arc, covered by the dense forest of the Wilderness, to strike at the isolated right flank of Hooker's right wing—the 11th Corps.[22]

Cannon were booming in the direction of Fredericksburg when the 154th New York was ordered into line at about 5 P.M. on May 1 and crossed the road to take position in a field. As Amos and his comrades of Company C listened, the distant artillery and musketry fire eventually petered out, but the soldiers continued to lay on their arms until about 10 P.M., when they rolled themselves in their blankets. A nearly full moon and a galaxy of bright stars lit the nighttime sky, and Captain Warner mused in his diary, "Under this beautiful canopy, thousands of intelligent beings are reposing, like myself not knowing but it may be the last night they may thus be permitted to enjoy the beautiful spectacle." The men nodded off to the sounds of shoveling, as work parties dug entrenchments nearby.[23]

By the morning of May 2, the green ground was scarred with brown lines of rifle pits, and immediately after the 154th New York finished a breakfast of hardtack and coffee, the regiment was ordered to occupy one of the pits. The nearby landscape was already familiar to Amos and the other Hardtacks from their sojourn of the previous day. Their rifle pit faced the woods at the southern edge of a clearing. The open space behind them was bisected by a road running east to west. On the south side of the road, near the 154th's position, stood a one-and-a-half-story wooden structure known as Dowdall's Tavern and several outbuildings. The former tavern and post office was home to a Baptist minister, the Reverend Melzi S. Chancellor, and his family; now it was also the headquarters of Generals Howard and von Steinwehr. A quarter-mile to the west, on the north side of the road, stood the Reverend Chancellor's sanctuary, the Wilderness Church. The Orange Plank Road and Turnpike formed a juncture at the Wilderness Church, ran in combination past Dowdall's Tavern, and less than two miles to the east, at a brick dwelling known as Chancellorsville, where General Hooker had established his headquarters, the two roads again parted.[24]

Hooker had concentrated the bulk of the right wing in a semicircle around Chancellorsville, and from there the line extended to the west, where the 11th Corps formed the extreme right. General von Steinwehr's 2d Division was positioned closest to the rest of the army, with Colonel Buschbeck's 1st Brigade in its rifle pits south of Dowdall's, and General Barlow's 2d Brigade entrenched north of the road. Next in line, north of the road near the Wilderness Church and in an adjacent farm clearing, was General Schurz's 3d Division. Prolonging the line along the turnpike until it tapered off in the dense Wilderness thickets was the 1st Division, commanded by Brigadier General Charles Devens.[25]

Hooker rode along the line that morning and was greeted with a loud, enthusiastic demonstration. "The cheers he received," Captain Warner noted, "must have plainly told him that he had the confidence of the 11th Corps at least." Unfortunately for both commander and men, that confidence was not reciprocated. Demonstrating the disdain for the 11th Corps prevalent throughout his army, Hooker had positioned it farthest from the enemy, where it was, so he thought, least likely to become engaged. But fate was about to play a most cruel trick on the general and the unlucky corps. While Amos and the rest of the Hardtack Regiment were hurrahing for Hooker, Stonewall Jackson was leading 28,000 battle-tested Confederates through the Wilderness, headed for the vulnerable right flank of the 11th Corps.[26]

Compounding the problem was a lack of vigilance on the part of General Howard. Several times as the day wore on, couriers arrived at Dowdall's Tavern to warn Howard of his corps' susceptibility to an attack from the west—worries shared by the rank and file of the 11th Corps. "During the day it was rumored that Jackson with a heavy force was advancing in our rear," Captain Warner noted, but he added, "Not much preparation seems to have been made to receive him in our vicinity." Reports of an enemy flanking maneuver were dismissed or ignored by Howard and his staff, and during the day Howard even rode away from his command, accompanied by General von Steinwehr and the corps' largest brigade—Barlow's—to join a distant attack on what proved to be Jackson's rear guard. That unfortunate move left the 11th Corps temporarily leaderless, reduced the remainder of the corps to about 9,000 men, and left Buschbeck's brigade as the only troops in the immediate area of Dowdall's Tavern.[27]

Despite the ominous signs, the afternoon passed quietly for the 154th, and at approximately 5 P.M. the regiment left the rifle pit and commenced preparing supper. Any threat from the enemy seemed to have disappeared, and throughout the 11th Corps, arms were stacked, cook fires were burning, music was playing, and soldiers were chatting, smoking, playing cards, and making arrangements for the night's sleep. Generals Howard and von Steinwehr rode up to Dowdall's Tavern, having left Barlow's brigade skirmishing in some distant woods, and Howard ordered the artillerymen of a nearby battery to unharness their horses and rest. As shadows lengthened around Dowdall's, Amos and the other Hardtacks relaxed; in the still, late afternoon air, insects buzzed, horses nickered, tunes floated faintly, conversation hummed, laughter pealed . . . and suddenly shots were fired.

They came from the west, from the far right of the corps, and the musketry quickly swelled to a thundering roar, punctuated by the boom of artillery and counterpointed by the high, keening wail of the rebel yell. Jackson's command, stretching for a mile into the forest on each side of the turnpike, had commenced its surprise attack on the unsuspecting, unprepared, and vastly outnumbered 11th Corps, shattering company after company and regiment after regiment as it rolled eastward with relentless force. Dense clouds of acrid white smoke—booming, crackling, flashing light—billowed through the woods and clearings like a mighty thunderstorm, scattering all in its path like leaves before the wind.

Colonel Jones quickly had the 154th New York under arms and in line, and Colonel Buschbeck ordered his brigade to take position in a shallow rifle pit dug in a north-south line astraddle the road just east of Dowdall's Tavern. The 154th New York was placed at the far left of the line. To the regiment's right were the 73d Pennsylvania, the 27th Pennsylvania, and the 29th New York. Built to face an attack coming from the east, the pit offered little shelter to Buschbeck's men as they lay and waited for the storm approaching from the west.

It was not long before the first fugitives were spotted coming down the road, and as Amos and the other Hardtacks watched in disbelief, the panicked men rushed right through Buschbeck's line without making any attempt to rally, and ran down the road into the woods to the rear. Behind them came a rising tide of rout: a mad jumble of soldiers, horses, mules, cattle, cannons, caissons, limber chests, and wagons, the panic-stricken men fleeing for their lives down the road and through the fields on both sides, cutting haphazardly through Buschbeck's regiments and, like their predecessors, refusing to re-form, for the most part. General Howard clutched a flag under the stump of his arm and with General von Steinwehr and various staff officers, tried desperately to rally the fugitives, with but little success. For about an hour and a half, the shattered remnants of two divisions poured in confusion past the Buschbeck line, forced to the rear by Jackson's approaching juggernaut. Devens's division had almost completely disintegrated. Schurz's men, farther from the initial point of the attack, fared a bit better and offered more resistance before they too were crushed. Falling back, a number of Schurz's men re-formed to the right of Buschbeck's brigade. It was about 6:30 P.M., and the Buschbeck line was all that was left of the 11th Corps on the field.

Circumstances could not have been worse for Sergeant Amos Humiston and his comrades of the 154th New York as they faced their baptism of fire. They were holding the exposed left flank of a small, poorly sheltered force, attempting to cover the demoralizing rout of their corps with no nearby reserves, and facing an enemy overwhelming in numbers, exultant with victory, and eager to destroy this last bit of opposition. In front of Buschbeck's men, the approaching Confederates filled the fields and swarmed through the adjacent forests as far as the eye could see. Behind Buschbeck's brigade, the 11th Corps reserve artillery was limbering up and disappearing down the Plank Road into the gloom of the Wilderness. It was more than a mile to the nearest Union reinforcements. As the setting sun neared the western horizon, the moment the Hardtacks had waited for, the time Amos and his companions had anticipated for seven months with mingled uncertainty, anxiety, impatience, and dread was at last at hand.

Positioned at the center of the regiment, the men of Company C heard Colonel Jones order Color Sergeant Lewis Bishop to raise the national flag, and Bishop stood and defiantly waved the banner, immediately drawing a concentrated fire. Then the colonel ordered his regiment to fire at will, and a deafening volley enveloped the rifle pit in smoke. Loading and firing as rapidly as they could, supported by the devastating fire of the few remaining artillery pieces, Buschbeck's men stunned and slowed the enemy's advance. But the Confederates were not to be stopped. Return fire quickly found its mark, dirt flew from the rim of the rifle pit, Sergeant Bishop's flag was ripped by bullets, and the sickening thud and whack of minié balls hitting flesh and bone began to be heard in the din. Bleeding men rolled in agony or lay stunned and immobile. Standing or crouching behind the line, several commissioned and noncommissioned officers toppled to the ground, among them Colonel Jones, severely wounded in his right hip. Balls began raking the rifle pit laterally, and then from the rear, as the long Confederate lines outflanked Buschbeck's force. From the field north of the road, the rebel yell raised to a higher pitch as the rallied men from Schurz's division, along with the 29th New York and the 27th Pennsylvania, gave way and scurried into the woods and down the road to the rear. As the Buschbeck line crumbled from right to left, part of the 73d Pennsylvania joined the retreat, but its left wing, seeing the 154th New York holding its position on the extreme left flank, remained at the rifle pit for another volley. Several hundred men from the two regiments were all that was left of the 11th Corps, and Colonel Jones, the highest-ranking officer still on the battlefield, realizing the command would soon be captured en masse, gave the order to retreat.

An open field about eight hundred feet wide lay between the rifle pit and the safety of the woods, and as Amos and the other Hardtacks broke into a run to cross the clearing, it was as if a hunter had flushed his game. The Confederate fire was furious and effective, and bodies spun, fell, and littered the field. Swarming over the rifle pit and field, the rebels captured scores of prisoners, including Colonel Jones and many other wounded. Into the darkened woods scrambled the survivors, clawing and tripping their way through the tangled underbrush, throwing away knapsacks and other accouterments, trying to stay together, but occasionally running into enemy squads and being forced to surrender. Sweating and panting, a core group reached a vacant log breastwork about a half-mile from Dowdall's, and there other survivors rallied to Lieutenant Colonel Loomis and the colors. During the brief pause, an inspection revealed some twenty bullets had pierced the national flag and three more had struck the flagstaff, one between the hands of Sergeant Bishop, who was miraculously unhurt.

What was left of the regiment continued the retreat, stumbling and struggling through the woods by the light of a full moon and emerging into the open near a plateau known as Fairview, not far from Chancellorsville, where a massive collection of artillery had been assembled. There the 154th New York was ordered to support a division of the 3d Corps, and behind those lines the regiment found the remainder of Buschbeck's brigade. Around midnight, Buschbeck was ordered to the rear of Hooker's headquarters at Chancellorsville, and Amos and the rest of the remaining bedraggled, numb, and exhausted Hardtacks collapsed on the ground and fell asleep.[28]

After the wild and terrible evening of May 2, the next few days were anticlimactic. Early on the morning of May 3, the 11th Corps marched down a road in the direction of United States Ford and was placed behind breastworks. Positioned there, well to the army's rear, it was reasoned the disgraced corps would be certain not to face the enemy again. From sunrise to about noon, the soldiers of the 154th New York listened as the battle raged around Chancellorsville. "The deafening thunder of the artillery and the awful roar of the musketry was terrible," Private Charles McKay re-

A Close Call at Chancellorsville

called, but, as anticipated, the 11th Corps remained unengaged. "Although we had no part in the fight of this day," Captain Warner wrote, "our position on the road leading to the River enabled us to see its effects in all their Horrors. While the battle lasted there was a constant stream of wounded going past, on horseback, on litters, on stretchers, on foot supported by friends on each side and without any aid. The sights were enough to make one sick of war and its attendant Horrors." At one point during the day, a group of prisoners was passing the 154th's position, and one of their guards was bearing a captured Confederate flag. Amos and the rest of Company C heard a thoughtless Hardtack shout, "Give me that rebel rag!" A bloodied young Confederate immediately looked him in the eye, gestured toward the front, and coolly responded, "There's lots of them just up yonder; go and get one." Both Yankees and Rebels shared a knowing laugh at the smart aleck's expense.[29]

That night the men lay on their arms and were roused and brought into line on a couple of occasions by picket firing, only to return to the breastworks and their fitful sleep. May 4 was relatively quiet, and the 154th lay in the rifle pits all day and all night. "Not much fighting this day," Captain Warner noted. "Both sides seem appalled by the carnage of yesterday." A number of men who had become separated from the regiment during the chaos of May 2 rejoined the 154th during the day, including a few from Company C, but Captain Warner recorded that seventeen of his men were still unaccounted for. Another quiet day passed on May 5, and in the afternoon the 154th was relieved by the 29th New York and left the breastworks as showers began to fall. It rained through most of the night. "We were almost without shelter or Blankets and no fires were allowed after dark," Captain Warner wrote, "so you may suppose we passed anything but a comfortable night." Early that evening, Lieutenant Colonel Loomis gathered the officers and ordered them to have their companies ready to march at any moment, but nobody knew where the next movement would lead.

On the wet morning of May 6, the regiment formed line to march before having a chance to make coffee. It then became evident that the entire army was retreating across the Rappahannock. The campaign was ending in defeat. "On the necessity I shall venture no opinion," Captain Warner commented about the move. "It probably took thousands as it did me by surprise." The men sloshed through the mud to United States Ford, crossed the swollen river on tossing pontoon bridges, and headed back to their old camp, which they reached on the morning of May 7 after trudging about twenty-five miles. At dilapidated Camp John Manley, Amos and his comrades fixed up shelters as best they could to get out of the intermittent rain. They cleaned their guns for inspection, and the officers filled out requisitions to replace clothing and equipage lost on the battlefield. "Thus ends Hookers Campaign No 1," Captain Warner wrote. "What has been accomplished I have little means of knowing and shall not venture an opinion."[30]

Camp John Manley was unusually quiet for the next few days, and the Hardtacks hastened to write home, to let their loved ones know they were all right, attempt to describe what they had been through, and try to put the overwhelming experience into perspective. They knew the campaign had been a failure, and that the rout of the 11th Corps had been a crucial turning point of the battle, but they also knew their regiment had performed courageously in its forlorn stand on the evening of May 2. Captain Warner wrote in his diary:

Nobly did the 154 respond to the call of duty, and bravely did she sustain the credit of old Cattaraugus. Not a man flinched amid the most withering fire of Shell Grape Canister & Musket Balls, while their deadly rifles made terrible havoc in the ranks of the advancing enemy. But numbers could not but prevail. Their ranks were filled as fast as they fell and they were fast turning our flanks. At last prudence became the better part of valor and our Colonel ordered a retreat. We now had an open field of about 50 rods to cross to reach a wood in our rear, and this crossing under the tremendous cross fire was terrible. Many was the poor fellow of the 154 who failed to reach the wood unharmed.[31]

Private James Washburn wrote to his parents:

You wanted to know how I felt when we went in the battle we had not much time to think the Rebs came on us by surprise as you might say they came in from the opposite way from what we were looking for them we knew nothing about this coming not more than 20 minutes before they attacked us. I did not feel as though I was going to get hurt we laid in the Rifle Pitts until we had orders to fall back but it was a chance that I came out alive. . . . our Brigadier General Bushbeck said that we fought the best of any new Reg't he ever saw.[32]

Some men sent accounts to their local newspapers, among them Private Glines, who wrote to the *Potter County Journal* in Coudersport, Pennsylvania. Glines presented a frank description of the regiment's retreat, and he also repeated a widespread but unfounded rumor that Stonewall Jackson's men were drunk when they made the attack:

The Rebels came on yelling like so many devils and were so drunk that they did not seem to think we were shooting at them until they were tipped over. We held them about thirty minutes, until they had us almost surrounded, and then we had orders to fall back, when you might have seen some tall running. When we left the rifle pits we had to run about sixty rods before we reached the woods, then the Rebels had a fair sight at us and the way the bullets flew was a sin to snakes. I began to think my time had come, but my legs were pretty good and they didn't stop until I came to a pretty good tree. I stopped and found myself minus knapsack, haversack and canteen. But the Rebels didn't give me time to think, so I had to "git" again. . . . We left quite a number of our men in the rifle pits; one man that lay by the side of me was shot through the head.[33]

Amos wrote to Philinda two days after returning to Camp John Manley, beginning his letter with a reassurance. "It is with plaisure that I addres a few lines to you," he told her, "to let you know that I am in the land of the living after the battle." Other than saying, "We had a hard fight," Amos did not attempt to describe the regiment's role in the battle. But he did tell Philinda that he had survived a close call on the evening of May 2. "[I] got away with a hole head but I got a wipe in the side with a spent ball that made me think of home," he wrote. "It struck on the short ribs just over the hart but glanced off if it had not I should not be writing to you now."[34]

Everyone who wrote about the battle referred to the regiment's staggering casualty count. "Now look at [us]," wrote Private Washburn, comparing the band of about 350 survivors to the roughly 950 men who had left Jamestown seven months before. "What a change," observed Captain Warner. "The 154 has gained a name," Amos declared, "but at what a loss." Of the 590 men in the regiment's line of battle at Dowdall's Tavern, at least 240 had been killed, wounded, or captured, one of the highest regimental losses in the Army of the Potomac, and a casualty rate of 40 percent. One out of every three men in Company C—nineteen of the fifty-seven in the fight—had become casualties. Four of them were reported to be killed, 5 were wounded, and the other 10 were missing and presumed captured.[35]

Among those reported killed in Company C was Private Seymour Sikes of Portville. "He was hit with a piece of shell in the head," Amos wrote. Private Martin Champlin of Portville was missing, and his fate was unknown. "That is all that is missing from our place," Amos notified Philinda. But the exact status of some of the company's casualties was uncertain, and as time passed, changes were made to the list. Meanwhile, as letters from survivors arrived and lists were published in area newspapers, families in Portville and other Cattaraugus County communities were plunged into mourning.[36]

Years later, surviving veterans of Company C would continue to ponder what had happened at Chancellorsville. In his postwar reminiscences Charles McKay declared, "Old Cattaraugus need feel no shame for the part played by the 'Hardtacks' on the field of Chancellorsville." Three decades after the battle, Lewis Warner commented, "The most unfortunate thing about the 154th was that we had not learned to run when we ought to have done so." In the middle of 1863, the question was whether the regiment had learned that lesson at Chancellorsville. The answer would not be long in coming.[37]

"I am tired and worn out with hard marching and hard fare," Amos informed Philinda in his letter of May 9, and he added just a few lines before closing:

I looked for a letter from you when I got back but did not [find one.] I am in hopes to get one to night I got the likeness of the children and it pleased me more than eney thing that you could have sent me how I want to se them and their mother is more than I can tell I hope that we may all live to see each other again if this war dose not last to long.[38]

His heart must have leaped with joy when he first saw the ambrotype. Eight-year-old Frank was sitting on the left in the mirror image, with six-year-old Alice on the right and four-year-old Fred in a high chair in the middle. Alice's dress and Frank's shirt were made from the same plaid material, no doubt sewn by Philinda. Fred was wearing a dark-colored suit with short trousers. All three children had solemn looks on their sweet faces and had sat rigidly still for the lengthy exposure to remain in tight focus. The likeness was framed in a gilt matte marked "Holmes, Booth & Hayden," a prominent New York City photographic supply manufacturer.[39]

For more than seven months, Amos had expressed his longing for home. Now he had a bit of home with him to cherish always, a picture that would convey precious memories forever. Now he had the children with him whenever he wanted them to be there.

Neither Amos nor Philinda had any idea of just how important the ambrotype would turn out to be.

NOTES

1. Stephen Welch diary, March 9, 15, 21, 1863, courtesy of Carolyn Stoltz; Martin V. B. Champlin to Sister Louise, March 30, 1863, courtesy of Richard D. Champlin.

2. Stephen Welch diary, March 22, 25, 27, 1863.

3. Ibid., March 26, 30, 1863; Martin V. B. Champlin to Sister Louise, March 30, 1863.

4. Stephen Welch diary, March 18, 19, 31, April 1 and 2, 1863; regimental return, March 1863, National Archives.

5. Franklin Ellis, ed., *History of Cattaraugus County, New York* (Philadelphia: L. H. Everts, 1879), 109, 280–282; Stephen Welch diary, March 16, 1863.

6. Charles W. McKay, "Three Years or During the War, with the Crescent and Star," in *The National Tribune Scrap Book* (Washington, n.d.), 125.

7. George W. Newcomb to Dear Wife, March 6, 1863, Lewis Leigh Collection, Book 36, #90, U. S. Army Military History Institute, Carlisle Barracks, Pa.

8. Company muster rolls, 154th New York, April 30, 1863, National Archives; descriptive book, Company I, 154th New York, National Archives; William Adams, ed., *Historical Gazetteer and Biographical Memorial of Cattaraugus County, N.Y.* (Syracuse: Lyman, Horton & Co., 1893), 208; registration form for Cadet Henry Martin, United States Military Academy Library.

9. Mark H. Dunkelman and Michael J. Winey, *The Hardtack Regiment: An Illustrated History of the 154th Regiment, New York State Infantry Volunteers* (East Brunswick, N.J.: Fairleigh Dickinson University Press, 1981), 49; John J. Hennessy, "We Shall Make Richmond Howl: The Army of the Potomac on the Eve of Chancellorsville," in Gary W. Gallagher, ed., *Chancellorsville: The Battle and Its Aftermath* (Chapel Hill: University of North Carolina Press, 1996), 23–25.

10. Stephen Welch diary, March 17, 1863; medical record card, Amos Humiston, copied from Register No. 353, Hospital No. 79, Page 54, National Archives.

11. Amos Humiston to Dear wife, April 3, 1863.

12. Stephen Welch diary, April 7, 1863; Lewis D. Warner diary, April 18, 1863, courtesy of John L. Spencer; Amos Humiston to Dear wife, May 9, 1863.

13. Mark H. Dunkelman and Michael J. Winey, "The Hardtack Regiment Meets Lincoln," *Lincoln Herald* 85, no. 2 (Summer 1983): 95–99.

14. Special muster roll, Company C, 154th New York, April 10, 1863, National Archives; medical record card, Amos Humiston.

15. Dunkelman and Winey, *The Hardtack Regiment*, 50–51; Stephen Welch diary, April 14–26, 1863.

16. Lewis D. Warner diary, April 27, 1863; Stephen Welch diary, April 27, 1863.

17. Lewis D. Warner diary, April 28, 1863; Stephen Welch diary, April 28, 1863; Dunkelman and Winey, *The Hardtack Regiment*, 51–52; John Bigelow, Jr., *The Campaign of Chancellorsville: A Strategic and Tactical Study* (New Haven: Yale University Press, 1910), 187–188.

18. Stephen Welch diary, April 29, 1863; Lewis D. Warner diary, April 29, 1863; Bigelow, *Campaign of Chancellorsville*, 136.

19. Lewis D. Warner diary, April 29–30, 1863; Stephen Welch diary, April 29–30, 1863; muster rolls, 154th New York, April 30, 1863, National Archives.

20. Timothy Glines, letter of May 9, 1863, published in the *Potter County Journal* (Coudersport, Pa.), May 27, 1863; Stephen Welch diary, April 30, 1863; Lewis D. Warner diary, April 30, 1863.

21. Lewis D. Warner diary, May 1, 1863.

22. Dunkelman and Winey, *The Hardtack Regiment*, 52–53; Bigelow, *Campaign of Chancellorsville*, 223; Mark H. Dunkelman, "Main Address," in *Dedication of*

the Chancellorsville Monument to the 154th New York Volunteer Infantry May 26, 1996 (154th New York Monument Fund, 1996), 12.

23. Lewis D. Warner diary, May 1, 1863.

24. Ibid., May 2, 1863; Bigelow, *Campaign of Chancellorsville*, 177–178; Noel G. Harrison, *Chancellorsville Battlefield Sites* (Lynchburg, Va.: H. E. Howard, 1990), 80–86.

25. Dunkelman and Winey, *The Hardtack Regiment*, 54; Bigelow, *Campaign of Chancellorsville*, Map 16, 285–286; Augustus Choate Hamlin, *The Battle of Chancellorsville* (Bangor, Me.: Published by the author, 1896), Map No. 1.

26. Lewis D. Warner diary, May 2, 1863; Stephen Welch diary, May 2, 1863.

27. Lewis D. Warner diary, May 2, 1863; Dunkelman and Winey, *The Hardtack Regiment*, 55.

28. Dunkelman and Winey, *The Hardtack Regiment*, 55–60; Dunkelman, "Main Address," in *Dedication of the Chancellorsville Monument to the 154th New York*, 13–16.

29. Dunkelman and Winey, *The Hardtack Regiment*, 62; McKay, "Three Years or During the War," 128.

30. Lewis D. Warner diary, May 4–7, 1863.

31. Ibid., May 2, 1863.

32. James W. Washburn to Absent Parents, May 12, 1863, National Archives.

33. Timothy Glines, letter of May 9, 1863, published in the *Potter County Journal* (Coudersport, Pa.), May 27, 1863.

34. Amos Humiston to Dear wife, May 9, 1863.

35. Ibid.; "Losses in the 154th Regiment," *Cattaraugus Freeman*, May 21, 1863; Schedule A, Casualties, accompanying Lieutenant Colonel Henry C. Loomis's official report of the Battle of Chancellorsville, May 21, 1863, in a regimental letterbook, Ellicottville Historical Society, Ellicottville, N.Y.; Dunkelman, "Main Address," in *Dedication of the Chancellorsville Monument to the 154th New York*, 17.

36. Amos Humiston to Dear wife, May 9, 1863.

37. McKay, "Three Years or During the War," 128; Adams, *Historical Gazetteer and Biographical Memorial of Cattaraugus County, N.Y.*, 1019.

38. Amos Humiston to Dear wife, May 9, 1863.

39. Carte de visite copies of the ambrotype by Wenderoth & Taylor and Wenderoth, Taylor & Brown, Philadelphia, in the author's collection; *American Presbyterian*, October 29, 1863; Floyd Rinhart and Marion Rinhart, *The American Daguerreotype* (Athens: University of Georgia Press, 1981), 316, 418.

CHAPTER 8

Gettysburg

ACRIMONIOUS FAULTFINDING ERUPTED in the aftermath of Chancellorsville, and the 11th Corps served as a convenient scapegoat for the loss of the battle. Abuse was heaped on the corps by the rest of the army and the press, with much of the criticism pointedly aimed at the German element. Members of the 154th New York were not immune to the bickering, and they assigned blame for the rout of their corps to whomever they saw fit. Many accused the Germans of cowardice; others cursed the stupidity of General Howard. Virtually all of them asserted the bravery of their stand in the Buschbeck line at Dowdall's Tavern. While Buschbeck's brigade received some recognition for its part in the battle from journalists and superior officers, the stigma of being associated with the "damned Dutchmen" was too much to overcome. The Hardtack Regiment was well aware it was part of a disgraced corps.[1]

Dispiriting too was the scene at Camp John Manley, where huts that had once held four occupants now had but one or two, or were empty. The soldiers languished in the desolate atmosphere. Aside from the usual drills and picket duty, inactivity ruled their lives; during one period in mid-May, Captain Warner did not bother to make an entry in his diary for four consecutive boring days. When something noteworthy did occur, it often seemed to add to the unpleasantness, particularly for Sergeant Amos Humiston.[2]

Company C received four months' pay on the evening of May 11, and Amos was issued an allotment check for forty dollars made out to Philinda. He promptly mailed it along with a letter, but it was lost in transit and never arrived in Portville, depriving his family of considerable much-needed income.[3] Two days later, on the night of May 13, Amos temporarily lost a mess mate when Corporal Joel Bouton accidentally shot himself in the toe while on picket, damaging it so badly it had to be amputated. Self-inflicted wounds were often desperate attempts to secure a discharge, but such was not the case with Bouton; within a month he was back on duty and ready to undertake the longest, hardest march the regiment had yet made.[4]

By the middle of May, the regiment's badly wounded had been recovered from the Chancellorsville battlefield, where they had lain without care for ten days, and most of them were transported to the 11th Corps hospital at Brooks Station, not far from Camp John Manley. Colonel Patrick Jones, hobbling on a pair of crutches made for him by a member of the regiment, left the 154th for home on May 17. On parole but not yet exchanged, the colonel would not return to duty with his regiment for six months. "We miss him considerable," wrote Private James Washburn. "He was a fine little fellow he was an Irish but he was smart."[5]

Among the severely wounded was Private Seymour Sikes. "We all made a mistake in regard to Seymour Sykes," Amos notified Philinda. "He was not kiled instantly as we surposed he was shot on Satureday night [May 2] and lay on the field until Tuesday [May 12] and sufferd a great deal but he was brought back on this side of the river and died in the hospital." Wounded in the head and hip, Sikes succumbed on May 19. With the wounded came news of other missing men. In Company C, Private Martin Champlin was reported killed, as were Privates Willis M. Guild of Ischua (whose brother Charles L. Guild was Amos's fellow sergeant) and Robert M. Grinard of Allegany.[6]

After morning inspection on Sunday, May 24, the Reverend Henry D. Lowing, the regimental chaplain and former pastor of a Congregational church in Cattaraugus County, held a service. During the scorching day, "hot enough to boil eggs," according to Amos, he wrote to Philinda. "We are laying in the old camp yet and do not know what we are going to do next enney more than you do," he informed her, "but think that we shal go over the river pretty soon again to see what the rebs are doing." Interrupted when mail was delivered to the regiment, Amos reported there was no letter for him. "Well I cannot help it," he commented, and resumed his writing. He was very anxious to know if Philinda had received the allotment check for forty dollars—"It is to mutch to loose." He closed with some typically tender thoughts of home, perhaps glancing at the ambrotype of the children as he wrote:

I would like [to be with] you to night and the little ones they will forget that [they] have got a pa but this thing cannot last a great while longer it seames to me I want you to write to [me] as often as you can and not wait for me and be a good girl and keep your courage up.[7]

It was the last letter Philinda received from her husband.

The next day was so cool that the men warmed themselves by fires. It was still cool on May 26, when Captain Warner surveyed the surrounding countryside, searching for a suitable site for a new camp. "Our camp will not do for a summer residence," Warner noted. "The decomposing remains of dead horses and mules, the entrails of Slaughtered Cattle the Garbage which has accumulated around the outskirts of our camp would soon under the heat of the sun become a fruitfull source of disease and death." Lieutenant Colonel Loomis and Surgeon Van Aernam selected a site the following day, and after dinner a detail of Hardtacks spent the afternoon clearing underbrush, digging sinks and springs, and laying out a new camp. The regiment moved on May 28, hauling camp equipage to the new site and pitching tents. For the next few days, the men fixed things up and policed the grounds, killing numerous blacksnakes. On Sunday, May 31, Chaplain Lowing's sermon was, "Those who fell at Chancellorsville," and the 154th's new camp was christened in honor of the regiment's slain adjutant.[8]

"Our Leut Colonel talks of resigning," Private Washburn wrote in late May. "If he does we loose all. . . . I hope that he will stay with us as long as we have to stay." But "Uncle Henry," as the men affectionately called Loomis, resigned and left the regiment on June 1, turning over command of the 154th to Captain Warner, the senior officer present. With First Lieutenant Henry Martin absent sick, Second Lieutenant Warren Onan on detached service in the ambulance corps, and First Sergeant Almon L. Gile at his Hinsdale home on a ten-day furlough, command of Company C devolved on Sergeant Charles Guild, and Amos became second in command. But that situation was short-lived. Gile returned from his furlough, and with the return to duty on June 10 of Major Daniel B. Allen, a lawyer from the Cattaraugus County town of Otto, Captain Warner resumed command of Company C.

In the meantime, some changes took place in the brigade. The same day Major Allen assumed command of the 154th, Colonel Charles R. Coster of the 134th New York took command of the 1st Brigade in the absence of Colonel Buschbeck, who was sick. Coster's regiment had joined the brigade in May in the aftermath of Chancellorsville. The 29th New York was mustered out when its two-year term of service expired in June. The changes evened the ethnic balance in the command, with the two German-American Pennsylvania regiments—the 27th and 73d—countered by the primarily native-born New Yorkers of the 134th and 154th Regiments.[9]

A large portion of the 154th New York was manning the picket line on the morning of June 12 when Captain Warner and a paymaster gathered the outposts and began paying the men. Companies A, B, and G had been paid when orders were received to return to Camp Noyes and prepare to march. After quickly packing up, the regiment took to the road in the early afternoon and marched to Hartwood Church, its old stopping place during the Chancellorsville campaign. The day's tramp was an exhausting one, as Captain Warner detailed in his diary that night. "This has been the hardest march we have had since entering the service . . . [made] at the hottest hour of a very hot day. That they were able to keep in line at all is a wonder. As it was several were obliged to fall out and drop behind or get their Knapsacks carried in the Ambulances."

In sweltering heat and choking dust, through countryside parched with drought, the march continued at a punishing pace for the next few days. Amos and his comrades were roused from sleep at 3 A.M. of June 13, made their coffee, and resumed the march at sunrise. Canteens were soon empty, and the men suffered greatly for want of water. No rain had fallen for more than a month, and springs and small streams were dry. A stifling cloud of dust was stirred up by shuffling feet, plodding hooves, and rumbling wheels, and a powdery layer caked sweaty skin and permeated uniforms and equipment all along the trudging column. Relief came at noon when the regiment halted for dinner and a three-hour rest. Many of the men stripped off their sweat-soaked wool uniforms and enjoyed a swim in a nearby millpond. Then the march continued until 6 P.M., when they collapsed and camped in a beautiful meadow in sight of the Orange and Alexandria Railroad near Catlett's Station, about thirty-five miles from their starting point of two days before.

Stiff and sore the next morning, Amos and his companions in Company C got breakfast and hoped to have a day's respite from the road. But the assembly was sounded at 8 A.M., tents were packed, knapsacks shouldered, and the men marched along the railroad, "enroute for somewhere," as Captain Warner put it. After a rest near Bristoe Station in the early afternoon, the march resumed. They passed the plains of Manassas as the sun neared the horizon and kept tramping until 10 P.M., when they reached Bull Run, crossed the stream, and camped on the northern bank. They had covered eighteen miles on the long day's march.

Their sleep was rudely interrupted at about 1 A.M. on June 15, when orders were received to issue three days' rations within two hours. During the interlude Amos and the other Company C boys made coffee and then tried to get back to sleep, only to be roused again at daylight by the sounds of reveille. When the march finally got underway at 8 A.M., the morning was the warmest yet encountered since leaving Camp Noyes. "The men were very much crippled with sore feet," Captain Warner reported, "and when we started we would have passed as a detachment of the Invalid Corps. However when we got warmed up (which was soon) we went easier." After trudging for two hours, the 154th reached the village of Centerville and halted. "We are to remain until further orders," Warner observed, "which I hope will give us time to heal our blisters and get rested, after as hard a three days tramp as often falls to the Soldiers lot." On June 16 the men enjoyed the luxury of resting in camp all day, "getting in condition for the work which may be in store," Captain Warner commented.

At 2 A.M. on June 17 Company C was roused with orders to march in an hour, and after a delay the men got underway at 4:30. They covered a dozen miles and reached Gum Springs by 9 A.M., had dinner at Farmers Church, and pushed on across Goose Creek, encamping on its western bank about four miles from Leesburg and the same distance from the Potomac River. "This has been the hardest days march yet," Captain Warner declared, "as we have come more than 20 miles and the heat and dust was really oppressive." Goose Creek was a godsend to the exhausted soldiers. "This stream affords the best bathing we have found in all our wanderings," Warner wrote, "and the boys were not slow in taking advantage of the fine opportunity to get rid of the dust which had accumulated in any amount upon their persons." Diving, dunking, splashing, and floating, Amos and his comrades washed their weariness away.

Another night's sleep was cut short just after 3 A.M. on June 18, when the regiment was wakened and told to be ready to march in an hour. But the order was soon countermanded and the men remained in camp until noon, when they backtracked down the road about a mile away from the creek and again stacked arms. "The weather was intensely hot and the men were scarcely able to remain in the ranks even for this short march," Captain Warner noted. But about the time they reached their new campground, clouds filled the sky and some rain fell. By nighttime, thundershowers were soaking the thirsty soil.

For the next five days, the 154th remained in the vicinity of Goose Creek. Intermittent rains continued to fall, and the temperature moderated. Amos and the other Hardtacks quickly discovered that nearby farms offered an abundance of provisions. "The boys have a fine time and high living on mutton Honey eggs milk warm biscuit cherries &c with which this country abounds," Captain Warner wrote. "We are in a section which has not been as yet overrun by hostile armies, and the inhabitants are good livers." Duty was light and consisted mainly of picketing. Twice the men were annoyed when the 154th was ordered to move its camp a short distance; once they moved and then immediately returned to their starting point, grumbling as they repitched their tents on the same ground they had just vacated. But most days Captain Warner observed in his diary that nothing of importance transpired.

If the stay near Goose Creek was a time of restoration, it was also one of speculation. For two days, heavy firing was heard coming from the west, in the direction of gaps in the Blue Ridge Mountains, but all Captain Warner could say about it was, "Some boddy is evidently getting hurt in that direction." Other than the marches of their own brigade, division, and corps, the men had no idea of the larger movements of the army or the corresponding movements of the enemy. In entries in his diary, Captain Warner voiced the uncertainty no doubt felt by Amos and everyone else in the regiment during the stay at Goose Creek:

We seem to be completely Isolated from the world. . . . The quiet is like unto the calm which preludes the coming storm Important events are undoubtedly near at hand. I have a presentment that we are on the eve of a great battle, But whether on this or the other side of the Potomac is more than I can tell. All sorts of rumors with regard to the position and doings of the Rebs are afloat in camp, and all are as such rumors are, perfectly reliable. Such as they are they are all we have as mental food, as we get neither mails or Newspapers here. . . . To be thus cut off from the world at a time when of all others one wants to know what is transpiring outside, When each day is developing anew what may decide the fate of a World, is to say the least anything but pleasant.

The absence of mail particularly galled the men. On June 21 Captain Warner noted they had been promised a delivery of mail and an opportunity to send letters, but were disappointed in both respects. "How many letters from home and Friends are delayed somewhere on the way while those friends are looking for answers thereto," he wondered. Amos must have been distracted to know that somewhere in transit was a letter from Philinda, with news of his loved ones and home. He also must have been frustrated at his inability to send word of his well-being and whereabouts to Portville.[10]

Midmorning on June 24 the Hardtacks returned to camp after a tour of picket duty and found the rest of the brigade waiting for them and ready to move. Coster's command marched ten miles without halting to the vicinity of Edward's Ferry on the Potomac River, which it reached at sunset. Early the next morning, the 154th crossed the river on a lengthy pontoon bridge to the Maryland shore. The regiment passed through the village of Poolesville at about 10 A.M., halted for dinner and a two-hour's rest west of Sugar Loaf Mountain, pushed on across the canal aqueduct over the Monocacy River, and at dusk crossed the tracks of the Baltimore and Ohio Railroad. With rain falling in the darkness, the men entered a narrow mountain gorge, broke into a trot, and kept up the punishing pace for about eight miles before they reached the village of Jefferson and encamped. "We have marched this day as much as 25 miles," Captain Warner recorded, "and the boys are jaded and tired with a wet uncomfortable night before them." Amos and the rest of Company C lay down on the sodden ground in their soaked uniforms and fell asleep.

Wet and stiff, Company C awoke to a chilly and rainy morning on June 26. At 10 A.M. orders were received to be ready to march in an hour, but it was not until about noon that the men got under way. Their route took them through the village of Middletown and along the National Road toward Boonsborough. As the road climbed South Mountain, Companies C, H, and a portion of K were sent ahead to establish an advanced picket post on the mountaintop. After a damp and disagreeable day's march of a dozen miles, the detached companies reached the Summit House tavern at Turner's Gap, and strung a line of pickets along the crest of the mountain.[11]

At dusk, the pickets of Company C heard the rhythmic pounding of a horse's hooves approaching from the west, and soon a rider galloped into view. Ordered to halt at a distance of fifteen paces, the gray-clad stranger dismounted and advanced on foot under the aim of the company's rifles. He said he was a Union scout and asked to be taken immediately to corps headquarters. Private Charles McKay was one of the men who accompanied the horseman to General Howard. "On the way back to camp he told me that Lee's army was in Pennsylvania," McKay wrote, "and that in all probability the battle of the campaign would be fought near Carlisle, Pa." At last, Amos and his comrades had an idea of the strategic situation, and knew why they had been pushed so hard on the recent grueling marches.[12]

Company C spent the pleasant day of June 27 on picket atop South Mountain, and Amos observed a landscape scarred by a battle fought nine months before. On the mild morning of June 28, Chaplain Lowing preached a sermon, and a large crowd of loyal local citizens visited the 154th New York's camp. In central Maryland, Amos and his comrades noticed an agreeable difference in the attitude of the populace compared to what they had experienced in Virginia. Union sentiment was widespread, and the residents along their path welcomed the New Yorkers with kind greetings and words of encouragement. They opened their larders to the Yankees and offered the soldiers milk, bread, pies, butter, and honey. After months of sour looks and bitter words from Virginians, the Marylanders' friendliness and support were a welcome change. The men particularly enjoyed the kind attention they received from the female portion of the population.[13]

Company C was inspected at noon that Sunday, and Captain Warner spent the next few hours working on returns. About 3 P.M. orders were received to march immediately, and the Hardtacks retraced their steps down the National Road through Middletown, over a gap in the Catoctin Mountains, and on to the city of Frederick, where they camped after dark and posted pickets. At daylight on the wet morning of June 29, the pickets were recalled, and the regiment marched. All day the rain fell, and Amos and the rest of Company C sloshed over sloppy roads for at least twenty miles before the column came to a halt. The exhausted men broke ranks and pitched their tents near the village of Emmitsburg, site of several Roman Catholic religious and educational institutions. "We bivouacked near the old Convent," Private McKay wrote, "and the nuns gave us nice, soft bread and sweet milk as long as their supply lasted."[14]

Rain continued to fall on the morning of June 30 and the regiment remained in camp until evening, when it moved a couple of miles to the north of the village. During the day, the 154th New York was mustered. The roll signed by Captain Warner for Company C recorded a total of 49 present, but 7 of them were on detached service in the brigade ambulance corps or division pioneer corps, leaving 42 soldiers to man a line of battle. The entire regiment listed 390 officers and enlisted men present, but detached and extra-duty soldiers reduced the total present and ready for action to 317 officers and enlisted men.[15]

Surviving letters and diaries written by members of Company C are strangely silent regarding news that swept through the army during the last days of June 1863. General Hooker resigned as commander of the Army of the Potomac and was replaced on June 28 by Major General George G. Meade, former head of the 5th Corps. Meade ordered Major General John F. Reynolds of the 1st Corps to take command of a provisional left wing of the army, composed of the 1st, 3d, and 11th Corps. Poised just south of the Mason-Dixon Line at or near Emmitsburg, Reynolds's expanded command was the closest Union infantry to the Confederate army, which was converging from the north and west on a county seat and college town about ten miles across the Pennsylvania line.[16]

Scattered showers fell lightly during the morning of Wednesday, July 1, 1863. Around daybreak a detachment of two hundred men was assembled in Coster's brigade—fifty from each of the four regiments. Captain Warner was detailed to command the detachment and lead it on a reconnaissance toward Sabillasville, Maryland, a hamlet some six miles west of Emmitsburg. Another officer of the 154th, Second Lieutenant Alonzo A. Casler of Company G, was also assigned to the detail. Exactly which fifty members of the Hardtack Regiment were part of the detachment went unrecorded, but it seems likely that Captain Warner chose a few members of his own Company C to accompany him. One thing is certain: as they marched away on their mission at 5 A.M. on that fateful day, Captain Warner and his scouting party had no idea how fortunate they were to have drawn the assignment.[17]

With 52 of its members gone on the reconnaissance to Sabillasville, the

154th New York was reduced to approximately 265 officers and men. The departure of Captain Warner also left Company C without a commissioned officer. First Sergeant Almon Gile was present, as were Sergeants Charles Guild and Amos Humiston and a half-dozen corporals, including Amos's mess mate, Joel Bouton. (Sergeant Lewis Bishop was with the color guard, carrying the regiment's national flag.) But all nine of the other companies were led by at least one commissioned officer, and Major Allen wanted the same for Company C. Consequently he assigned Second Lieutenant John "Jack" Mitchell of Company D to temporary command of Company C. Come what may during the ensuing hours, Amos and his company comrades would have to do without the leadership of their tried and true Captain Warner, and rely instead on the judgment and example of an officer not well known to them.[18]

Leaving their knapsacks and baggage at Emmitsburg, the Hardtacks commenced the march at 8 A.M. and two hours later crossed into Pennsylvania. The morning showers gave way on a soft, southerly breeze to a cloudy, humid day. As batteries of artillery rumbled by at a full gallop on the road, the infantrymen took to the adjacent fields and woods. Their steady pace was pushed to the double-quick when General Reynolds ordered the 11th Corps to hurry forward as rapidly as possible. About six miles into the march, after the 154th New York crossed Marsh Creek, the reason for their haste became obvious. "As we reached the high ground north of that stream," Private McKay recalled, "the rattle of musketry and roar of cannon told us that our long race after the enemy was ended." There was fighting up ahead, and with each loping stride Amos and his comrades drew closer to the conflict.

At approximately 3 P.M. the regiment left the road and crossed the fields to Evergreen Cemetery, on a hilltop at the southern outskirts of the town of Gettysburg. "We stacked arms among the old gravestones," Private McKay wrote, "and watched with wondering eyes the scene that presented itself in plain view just across the valley." It was a dramatic panorama. Below Cemetery Hill spread a web of streets and the crowded rooftops and spires of Gettysburg. From the town, ten roads slanted to the horizon in ten different directions, intersecting a patchwork of yellow and green fields and orchards stitched together by post-and-rail fences. In distant fields to the west and north of the town, billowing clouds of gun smoke marked the lines of the contending armies. The entire 1st Corps and the 1st and 3d Divisions of the 11th Corps were battling the enemy on those hazy ridges and plains, and the terrific din of musketry and artillery signaled a major battle. General Reynolds had been killed, and General Howard had assumed command of the Federal forces as the senior officer on the field, with General Schurz taking Howard's place as commander of the 11th

Corps. On Cemetery Hill, General von Steinwehr's two brigades—Coster's and Colonel Orland Smith's—formed the Union army's only available reserve.[19]

As they rested after a tiring march of more than ten miles, Amos and his comrades rummaged through their haversacks, had a quick lunch of hardtack and salt pork, filled their canteens, inspected their ammunition, and cleaned and loaded their Enfield rifles. A number of panting stragglers caught up with the regiment during the interlude. Amid the cemetery's wrought iron fences and marble headstones, the men anxiously waited to see if they would be put into the fight. Meanwhile, Major General Jubal A. Early's Confederate division advanced toward Gettysburg from the northeast on the Harrisburg Road, and in combination with other Southern forces broke the 11th Corps line north of the town and sent it reeling in retreat. At about the same time, other Confederate brigades attacking from the west began to force back the 1st Corps. The entire Union position was collapsing, and the crisis of the day's fighting had come. After refusing repeated and desperate pleas for reinforcements from General Schurz earlier in the day, General Howard at this critical time finally relented. Coster's brigade was ordered forward to cover the retreat of the 11th Corps—the same dangerous role the brigade had played at Chancellorsville.[20]

At about 3:30 P.M., Sergeant Amos Humiston took his place in Company C's line, and the 154th New York followed Colonel Coster and the 134th New York out of Evergreen Cemetery and down Baltimore Street into the town, trailed by the 27th and 73d Pennsylvania Regiments. As Coster's brigade double-quicked through Gettysburg's streets, "all around was confusion and disaster," Private McKay remembered. The sidewalks were lined with wounded, bloodied men were being carried to the rear, stragglers and shirkers milled aimlessly, and Coster's column had to force its way against a rising tide of retreat as fleeing Union soldiers swarmed the streets, seeking the shelter of Cemetery Hill. Adding to the unnerving scene, the brigade came under fire of Confederate artillery, and shot and shells began to shriek overhead. "Under such circumstances," Charles McKay thought, "it requires the steadiness of veterans of unswerving courage to advance and meet the victorious foe." But before Coster's brigade could meet the enemy face to face, it was weakened by a command decision. General Schurz met Coster in town to guide him to his position, and one of those two officers crippled the brigade by detaching the 280-man 73d Pennsylvania and deploying it as a reserve along the railroad track, near the depot. Coster's force was thereby reduced to approximately 980 men: about 440 in the 134th New York, 275 in the 27th Pennsylvania, and 265 in the 154th New York.[21]

After crossing the railroad, the three remaining regiments hurried down

Gettysburg

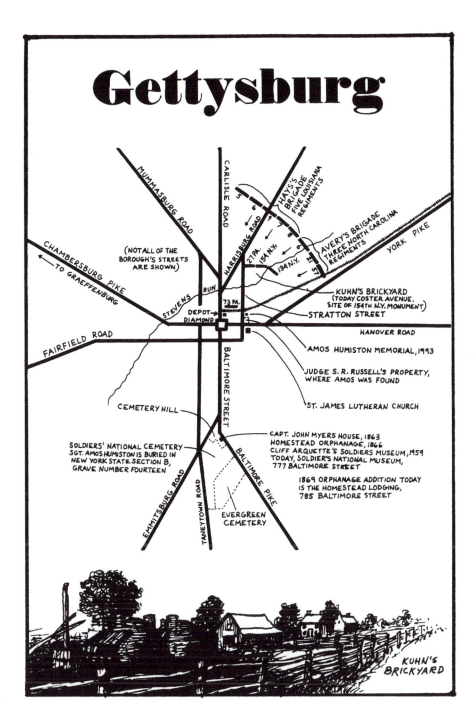

MUMMASBURG ROAD

CARLISLE ROAD

HARRISBURG ROAD

5
6
7
HAYS'S BRIGADE FIVE LOUISIANA REGIMENTS

AVERY'S BRIGADE THREE NORTH CAROLINA REGIMENTS

YORK PIKE

CHAMBERSBURG PIKE
TO GRAEFFENBURG

(NOT ALL OF THE BOROUGH'S STREETS ARE SHOWN)

27 PA.
154 N.Y.
134 N.Y.

STEVENS RUN

73 PA.

DEPOT→
DIAMOND

KUHN'S BRICKYARD (TODAY COSTER AVENUE, SITE OF 154th N.Y. MONUMENT)

STRATTON STREET

FAIRFIELD ROAD

HANOVER ROAD

BALTIMORE STREET

AMOS HUMISTON MEMORIAL, 1993

JUDGE S. R. RUSSELL'S PROPERTY, WHERE AMOS WAS FOUND

ST. JAMES LUTHERAN CHURCH

CEMETERY HILL

CAPT. JOHN MYERS HOUSE, 1863
HOMESTEAD ORPHANAGE, 1866
CLIFF ARQUETTE'S SOLDIERS MUSEUM, 1959
TODAY, SOLDIER'S NATIONAL MUSEUM,
777 BALTIMORE STREET

SOLDIERS' NATIONAL CEMETERY
SGT. AMOS HUMISTON IS BURIED IN
NEW YORK STATE SECTION B,
GRAVE NUMBER FOURTEEN

1869 ORPHANAGE ADDITION TODAY
IS THE HOMESTEAD LODGING,
785 BALTIMORE STREET

BALTIMORE PIKE

EMMITSBURG ROAD

TANEYTOWN ROAD

EVERGREEN CEMETERY

KUHN'S BRICKYARD

Stratton Street to the northeastern outskirts of town, across a meandering little stream called Stevens Run, and out to a two-story brick house, the dwelling of brickmaker John Kuhn and his family. Coster's line filed to the right through a carriage gateway and down a swale into Kuhn's brickyard, an irregular pentagonal lot of a few acres, bounded by a stout post-and-rail fence, and crossed near its southeast edge by Stevens Run. Behind Kuhn's house stood a wooden barn or shed and the beehive-shaped brick kilns. Nearby was the pug mill, a large, upright barrel in which plowed clay was mixed with water. Scattered about the yard were dozens of wooden molds, stacks of plank pallets, and other implements of the brickmaker's trade.

At Coster's center, the 154th New York formed in line of battle in front of the kilns, and advanced a few yards to the fence at the brickyard's northern boundary. There, Private McKay wrote, "we were ordered to kneel and reserve our fire until the enemy were close enough to make our volley effective." Directly behind Company C's line, Lieutenant Mitchell and Sergeants Gile, Guild, and Humiston took their places. To the company's left was the regimental color guard, with Sergeant Lewis Bishop under the national flag and Corporal Albert Mericle of Company H bearing the state flag. On the 154th's right, the 134th New York prolonged the line along the fence as it angled to the southeast and crossed Stevens Run. On the 154th's left, the 27th Pennsylvania took shelter along the fence where it ran up the slope toward Stratton Street.[22]

From his position at the right of the 154th's line, Major Allen noted that the terrain presented visibility problems. In front of the regiment's line, a wheat field climbed a gentle swell, blocking any view of the advancing enemy. To the left, the slope rising to Stratton Street obstructed observation of enemy progress on the brigade's left flank. Colonel Coster was stationed there, and Dan Allen was relying on the brigade commander to send word should any difficulties arise on the left.[23]

Coster's brigade had scarcely taken position behind the fences in Kuhn's brickyard when the Confederate attack reached it. Suddenly the enemy line crested the slope in the wheat field in front of the 154th New York, presenting an awe-inspiring and intimidating sight to Amos and his comrades. "I shall always remember how the Confederate line of battle looked as it came into full view and started down towards us," Charles McKay wrote years later. The enemy advanced in well-kept lines as if on parade, trampling the wheat as they marched, their many battle flags snapping in the breeze. Two entire brigades of General Early's Division made the attack. On the Confederate right was the brigade commanded by Brigadier General Harry T. Hays, consisting of the 5th, 6th, 7th, 8th, and 9th Louisiana Regiments. The Louisianians charged down both sides of the Harrisburg

Road toward the junction with Stratton Street and the brickyard. On the enemy's left, approaching the brickyard through the fields and straddling Stevens Run, was Colonel Isaac E. Avery's Brigade, including the 6th, 21st, and 57th North Carolina Regiments. Totaling approximately 3,000 men, the Confederates outnumbered Coster's brigade by more than three to one, and their long lines extended well beyond both flanks of the Union position.

As at Chancellorsville two months before, the stand of the 1st Brigade at Gettysburg on July 1 delayed the Confederate attack long enough to allow other elements of the 11th Corps to make good their retreat. As at Chancellorsville, the brigade paid a high price in blood for its bravery. And as at Chancellorsville, the brigade's brief stand came to a quick and tragic end.[24]

As soon as the Confederates came into view, Coster's men opened fire. The brickyard fence erupted in a sheet of flame and a billow of smoke, and the enemy line staggered. The Confederates unleashed a volley of their own, and the firing became general. Steadying their Enfields on fence rails, reloading as rapidly as they could, some of the Hardtacks leveled as many as six to nine shots apiece at the enemy. During those minutes, Confederate fire began to penetrate the fence's slight shelter. In Company C, a ball grazed Charles McKay's scalp, and the wound bled profusely, matting his long hair and soaking his jacket. Another ball smashed into Corporal Joel Bouton's skull, and Amos's mess mate fell, instantly killed.[25]

On Coster's right, Avery's North Carolinians outflanked the 134th New York and opened a murderous enfilading fire on the brickyard line, devastating the 134th and raking the position of the 154th. Shattered by gunfire and in danger of being surrounded, the survivors of the 134th broke into retreat, leaving almost 200 of their comrades killed and wounded in the brickyard and nearby fields, and another 60 or so in the hands of the enemy. Observing the withdrawal of the 134th, Major Allen saw his own regiment had quickly become vulnerable to capture, and despite having received no word from Colonel Coster, he immediately ordered the 154th to retreat to the left, in the direction of the carriage gateway and Stratton Street. The Hardtacks pulled away from the fence, rushed across the brickyard, and found to their great surprise that the 27th Pennsylvania had already abandoned its position. Stratton Street and the surrounding lots and fields were swarming with exultant Confederates.[26]

Meanwhile, one officer disregarded Dan Allen's order to retreat. Apparently unaware of the precarious situation and inspired by the effectiveness of his men's fire, Lieutenant Jack Mitchell shouted to Company C, "Boys, let's stay right here!" According to Private McKay, the response was unanimous. "I do not think a man in Co. C hesitated," McKay wrote; "all came back to the fence and commenced to fire again as fast as we could load our muskets." But after a minute and another round or two, Mitchell realized he had made a foolhardy decision. "Boys, we must get out of here!" he yelled, and Company C ran back past the kilns and headed to Stratton Street.

Jack Mitchell, Amos Humiston, Charles McKay, and the rest of Company C rushed to the carriage gateway and found the street crowded with fellow Hardtacks, disarmed and sitting on the ground as prisoners of war. As more than one member of the 154th New York put it, the regiment had been "gobbled up" by the enemy after a brief but furious hand-to-hand fight, which continued to eddy and swirl in the brickyard and street and nearby lots. The few Hardtacks who were able to escape, one member of the regiment declared, were the fastest runners and the most exposed to danger.

Near the gateway, McKay heard two mounted Confederate officers shout to Private Addison L. Scutt of Company C, a twenty-eight-year-old Portville lumberman, "Throw down your gun! Surrender!" When Scutt refused, one of them slashed the stubborn Yankee across the head with a saber. Witnessing that, McKay and Private Albert Hall made a dash for Stevens Run, splashed through the stream, tried to hide as best they could behind the low bank, and finally reached the relative safety of a retreating Union artillery piece. Somehow, despite his head wound—and after being literally within reach of the Confederate officer—Private Scutt also managed to escape.[27]

Most of the men of Company C were not so fortunate. Lieutenant Mitchell was captured; so were Sergeants Gile and Guild. Of the five corporals left after Joel Bouton was killed, two were wounded, and the other three were captured. Sixteen of Company C's privates were captured, and two of them were also wounded. Men who escaped the trap at the brickyard gate were run down and captured or shot by their pursuers. Color bearers Lewis Bishop and Albert Mericle were both mortally wounded, and after a mad scramble, the flags of both the 154th and 134th New York were rescued by members of the two regiments.[28]

Sergeant Amos Humiston survived the firestorm at the brickyard fence. Somehow he was able to escape the melee near the carriage gateway. He fled up Stratton Street, across Stevens Run, past the railroad, heading toward the shelter of Cemetery Hill, running for his life, with the enemy close behind him.

While the 154th New York marched to Gettysburg and was virtually destroyed on July 1, Captain Warner and his lucky detachment made an uneventful reconnaissance to Sabillasville. "Nothing of importance attended the march," Warner noted in his diary. On their return to Emmitsburg, the men discovered the regiment had marched to Gettysburg and heard reports of the battle there. Warner marched his squad a couple of miles north, lodged it in a stone barn, and left it in charge of Lieutenant Casler while he rode on to Gettysburg to see what was happening. He arrived at Cemetery Hill after dark, and was shocked to find Major Dan Allen, two other officers, and fifteen men were all that was left of the 154th. Among the many missing was Sergeant Amos Humiston.[29]

Colonel Coster ordered Warner to return to his detachment and get the men to Gettysburg as soon as possible. Warner returned to the stone barn, imparted the sad news about the regiment to the men, and got them marching as fast as he could move them. They reached Cemetery Hill at midmorning of July 2, and what was left of the 154th and 134th New York was temporarily consolidated under the command of Major Allen. That night Coster's brigade took part in the repulse of an attack on East Cemetery Hill (made, ironically, by Hays's and Avery's Brigades), but the New Yorkers played a supporting role as the 73d Pennsylvania, held in reserve the previous day, took the lead in repulsing the enemy. For two hours the Hardtacks hugged the ground, Captain Warner noted, "with shells canister round shot and RR slugs flying around & over in plenteous profusion." Two members of the 154th were wounded during the barrage.[30]

The Hardtacks spent the night behind a low stone wall in Evergreen Cemetery. On the afternoon of July 3, they lay low under another bombardment, described by Captain Warner as "the greatest Artillery duell I ever witnessed." Then they observed the defeat of the massive Confederate charge on the Union center, which was greeted with hearty cheers by the victorious Yankees.

Rain fell in the morning and afternoon of Independence Day. At 7 A.M. Coster's brigade marched down Cemetery Hill into the center of Gettysburg, which had been evacuated by the enemy. "My opinion is that they are on the retreat from here," Captain Warner wrote, "they have had enough of us at this place." But although the Confederates had abandoned the town, they held their lines in the nearby countryside. Coster's men were divided into detachments and assisted the pioneers in barricading various streets. That night the Hardtacks bivouacked in the town.

More rain fell on the morning of July 5, and word was received that Lee's army had retreated during the night. The Confederates had taken "French leave," Captain Warner wrote lightheartedly, "without even the politeness of saying good bye to the citizens of Gettysburg or thanking them for their generous hospitality." He added, "What course they have taken of course I know not, but venture to predict that the shortest course towards Dixie is where they have left their tracks." At 10 A.M., the 154th New York was ordered to recall its pickets and be ready to march at a moment's notice. But after forming in line, no further orders were received, and the men spent the remainder of the day relaxing. It was nearly nighttime before the regiment marched out of Gettysburg, crossed Cemetery Hill, and headed down the road toward Emmitsburg, in pursuit of the defeated enemy.[31]

In the four days after the brickyard fight, about forty Hardtacks who were separated from the 154th in the chaos of the battle and the subsequent wild scramble through town rejoined the regiment. Despite their return, the casualty count remained high: 207 of the 265 men who went into the brickyard fight were listed as killed, wounded, or missing, for a loss of 78 percent. As was the case after Chancellorsville, there was much uncertainty about the fates of the missing. It seemed that most of them had been captured, but exactly who were now prisoners of war and who were still lying on the field dead or wounded was unknown. None of the men who returned to the regiment during its stay at Gettysburg had any knowledge of what had happened to Sergeant Amos Humiston.[32]

On July 4 and 5, for more than a day and a half, the 154th New York was posted within a few blocks of where the regiment fought on July 1. If they had a chance, it seems likely that the men would have tried to search for killed or wounded comrades on their recent battleground. But if any of the Hardtacks returned to Kuhn's brickyard and the surrounding Stratton Street neighborhood, it went unrecorded. And if any of the regiment's dead were found and laid to rest, Major Allen most likely would have noted that fact in his official report, or Captain Warner would have commented on it in his diary. Neither man did. During their thirty-six hours in Gettysburg in the aftermath of the battle, none of the Hardtacks spotted Sergeant Humiston.

At least a dozen members of the 154th New York stayed behind when the regiment marched away from Gettysburg, detailed as nurses in the 11th Corps hospital, located about a mile south of Cemetery Hill. There they remained for the rest of the month, caring for their wounded comrades and assisting the surgeons and stewards. In August they moved to the recently established general hospital, Camp Letterman, on the York Pike about a mile east of Kuhn's brickyard. They issued rations, clothing, and medicine, did laundry, bathed and bandaged patients, held arms and legs during amputations, nursed some men to health, sent some to hospitals in northern cities, and consoled others as they died.

In their free time, the Hardtack nurses read Gettysburg newspapers, chatted with Gettysburg civilians, strolled Gettysburg streets, and wandered the Gettysburg battlefield. But none of them learned what had happened to Amos Humiston.[33]

NOTES

1. Mark H. Dunkelman and Michael J. Winey, *The Hardtack Regiment: An Illustrated History of the 154th Regiment, New York State Infantry Volunteers* (East Brunswick, N.J.: Fairleigh Dickinson University Press, 1981), 61, 63; Mark H. Dunkelman, "Main Address," in *Dedication of the Chancellorsville Monument to the 154th New York Volunteer Infantry May 26, 1996* (154th New York Monument Fund, 1996), 17–20.

2. Dunkelman and Winey, *The Hardtack Regiment*, 67; Lewis D. Warner diary, May 18–21, 1863, courtesy of John L. Spencer.

3. Dunkelman and Winey, *The Hardtack Regiment*, 65; Amos Humiston to Dear wife, May 24, 1863; *American Presbyterian*, December 17, 1863, 201.

4. Lewis D. Warner diary, May 13, 1863; Thaddeus L. Reynels to Dear friends at home, May 20, 1863, National Archives.

5. Dunkelman, "Main Address," in *Dedication of the Chancellorsville Monument to the 154th New York Volunteer Infantry*, 17; Dunkelman and Winey, *The Hardtack Regiment*, 66; James W. Washburn to Dear Parents, May 24, 1863, National Archives.

6. Amos Humiston to Dear wife, May 24, 1863; James W. Washburn to Dear Parents, May 24, 1863, National Archives.

7. Lewis D. Warner diary, May 24, 1863; Amos Humiston to Dear wife, May 24, 1863.

8. Lewis D. Warner diary, May 25–June 1, 1863; Dunkelman and Winey, *The Hardtack Regiment*, 67.

9. James W. Washburn to Dear Parents, May 24, 1863; Lewis D. Warner diary, June 1, 10, 1863; muster roll, Company C, 154th New York, June 30, 1863, National Archives; Dunkelman and Winey, *The Hardtack Regiment*, 67, 154; Frederick H. Dyer, *A Compendium of the War of the Rebellion* (Dayton, Ohio: Press of Morningside Bookshop, 1978), 319; Frederick Phisterer, *New York in the War of the Rebellion 1861 to 1865* (Albany: Weed, Parsons and Company, 1890), 395, 479; William T. Levey, *The Blue and the Gray: A Sketch of Soldier Life in Camp and Field in the Army of the Civil War* (Schenectady, N.Y.: Roy Burton Myers, Publisher, 1904), 7.

10. Lewis D. Warner diary, June 12–21, 1863.

11. Lewis D. Warner diary, June 24–25, 1863; Dunkelman and Winey, *The Hardtack Regiment*, 69.

12. Charles W. McKay, "Three Years or During the War, with the Crescent and Star," in *The National Tribune Scrap Book* (Washington, n.d.), 130.

13. Lewis D. Warner diary, June 27–28, 1863; Dunkelman and Winey, *The Hardtack Regiment*, 69–70.

14. Lewis D. Warner diary, June 28–29, 1863; Charles W. McKay, "Three Years or During the War," 130.

15. Muster rolls for the field and staff and all ten companies, 154th New York, June 30, 1863, National Archives.

16. Dunkelman and Winey, *The Hardtack Regiment*, 70–71; Edwin B. Cod-

dington, *The Gettysburg Campaign: A Study in Command* (Dayton, Ohio: Morningside Press, 1994), 122, 130–133, 209–210, 231–232.

17. Lewis D. Warner diary, July 1, 1863; Lieutenant Colonel Dan B. Allen to New York State Adjutant General John Sprague, July 1863, in Regimental Letterbook, Ellicottville Historical Society; Dunkelman and Winey, *The Hardtack Regiment*, 71, 77; Mark H. Dunkelman and Michael J. Winey, "The Hardtack Regiment in the Brickyard Fight," *Gettysburg Magazine*, no. 8 (January 1993): 19.

18. Muster rolls, 154th New York, June 30, 1863, National Archives; McKay, "Three Years or During the War," 131.

19. Dunkelman and Winey, *The Hardtack Regiment*, 71; Dunkelman and Winey, "The Hardtack Regiment in the Brickyard Fight," 19; Coddington, *The Gettysburg Campaign*, 268–269, 278–280, 287–288; McKay, "Three Years or During the War," 130.

20. Dunkelman and Winey, *The Hardtack Regiment*, 71–72; Dunkelman and Winey, "The Hardtack Regiment in the Brickyard Fight," 19; Coddington, *The Gettysburg Campaign*, 287–292, 302–305; Warren W. Hassler, Jr., *Crisis at the Crossroads: The First Day at Gettysburg* (University: University of Alabama Press, 1970), 75–81.

21. Dunkelman and Winey, "The Hardtack Regiment in the Brickyard Fight," 19–20; McKay, "Three Years or During the War," 131.

22. Dunkelman and Winey, "The Hardtack Regiment in the Brickyard Fight," 20, 22; McKay, "Three Years or During the War," 131; muster roll, Company C, 154th New York, June 30, 1863, National Archives.

23. Daniel B. Allen, "Address at Dedication of Monument," in New York Monuments Commission for the Battlefields of Gettysburg and Chattanooga, *Final Report on the Battlefield of Gettysburg* [hereafter *New York at Gettysburg*] (Albany: J. B. Lyon Company, 1902), Vol. 3, 1051.

24. Hassler, *Crisis at the Crossroads*, 82; A. Wilson Greene, "From Chancellorsville to Cemetery Hill: O. O. Howard and Eleventh Corps Leadership" in Gary W. Gallagher, ed., *The First Day at Gettysburg: Essays on Union and Confederate Leadership* (Kent, Ohio: Kent State University Press, 1992), 81–82. Hassler states, "Despite overwhelming pressure and grave menace, Coster's small brigade managed to delay the Southerners long enough to allow [Brigadier General Adelbert] Ames to withdraw his First Division from its threatened and critical position at the Almshouse line. In buying this invaluable time, however, Coster's men suffered fearful casualties from the severe enemy fire." According to Greene, "Coster's men, as much as any other unit in the Eleventh Corps, belied their reputation as demoralized cowards. . . . Coster's brigade contributed significantly to the extrication of the Eleventh Corps north of Gettysburg."

25. Dunkelman and Winey, "The Hardtack Regiment in the Brickyard Fight," 21; E. D. Northrup, "Historical Sketch," in *New York at Gettysburg*, Vol. 3, 1055; McKay, "Three Years or During the War," 131; "Register of Deaths," descriptive book, Company C, 154th New York, National Archives.

26. Dunkelman and Winey, "The Hardtack Regiment in the Brickyard Fight," 21; Hassler, *Crisis at the Crossroads*, 148.

27. McKay, "Three Years or During the War," 131–132; Dunkelman and Winey, "The Hardtack Regiment in the Brickyard Fight," 21–22.

28. Muster roll, Company C, 154th New York, August 31, 1863; "Schedule A embracing a list of the killed wounded & missing in the action of Gettysburg, Pa. July 1st 1863," accompanying Lieutenant Colonel Dan B. Allen to New York State Adjutant General John Sprague, July 1863, in Regimental Letterbook, Ellicottville Historical Society; Dunkelman and Winey, "The Hardtack Regiment in the Brickyard Fight," 22, 28.

29. Lewis D. Warner diary, July 1, 1863; Dunkelman and Winey, *The Hardtack Regiment,* 77.

30. Lewis D. Warner diary, July 2, 1863; Dunkelman and Winey, "The Hardtack Regiment in the Brickyard Fight," 24.

31. Lewis D. Warner diary, July 3–5, 1863.

32. As best can be determined, the regiment's casualties at Gettysburg totaled 5 killed, 6 mortally wounded, 23 wounded, 8 wounded and captured, and 165 captured. Of the captives, 60 died as prisoners of war, 2 had no further record and probably also died, and 1 was reported dead. "Schedule A embracing a list of the killed wounded & missing in the action of Gettysburg, Pa. July 1st 1863," accompanying Lieutenant Colonel Dan B. Allen to New York State Adjutant General John Sprague, July 1863, in Regimental Letterbook, Ellicottville Historical Society; regimental muster rolls, August 31, 1863, National Archives; New York State Adjutant General, *Annual Report of the Adjutant General of the State of New York* (Albany: Brandow Printing Company, State Legislative Printers, 1905, Serial No. 39), 1090–1232; Mark H. Dunkelman, " 'We Were Compelled to Cut Our Way Through Them, and in Doing so Our Losses Were Heavy': Gettysburg Casualties of the 154th New York Volunteers." *Gettysburg Magazine,* no. 18 (January 1998): 34–56.

33. Regimental muster rolls, August 31, 1863, National Archives.

Philinda Humiston. The earliest known portrait of Amos's wife is this carte de visite by Tipton & Myers of Gettysburg, most likely a copy of an earlier image. *Courtesy of David Humiston Kelley.*

Dr. John Francis Bourns. His only known portrait pictures the controversial doctor later in life, years after he publicized the death of Gettyburg's unknown soldier. *Courtesy of Mary A. Parker.*

Monument to the 154th New York at Gettysburg. When dedicated in 1890, John Kuhn's brick kilns and the fence enclosing his brickyard had been torn down, the town had expanded toward the site, and a tall tower (to the left on skyline) had been added to St. James Lutheran Church. The monument marks the center of the regimental line. Amos's race for life carried him from this position toward the church. *New York Monuments Commission. "Final Report on the Battlefield at Gettysburg," vol. 3. Albany: J.B. Lyon, 1902.*

Early carte-de-visite copy of the ambrotype of the Humiston children. Amos and the children (from left to right, Franklin, Frederick, and Alice) were still unidentified when James E. McClees produced this image. Frank's hair has a slightly rumpled look that was retouched and disappeared in subsequent copies. A handwritten notation on the reverse reads, "Copy of a picture found in the hand of a dead Soldier on the Battle field of Gettysburg." *Courtesy of Dean S. Thomas.*

"An Incident of Gettysburg–The Last Thought of a Dying Father." Amos Humiston had been identified when this imaginary depiction of his famous death pose was published. *"Frank Leslie's Illustrated Newspaper,"* *January 2, 1864.*

Robert Whitechurch's engraving of the Humiston children. The children's faces, Philadelphian John Mears stated in 1866, were almost as familiar to the American people as were Lincoln's or Grant's. *Author's collection.*

Amos Humiston, retouched to be a soldier. This rare version of the Frederick Gutekunst carte-de-visite, possibly a prototype made for Philinda's approval, was produced without the printed identification on the front or the explanation on the reverse that was common in copies offered for sale. The image was made by adding a beard and uniform to the ambrotype portrait of Amos. *Courtesy of David Humiston Kelley.*

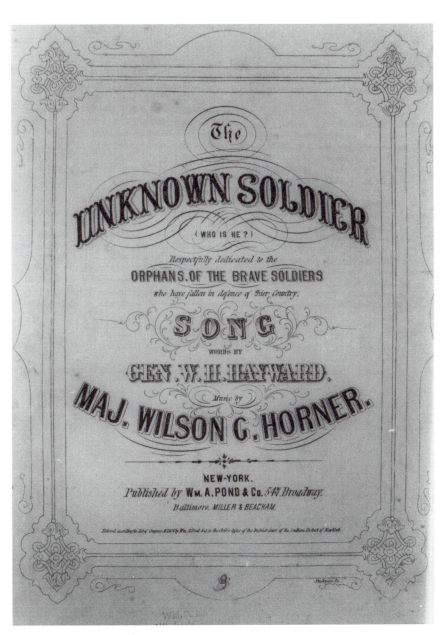

"The Unknown Soldier (Who Is He?)" sheet music. Dr. Bourns debuted William H. Hayward's poem at the 1864 Portville Presbyterian Church meeting. Pond and Company's publication of the song featured ornate typography but no illustration on its cover. *Author's collection.*

"The Children of the Battle Field" sheet music, first edition. Published in April 1864, the cover featured an unpolished lithograph of the children by T. Sinclair of Philadelphia. *Author's collection.*

The Humiston children in Gettysburg, first pose. One of several cartes-de-visite of Frank, Alice, and Fred taken during their Gettysburg years by Tipton & Myers. According to Miss Latimer, the children were photographed soon after their arrival at the Homestead in the autumn of 1866; this would appear to be that pose. *Courtesy of David Humiston Kelley.*

The Captain John Myers house during renovation. Workers posed for an unknown photographer as the Homestead orphanage took shape on the Baltimore Pike in Gettysburg in the summer of 1866. *Courtesy of Henry Deeks.*

The Humiston children in Gettysburg, final pose. Albumen photograph by Tipton & Myers, dated by Alice to 1869. Forsaking their usual pose, Alice and Fred deferentially stand on either side of their seated older brother, Frank, and rest their hands on his shoulders. It is the children's last known pose together. *Courtesy of David Humiston Kelley.*

General Grant's visit to the Homestead in June 1867. Centered between the two groups of orphans are (left to right) Governor Geary, General Crawford, General Grant, and General Porter. The printed caption on Charles J. Tyson's mounted photograph remarked of the orphanage building, "It is used until a more commodious and suitable structure can be erected to shelter its present fatherless inmates, with many other soldiers' orphans in different States of the Union, awaiting admission to the institution." *Library of Congress.*

Hobbles used by Mrs. Carmichael at the "Soldiers Orphans Homestead" Gettysburg Pa.

Rosa Carmichael's shackles. Photographic evidence of the matron's cruelty, obtained by Gettysburg's Corporal Skelly Post, Grand Army of the Republic, after the Homestead was shut down. *Courtesy of William J. Little and Larry R. Runk.*

Children playing at the Homestead. Tipton captured the yard in an 1874 view, with the new addition at left and the Myers house at center. One of the women looking on could be the notorious Rosa J. Carmichael, who became admistrator of the orphanage in 1870. *Tipton Collection, National Archives.*

Fred and Nettie (Orne) Humiston with daughter Doris. Doris was born in 1897; Fred and Nettie's daughter Eleanor arrived in 1906. Fred was a successful traveling salesman out of West Somerville, Massachusetts. *Courtesy of David Humiston Kelley.*

Frank Humiston (top) and family. Middle row, left to right: Carrie (Tarbell) Humiston, Frank, Helen. Foreground, left to right: Alice, Ruth. This picture was taken circa 1895, prior to the arrival of babies John and Freda. Frank was the beloved town doctor of Jaffrey, New Hampshire, for a quarter-century. *Courtesy of David Humiston Kelley.*

Alice Humiston in her pigeon roost. She purchased Westview, her farm in North Leominster, Massachusetts, in 1906. Raising chickens was one of Alice's many occupations; Westview was one of many homes. *Courtesy of David Humiston Kelley.*

Philinda Barnes with granddaughter Alice M. Humiston. The only known photograph of Philinda in her later years, taken circa 1895. *Courtesy of David Humiston Kelley.*

Cliff Arquette's Soldiers Museum. The renovated Homestead building was still recognizable when Arquette opened his museum in 1959. The inset in this photo postcard published by the Lane Studio in Gettysburg shows Arquette in his familiar role as Charlie Weaver. *Courtesy of Allan L. Cox.*

The Amos Humiston Memorial. The only monument to an individual enlisted man on the Gettysburg battlefield. *Author's photograph*.

CHAPTER 9

Whose Father
Was He?

GETTYSBURG IN THE aftermath of the great battle was an appalling place. Acres of trees were damaged by bullets and shells, some of them killed by the leaden storm, others crippled with bark and limbs peeled and shot away. Rocks were pocked and scraped and splintered. Hastily built breastworks and barricades scarred hillsides, fields, and streets. The ground was ripped and plowed by shot and shell, cut by the wheels of artillery, ambulances, and wagons, and trampled by the ebb and flow of the contending armies into a bog of mud and ground-up grass and grain. Property damage was extensive. Fields, crops, and gardens had been devoured by man and beast, fences were destroyed, furniture and household goods were scattered, windows were shattered, signs were shot through, wooden houses were perforated with bullets, brick houses were splattered with lead, and the occasional dwelling, barn, and warehouse was burned. In Evergreen Cemetery, where the 154th New York had been posted for much of the three days of battle, headstones and fences were smashed and knocked down.

Wrecked caissons and wagons littered twenty-five square miles of battlefield. Shells, cannonballs, and musket balls were everywhere, embedded in trees, fences, and houses, and dotting the surface of the ground. Unexploded shells would maim or kill the curious who handled them in days and months to come. At least three thousand mangled, swollen, and fetid dead horses rotted on the battlefield, clumps of them marking positions where batteries had been decimated. Offal and bones of butchered cattle, sheep, and hogs were scattered widespread, evidence of a heavy loss of local livestock, and loose animals strayed over the battlefield. Swarms of flies covered decaying flesh in crawling, buzzing black masses. Notable by their absence were scavenging birds. Crows and vultures had been scared away by the tremendous noise of the battle and the acrid stench of burned gunpowder. Birds of all kinds had in fact fled Gettysburg, and no cheerful birdsong was to be heard.

And everywhere were the grotesque, decomposing corpses and body parts of men, transforming Gettysburg into a vast city of the dead. More than seven thousand slain soldiers from North and South lay on the battlefield—by comparison, the population of the borough was twenty-four hundred—and in the coming days and weeks another four thousand maimed men would die of their wounds. Swollen (sometimes to the point of bursting open), blackened, blistered, their eyeballs protruding, their mouths fixed in ghastly grins, mutilated and disfigured, the dead lay sprawled in countless contorted poses, their uniforms stiff with dried blood. Maggots devoured flesh, and beetles, spiders, millipedes, and mites crawled over the corpses. Wild animals, stray dogs, and loose hogs also preyed on the dead. An impermeable, putrid stench hung in the air. Despite the summer heat, Gettysburg residents shut their windows to avoid the foulness, and when they ventured outdoors, they carried bottles of peppermint or pennyroyal to counteract it. Burial squads, composed of Union pioneers and infantry details, Confederate prisoners and pressed citizens, were issued whiskey to deaden their senses to the stink.[1]

An assistant quartermaster, Captain William G. Rankin, superintended the burial operations in the days after the battle. By July 7 his squads had interred the Union dead. All over the battlefield, positions of regiments and brigades were marked by clusters of the slain. Where the dead were the thickest, corpses were laid in rows and buried in trenches. Frequently a burial squad tied a rope or belt around a dead man's legs or chest and dragged him to his place in a row. Individual graves were dug for isolated victims. Rankin's men typically used poles or fence rails to roll a corpse directly into a grave or onto a litter to be carried to the nearest grave site. The Union and Confederate dead were strictly segregated, laid in separate rows and buried in separate trenches. Graves were marked by crude wooden headboards with carved or penciled inscriptions, if the individual's identity could be ascertained. Boards from ammunition or ration boxes served the purpose best, but shingles, fence rails, floorboards, chiseled rocks, piles of stones, and leather cartridge box flaps were also used as needed.[2]

No corpses the gravediggers found were more repulsive than the Union dead on the battlefield of July 1. The Confederates had made little effort to bury their enemy, and the Southerners controlled the field of the first day's fight until the retreat on July 5. Consequently the corpses found north of Gettysburg were in the most advanced state of decomposition. When the burial squads reached the neighborhood of John Kuhn's brickyard, they dragged more than fifty moldering Union soldiers into rows near Stevens Run and buried them. Among them were some dead of the 154th New York, including Corporal Joel Bouton. Nearby, where the railroad crossed Stratton Street, they buried a solitary Yankee and two Confederates.[3]

If the dead were ineffably hideous, their detritus was ineffably sad. Mile after mile of the Gettysburg countryside was littered with muskets, knapsacks, haversacks, cartridge boxes, cap pouches, shreds of clothing, shoes, papers, bibles, photographs, envelopes, and letters that would never be answered or sent. Every bit and scrap represented an individual soldier, but in most cases it was impossible to link a belonging to its owner. Even when an item obviously belonged to a soldier, it did not always serve to identify him. Scattered near a dead Confederate on the first day's field were letters and a photograph of his South Carolina fiancée, torn to pieces. The burial squad who found him surmised the man had ripped apart the items before he died to prevent them from becoming souvenirs. Another sad example was afforded by a dead Yankee who was believed to be a member of the 9th Massachusetts Battery. A New York colonel came across the soldier and recovered photographs of a woman and two young children from his person. The pictures and the story behind them eventually made their way to the office of Governor John A. Andrew of Massachusetts, but state officials were unable to verify the man was a member of the 9th Battery, let alone identify him for certain. The anonymous soldier remained unidentified in his anonymous grave, and the woman and her children remained unaware of their loved one's fate.[4]

Every now and then, a personal item was definitely linked to a particular soldier, and on some lucky occasions, an artifact served to identify a corpse. Two cases involved privates found on the southern portion of the battlefield. A Pennsylvanian was identified by a silver medal found clutched in his hand. Another soldier was found missing his hat, shoes, and socks, but inside one of his pockets the burial squad found a gold locket with a photograph of his wife or sweetheart, along with her name and address.[5]

And so some of the Gettysburg dead were identified in a fortuitous manner by a letter, a photograph, an inscribed testament or diary, a stencil plate, or an identification disc found on their bodies. But their stories remained unknown to the general public, merely noted in passing by the members of the burial squads who found them. One such soldier's story, however, made headlines in newspapers across the North and captured the imagination of millions. But as famous as that story became, it came very close to being another forgotten tale of the battlefield.

Exactly who found Amos Humiston remains a mystery. Precisely when and where he was found are also uncertain. The exact details have long since passed away, along with the family who made the discovery and retrieved and preserved the single, sad clue to his identity, the ambrotype of his three children. And the story of the dead soldier and the ambrotype most likely would have remained nothing more than a family legend had it not been for an accident on a mountain road.

Amos was probably found on July 5, or at most a day or two later, located as he was in a residential neighborhood. The only accounts to specify even vaguely when he was found merely stated it was soon after the battle, when the dead were being buried.[6]

Where Amos was found also went unspecified. Early accounts indicated he had crawled to a sheltered or secluded spot or the shade of a tree after he was mortally wounded, but gave no exact location. The only definite description of where Amos was discovered was not made until after the war was over, in a statement by David Wills, the Gettysburg attorney who played a leading role in establishing the Soldiers' National Cemetery and hosted Abraham Lincoln when the president came to town to attend the cemetery's dedication. In August 1865, Wills pinpointed the spot where Amos was found: "on Stratton street, in Gettysburg, along the property of Judge Russell."[7]

Judge Samuel Riddle Russell's property, enclosed by a whitewashed board fence, was situated on the northeastern corner of York and Stratton streets, less than a quarter-mile south of John Kuhn's brickyard. A Gettysburg native and son of a Revolutionary War veteran, Russell had been a lawyer in his home town since 1823 and a judge since 1851, and was well known to his townsmen as a picturesque old gentleman who dressed in old-fashioned clothes, including a silk stock. His quaint clapboard house, one of the oldest in the borough and his 1801 birthplace, fronted on York Street. Adjoining it on the Stratton Street side was an undeveloped lot, and in the corner of the lot at the intersection of York and Stratton streets some small trees grew inside the fence. Directly across York Street loomed St. James Lutheran Church, a large brick structure topped with a cupola. It seems that the secluded, sheltered spot Amos Humiston found after he was shot was somewhere in Judge Russell's fenced lot.[8]

The exact nature of Amos's mortal wound went unrecorded, as did a detailed description of his death pose. One account noted that he had thrown away most of his accouterments; another stated that he was found without any of his equipment. (Along with the rest of the 154th New York, Amos had left his knapsack at Emmitsburg on the morning of the day he was killed, but it is certainly possible that he threw aside other items during his race from the brickyard.) All accounts agreed, however, that nothing was found on his body to help identify him—no company letter or regimental numbers on his cap, no corps badge on his jacket, no sergeant's chevrons on his sleeves, no identification disc, no letters or diary or any other personal item. All he had, clutched in his hands, was the ambrotype of his three children.[9]

Skies were overcast, and rain fell intermittently for several days after the battle. It might have been a glint of light from the glass of the ambrotype or the gilt of its matte that drew whoever spotted the sodden corpse to come closer for a second look. And when that person removed the picture from the bloody, stiffened hands and stared at the sweet faces of the children, he knew he had come upon an extraordinary example of a father's love. In his last moments, this soldier had chosen to carry the sight of his little ones with him into eternity. As death approached, his heart had reached for home.

Who found him? The earliest accounts stated he was discovered by a Miss Schriver, daughter of Gettysburg's postmaster. In the latter detail, the newspapers were mistaken. Big, brawny Benjamin Schriver was well known in Gettysburg and throughout Adams County, but in 1863 he and his family were no longer living in the borough. The year before, the Schrivers had moved to Graeffenburg, a hamlet in the mountains on the border of Adams and Franklin counties, about thirteen miles west of Gettysburg on the Chambersburg Pike. There, Ben Schriver was Graeffenburg's postmaster and proprietor of the Graeffenburg Springs tavern, where he lived with his second wife, Maria Forrey Schriver, and their three daughters: fourteen-year-old Jane, ten-year-old Anna, and eight-year-old Louisa. The four adult children of Ben Schriver's first marriage, to the late Sarah Deardorff—including the youngest, Emma, age twenty-two—had long since left his household.[10]

Schriver was fifty-seven years old in the summer of 1863. He had served as sheriff of Adams County for three years in the late 1840s, and from 1854 to 1861 he was a licensed tavernkeeper and proprietor of the Wagon Hotel at the intersection of Baltimore Street and the Emmitsburg Road in Gettysburg, at the foot of Cemetery Hill. The Wagon Hotel catered to teamsters and was not considered one of Gettysburg's finer inns. A massive man, renowned for his strength, Ben Schriver was fully capable of handling any rowdy customers who got out of hand in his barroom. He was, in fact, champion of the brawls that quadrennially erupted in Gettysburg on presidential election days. It was customary for the staunch Whig (later a Republican) to take post during the voting at the Adams County Court House on the town square and take on all Democratic comers. As a general rule, his opponents left with battered heads, cursing, "Damn Ben Schriver!"[11]

How could one of the young daughters of this rough-and-tumble tavern keeper, living more than a dozen miles away from Gettysburg, have found Amos Humiston and his ambrotype? That question is both complicated by and perhaps answered by the 1865 testimony of David Wills, who stated that Amos was found by Mr. Peter Beitler.[12]

The connection between thirty-one-year-old Peter Beitler and the Schriver family was an intimate one. On April 5, 1859, Beitler married Emma Schriver, Ben's daughter. In March 1860 a son, Andrew, was born to the couple. Two months later, a census taker recorded the family to be near neighbors to John Kuhn's brickyard. Peter worked as a granite cutter, and an eighteen-year-old boy was living with the family as an apprentice.[13]

Peter, Emma, and little Andrew Beitler presumably were still living in the vicinity of Kuhn's brickyard in July 1863, placing them on a daily basis in close proximity to where Amos was found. At the time, Emma was about five months pregnant with another child, a circumstance that could well explain the presence of one of the younger Schriver girls in Gettysburg. In the family plot in Evergreen Cemetery are the undated headstones of four stillborn Beitler children, indicating Emma Schriver Beitler experienced chronic problems in pregnancy. As her confinement approached, Emma possibly had one of her young stepsisters come to Gettysburg to help care for young Andrew and assist with household chores. And if Jane Schriver— or Anna or Louisa—was indeed staying with the Beitler family after the battle, she quite likely was the Miss Schriver who came across the dead soldier clutching the ambrotype.[14]

With the frustrating lack of corroborative evidence, it is impossible to say which of the Schriver sisters—or Peter Beitler, as David Wills later asserted—found Amos Humiston. What is certain is that the unknown soldier was subsequently buried on Judge Russell's lot, and that the ambrotype was given to Ben Schriver, who probably hurried into town to make sure his relatives were all right and witness the effects of the battle. Back at Graeffenburg Springs, the curio was no doubt displayed by the innkeeper to fascinated patrons, and perhaps even earned a place of honor propped on the back bar. It certainly must have inspired many earnest conversations on the horrors of the war and the recent battle, and the poignant fate of the three orphaned children. Chances are the ambrotype would have remained a barroom curiosity for a few months—until Ben Schriver died in January 1864—and then gotten lost in family clutter, its story eventually forgotten. But that summer a vehicle broke down on the road running from Chambersburg to Gettysburg, and Dr. John Francis Bourns and three other stranded travelers entered the tavern.[15]

All four men were headed to Gettysburg to care for the wounded in the wake of the battle. The conversation that ensued at Graeffenburg Springs can be imagined: Ben Schriver's hearty welcome, the explanation of their plight by the strangers, the tavern keeper's offer of hospitality, the travelers' announcement of the purpose of their journey. Then Schriver showed the ambrotype of the three children to the men, and told them the story of its discovery. Dr. Bourns immediately realized the photograph was a vital clue to the identity of the fallen father. He convinced Schriver to give him the ambrotype, explaining that when his work in Gettysburg was finished, he would use the picture to discover who the children were. When Dr. Bourns and his companions left Graeffenburg after their vehicle was repaired, he took the ambrotype with him.[16]

With that transaction, the fate of the children and their mother was forever changed. Unbeknown to them, a man had entered their life who would reveal to them their fate and then personally change its course. Dr. Bourns would become a hero of the story to the general public, but to the bereaved family, his shining reputation as a benevolent philanthropist, made on their behalf, ultimately would be tarnished. According to their later testimony, he would alternately console them and confound them, favor them and frustrate them, aid them and cheat them.

He was a complex man, learned, devout, cultivated, and creative. He preferred to call himself J. Francis Bourns, although his true surname was Burns. He was forty-nine years old in the summer of 1863 and a resident of Philadelphia, who spent his summers at the old Burns family homestead, a farm in Franklin County, Pennsylvania. There, near the village of Roadside and the town of Waynesboro, his Scottish grandfather had been one of the first settlers to put down roots in the early 1770s. There, John Francis was born on May 17, 1814, the eldest son of Jeremiah and Sarah (Renfrew) Burns, and the second of eight children who would survive infancy. In his boyhood he attended the nearby district school and helped his father and brothers on the farm until 1830, when the local schoolmaster suddenly resigned. Sixteen-year-old Francis took the position and taught for several years, constantly expanding the school's curricula. He left his post for about six months to study Latin at the Chambersburg Academy in the Franklin County seat and then resumed teaching, initially in Waynesboro and later in Shippensburg.

In the early 1840s Bourns decided to study medicine and went to Philadelphia, where he graduated from the University of Pennsylvania School of Medicine in July 1849. Armed with his degree, he returned to the Roadside homestead intending to open a practice in the Waynesboro area. But he discovered he would have a difficult time earning a living in his home neighborhood, so he returned to Philadelphia and opened what developed into a successful practice. By the summer of 1863, he was living on Spring Garden Street in the city.

On Christmas Day of 1829, fifteen-year-old Francis began chronicling his life in a diary, which he kept until 1850, after he had completed his education. Entries in the three volumes reveal a rather sickly young man who was also perhaps affected by a bit of hypochondria. He had bouts with the measles and smallpox, complained of a heart ailment, and several times a month recorded headaches, intestinal problems, or feeling unwell in general. He used opium to relieve his abdominal pains.

He spent as much time examining the state of his soul and his mind as he did his body. His parents were both Covenanters, adherents of the iron-bound, strict old Scottish Presbyterian creed, and Francis was raised as a Covenanter. But as that church gradually waned as a separate entity, he and the rest of the Burns family joined the mainstream Presbyterian church. Again and again, he poured out his thoughts on religion to his diary, critiquing sermons he had heard, describing discussions he had engaged in with friends, wrestling with his own ideas regarding the teachings of the church.

If he was somewhat mistrustful and self-righteous, he could also be quite tolerant and open-minded. He loved learning, literature, poetry, art, and music. He was eight or nine years old, he said, when he read his first book voluntarily (*Pilgrim's Progress*). Between 1822 and 1842 he read 125 books in addition to school books, and listed them all in his diary: works of history, biography, and religion; fairy tales, novels, verse, travel books, and political books. He read Homer and Plutarch and Scottish history and the lives of American Revolutionary patriots and Charles Dickens and Sir Walter Scott. He read books about flowers and became an accomplished gardener. He wrote poetry and articles for the local newspaper, the *Waynesboro Village Record*. He joined a debating society and established a library society with a friend. He played the violin, the flute, and the accordion, and sang with the choral society.

There was a poignant aspect to this accomplished man's life: he was unable to find a wife. He always had many friends, both male and female, and he seemed to have good relationships with women. But something seemed to go wrong between him and every woman he took a romantic interest in. Five times he fell in love during the years he kept his diary, and although in each case the woman seemed to be attracted to him, he never was able to carry out a serious courtship, and the relationships dissolved.

Francis Bourns was an ardent abolitionist, a steadfast Whig, and a patriotic American. Every Fourth of July he described in his diary as a special day in his life. Also special to the bachelor was his family. The Burnses were an affectionate clan, and the large number of relatives in the vicinity of the homestead maintained close relationships with him and his parents and siblings. Special to him too was the Franklin County countryside. He took comfort in the beauty of the mountains and landscape around Roadside and Waynesboro, and he loved to pass time on the banks of Antietam Creek, which meandered through the Burns property.[17]

Spending his summers at the old homestead, Dr. Bourns was a familiar figure on the streets of Waynesboro. It seems likely he was there in the first days of July 1863, and there received word of the terrible battle that raged at Gettysburg, only about twenty miles east on the Fairfield Road. It also seems that Dr. Bourns did not travel directly from Waynesboro to Gettysburg, but instead first went to Chambersburg, a designated rendezvous for civilian physicians heading to the battlefield to tend the wounded. That was a fortunate circumstance. Had he gone from Waynesboro straight to Gettysburg, he would not have passed through Graeffenburg. By approaching Gettysburg from Chambersburg, his route took him right through that place, where the auspicious breakdown put him at the door of Ben Schriver's tavern.

Francis Bourns's mission to Gettysburg was twofold: he went to care for the wounded soldiers as both a volunteer physician and a delegate of the United States Christian Commission (USCC).[18]

There was a staggering amount of work to be done. More than 14,000 Union soldiers were wounded in the battle, and another 6,800 Confederate wounded were left behind when their army retreated. Of the more than 650 surgeons and assistant surgeons present for duty with the Union forces at Gettysburg, only 106 were left behind to care for the multitude of wounded in the aftermath of the battle. (Expecting another imminent battle, which never came, the army wanted most of its medical officers at the front.) But much of the surgeons' more grisly work was finished by the time the Federals departed Gettysburg in pursuit of the enemy. "The greater portion of the surgical labor was performed before the army left," reported Surgeon Jonathan Letterman, medical director of the Army of the Potomac. "The time for primary operations had passed, and what remained to be done was to attend to making the men comfortable, dress their wounds and perform such secondary operations as from time to time might be necessary."[19]

There were still many tasks to occupy physicians, but Francis Bourns and the other civilian doctors who converged on Gettysburg after the battle often found themselves less than welcome by their military counterparts. Army surgeons branded the civilian volunteers unreliable adventurers and condemned them as interested mainly in performing amputations. Surgeon Letterman emphatically declared, "An army must rely upon its own Medical officers for the care of the sick and wounded."[20]

If Dr. Bourns's medical work at Gettysburg was limited by the hostility of military surgeons, his chores for the USCC were boundless. Founded at a convention of the Young Men's Christian Association in New York City in 1861, the commission's stated object was "to promote the spiritual and temporal welfare of the brave men in arms to put down a wicked rebellion." To accomplish its goal, the USCC relied on three mainstays: men, stores, and publications. The men were unpaid volunteers, ministers or laymen, who were sent as delegates to battlefields, hospitals, and camps, where they distributed the stores and publications to soldiers and sailors. Stores included clothing, bedding, other dry goods, stationery, food, beverages, and stimulants. Publications were strictly of the religious variety: bibles, testaments, books, papers, and tracts.[21]

Francis Bourns is not listed in a published roster of USCC delegates or in surviving registers of commission delegates. He went unrecorded along with hundreds of other volunteers who arrived at Gettysburg in the wake of the battle as special "battlefield delegates" and "minute men," who served on a temporary basis until the emergency for which they had volunteered eased.[22]

A great stream of USCC supplies flowed to Gettysburg in the days and weeks after the battle. About thirty delegates and eighty boxes of stores reached the battlefield from commission headquarters in Philadelphia two days after the Confederate retreat, and in subsequent days men and goods arrived regularly from Philadelphia and other cities and towns. Headquarters were established in the office of Robert G. Harper, editor of one of Gettysburg's three newspapers (the *Adams Sentinel and General Advertiser*), and a supply depot was situated in John L. Schick's store on the town square. Stations were set up at the various corps hospitals and the makeshift hospitals in churches, houses, and other buildings in town. Union and Confederate alike were cared for, although some delegates were reluctant to treat the enemy. USCC representatives fed, bathed, bandaged, and clothed the wounded. They gave them tracts, newspapers, books, and testaments. They wrote letters for them, preached to them, read the Bible to them, and prayed with them. They comforted them as best they could, and when nothing more could be done, they buried them.

In early August, with many of the wounded having been sent to hospitals in Northern cities, the corps hospitals were disbanded and the remaining wounded consolidated at a new general hospital, Camp Letterman, south of the York Pike. The USCC's field organization was broken up, and the supplies and work were turned over to a special Gettysburg Army Committee of the commission, headed by prominent Gettysburg citizen and lawyer Robert G. McCreary. Tents were pitched at Camp Letterman to store supplies and accommodate a dozen delegates, and they manned their post until the hospital was finally closed in late November.

Whose Father Was He?

More than four hundred USCC delegates served at Gettysburg from the days immediately after the battle until the last of the wounded were transferred, each working for two weeks or more. The USCC's chairman, dry goods importer George H. Stuart, came from Philadelphia to visit the hospitals and speak with the wounded and dying, who expressed gratitude for the work done on their behalf. Surgeons calculated that more than a thousand lives were saved by the timely relief and stores provided by the commission, and clergymen reported that more than a thousand souls were saved by its work—numbers that the USCC believed were underestimated. "No one who labored at Gettysburg as a delegate of the Christian Commission," the USCC reported, "can help being thankful for the part he was permitted to bear in the work there accomplished, or cease to pray for the continued and increased prosperity of the organization which he there represented."[23]

When and for how long Dr. Bourns worked in Gettysburg's hospitals is not known. He did not attempt to begin his crusade to identify the unknown soldier during his stay in Gettysburg; he would wait to do that on his return to Philadelphia. But he did make sure one task was taken care of while he was on the battleground: he convinced friends to mark the unknown father's grave on Judge Russell's lot in a permanent manner. After the man was identified—if the doctor's plan worked—he could be disinterred and transported to a cemetery in his home town, wherever that might be.[24]

Since its discovery, the ambrotype had traveled from Gettysburg to Graeffenburg by means of the Schriver family, and from Graeffenburg back to Gettysburg with Francis Bourns. Now it went to Philadelphia, where the doctor knew he would find the resources he needed to solve the mystery of Gettysburg's unknown soldier. With a population of more than a half-million, Philadelphia was the second largest city in the country, and Dr. Bourns's Spring Garden Street residence was just blocks from its commercial center. Within a short walk of the historic heart of the city at Independence Hall were the bankers and brokers of Third Street, the crowded shops of Second Street, the wholesale houses of Market Street, and the newspaper, telegraph, and express offices of Chestnut Street. Stretched across Bank Street, a banner marked the location of the central office of the USCC, in the commercial buildings of Stuart & Brother. "Here it is," a commission report described the location of its office, "surrounded by the clatter of traffic, the fever of greenbacks and gold, the rush of hurrying feet, the din of rattling wheels, the click, click, click of the news, the clangor of the press, the babel of tongues, all the kingdoms of the world and the glory of them in a focus!"[25]

Gettysburg's Unknown Soldier

By harnessing some of that energy, Dr. Bourns hoped to reveal the identities of the children in the ambrotype and their father. Newspaper publishers and photographers were essential to the success of his plan, and Philadelphia was rich in both. The city was home to a dozen daily and eighteen weekly English-language newspapers and three others published in German. From the more widely circulated newspapers, the doctor knew, the story of the dead soldier and the ambrotype would spread across the land. Philadelphia's photographers had occupied a prominent place in their profession since the introduction of the daguerreotype to America more than two decades before. They could provide him with plenty of copies of the picture of the children, and those copies were an integral part of his idea.

Photographic copies of the ambrotype, however, did not figure into his plan for the initial stage of the publicity campaign. The newspapers, magazines, and books of the day could not print photographic reproductions. Photographs were the basis for some of the pictures presented in the nationally distributed illustrated papers—notably *Harper's Weekly* and *Frank Leslie's Illustrated Newspaper*—but they merely served as models for the woodcuts that filled the pages of those popular publications. The only graphic devices found in typical newspapers were crude cuts illustrating advertisements. When the story of the unknown soldier was publicized, the ambrotype would be described in words, not depicted pictorially.

Bourns nevertheless approached photographers first, before he went to the newspapers. He wanted to obtain copies of the ambrotype for two reasons. After the story appeared in the papers, he would receive inquiries about the picture, and he wanted to have copies on hand to send to those correspondents. And if his plan worked and the soldier's family was located, he wanted to donate profits from the sale of copies to support the three orphans. What he needed was a supply of inexpensive copies that could be replenished with ease when necessary.

A relatively new photographic process made that possible. The carte-de-visite was a small paper photograph mounted on a card measuring about two and a half by four inches, about the size of a calling card—hence its name. Cartes-de-visite could be reproduced in multiple copies from their glass plate negatives, which were exposed in cameras with multiple lenses. A European import, the format arrived in the United States in the late summer of 1859. By the following spring, dozens of American photographers, including some in Philadelphia, were making cartes-de-visite, and by the end of 1860 the style was a major fashion in the country. Albums to hold the little pictures were introduced, and quickly became common and treasured family possessions. The war greatly spurred the spread of the carte-de-visite, with soldiers and their families and friends all eager to exchange portraits. Affordability was an important factor in their popularity: the price was generally $2 to $3 for a dozen cartes.[26]

Making copies of photographs was an important part of a photographer's studio work. Since the introduction of the carte-de-visite, photographers had notified the public in advertisements that they could copy daguerreotype and ambrotype portraits in the new format, so Dr. Bourns knew cheap copies of the dead soldier's ambrotype could be readily had. What he also wanted were copies of good quality, and so he had more than one photographer try their hands.[27]

Philadelphia's most popular photographers had studios on Chestnut Street, and James E. McClees was among the most prominent. McClees learned the daguerrean trade in 1844 and over the years experimented with several different photographic processes, produced a series of photographs of the city's public buildings, and wrote a book, *Elements of Photography*. In copying the ambrotype for Bourns, McClees produced a vignetted effect by shading off the edges during the printing process. The result was an oval-shaped image of the children, with faded edges and no discernable background.[28]

When the Chestnut Street studios of H. C. Phillips & Brother and Wenderoth & Taylor produced cartes for Dr. Bourns, they too vignetted the image, but they apparently made copies from a retouched print. The hair of all three children was touched up, with a clearly defined highlight brushed into Frank's. The size of the vignette was also made slightly larger on the Phillips & Brother and Wenderoth & Taylor cartes. And while McClees made his cartes in the vertical format, the Phillips brothers made their cartes horizontal, and Wenderoth & Taylor made copies in both formats.[29]

Dr. Bourns would return to all three photographers—and another well-known Philadelphia cameraman, Frederick Gutekunst—for more copies of the carte as events unfolded. Judging from the amount of work he gave them, he appears to have been most pleased with the firm of Wenderoth & Taylor, whose Chestnut Street studio was next door to that of James McClees. The principal in the firm, Frederick A. Wenderoth, was a painter in Charleston, South Carolina, in the late 1850s, one of many painters who put aside their brushes to take up the camera. Wenderoth worked for the Philadelphia studio of Broadbent & Company from about 1860 until 1863, when he took over the firm and changed its name. Wenderoth and his employees were to become very familiar with the faces of the three children over the next few years.[30]

With good-quality carte-de-visite copies of the ambrotype in hand, Dr. Bourns was ready to proceed with the second part of his plan. He then turned to Philadelphia's newspapers.

Gettysburg's Unknown Soldier

The story broke on October 19, 1863. The *Philadelphia Press* of that date ran a short item:

A Gettysburg Relic

An interesting relic has been obtained from the field of Gettysburg, by a member of the family of Benjamin Schriver, Esq., of Graefenberg. The relic consists of a daguerreotype of three children—two little boys and a little girl. It was found clasped between the hands of a Union soldier, whose eyes were intently fixed upon it. The gaze of the dying man appears to the last to have been concentrated upon these objects of his tenderest affection. The name of the dead soldier is not known, but his remains are protected within a secluded and honored grave. The daguerreotype is now in the hands of Dr. Burns, of this city.[31]

That article must not have been entirely pleasing to Dr. Bourns. Not only had the *Press* misspelled his name and misidentified the ambrotype as a daguerreotype, it had offered no detailed description of the picture, which was essential to his plan. The same day, a much more satisfactory story ran in the *Philadelphia Inquirer*, under an eye-catching headline:

Whose Father Was He?

After the battle of Gettysburg, a Union soldier was found in a secluded spot on the field, where, wounded, he had laid himself down to die. In his hands, tightly clasped, was an ambrotype containing the portraits of three small children, and upon this picture his eyes, set in death, rested. The last object upon which the dying father looked was the image of his children, and as he silently gazed upon them his soul passed away. How touching! how solemn! What pen can describe the emotions of this patriot-father as he gazed upon these children, so soon to be made orphans! Wounded and alone, the din of battle still sounding in his ears, he lies down to die. His last thoughts and prayers are for his family. He has finished his work on earth; his last battle has been fought; he has freely given his life to his country; and now, while his life's blood is ebbing, he clasps in his hands the image of his children, and, commending them to the God of the fatherless, rests his last lingering look upon them.

When, after the battle, the dead were being buried, this soldier was thus found. The ambrotype was taken from his embrace, and has since been sent to this city for recognition. Nothing else was found upon his person by which he might be identified. His grave has been marked, however, so that if by any means this ambrotype will lead to his recognition he can be disinterred. This picture is now in the possession of Dr. BOURNS, No. 1104 Spring Garden street, of this city, who can be called upon or addressed in reference to it. The children, two boys and a girl, are, apparently, nine, seven and five years of age, the boys being respectively the oldest and youngest of the three. The youngest boy is sitting in a high chair, and on each side of him are his brother and sister. The eldest boy's jacket is made from the same material as his sister's dress. These are the most prominent features of the group. It is earnestly desired that all the papers in the country will draw attention to the discovery of this picture and its attendant circumstances, so that, if possible, the family of the dead hero may come into possession of it. Of what inestimable value will it be to these children, proving, as it does, that the last thoughts of their dying father was for them, and them only.[32]

Nineteenth-century Americans were highly receptive to this story. Death shadowed their society, casting its darkness into the lives of all, always ready to cloud thoughts. People were grimly aware of the tentativeness of life. The average life expectancy at birth was approximately forty years. Child mortality rates were frightful. Some folk did not name their babies for months, for fear of losing them. Others dreaded receiving letters, afraid of learning of a loved one's demise. Yet most were resigned to providence and humbly accepted God's will. How one died was deemed important, and to ask for and receive the details of a person's passing was common. To be prepared for one's own demise—at any place and any time—was wise.

Death was most often an intimate family affair. Relatives and friends cared for the dead and dying, gathered by their bedsides, prepared their corpses for burial. The deathbed was a sacred spot, the place where—ideally—loved ones could witness a peaceful passing, and provide the departed with comfort and reassurance. With everyone solemnly aware of death's presence, the family circle closed around its loved one, hoping for a submissive but triumphant release from a troubled world. To be present at the deathbed was regarded as a great privilege; to be unable to attend was considered a distinct deprivation. To die away from the family circle, unattended and alone, was a frightful prospect.[33]

The war changed all that. America's sons, brothers, and husbands were now dying in droves, far from home and the comfort of the family circle. Some were embalmed and sent home in cheap coffins, to rest in family plots, church graveyards, or hometown cemeteries. More found dismal final resting places in the soil of Virginia or Tennessee or Maryland or Pennsylvania. Their family in the army—their comrades of company and regiment—tried to gather by their deathbeds in the hospitals, and succor them where they fell on the battlefields, but all too often men died alone, as this soldier had at Gettysburg. None of his comrades had been there to comfort him, to write the fateful letter to his family, to mark his lonely grave. But this soldier, it seemed, had not died alone after all—he had brought his family to his deathbed, after a fashion. The last thought of this dying father was to close his family circle around him. The pathos of his dying act consequently struck a profound note in the nation's collective consciousness.

After the *Press* and the *Inquirer* broke the story, other Philadelphia newspapers carried articles about Gettysburg's unknown soldier. None of them, however, matched the *Inquirer*'s account for emotion and drama. The day after the *Press* and *Inquirer* stories ran, on October 20, the *Daily Evening Bulletin* printed a terse piece given mainly to a description of the children. The *Philadelphia Daily Age* described "A Dear Picture" on October 21. The *Philadelphia North American and United States Gazette* ran a short item on November 4 under the headline, "The Soldier's Children," describing how the soldier "had dragged himself to a lonely spot, and there breathed out his soul with the images of his loved ones before him."[34]

It was the *Inquirer*'s dramatic "Whose Father Was He?" story that gained the widest circulation. It was reprinted, virtually verbatim, in newspapers across the North. The *Albany Evening Journal* ran it on October 31. Readers in Gettysburg perused it on the front page of the November 3 *Adams Sentinel and General Advertiser*. Two days later, whalemen in New Bedford read the story in the *Republican Standard*. It appeared on the front page of the *Waynesboro Village Record* in Dr. Bourns's home town on November 13. And about a month after it first appeared in Philadelphia, the story reached Cattaraugus County. The *Cattaraugus Freeman* carried "Whose Father Was He?" in its issue of November 18, and the *Olean Times* ran it about the same time. By then, however, the question in the headline had been answered.[35]

In addition to its numerous secular newspapers, Philadelphia boasted a sizable religious press. The city was a Presbyterian publishing center, home to about a dozen periodicals of that faith during the war era, among them the weekly *American Presbyterian*. Dr. Bourns apparently visited the Chestnut Street office of that newspaper about a week after "Whose Father Was He?" ran in the *Inquirer*, to show the ambrotype and relate the story. The Reverend John W. Mears, ordained minister, author, and editor of the *American Presbyterian*, published a piece in the October 29 issue of his paper. Like those in other papers, it was a straightforward account, much less dramatic than the *Inquirer*'s version. The article twice misidentified the type of photograph found in the unknown soldier's hand, in both the headline and the body of the story, but otherwise it was accurate, if terse and unsentimental:

The Dead Soldier and the Daguerreotype

An interesting and touching relic from the battle-field of Gettysburg, is in possession of J. F. Bourns, M.D., No. 1104 Spring Garden St., Philadelphia. It is a Melainotype, or Ambrotype on iron, of three children, two boys and a girl, and was taken from the hands of a dead soldier belonging to the Union army. He had been mortally wounded, and crawled to a sheltered spot, where his body was found, with

Whose Father Was He?

the picture of his children so placed within his folded hands that it met his dying gaze. There was no clue to his name or regiment, or his former place of residence, but his grave is marked, and it is hoped that he may be identified by the picture of his children.

The little ones have all interesting faces, and would seem to be nine, seven, and five years of age. The youngest is seated on a high chair, with his brother on his right hand, and his sister on his left. The little girl has a plaid dress, and the oldest boy a jacket of the same material. The miniature has a flat gilt frame, and may have been sent from home in a letter. On the frame, faint but traceable, is the inscription: *"Holmes, Booth & Haydens. Superfine."* Our exchanges, by copying this notice, may bring some comfort to a widow and orphans, by giving them intelligence of the hero's last resting-place. Dr. Bourns will give further information to those who desire it.[36]

The *American Presbyterian* article was also reprinted, although to a lesser extent than the *Inquirer*'s story. It was paraphrased and credited, for example, under the headline "An Affecting Incident," in the November 7 issue of the *Calendar*, published in York, Pennsylvania. It ran in the *New York Observer* and then was picked up by the weekly Boston magazine, *Living Age*. But it was an original issue of the *American Presbyterian* that proved to be the key that unlocked the ambrotype's secret. Over the next few days, a copy of the paper made its way to Portville, New York, where it was received by a single subscriber.[37]

NOTES

1. Gregory A. Coco, *A Strange and Blighted Land; Gettysburg: The Aftermath of a Battle* (Gettysburg: Thomas Publications, 1995), 5–79; Gerard A. Patterson, *Debris of Battle: The Wounded of Gettysburg* (Mechanicsburg, Pa.: Stackpole Books, 1997), 1–4; William A. Frassanito, *Early Photography at Gettysburg* (Gettysburg: Thomas Publications, 1995), passim.

2. Coco, *A Strange and Blighted Land*, 85, 87–90, 102–106; Patterson, *Debris of Battle*, 28–31.

3. Coco, *A Strange and Blighted Land*, 94; *Elliott's Map of the Battlefield of Gettysburg Pennsylvania*.

4. Coco, *A Strange and Blighted Land*, 17; Henry Deeks, "Civil War Images," *Civil War News* (July 1996); J. Frank Hanley, *The Battle of Gettysburg* (Cincinnati: Jennings and Graham, 1912), describes two other examples (p. 75): "Here is a captain. In his stiffening fingers, a woman's photograph, splattered with blood; on his face, a look of love and yearning tenderness. . . . Here is a baby's likeness, smeared with the blood of bruised and bleeding lips."

5. Coco, *A Strange and Blighted Land*, 70, 90–91.

6. "The Dead Soldier Identified," *American Presbyterian*, November 19, 1863, 186; "Whose Father Was He?" *Philadelphia Inquirer*, October 19, 1863, 4.

Gettysburg's Unknown Soldier

7. "The Dead Soldier Identified," 1863, 186; "Whose Father Was He?" 4; "Amos Humiston," *Owego Times*, February 4, 1864; "Sergeant Humiston," *Gettysburg Compiler*, September 4, 1865, quoting a letter by David Wills of August 10, 1865.

8. William A. Frassanito, *Gettysburg Bicentennial Album* (Gettysburg: Gettysburg Bicentennial Committee, 1987), 27–28, 127–128; Frassanito, *Early Photography at Gettysburg*, 32, 116–118; J. Howard Wert, *A Complete Hand-Book of the Monuments and Indications and Guide to the Positions on the Gettysburg Battle-Field* (Harrisburg: R. M. Sturgeon & Co., 1886), 179; W. C. Storrick, *Gettysburg: The Place, the Battles, the Outcome* (Harrisburg: J. Horace McFarland Company, 1932), 86.

9. "The Dead Soldier and the Daguerreotype," *American Presbyterian*, October 29, 1863, 174; "The Dead Soldier Identified," 186; *The United States Christian Commission at Gettysburg* (N.p., n.d), unpaginated; "Whose Father Was He?" 4. The poem "The Dead Soldier's Children," by K.H.W., *Philadelphia Photographer* (1, no. 1 (January 1864): 15, discussed in Chapter 11, specified Amos was wounded three times: "One grazed his cheek, one broke an arm, the third his breast had sought." Where K.H.W. came up with those details is unknown, but they are suspect when the unreliability of other information in the poem is considered.

10. "The Dead Soldier Identified," 186; Isaac G. Ogden to Editor, *Olean Times*, in the *Cattaraugus Freeman*, December 16, 1863; 1850 U.S. Census, borough of York, Pennsylvania; 1860 U.S. Census, borough of Gettysburg, Pennsylvania; map of Adams County, Pennsylvania, Accession No. 4131, and marriage records, Adams County Historical Society, Gettysburg; Dr. Charles H. Glatfelter, director, Adams County Historical Society, to author, November 2, 22, 1995.

11. Evergreen Cemetery records, Benjamin Schriver, Adams County Historical Society; Glatfelter to author, November 2, 1995; Frassanito, *The Gettysburg Bicentennial Album*, 12; J. Howard Wert, "Old Time Notes of Adams County, [Gettysburg] Star and Sentinel*, August 29, 1906: 1.

12. "Sergeant Humiston," *Gettysburg Compiler*, September 4, 1865, quoting a letter by David Wills of August 10, 1865.

13. 1860 U.S. Census, borough of Gettysburg; Evergreen Cemetery records, Beitler family, Adams County Historical Society.

14. Evergreen Cemetery records, Beitler family, Adams County Historical Society.

15. "Sergeant Humiston," *Gettysburg Compiler*, September 4, 1865, quoting a letter by David Wills of August 10, 1865; "The Dead Soldier Identified," 186; death record, Benjamin Schriver, Adams County Historical Society; *The United States Christian Commission at Gettysburg*.

16. *The United States Christian Commission at Gettysburg*; "Interesting Details of a Charity Meeting at Portville," *Cattaraugus Freeman*, January 20, 1864.

17. "Burns," *Waynesboro Village Record*, December 28, 1899 (obituary of Dr. J. Francis Bourns); Mary A. Parker to author, April 15, 1996.

18. *The United States Christian Commission at Gettysburg*.

19. Surgeon General Joseph K. Barnes, U. S. Army, *Medical and Surgical History*

of the War of the Rebellion (1861–65) (Washington: Government Printing Office, Second Issue, 1875), Medical Volume, Part First, Appendix, "Report on the Operations of the Medical Department at Gettysburg by Surgeon Jonathan Letterman," 140–142.

20. Coco, *A Strange and Blighted Land*, 239.

21. United States Christian Commission, *Facts, Principles, and Progress* (Philadelphia: William S. & Alfred Martien, 1864), 7–10, 32–33.

22. *The United States Christian Commission at Gettysburg*; Lemuel Moss, *Annals of the United States Christian Commission* (Philadelphia: J. B. Lippincott & Co., 1868), 604–613; Michael P. Musick, National Archives, to author, December 30, 1996, January 30, 1997.

23. United States Christian Commission, *United States Christian Commission for the Army and Navy. For the Year 1863. Second Annual Report* (Philadelphia: United States Christian Commission, 1864), 67–86; Andrew B. Cross, *Battle of Gettysburg and the Christian Commission* (N.p., n.d.), 18–23.

24. "The Dead Soldier Identified," 186; "Whose Father Was He?" 4.

25. United States Christian Commission, *Second Annual Report*, 238.

26. William C. Darrah, *Cartes de Visite in Nineteenth Century Photography* (Gettysburg: W. C. Darrah, Publisher, 1981), 1–9, 12, 19.

27. Ibid., *The United States Christian Commission at Gettysburg*.

28. Kenneth Finkel, *Nineteenth-Century Photography in Philadelphia* (New York: Dover, 1980), 53, 218, 221; carte de visite by J. E. McClees, Artist, 910 Chestnut Street, Philadelphia, courtesy of Dean S. Thomas of Gettysburg.

29. Darrah, *Cartes de Visite in Nineteenth Century Photography*, 84–86; William Gladstone, "The Children of the Battle Field," *Military Images* 2, no. 5 (March–April 1981): 8–9; Kathleen Collins, "Photographic Fundraising: Civil War Philanthropy," *History of Photography* 11, no. 3 (July–September 1987): 181–184.

30. Finkel, *Nineteenth-Century Photography in Philadelphia*, 3, 54, 107, 219.

31. *Philadelphia Press*, October 19, 1863, 4.

32. *Philadelphia Inquirer*, October 19, 1863, 4.

33. Lewis O. Saum, "Death in the Popular Mind of Pre–Civil War America," in David E. Stannard, ed., *Death in America* (Philadelphia: University of Pennsylvania Press, 1975), 30–48.

34. "Dr. J. F. Bourns," *Philadelphia Daily Evening Bulletin*, October 20, 1863, 4; "A Dear Picture," *Philadelphia Daily Age*, October 21, 1863, 4; "The Soldier's Children," *Philadelphia North American and United States Gazette*, November 4, 1863, 2.

35. *Albany Evening Journal*, October 31, 1863, 2; *Adams Sentinel and General Advertiser*, November 3, 1863, 1; *New Bedford Republican Standard*, November 5, 1863, 4; *Waynesboro Village Record*, November 13, 1863, 1; *Cattaraugus Freeman*, November 18, December 16, 1863.

36. *American Presbyterian*, October 29, 1863: 174; Frank Luther Mott, *A History of American Magazines 1850–1865* (Cambridge: Belknap Press of Harvard University Press, 1957), 62–63; "Commendation from the Rev. John W. Mears,"

in James G. Clark, "The Children of the Battle Field" sheet music (Philadelphia: Lee & Walker, 1864).

37. *The Calendar*, York, Pa., November 7, 1863; *Living Age*, 3d ser., December 5, 1863, 453; "Sketch," James G. Clark, "The Children of the Battle Field" sheet music.

CHAPTER 10

A Widow and Her Orphans

LIFE WAS WRENCHED out of place for Philinda Humiston in the aftermath of the Battle of Gettysburg. No word came from Amos, and news about his regiment was unsettlingly vague. A week after the battle, the *Cattaraugus Freeman* printed a false report that the 154th New York had been detached from the Army of the Potomac before the battle and consequently was not present at Gettysburg. The *Freeman* of the following week acknowledged the 154th had been at Gettysburg, but speculated that it "probably did not participate in the engagement." Only sketchy details emerged in subsequent weeks, but it was revealed that most of the regiment was missing. A list of the 154th's casualties was never published. The survivors were too few and too uncertain to notify the homefolk adequately of the fate of their comrades.[1]

Philinda went about her daily tasks gripped with uncertainty about her husband's fate. Amos must have regularly intruded on her thoughts, no matter how busy she was—and she had enough chores, no doubt, to keep her occupied during almost every waking hour, with only her young children for helpers. She also had to earn a living. The Reverend Isaac Ogden described the Humistons as living in needy circumstances. An anonymous visitor described the family's home as a "very humble dwelling . . . a little house in the country, in a new-cleared spot, dreary and desolate, half a mile or more from any other dwelling." (Presumably this was the house they had moved to in November or December 1862.) Money was a constant problem. The forty-dollar allotment check Amos sent after Chancellorsville had never arrived. Philinda earned only meager amounts of money by taking in sewing. Fortunately, Portville kept the promise it had made to Amos before he enlisted. The Humistons and other soldiers' families received aid from benevolent townspeople.[2]

Nevertheless, Philinda struggled to keep Frank, Alice, and Fred well fed, comfortably clad and shod, and healthy—a worrisome endeavor when epidemics of diphtheria, smallpox, and other contagious diseases all too often sent children to early graves. After Gettysburg, caring for the children took on a distressing new dimension: the agony of trying to answer their questions about their father.

Children throughout the stricken country were caught up in the war, and its impact was devastating. With fathers and older brothers absent at the front, youth solemnly took on new worries and responsibilities. Many battled extreme material and emotional hardships. But there was also a playful response to the war, as youngsters fit the conflict into their lives as meaningfully as they could. Boys mimicked adults and played soldier, forming companies and drilling with broomsticks and pokers. Girls followed the news in the illustrated weeklies and clipped maps and woodcuts to paste in scrapbooks. Children made miniature panoramas of war scenes, collected cartes-de-visite of generals, produced theatricals with war themes, and posed for photographs dressed in military-style garb, carrying miniature weapons and drums.[3]

Little Frankie, Allie, and Freddy Humiston no doubt shared the war excitement with their playmates, especially when their pa volunteered for the army. He was one of Portville's heroes, fighting to uphold the old flag and the Union, and his children must have been proud of him. As long as his letters came, everything was all right. Pa had survived the harshness of army life, recovered from his illnesses, and luckily escaped harm at Chancellorsville. Surely he would return when the war was won, lift them in his strong arms, and hug and kiss them, as he had so many times before. But then came Gettysburg, and their world was knocked askew. What had happened to their pa?

Days, weeks, and months dragged by. The haze, heat, and humidity of July and August gave way to the more moderate days of September and October. Summer's dense green surrendered to autumn's array of color. Farmers harvested their crops, and the first snows whitened the landscape. Still no word reached Philinda about Amos. As she was putting Freddy to bed one night, the little boy talked about the snow outside, about how Amos had promised the children new sleds and sleighs, about how he dreamed of his pa every night, and he asked his mother when his father would return. Philinda could only respond with a tight hug.[4]

During the first days of November, a lone copy of the October 29 *American Presbyterian* reached Portville. The unknown subscriber (probably Reverend Ogden) shared it with friends and the paper passed from hand to hand. For several days, the piece about the dead soldier and the photograph of his three children caused much comment and aroused many tender sympathies in the village. Then the *Presbyterian* reached the hands of a woman—long since anonymous—who realized the article could pertain to her friends the Humistons. She carried the paper to the Humiston home, where Philinda, stunned and heartsick, read the description of the picture and realized that it matched exactly the features of the ambrotype she had sent to Amos.[5]

The likelihood that Amos could be the unknown soldier was unsettlingly strong but still uncertain. The Philadelphia doctor would have to be contacted for more information. Philinda herself did not write to Dr. Bourns. With her friends acting as intermediaries, Portville's postmaster, Dr. Thomas S. Jackson, handled the correspondence. Jackson summarized the facts in a letter to Dr. Bourns, describing how Mrs. Humiston learned of the dead soldier and his picture in the *American Presbyterian*, how she had sent her husband a photograph like the one described, how she had not heard from him since the Battle of Gettysburg, and how she anxiously awaited a reply.[6]

Meanwhile, in Philadelphia, Dr. Bourns was becoming discouraged. Since the publicity began, he had received many affecting inquiries from throughout the North. Some of the letters came from soldiers' wives who had not heard from their husbands since Gettysburg. Others came from soldiers who had survived the battle but could not learn the fate of comrades. All had received a reply and a carte-de-visite copy of the ambrotype. But no identification had been made.[7]

Despite Dr. Bourns's uncertainty of locating the soldier's family, the cartes-de-visite were offered for sale to the public. The *Philadelphia North American and United States Gazette* admitted on November 4 that "all efforts to ascertain his name or regiment have been to this time unavailing," but optimistically noted that the photograph had been copied "for the benefit of the fatherless children. . . . This likeness will grace any lady's album." The *Philadelphia Inquirer* of the same day announced that the picture of the children was for sale at two Chestnut Street locations, McAllister and Brother's photography shop and Martien's store. The *Inquirer* item indicated that the goal of identifying the soldier was still in sight, but should the effort fail, another cause was contemplated: "It is hoped by this means the family of the deceased will soon be found, when the original, from which the pictures are taken, may be placed in their possession. The proceeds from the sales of the pictures will be given to the family of the deceased if found, and should no information of their whereabouts be revealed, the proceeds will be devoted to some benevolent institution for the benefit of the soldiers."[8]

The break Dr. Bourns had been looking for finally occurred early in

November when a letter with a Portville postmark arrived at 1104 Spring Garden Street. Postmaster Jackson's message convinced Bourns that the mystery of the dead soldier was on the verge of being solved. The doctor immediately responded by sending a carte de visite via express mail. He felt confident enough about the development to share the news with John Mears, who ran a carefully worded story in the *American Presbyterian* of November 12: "The ambrotype found on the Gettysburg battle-field, in the hands of a dead Union soldier, it is hoped, has been identified, through the notice published in the *American Presbyterian*, a week or two ago." The paper promised to print the results of the correspondence, "if they prove satisfactory," the following week. "Meanwhile, efforts through the public press will not be intermitted to discover the true party, if it be not already found." The cartes-de-visite were in great demand, the *Presbyterian* noted. Several religious organizations were now offering them for sale: the Sunday School Union, American Tract Society, and Presbyterian House on Chestnut Street and the Baptist Publication House on Arch Street. The proceeds were to be reserved for the benefit of the family, "when discovered," and "the wide distribution of the picture will also aid in the work of discovery."[9]

About the same time that readers in Philadelphia were absorbing this tentative news, the heartrending discovery was made in Portville. Philinda Humiston was handed the envelope, newly arrived from Philadelphia; she opened it and removed the carte-de-visite, stared at the familiar faces of her three children, and finally knew for certain that she was a widow and little Frank, Alice, and Fred were orphans.

Initially, the Humistons' grief was private. For a week or so they shouldered their sorrow in relative anonymity, with only their Portville friends and whatever family members Philinda managed to contact offering condolences and consolation. But when word that the mystery was solved reached Dr. Bourns, a second great wave of publicity spread from Philadelphia across the North. From then on, the Humistons' loss was weighted with the burden of celebrity. Now that the public could put names to the three sweet faces in the famous picture, Frank, Alice, Fred, and their mother would mourn Amos Humiston at the center of a vast outpouring of public empathy and interest.

Thomas Jackson quickly sent word of Philinda's confirmation to Dr. Bourns, who immediately conveyed it to John Mears. On November 19— exactly one month after the *Philadelphia Inquirer* had first asked, "Whose Father Was He?"—the *American Presbyterian* broke the story under the headline, "The Dead Soldier Identified." The article recounted the Humistons' reaction on seeing the carte-de-visite in dramatic terms:

A Widow and Her Orphans

It was the identical picture! The dread certainty of widowhood and orphanage flashed upon the group with this discovery; yet the severity of the blow was tempered by the dying affection of the father, by the tender romance of mystery which enveloped the facts and by the wide-spread interest the case had awakened in patriotic minds.

The item closed with a look into the future, for the story had not ended with the identification of the soldier and his family:

Dr. Bourns proposes to visit Portville and return the ambrotype with his own hands. He is promised an enthusiastic reception by the people who take a lively interest in the family. It is hoped that a sufficient sum of money will be raised by the sale of the photograph or otherwise to give each of the children a good education. Indeed, the idea has suggested itself to some large minds among us, that the interest occasioned by this beautiful event might be turned to the account of soldiers' orphans generally; and that an effort might at this time be successfully made to found and endow in this city a Soldiers' Orphans' Asylum on a large scale. We trust such may be the result.[10]

A seed had been planted. Nurtured by the inspiration of Amos Humiston, nourished in the fertile soil of public patronage, a sturdy tree would grow and flourish. Standing strong and tall, its spreading branches would offer shelter to many. Then, sadly and quite suddenly, the tree would rot from within, break, and topple to the ground.

News of the identification spread quickly. The day after the *American Presbyterian* published its story, on November 20, the *Philadelphia Daily Evening Bulletin* carried the tidings under the headline, "Identity Ascertained." A day later, the *Philadelphia Inquirer* carried a short item announcing the family had been located. "The wide circulation given to the notice which appeared in this paper, and which was copied into other papers, both secular and religious, has had its desired effect," the *Inquirer* stated, choosing not to credit the *Presbyterian* specifically for solving the mystery. The *Philadelphia Daily Age* reported the discovery on November 23. "The children are poor," the item stated, "and it is proposed to educate them in the Gettysburg seminary."[11]

The *Daily Evening Bulletin*'s story, "Identity Ascertained," was widely circulated. The *Baltimore Clipper* ran it, with slight modifications, on November 23. People in Gettysburg read it on November 30 in the *Gettysburg Compiler*. Readers in Dr. Bourns's home town found it in the December 4 *Waynesboro Village Record*. In Amos Humiston's home town, folks read it in the December 31 *Owego Times*.[12]

The news reached Cattaraugus County readers in the pages of the *Cattaraugus Union*, Ellicottville's Democratic rival to the *Cattaraugus Freeman*. "The touching story," declared the *Union*, "has made every body in the land who has read it weep."[13]

Philinda clipped and saved an article noting the emotional impact of the story on the general public:

> The incident was one which affected many hearts, as it illustrated the undying love of a father who had left his happy home circle to offer his life on the altar of his country. . . . The bereaved widow will now have the mournful satisfaction of learning the circumstances of her husband's death, and of regaining the precious relic which had been one of his last consolations.

The article encouraged "every one who has an album" to purchase one of the cartes de visite, "to promote the philanthropic object of its publication," and noted that copies could be obtained through the mail from Dr. Bourns at five for a dollar.[14]

While reports of the identification circulated, the Philadelphia press covered new developments in the story. The *Philadelphia North American and United States Gazette* noted that the Episcopal Book Store on Chestnut Street had been added to the list of religious institutions offering the carte-de-visite for sale. "These prominent places are generously offered without any charge," the paper observed, "as depositories for the sale of the photographs." The *American Presbyterian* reiterated Dr. Bourns's desire to pay an early visit to Portville to return the ambrotype to the Humistons and, it was hoped, to present the family with a substantial amount of money. More than seven hundred copies of the carte-de-visite had been sold, the paper noted, but the profits were small and accumulated slowly. Consequently the *Presbyterian* appealed for donations, hoping to raise a purse of $500, and invited readers to leave their names and contributions at its Chestnut Street office. A week later, the *Presbyterian* announced that new subscribers to the paper would receive a large photograph of the Humiston children (oval albumen prints, about nine inches long and seven inches high, produced by Wenderoth & Taylor), a value of one dollar.[15]

Additional information about Amos and his family emerged from Portville in mid-December, when the Reverend Isaac Ogden responded to an inquiry from *American Presbyterian* editor John Mears. Mears printed Ogden's letter in the *Presbyterian*'s December 17 issue, and the *Philadelphia Daily Evening Bulletin* copied it in on the front page of that night's edition. Ogden's letter, Mears noted in a brief side story, "guarantees any who may feel disposed to render assistance, against a misappropriation of their contributions." Mears reported that the people of Portville were planning to demonstrate their support of the bereaved family when Dr. Bourns visited their town.

In his letter, the Portville pastor related a brief account of Amos's life, described his enlistment, and offered hope that Amos turned to God in his final moments:

May we not hope that while life was slowly ebbing away on that bloody battle-field, while this thoughts were evidently on his distant home, as is evidenced by the ambrotype of his children found in his hands when dead, that his thoughts and prayers also went up to Him who said to one of old, praying, "Lord remember me": "This day thou shall be with me in Paradise."

Philinda Humiston had turned to God in her affliction, Ogden reported. "Mrs. H. recently made a public profession of her faith in Christ," Ogden wrote, "and united with the Presbyterian Church of this place. . . . She bows with Christian submission to the Providence which makes her a widow, and her children fatherless." Little Frank, Alice, and Fred, "bright, active and intelligent," according to Ogden, were members of the church's Sunday school.

The hand of God was to be seen in what had happened to Amos and what was happening as a result, Isaac Ogden believed. "It was certainly a remarkable Providence which made his attachment to his family the means of his recognition; and also the means of awakening so lively an interest in his bereaved family. May God abundantly bless all who, though at a distance, are thus practically, 'visiting the widow and the fatherless in their affliction.' "[16]

Ogden also strove to interest his neighbors in the plight of the Humiston family. In a letter to the editor of the *Olean Times*, later reprinted in the *Cattaraugus Freeman*, he described how Dr. Bourns and others in Philadelphia were raising funds for the bereft family, and issued a challenge to readers:

Why should not the citizens of Cattaraugus County aid in this work? The family are in needy circumstances, and Mr. HUMMISTON was our soldier, enlisted for our defence, and laid down his life that we might enjoy the quiet of our homes and the protection of a good government. Why cannot some five hundred or more of those photographs be sold in our County? Every family would prize such a photograph as commemoration of the most touching incident of the war; and besides in this way, we would be helping a needy and most worthy family.[17]

Word of Sergeant Humiston's fate reached his comrades of the 154th New York Volunteers in Lookout Valley, Tennessee, in December. An official "Inventory of Effects and Final Statement" was filed for Sergeant

Humiston on December 20. On Company C's muster roll for December 31, Amos was finally listed as having been killed at Gettysburg, "according to recent information." Major Lewis D. Warner, former captain of Amos's Company C, testified to Sergeant Humiston's good qualities as a soldier in a letter sent to Portville. Reverend Ogden quoted Warner's opinion of Amos in the *American Presbyterian:* "He was always cheerful, prompt to do duty, free from vicious habits, and always thought much of his absent family."[18]

On the same day that Sergeant Humiston's "Final Statement" was filled out in Tennessee, Private John W. Summers, a member of Battery B, 1st Pennsylvania Light Artillery, Army of the Potomac, addressed a letter to the widow Humiston. "I had formed considerable acquaintance with your husband before the battle of gettysberg," Summers wrote. "I saw Sergt. H. when he marched in to the fight but I never saw him afterwards." Summers had learned with "deep sorrow" of his friend's death. Amos "had many friends and I often thought of the love he had for those he left behind I had frequently heard him speak of you and his Children." The artilleryman added:

I would not wish to add any sorrow to the bereaved, but he died a good soldier and a good man covered with honor and Glory, no more to hear the bugle or the drum or the roar of canons, at rest wrapt in a soldiers grave and resting will he continue until the graves shall give up their dead and may kind Providence smile upon you and may guardian angels protect his children through this toilsome world and may you all meet again where parting is no more is the prayer of the writer you no doubt are lonesome but we have few joys in this world.[19]

It is ironic that of all the letters of condolence Philinda Humiston surely received, this is the only one that has been preserved, because for all of its touching and apparently heartfelt sentiments, John Summers's letter was based on a falsehood. His battery was in the 1st Corps, and consequently Summers could not have formed a "considerable acquaintance" with Amos Humiston, a member of the 11th Corps. Nor could Summers have seen Amos march into the fight at Gettysburg, because his battery was already in action west of the town when the 154th New York arrived at Cemetery Hill and hurried out to Kuhn's brickyard. In fact, the chances John Summers ever met Amos Humiston are virtually nil.

The sketchy details regarding Amos in Summers's letter were no doubt gleaned from one of the newspaper or magazine stories then in circulation. But why would Summers deceive Philinda about knowing her husband? He himself provided the answer in his letter: he was an admittedly lonesome

A Widow and Her Orphans

soldier seeking correspondents. As a purported friend of her late husband, he hoped to exchange letters with the widow. In his artful deception, Summers produced an entirely plausible letter. Philinda was certainly touched by it, but whether she replied to Summers is unknown.[20]

The *American Presbyterian* revealed the identification of Amos Humiston on November 19, 1863—by coincidence the same day that President Abraham Lincoln delivered his timeless address at the dedication of the Soldiers' National Cemetery at Gettysburg. By then perhaps twelve hundred of the Union dead had been reinterred on Cemetery Hill—about a third of the eventual number—but Amos still rested in his unknown's grave on Judge Samuel Russell's lot. At some point after the *Gettysburg Compiler* carried the story of the identification on November 30, David Wills ordered Amos's body disinterred and reburied in the Soldiers' National Cemetery.

In the summer of 1863, Wills was appointed by Governor Andrew G. Curtain of Pennsylvania to coordinate the establishment of a cemetery for the Union dead at Gettysburg. After some unseemly wangling between Wills and David McConaughy, another Gettysburg attorney and president of the board of Evergreen Cemetery, the former purchased seventeen acres on Cemetery Hill from the latter at a good price. William Saunders, a landscape architect employed by the U.S. Department of Agriculture, designed the cemetery as a semicircle of graves, in sections by state, radiating from a proposed central monument. Wills sought bids in October for the disinterment, removal, and reburial of the remains, and the contract was awarded to Franklin W. Biesecker at $1.59 per body. Biesecker hired Samuel Weaver, pioneer Gettysburg photographer and teamster, to superintend the exhumation of bodies on the battlefield, and Joseph S. Townsend to survey the cemetery and superintend interments. Weaver in turn hired Basil Biggs, a black Gettysburg-area resident, and a crew of black workmen, to disinter corpses and put them in coffins. The work commenced in October 1863 and was completed the following March.

In reporting the results of his work, Weaver noted the particularly poor condition of the dead on the battlegrounds of July 1. Most of them were unidentified, and because of the relatively long time that had elapsed before they were buried, their corpses were in particularly poor condition. "They were generally covered with a small portion of earth dug up from along side of the body," Weaver wrote. "This left them much exposed to the heat, air, and rains, and they decomposed rapidly, so that when these bodies were taken up, there was nothing remaining but the dry skeleton."

At an unknown date, Samuel Weaver, Basil Biggs, and their crew parked their wagon near the intersection of Stratton and York streets, entered Judge Russell's lot, and located the headboard marking Amos's grave.

Biggs's men dug up Amos's corpse, and Weaver went through the clothing's rotting pockets with an iron hook, searching for effects. Under Weaver's watchful eye, the workmen gently placed the remains in a white pine coffin, careful not to overlook any hair or bone. One of the men nailed Amos's headboard to the side of the coffin. Weaver wrote Amos's name, company, and regiment atop the coffin, assigned it a number, and entered the information in a record book. The box was loaded on the wagon, and when the crew had a full load of about a half-dozen coffins, they headed to the cemetery.

On Cemetery Hill, Joseph Townsend measured the depth of a newly dug trench at three feet. Slightly beyond the head of the trench, workmen built a sunken stone wall, the foundation for future permanent headstones. The coffins of several members of the 157th New York Volunteers were lowered into the excavation, side by side. Then a freshly inscribed wooden headboard was nailed to the head of Amos's coffin, Townsend entered Amos's information in his own register, and his workmen lowered the coffin into the trench. After filling the row with coffins of members of the 134th New York and other regiments, the workmen shoveled fill into the trench, taking care not to obscure the lettering on the headboards. Later, in the summer of 1865, permanent granite markers were installed on the stone foundations. Sergeant Humiston's name was chiseled on the stone marking Grave Number 14, Section B, in the New York State portion of the Soldiers' National Cemetery.

Samuel Weaver later reported that he was able to identify a number of soldiers by effects found on their exhumed remains. "They were discovered in various ways," he wrote. "Sometimes by the pocket diaries, by letters, by names in Bible, or Testament, by photographs, names in pocketbooks, descriptive list, express receipts, medals, names on some part of the clothing, or on belt, or cartridge-box, &c., &c." A list of articles taken from soldiers' corpses filled eight pages in a published report and included seventeen ambrotypes. But like the handful of soldiers who were identified by means of personal items when they were buried on the battlefield, the soldiers identified during the reburial operations remained anonymous to the public at large. Only Amos Humiston, because of the unique circumstances of his case, was thrust into fame.[21]

On the final day of 1863, the *American Presbyterian* cited another touching case of a widow and orphan that had come to the attention of Francis Bourns, and reiterated its proposal for a soldiers' orphans' home with an impassioned plea:

The efforts of Dr. Bourns in behalf of the widow of the fallen Sergeant Hummiston, have not only called forth a great deal of interest in the public generally, but have awakened hope in the minds of others similarly situated with that bereaved family. The widow of a Pennsylvania soldier, who died in the service last summer in Missouri, and who was the son of a Presbyterian elder, sends Dr. B. a photograph of her child, who, with herself, is now entirely dependent upon the proceeds of the mother's needle for support. Would it not be interesting to have a collection of photographs of soldiers' orphans? Would not their mute faces stimulate our sense of obligation to those who, for our sakes, have been brought to orphanage and dependence? For our part, we welcome any and every suitable means of keeping alive the national conscience on this subject. We will surrender our office walls as a gallery of photographs of these objects, whom we regard as constituting one of our most solemn trusts as a people.

When will Pennsylvania bestir herself, as we believe New York has already done, to provide a home, an education and a support, so far as they are needed, for the orphans of her fallen heroes? When shall the corner-stone of a structure for this purpose be laid—as we think it should be—upon the crest of Cemetery Hill, close by the side of the illustrious dead of Gettysburg?[22]

Pennsylvania would indeed bestir herself, spurred by Governor Curtain, who became deeply committed to the cause as the result of a pathetic incident that occurred on Thanksgiving Day 1863. That morning two children clothed in rags, a soldier's orphans whose mother had since died, begged for bread at the executive mansion in Harrisburg. They were met by the governor himself, and he was deeply moved by their plight. Curtain brooded about the encounter while attending church that day, and resolved to involve his state in the care of soldiers' orphans. During 1864 legislation was passed, a bureau was established, a superintendent of soldiers' orphans was appointed, orphanages and orphans' schools were opened, and Pennsylvania took the lead among the states in the work. But the idea that the Humiston incident could somehow inspire an institution to benefit soldiers' orphans continued to glimmer, never totally eclipsed by the commonwealth's productive efforts.[23]

In the meantime, the story of the Humistons continued to reach across the land, and the family reluctantly found it was famous.

NOTES

1. *Cattaraugus Freeman*, July 9, 16, 23, 30, 1863.

2. "Sergeant Hummiston's Family," *Waynesboro Village Record*, January 22, 1864, 1; Isaac G. Ogden, "Sergeant Hummiston and His Family," *American Presbyterian*, December 17, 1863, 201; Isaac G. Ogden, "Editor Olean Times," *Cattaraugus Freeman*, December 16, 1863.

3. James Marten, "Stern Realities: Children of Chancellorsville and Beyond," in Gary W. Gallagher, ed., *Chancellorsville: The Battle and Its Aftermath* (Chapel Hill: University of North Carolina Press, 1996), 225–231.

4. Miss E. Latimer, *Idyls of Gettysburg* (Philadelphia: George Maclean, 1872), 76.

5. *The United States Christian Commission at Gettysburg* (n.p., n.d.), unpaginated.

6. "Sergeant Hummiston's Children," *American Presbyterian*, December 3, 1863, 194; "Sketch," in James G. Clark, "The Children of the Battle Field" sheet music (Philadelphia: Lee & Walker, 1864); William Adams, ed., *Historical Gazetteer and Biographical Memorial of Cattaraugus County, N.Y.* (Syracuse: Lyman, Horton & Co., October 1893), 171.

7. *The United States Christian Commission at Gettysburg*; "Sketch," in Clark, "The Children of the Battle Field" sheet music; "Story," undated broadside published by the Office of the National Homestead, Philadelphia.

8. *Philadelphia North American and United States Gazette*, November 4, 1863, 2; *Philadelphia Inquirer*, November 4, 1863, 4.

9. "The Ambrotype Found on the Gettysburg Battle-field," *American Presbyterian*, November 12, 1863, 182.

10. "The Dead Soldier Identified," *American Presbyterian*, November 19, 1863, 186.

11. "Identity Ascertained," *Philadelphia Daily Evening Bulletin*, November 20, 1863, 4; "The Children of the Deceased Hero," *Philadelphia Inquirer*, November 21, 1863, 9; "Discovered," *Philadelphia Daily Age*, November 23, 1863, 3.

12. "Identity Ascertained," *Baltimore Clipper*, November 23, 1863, 4; "Identity Ascertained," *Gettysburg Compiler*, November 30, 1863; "Identity Ascertained," *Waynesboro Village Record*, December 4, 1863; "Identity Ascertained," *Owego Times*, December 31, 1863.

13. "The Name of the Dead Soldier," *Cattaraugus Union*, December 11, 1863.

14. "Identification," unidentified, undated clipping, courtesy of Allan L. Cox.

15. "The Hummiston Orphans," *Philadelphia North American and United States Gazette*, November 26, 1863, 2; "Sergeant Hummiston's Children," 194; "New Premium Offered, *American Presbyterian*, December 10, 1863, 198.

16. "Sergeant Hummiston and His Family," *American Presbyterian*, December 17, 1863, 201; "Rev. Mr. Ogden's Letter," *American Presbyterian*, December 17, 1863, 202; "Sergeant Hummiston and His Family," *Philadelphia Daily Evening Bulletin*, December 17, 1863, 1; "Sergeant Hummiston's Children," *American Presbyterian*, December 3, 1863, 194. Philinda was examined for membership in the church on November 21, 1863, and admitted as a communicant the next day. Session minutes, Portville Presbyterian Church, courtesy of Ronda S. Pollock.

17. "Editor Olean Times," *Cattaraugus Freeman*, December 16, 1863.

18. Quarterly Returns of Deceased Soldiers, Fourth Quarter, 1863, 154th New York Volunteers, National Archives; muster roll, Company C, 154th New York, December 31, 1863, National Archives; "Sergeant Hummiston and His Family," *American Presbyterian*, 201.

19. John W. Summers to Mrs. Hummiston Dear Lady, December 20, 1863, courtesy of Allan Cox.

20. Summers became another victim of the war. He was wounded at Petersburg,

A Widow and Her Orphans

Virginia on April 2, 1865, and died fifteen days later. Samuel P. Bates, *History of Pennsylvania Volunteers* (Harrisburg: B. Singerly, State Printer, 1869), Vol. 2, 978.

21. "Sergeant Humiston," *Gettysburg Compiler*, September 4, 1865; *Revised Report of the Select Committee Relative to the Soldiers' National Cemetery, Together with the Accompanying Documents, as Reported to the House of Representatives of the Commonwealth of Pennsylvania* (Harrisburg: Singerly & Myers, State Printers, 1865), 3, 7–12, 14–15, 64, 134–141, 147–152; Gregory A. Coco, *A Strange and Blighted Land; Gettysburg: The Aftermath of a Battle* (Gettysburg: Thomas Publications, 1995), 109–122; William A. Frassanito, *Early Photography at Gettysburg* (Gettysburg: Thomas Publications, 1995), 167–173.

22. "Gallery of Soldiers' Orphans," *American Presbyterian*, December 31, 1863, 210.

23. James L. Paul, *Pennsylvania's Soldiers' Orphan Schools* (Harrisburg: Lane S. Hart, 1877), 17, 31–53.

CHAPTER 11

Celebrity

PUBLICITY CONTINUED TO spread the Humiston story during the last days of 1863 and the beginning of 1864. The day after the *American Presbyterian* printed Isaac Ogden's account of "Sergeant Hummiston and His Family," the *Philadelphia Inquirer* excerpted it. "We append a brief sketch of his history, the first, we believe, that has been published," the *Inquirer* shamelessly claimed. On Christmas Day 1863 the *Inquirer* warned the public that an unscrupulous photographer had pirated the popular photograph of Sergeant Humiston's children, "and is thus defrauding the orphans of the money which should be given for their support." The same item noted that Dr. Bourns expected to leave that morning on his trip to Portville to visit the Humiston family.[1]

Various publications ushered in the New Year with Humiston stories. The *Portrait Monthly*—a magazine published in New York, full of biographies and woodcuts of generals and "sketches of departed heroes"—printed the "Whose Father Was He?" article in its January 1864 issue. The question was answered in the February number with the "Identity Ascertained" piece.[2]

Although it saw some circulation in magazines, the Humiston tale primarily appeared in newspapers. General monthly magazines of the war years tended to avoid literature of the conflict. Editors knew that the public sought to escape the war's burdens, and they shaped the content of their publications accordingly. Most often, magazine articles offered readers a respite from the battlefield's horror, rather than confront them with it in stories like that of the dead soldier and his ambrotype.[3]

The Humiston story received its widest circulation when it ran in the January 2, 1864, issue of the popular, nationally distributed *Frank Leslie's Illustrated Newspaper*. A fanciful woodcut after an unnamed artist pictured "An Incident of Gettysburg—The Last Thought of a Dying Father." The illustration depicted Amos lying in a bleak landscape, ambrotype clutched to his chest, his rifle, cartridge box, and forage cap by his side. Dead horses and another dead soldier sprawled in the background near abandoned artillery pieces. Vultures circled the sky. The scene was wholly imaginary, but the accompanying short article praised the artist nonetheless:

One of the most touching scenes of the battlefield of Gettysburg, called up more vividly now by the recent great solemnity at that hallowed ground, was the finding among the slain the body of a Union soldier who, receiving his death wound, had, as life ebbed slowly away, drawn from next his heart the likeness of his motherless children, and gone to his Maker with it pressed to his lips. This touching scene affected all. The most earnest search was made to discover the hapless children of so devoted a father, who proved to be a volunteer from New York. Our Artist has happily caught the spirit of the scene, and words would but mar the impression.[4]

The author took a few liberties with the story by adding some melodramatic touches: the expiring kiss, the "motherless" children. It is also interesting to note that Amos Humiston had been reduced to anonymity in his own tale, referred to simply as "a volunteer from New York."

Curiosity about the celebrated soldier motivated some bureaucrats in his home state to try to find out more about him. A representative or correspondent of the Bureau of Military Statistics gathered information about Amos from relatives, and a brief biographical sketch was included in the bureau's first annual report, issued in January. A copy of the famous ambrotype was framed for the bureau's collection of artifacts, and the public was informed it could order copies at the bureau's Albany office. Newspapers reprinted the biographical sketch, among them the *Owego Times*, whose readers now realized that the hero of the story was a former hometown boy.[5]

When the great Metropolitan Fair was held in New York City in 1864, the Bureau of Military Statistics loaned the framed picture of the Humiston children for exhibition. A photograph taken at the fair captured it on display along with a large quantity of artfully arranged weapons, uniforms, and other military objects. The bazaar was one of a series held in cities and towns in the North to benefit the United States Sanitary Commission, a soldiers' relief agency similar in purpose to the USCC (but lacking the religious element). The Metropolitan Fair opened on April 4 in specially constructed buildings in and near Union Square and had a lucrative nineteen-day run, earning more than a million dollars for the Sanitary Commission's treasury.[6]

Framed with the large-sized print of the Humiston children on display at the sanitary fair was a carte-de-visite reproduction of the ambrotype portrait of Amos Humiston. Philinda Humiston evidently had the ambrotype copied, perhaps at the request of the Bureau of Military Statistics, perhaps to provide family members with a memento of Amos. The copy work was done by ambrotypist and photographer Mason Otis of Cuba, New York, a village in Allegany County about fifteen miles from Portville.[7]

In a Sanitary Commission catalog of the many items on display at the Metropolitan Fair, the Humiston images led off the list of portraits, photographs, and drawings. A short paragraph recounted the story: "These pictures [of the children] are being sold for the benefit of the family, and further facts can be ascertained at the Bureau of Military Statistics concerning them."[8]

Sales of the cartes-de-visite of the Humiston children continued to be brisk. Now that the family had been identified, the Philadelphia photographers producing the photographs made some changes. Frank, Fred, and Alice were named in a caption on the face of the mount, and a short explanation was printed on the reverse: "This is a copy of the Ambrotype found in the hands of Sergeant Humiston of the 154th N.Y. Volunteers as he lay dead on the Battle field of Gettysburg. The proceeds of the sale of the copies are appropriated to the support and education of the Orphan Children." Certain businesses were authorized as agents for the sale of the cartes-de-visite. In Gettysburg, for example, Dr. Robert Horner offered them at his drugstore for twenty-five cents apiece. "They are executed in very handsome style," the *Gettysburg Compiler* commented, "and no doubt will command a ready sale."[9]

The *American Presbyterian* continued to offer the "very elegant large size photograph" of the children as a premium. "We are filling orders almost every day to those procuring us new subscribers," the paper reported in January 1864. It also noted that the picture had been "improved considerably by several of our city artists so that the blemishes on the original plate are no longer reproduced in the new picture."[10]

The popularity of the children's photograph did not deter the Philadelphia engraver Robert Whitechurch from producing an exquisite engraving of the trio. A native of England, Whitechurch took up engraving at about thirty years of age, and after three years of study he came to America in 1848. In Philadelphia he built a reputation as an excellent engraver of portraits and banknotes in the line and stipple style. His fine depiction of Frank, Fred, and Alice was framed by an ornate shield, surmounted by an eagle, with a flag motif and an inscription: "Portraits of the Children of Sergeant Amos Humiston, from the Ferrotype found upon his Breast on the Field of Gettysburg." No caption indicated the Whitechurch engraving was sold to benefit the Humistons, but it seems probable that the artist donated his profits to the family.[11]

With the children's image selling so well, another Humiston photograph was issued in Philadelphia. The highly regarded photographer Frederick Gutekunst copied Amos's life portrait and retouched it to add a beard and a uniform jacket, creating a bust image of Amos as he appeared as a soldier. Printed under the photographer's imprint on the reverse of the carte was a brief summary of the story. Gutekunst, who also produced a fine carte-de-visite version of "The Soldier's Children," implicitly passed Amos's spurious wartime portrait off as genuine. "After the discovery of his family," the caption stated, ". . . the original of this photograph was obtained." Like the image of the children, the portrait of Amos was "sold for the assistance of the dependent orphans." While patrons listened to organ music while waiting to be photographed at Gutekunst's popular Arch Street studio, a photo-reproduction business on the premises produced Humiston cartes-de-visite by the hundreds.[12]

The Humiston story made its first known appearance in a book in 1864. Horatio B. Hackett, a professor of theology and author of several religious books, was collecting material "illustrative of religious faith and principle, patriotism and bravery in our army," when he came across "The Dead Soldier and the Daguerreotype" in the *American Presbyterian*. Hackett paraphrased the article for his book, and before *Christian Memorials of the War* was published, he was able to add a footnote mentioning the identification of the fallen father.[13]

By the time Hackett's book was released, another poignant chapter had been added to the Humiston story.

Four of Portville's leading citizens were on hand to greet Dr. J. Francis Bourns when he arrived at the Erie Railroad depot in Olean on Saturday, January 2, 1864. The party traveled six miles to Portville, where Dr. Bourns was welcomed by the Reverend Isaac Ogden at his parsonage, next to the Presbyterian church on Main Street. With Pastor Ogden were the Humistons' good friend, blacksmith Adam T. Warden, and the Reverend John Heyl Vincent. (Vincent was in Portville by happenstance. He was on his way home to Illinois after returning from a lengthy tour of Europe, Egypt, and Palestine, and had stopped in Portville to visit his wife Elizabeth's family, the Dusenburys. Known as an impressive orator and an expert on Sunday school education, the balding, bearded Methodist clergyman could also boast a personal friendship with the Union's preeminent general, Ulysses S. Grant.)[14]

Bourns, Vincent, and their Portville hosts chatted at the parsonage for about an hour, and then Adam Warden went ahead to notify Philinda Humiston of the impending visit. A short while later, Ogden, Vincent, and Bourns proceeded to the Humiston home. Philinda and the children greeted the visitors with what the men described as a quiet but warm-hearted welcome. "There was no *scene*—no acting," they reported, "but undemonstrative as was the feeling of the occasion, it was deep and tender." Philinda invited her guests to sit, and when the four men settled themselves across from the family, they were touched to note that the children had inadvertently assumed the same pose as in the famous photograph: Fred in a high chair, Frank on his right and quiet, steady Alice on his left. Philinda sat beside the children, succeeding admirably in an effort to remain composed.

A few minutes of conversation led the way for Dr. Bourns to produce the ambrotype and gently hand it to Philinda. "When the relic, stained with the blood of her own husband, was presented to the wife," Pastor Ogden observed, "her hands shook like an aspen leaf, but by a strong effort she retained her composure." Doctor Bourns suggested that it would be proper to thank God for his wonderful kindness and strange providence in rewarding the prolonged efforts to find the family, and relieving them of their anxiety. The two clergymen promptly agreed, and the entire party dropped to their knees, little Freddy quick to kneel beside his new-found friend, Dr. Bourns.

In his prayer, the Reverend Ogden declared that the hand of divine providence was so clearly seen in the events that had led to the current occasion that a most devout acknowledgment of the goodness of God was an impulse and a duty. The Reverend Vincent followed with an eloquent and touching prayer of thankfulness and praise to the God of the widow, and the Father of the fatherless. "It was a scene for some master painter," Ogden thought; "one, we believe, that angels and the God of angels looked down upon with interest and delight."

The mood lightened when Bourns presented the children with several books, New Year's presents sent from Philadelphia by George Stuart, USCC chairman. The youngsters were delighted with the gifts, and while they paged through the little volumes, Dr. Bourns took Philinda aside. He handed her the money collected from sales of the children's picture and stressed to her that it was not a charitable contribution, but rather "an expression of a felt obligation from many warm hearts that sympathized with her in her sorrow." Philinda stammered an appreciative response, and the four gentlemen bid the family farewell.

A crowd filled the Portville Presbyterian Church the following day, Sunday, January 3, to attend a "Union meeting" and public reception for Dr. Bourns. Philinda and the three children were ushered to a front pew. After the usual worship service, Pastor Ogden delivered an address of welcome, assuring Bourns that Portville greeted him with great pleasure as a respected, admired, and distinguished philanthropist and friend. "The love of a parent for his children, and the love of a patriot for his country, are among the strongest emotions of the soul," Ogden declared, "and both were developed in the noble-hearted Humiston. His body, mouldering beneath the sod, attests the one, and the blood-stained ambrotype the other. The strong love of that dying father for his children has reached across the intervening months, and is the real cause of this assemblage."

Doctor Bourns expressed his hearty thanks for the kind reception and delivered to the rapt audience a vivid account of his role as the story unfolded. At its close, the Reverend O. S. Chamberlayne, pastor of the Portville Methodist Episcopal Church, took the pulpit and offered resolutions of thanks to the doctor on behalf of the family, the citizens of Portville, and the widows and orphans of the war. The resolutions were seconded in eloquent speeches by lumber tycoon William Wheeler and Pastor Vincent. "Who can tell what may spring from this little incident that has thrilled the heart of the nation?" Vincent asked. "Humiston while dying looked at his children, till a film grew over his eyes, and his hands dropped in death. That last lingering look was a rich legacy indeed. It may lead to the founding of asylums for thousands of orphaned ones over the land."

The resolutions were adopted by a unanimous vote, and Dr. Bourns returned to the podium. William H. Hayward of Baltimore had composed a poem, the doctor announced, and sent it to him to be used for the benefit of the Humiston family. Bourns then gave Hayward's verses their first public reading. "The Unknown Soldier! Who Is He?" was cleverly written in the first person from the viewpoint of the mortally wounded Amos Humiston. It was a "poetic gem," thought Pastor Ogden.

An announcement was made that Dr. Bourns had brought copies of the ambrotype to sell for the benefit of the Humistons. Photographs in different sizes were distributed throughout the church and sold in large numbers. The cartes-de-visite sold out, and a total purse of $51 was turned over to Philinda. Bourns promised that when he returned to Philadelphia, he would send a new stock of photographs to Portville.

At some point during his Portville stay, Dr. Bourns reportedly made arrangements for the Humistons to move from their isolated home into comfortable quarters in the village, close to the schoolhouse and church. This arrangement would supposedly be temporary, until ample means were provided for the family's future support.

After Bourns had returned to Philadelphia, Pastor Ogden reflected on the success of the visit and the possibilities inspired by the Humiston story. "It is the design of the Dr. and his friends in Philadelphia, to turn this most touching incident to a larger account than simply to provide comfortably for the family of Sergeant Humiston," Ogden wrote. "It is hoped that interest enough will be awakened in this subject to secure a fund to aid the families of deceased soldiers all over the land. . . . It would be a remarkable illustration of Providence, if from the little ambrotype found in the dead soldier's hands, should spring a great national charity. Small beginnings often grow to a great conclusion."[15]

An extensive account of the Portville proceedings written by Ogden made the rounds of the newspapers—from the *Olean Times* to the *Cattaraugus Freeman* and the *Owego Times*, and from the *American Presbyterian* to the *Albany Evening Journal* and other papers in condensed form. *Presbyterian* editor John Mears found in the Portville events "full justification of all the interest which we or others have taken in the pathetic case of Humiston and his family," and emphasized, "It is no mere flush of sentimentalism which gives that portrait and the happily discovered family such a place in our hearts." Mears again exhorted the public to make a commitment to care for soldiers' orphans and complimented Governor Curtin for his recent efforts in that regard.[16]

Around the time of Dr. Bourns's visit to Portville, the Humiston story was embraced by two popular American art forms, poetry and song. Prior to its public debut by Dr. Bourns, and before Amos Humiston was identified, William Hayward published "The Unknown Soldier! Who Is He?" as a broadside. An explanatory paragraph introduced the poem, described the ambrotype, and provided readers with Dr. Bourns's address. Hayward included "The Unknown Soldier!" in a collection of his poems published in 1864. A slightly condensed version of the *Philadelphia Inquirer*'s "Whose Father Was He?" article served as an introduction, and a note at the end of the verses announced that the unknown had since been identified. "We make no pretensions to being a poet," Hayward wrote in the preface to his book, "but have written merely for pastime and amusement, and to preserve in a crude manner, the remembrance of many little incidents of loyalty and affection upon the battle-field, on the part of our brave boys, who are now offering their lives in defence of their Flag and the Flag of their Fathers."[17]

Hayward's verses were set to a tune written by Wilson G. Horner, director of the National Union Musical Association of Baltimore. The song was published as sheet music, "respectfully dedicated to the orphans of the brave soldiers who have fallen in defence of their country," simultaneously by the New York firm of William A. Pond and Company and by Miller & Beacham of Baltimore. The same "Whose Father Was He?" paragraphs that introduced "The Unknown Soldier!" in Hayward's 1864 book prefaced the song. No mention of Amos was included, however, indicating that the sheet music, like the broadside, was published before he was identified. There was no notice indicating profits from the sheet music were to go to the Humistons, but it is possible that was the intention, in accordance with Hayward's purpose in writing the poem. ("The Unknown Soldier!" is reproduced in the appendix.)[18]

Perhaps the first poem inspired by the Humiston story was written by "Walter," a Union sailor aboard the side-wheel steamer *Philadelphia*, the flagship of the South Atlantic Blockading Squadron. Walter's effort reveals how rapidly the Humiston story spread. The *Philadelphia* was stationed off Morris Island, near Charleston, South Carolina, when Walter composed "The Little Ones" on October 24, 1863—a scant five days after the "Whose Father Was He?" story first appeared in the *Philadelphia Inquirer*. He was just as quick to disseminate his work: the verses appeared on the front page of the November 8 issue of the *Philadelphia Sunday Dispatch*. "The Little Ones" was also published as a broadside by an unknown printer. Walter's verses followed Amos from his tearful farewell to the children at home to his final words to their pictured form on the battlefield ("God keep ye dear, dear little ones!"), and encouraged the orphans to look to Jesus for protection.[19]

At a later date an anonymous author composed "The Three Watchers," verses "of touching beauty and power," in the opinion of Francis Bourns. The poet described the children at home, faces pressed to the windowpane as they awaited their father's return, and then abruptly shifted to the battlefield, where the same "three little cherub faces smile through the bloodstained glass" of the ambrotype. Like Walter's poem, "The Three Watchers" incorporated a strong religious message, with the orphaned children finding ultimate solace in God.[20]

A new journal titled the *Philadelphia Photographer* published a poem inspired by the Humiston story, "The Dead Soldier's Children," in its January 1864 inaugural issue. The poet, identified only by the initials "K.H.W.," had composed the verses before Amos's identity was determined. In them, the unknown soldier was discovered by a burial squad, and "as they lift to lay him in his grave, a card falls flutteringly." "And by this little picture's aid," hoped K.H.W., "their father's fate be known." In a footnote, the publication's editor briefly related the story, noted that the identification had been made, and remarked on the key role photography had played in the events. "The picture has been copied by some of our best Photographers, and is being sold in large quantities by several leading houses," he wrote. "Being so intimately connected with the art we advocate, we give it this notice, and publish the above beautiful lines inspired by looking upon their three tiny faces."[21]

The most popular poetic and musical effort inspired by the Humiston story was the winner of a contest sponsored by the *American Presbyterian*. John Mears announced the competition in the issue of December 17, 1863, suggesting the incident of the fallen father was "a suitable topic for our lyrical contributors." A cash award was offered for the chosen poem, and January 15, 1864, was set as the deadline. But only three poems had been received by that date, and in the meantime, Mears had neglected to make more announcements regarding the contest, "having overlooked the matter in the press of business attendant upon the opening year." (Among that business was an expansion of the paper from four to eight pages per issue.) The editor now renewed the call for poems and extended the deadline to February 1, 1864. That request brought several more responses.

The winning poem was written by one of the country's most popular entertainers, James Gowdy Clark, a poet, composer, and balladeer who routinely filled halls during his tours of the North. Clark's songs and poems were widely reprinted in newspapers, and his compositions were popular sellers as sheet music. A poem written by the celebrated vocalist, John Mears knew, would see a wide circulation beyond the pages of the *American Presbyterian*. "Out of several pieces sent us on the death of Sergeant Humiston," Mears wrote in announcing the contest winner, "we unhesitatingly give the preference to the following simple, sweet verses, very well adapted to music, which the author has already provided for them, and will soon publish." Mears described Clark as "an adept in this kind of work," and predicted the poet's verses would rival his previous compositions in popularity.[22]

Clark had been a professional musician for a decade when the Civil War broke out. Born in central New York State in 1830, he showed a boyhood aptitude for setting his favorite poems to melodies. After an unsuccessful stint clerking in a store, the young man dedicated himself exclusively to his music. His breakthrough came when his mother asked him to write a hymn and was overcome by teary emotion on reading the result. The verses circulated widely in the press, appeared in hymnals, inspired scores of imitations and plagiarisms, and launched the career of a prolific songwriter and poet.

Clark took to the road about 1851 as musical director of Ossian's Bards, a popular concert troupe organized and run by Ossian E. Dodge, a well-known humorist. Clark's compositions for the Bards were published by a Boston firm in alliance with publishers in other large cities, and proved to be hits. When the group disbanded, Clark toured as a solo artist. His concerts were a crowd-pleasing combination of sentimental and humorous songs, and lectures and recitations. He prided himself on attracting the more cultured and refined elements of the communities in which he appeared. Clark publicized his concerts by sending notes to newspaper editors along with a gushing blurb from a review: "He is the best ballad singer in America. He is the best ballad writer living. He is a whole-souled man. He is a Christian gentleman. He can make you laugh, he can make you cry. Do not stay at home. He will civilize you, humanize you, and delight you."

When the war opened, Clark was living with his wife and two young daughters in Dansville, New York, and was a familiar figure in concert halls in the western part of the state. (He made a swing through Cattaraugus County in October 1863 and appeared in Olean and Ellicottville, among other towns.) He was of prime age for a soldier but chose not to enlist. About a month after the Battle of Gettysburg, the *Cattaraugus Union* reported that Clark had been drafted and sarcastically suggested he would be singing a new song: "We are coming with $300, Father Abraham"—a play on the title of a popular song written by one of Clark's competitors to celebrate the volunteers of 1862, "We Are Coming Father Abraham, Three Hundred Thousand Strong," and an insinuation that Clark would pay the $300 fee to hire a substitute rather than serve himself. But Clark served the Union in his own way, expressing staunch support of the cause in patriotic verse and song, and enhancing home front morale with his performances. When he sat down at his melodeon to entertain wartime audiences, the program included his popular compositions "Let Me Die with My Face to the Foe," "The Voice of the Army," "The Sword That My Brave Boy Wore," and other martial songs. His war poetry, widely reprinted in the press, reached soldier and civilian alike, and he gave concerts to benefit the Sanitary Commission and the Soldiers' Aid Society.[23]

What better bard to interpret the Humiston story? Clark's finished poem featured some rhythmic repetition and a catchy title—"The Children of the Battle Field"—that soon became synonymous with the well-known image of Frank, Fred, and Alice Humiston. Each of the three verses began with the line, "Upon the field of Gettysburg," and ended with a prayer by Amos as the refrain: "Oh! Father, shield the soldier's wife, and for his children care." The first verse had Amos—a hero of the North who had rushed from his happy home to defend freedom, albeit "a man of humble fame"— gazing at the picture of his children while waiting to enter the fray. In the second verse Amos braved "the awful flood of shot, and steel, and shell," as the battle raged, a "Champion of the Free." A full moon illuminated the battlefield's pale corpses in verse 3, and Amos was depicted in his famous pose, staring at the image of his children, "three sweet stars" arisen in memory's sky to light his way over the sea of death.

Clark's poem was published in the February 4, 1864, issue of the *American Presbyterian* and subsequently circulated in the newspapers. The *Cattaraugus Freeman* printed it on February 10, 1864, noting that it came from "the pen of a gifted and valued friend."[24]

The music Clark composed for his verses included a straightforward melody in the key of A flat, set to 2/4 time. A dramatic touch was added by drawing out the line "and for his children care" with extended rests over a minor chord, and returning to the major to repeat the line. The result, a polished production by a veteran songsmith, was published by the Phila-delphia firm of Lee & Walker in April 1864. About the time the sheet music was issued, Clark sang the song to great applause at the Union League in Philadelphia, and the *American Presbyterian* reprinted the poem in its columns.[25]

"The Children of the Battle Field" was dedicated by Clark to Dr. Bourns, "honored for his living patriotism and philanthropy." The front cover of the April 1864 edition featured a rather crude lithograph of Frank, Fred, and Alice. A second edition, published in October 1864, was graced with a finer lithograph of the children set within a flag-motif shield draped in foliage. An introductory page contained a sketch of the Humiston story, a commendation by *American Presbyterian* editor John Mears, and a notice: "The net proceeds of the sales of this Music are reserved for the support and education of the Orphan Children." The sheet music sold for fifty or sixty cents a copy, higher than average (Hayward and Horner's "The Un-known Soldier!" sheet music sold for a quarter or thirty cents), but the price did not deter the public from buying it in large quantities.[26]

Clark immediately added "The Children of the Battle Field" to his con-cert repertoire, and it proved to be one of his most popular war songs. When he toured Cattaraugus County late in 1864, the *Cattaraugus Free-man* described his compositions, including "The Children of the Battle Field," as "beautiful creations of genuine poetic genius," and praised the "fervor and pathos" of Clark's singing. "No one can hear him without loving the man," the paper declared, "and forming high resolves to lead a better life." Clark himself was apparently pleased with his prize-winning effort. When two anthologies of his poems and songs were published dec-ades after the war, "The Children of the Battle Field" was included in both.[27]

Of course, the *American Presbyterian* endorsed Clark's sheet music. "The music is very pleasing," editor Mears wrote, "and the song well worth possessing as a worthy memorial of one of the most touching incidents of the war." The newspaper offered a copy as a premium to new subscribers from October 1864 until February 1865, noting in each issue that the song had been sung to great applause, "especially in Western New York." (The song is reproduced in the appendix.)[28]

In addition to the poems and songs written specifically to commemorate the Humiston story, Amos's tale seems to have inspired other verse. Surely echoes of the Humiston incident were to be heard in W. A. Devon's poem, "The Night After the Battle," in which a soldier kissed the bloodstained photograph of his sweetheart as he died. And in a poem titled "Carte de

Visite," by an anonymous author, a furloughed soldier, visiting a young woman, shows her the photograph of a dead comrade. With a "passionate, hopeless, heart-broken wail," she discovers it is a portrait of her lover.[29]

Amos's story also brought forth genuine accounts of similar incidents. A Rochester, New York, correspondent of the *American Presbyterian* wrote of an encounter with a soldier in a horse car. The veteran told of tending to the wounded and dying after a bloody battle during the Seven Days fighting in 1862. He found a dead comrade leaning against a fence in a sitting posture. "With one cold hand he was still clasping his gun, and in the other, extended at arm's length, there rested a fair daguerreotype of what was supposed to be a daughter; and his leaden eye balls were still turned in that direction, as though he were gazing upon the precious face and form." The soldier who found the corpse, himself a father, was overcome by his discovery and burst into tears at the sight. He gently removed the picture, and sent it to the dead man's surviving relatives, where "a precious relic in some home circle that must be." Although that fallen father's identity was never in doubt, John Mears still thought his story was "A Match for Humiston."[30]

James G. Clark's song title became so closely linked to the Humiston story in general, and the image of the children in particular, that it was used to name a new edition of the carte de visite published by the expanded Philadelphia firm of Wenderoth, Taylor & Brown. The carte also included a notice below the usual inscription on the back: "This Picture is private property, and can not be copied without wronging the Orphans for whom it is published. Philadelphia, Dec. 3d, 1864. J. Francis Bourns."[31]

The Humistons were firmly embedded in American popular culture in 1864. Newspaper stories, photographs, poems, and songs had made their sad tale a familiar one to hundreds of thousands of Northerners. Thousands of them responded to the pathos by purchasing cartes-de-visite and sheet music, but what happened to the money raised by those sales is shrouded in mystery. Evidence indicates the Humistons did not benefit greatly from the philanthropic efforts made on their behalf. More seriously, fifty years after the war, the family claimed they were cheated by Dr. Bourns, insinuating that he appropriated the money for his own use.

"It is believed that my mother received a portion of the money raised by the sale of the pictures," Alice Humiston told a reporter for a Gettysburg newspaper in 1914. "This is not so. . . . The public may as well know this side of the story as the other." Alice sent a clipping of the resulting article to her brother Fred, along with a letter explaining her relief in breaking the family's long silence. "To tell the truth I was glad of the chance to tell our side of the case," she wrote. "Mother and I threshed the thing out more than once and I certainly understand the situation much better than I would have if it had not been so." Nonetheless, revealing her accusation had been made with some reluctance, Alice admitted: "Frank and I have always agreed as to how things were and how they should have been, and we did not see any necessity of letting Tom, Dick and Harry into the situation." Bourns had taken advantage of Philinda Humiston's naiveté to enrich himself, Alice claimed. "If Mother had been older and a little more used to the ways of the world Dr. Bourns would not have sit at his ease all his life and she living the way she had to. I boil every time I think of it."[32]

Philinda Humiston's work as a seamstress and Portville charity brought in some money. A reliable source of income, albeit a minimal one, was eventually provided by the federal government. On June 8, 1864, Philinda appeared before the prothonotary of the McKean County Court of Common Pleas in Smethport, Pennsylvania, and signed an application for a widow's army pension. A clerk filled in the blanks on a printed document as Philinda provided information. Two Smethport acquaintances signed the document as witnesses. Philinda appointed her uncle, William A. Williams of Smethport, who was present with his wife, as her agent and attorney in presenting the claim.

The application slowly worked its way through the bureaucracy, but months passed without a resolution to the case. The Pension Office in Washington apparently requested additional proof of the marriage. Morris and Sarah Humiston and the Reverend Asa Brooks swore out depositions in Tioga County in the spring of 1866 attesting to Amos and Philinda's wedding. Philinda was finally admitted to the rolls on May 26, 1866, to receive a pension of eight dollars a month. Her certificate was dated June 5, 1866—three days short of a year after she applied. The payments were retroactive to July 1, 1863, the date of Amos's death.[33]

In the meantime, the Humistons scraped by. A new round of publicity made the papers in May 1865, about a month after the war ended, announcing that "some benevolent persons" in Philadelphia and New York were endeavoring to raise a fund for the support and education of the Humiston children through sales of the cartes-de-visite. "A small sum has already been paid over to Mrs. Humiston," the *New York Times* noted, "but quite insufficient for the support of herself and children."[34]

A few months later, a new version of the "Children of the Battle Field" carte-de-visite was issued by Wenderoth, Taylor & Brown. An added notation indicated that the beneficiary of sales of the picture had changed: "The copies are sold in furtherance of the National Sabbath School effort to found in Pennsylvania an Asylum for dependent Orphans of Soldiers; in memorial of our Perpetual Union. This Picture is private property, and can not be copied without wronging the Soldiers' Orphans for whom it is published. Philadelphia, Sept. 23d, 1865. J. Francis Bourns."[35] The long-hoped-for dream of a soldiers' orphans' home, voiced so often by the *American Presbyterian*, was at last being realized. But was it being realized to the detriment of the Humiston family?

Dr. Bourns evidently did make good on his promise to find the Humistons a new home in Portville. It was reported that a comfortable house in the village was purchased for them from the profits from the photographs and the "Children of the Battle Field" sheet music. Writing to a supporter in the summer of 1865, Dr. Bourns declared that "the widow Humiston and her three little ones are in comfortable possession of their new home—a house and lot—I have been able to purchase for them at Portville, New York." The doctor also asserted he was providing for the family's support. "From the first, after effecting their discovery," he wrote, "I have been enabled to furnish them with support; and my confident trust is to have it in my power to provide amply for their future, including the education of the children."[36]

But the Humistons felt that they were defrauded by Dr. Bourns in the Portville real estate transaction in addition to being bilked of the profits from sales of the photographs and sheet music. In her postwar accusations, Alice Humiston charged the doctor with swindling the family when the house was sold: "Even the money gotten for the sale of the property in Portville, purchased out of the fund . . . was appropriated and never one cent returned."[37]

No evidence of the purchase or sale of the Portville house has been uncovered, and exactly when the Humistons occupied it is unknown. When a New York State census taker visited the village in 1865, he found Philinda and the children living in the household of Lanson Smith, a fifty-two-year-old mechanic, his thirty-seven-year-old wife, Arley, and their fourteen-year-old son, C. H. A year later, the Humistons left Portville.[38]

Let us care for the soldiers' widows and orphans, President Lincoln admonished the nation in his second inaugural address in March 1865. A few weeks later, the president was dead and the war was over. The country began the process of putting the conflict behind it and struggling with the issue of reconstruction. It seemed that the tale of the Humistons would recede into memory, a well-known anecdote of the war days. But that summer an astonishing report put the family back into the newspapers.

The *Baltimore Clipper* broke the story on August 22, 1865, under the headline, "An Affecting Story Spoiled." Sergeant Humiston had returned to his family and home in Portville! He had not been killed at Gettysburg as supposed, the *Clipper* reported, but captured and confined as a prisoner of war, and just recently released. "Is not the Sergeant unwise to relinquish so envious a fame and spoil such a touching story by returning to this life?" the writer wondered. The Baltimore paper attributed the account to the *Olean Times*, but hedged the story with a disclaimer: "Precisely how much of fact, of mistake, and of humbug are mixed up with the whole affair we are at present unable to determine."[39]

Such miraculous resurrections were not unheard of. Two dramatic examples involved members of the 154th New York. Private William Cone of Company I was reported killed at Chancellorsville, a funeral sermon was preached in his home town of Salamanca, and his wife applied for his bounty money and back pay. "Luckily, however, she was in no hurry to marry again," the *Cattaraugus Freeman* reported seven months after the battle, "for a few weeks ago her husband came home all right, having only been wounded and a prisoner in Rebel hands." In a similar case, Private Robert Grinard of Amos's Company C was also reported killed at Chancellorsville. His funeral sermon was delivered, and an attorney secured his bounty, pay, and a pension for his Allegany wife and family. After two years of grief, the Grinards were becoming reconciled to his death when he arrived home in good health in August 1865. "It is said his wife was about to be married again," the *Cattaraugus Union* reported, "and Mr. Grinard seems to have arrived none too soon. He claims to have been a prisoner for more than two years."[40]

There was no such happy ending to the Humiston story. As quickly as the Baltimore report circulated, articles ran to refute it. Francis Bourns wrote to Isaac Ogden in Portville regarding the account, and the doctor released the minister's reply to the press: "There is not a word of truth in the absurd rumor." A passage from a letter written by Gettysburg's David Wills also debunked the story, relating how Sergeant Humiston was buried on Judge Russell's lot and later reinterred in the Soldiers' National Cemetery.[41]

Amos Humiston never returned to Portville. Instead, Philinda, Frank, Alice, and Fred joined him in Gettysburg.

NOTES

1. "Sergeant Hummiston and His Family," *Philadelphia Inquirer*, December 18, 1863, 2; "The Photograph of Sergeant Hummiston's Children," *Philadelphia Inquirer*, December 25, 1863, 1.

2. "Whose Father Was He?" *Portrait Monthly* (January 1864): 107; "Identity Ascertained," *Portrait Monthly* (February 1864): 119; Frank Luther Mott, *A History of American Magazines 1850–1865* (Cambridge: Belknap Press of Harvard University Press, 1957), 176.

3. Mott, *A History of American Magazines 1850–1865*, 493.

4. Illustration, "An Incident of Gettysburg—The Last Thought of a Dying Father," and article, "Reminiscence of Gettysburg. The Last Thought of a Dying Father," *Frank Leslie's Illustrated Newspaper*, January 2, 1864, 235, 236.

5. Lois Ann (Humiston) Goodwin to My Dear Niece Alice [Humiston], September 8, 1896, courtesy of David Humiston Kelley; New York State Bureau of Military Statistics, *First Annual Report of the Chief of the Bureau of Military Statistics* (N.p., January 29, 1864), 32; "Amos Humiston," *Owego Times*, February 4, 1864.

6. William Y. Thompson, "Sanitary Fairs of the Civil War," *Civil War History* 4, no. 1 (March 1958): 58–60.

7. Robert C. Marcotte to Editor, *Military Images* 3, no. 1 (July–August 1981), 3; Ellsworth Swift to author, September 13, 1996. Otis opened his Cuba studio about September 1863 and operated it until December 1865. *Cuba True Patriot*, September 4, 1863, December 1, 15, 1865.

8. United States Sanitary Commission, Department of Arms and Trophies, Metropolitan Fair, *Catalogue of the Museum of Flags, Trophies and Relics* (New York: Charles O. Jones, 1864), 52.

9. Kathleen Collins, "Photographic Fundraising: Civil War Philanthropy," *History of Photography* 11, no. 3 (July–September 1987): 181; William Gladstone, "The Children of the Battle Field," *Military Images* 2, no. 5 (March–April 1981): 9; "Our Citizens Are Familiar with the Story of Sergeant Humiston," *Gettysburg Compiler*, February 8, 1864.

10. "Sergeant Hummiston's Children," *American Presbyterian*, January 7, 1864, 5.

11. W. S. Baker, *American Engravers and Their Works* (Philadelphia: Gebbie & Barrie Publishers, 1875), 182–183.

12. Cartes-de-visite of "Sergt. Amos Humiston, Of the 154th N.Y. Vols." and "Frank, Frederick & Alice," by Frederick Gutekunst, 704 & 706 Arch Street, Philadelphia, courtesy of Henry Deeks; Kenneth Finkel, *Nineteenth-Century Photography in Philadelphia* (New York: Dover, 1980), 3, 218.

13. Horatio B. Hackett, *Christian Memorials of the War: or, Scenes and Incidents Illustrative of Religious Faith and Principle, Patriotism and Bravery in Our Army, with Historical Notes* (Boston: Gould and Lincoln, 1864), 201.

14. Isaac G. Ogden, "Interesting Details of a Charity Meeting at Portville," *Cattaraugus Freeman*, January 20, 1864; "Sergeant Hummiston's Family," *Waynesboro Village Record*, January 22, 1864; Leon H. Vincent, *John Heyl Vincent: A Biographical Sketch* (New York: Macmillan, 1925), 49–51, 53–80, 116–132, 158–160, 185, 201; Ruth K. McGaha, "The Journals of S. Elizabeth Dusenbury, 1852–1857; Portrait of a Teacher's Development" (Ph.D. diss., Iowa State University, 1990), 226.

15. Ogden, "Interesting Details of a Charity Meeting at Portville," 1; "Sergeant Hummiston's Family," *Waynesboro Village Record*, January 22, 1864.

16. Ogden, "Interesting Details of a Charity Meeting at Portville," 1; "Interesting Details of a Meeting at Portville," *Owego Times*, February 4, 1864; "The Dead

Celebrity

Soldier's Ambrotype of His Three Children," unidentified clipping, reprinting an item from the *Albany Evening Journal*; "Dr. Bourns at Portville," *American Presbyterian*, January 14, 1864, 12; "Dr. Bourns in Portville," *American Presbyterian*, January 21, 1864, 19; "Dr. Bourns at Portville," *American Presbyterian*, January 28, 1864. John Heyl Vincent also wrote an account of the Humiston incident and the Portville proceedings, which was published in midwestern newspapers. According to Vincent, Bourns abandoned his medical practice during part of 1864 to devote himself to promoting the orphan relief drive. His plan was to raise $1,000 for each of the Humiston children and devote additional funds to other needy orphans. An inner voice had told Bourns, "From the father's last look there may come means to provide for hundreds and thousands of helpless ones." Vincent also reported that Bourns presented an enlarged, tinted copy of the children's portrait to the family during his visit to the Humiston home. Of that visit, Vincent wrote, "It was a touching scene. The plain, quiet home—the simple-hearted children, delighted with these little gifts from strangers—the stricken widow, trembling as she grasped and gazed long upon the sacred relic, and wondered at the Providence which made it such a minister of aid and consolation." "The Dead Soldier and the Ambrotype," *Lafayette [Indiana] Daily Journal*, June 22, 1864. My thanks to Mark D. Jaeger of West Layfayette, Indiana, for bringing this article to my attention.

17. Wm. H. Hayward, Esq., "The Unknown Soldier! Who Is He?" broadside, n.p., 1863, courtesy of Michael J. Winey; William H. Hayward, *Camp Songs for the Soldier and Poems of Leisure Moments* (Baltimore: Henry A. Robinson, 1864), 3, 28–30.

18. Gen. W. H. Hayward and Maj. Wilson G. Horner, *The Unknown Soldier (Who Is He?)* (New York: William A. Pond & Co.; Baltimore: Miller & Beacham, n.d.).

19. Walter, "The Three Little Ones," *Homestead Journal* 1, no. 1 (January 1869): 3; *Philadelphia Sunday Dispatch*, November 8, 1863: 1; broadside version in the C. Fiske Harris Collection on the Civil War and Slavery, Providence (Rhode Island) Public Library; Paul H. Silverstone, *Warships of the Civil War Navies* (Annapolis: Naval Institute Press, 1989), 109.

20. "The Three Watchers," "The Poems," *Homestead Journal* 1, no. 2 (March 1869): 1, 11.

21. K.H.W., "The Dead Soldier's Children," and editor's footnote, *Philadelphia Photographer* 1, no. 1 (January 1864): 15.

22. "Poem Wanted," *American Presbyterian*, December 17, 1863, 201; "The Prize Poem," *American Presbyterian*, January 21, 1864, 21; "The Prize Poem," *American Presbyterian*, February 4, 1864, 33.

23. George Birdseye, "America's Song Composers. XIV.—James G. Clark," *Potter's American Monthly* (July 1880): 20–24; James Gowdy Clark, *Poetry and Song* (Boston: D. Lothrop and Company, 1886); James Gowdy Clark, *Poems and Songs by James Gowdy Clark* (Columbus, Ohio: Press of Champlin Printing Co., 1898); B. O. Flower, "James G. Clark, the American Laureate of Labor," *Arena* (January 1898): 54–67; B. O. Flower, *A Poet of the People and After Sixty Years* (N.p., n.d.); William Conklin, compiler, *Boyhood Reminiscences with Other Sketches [of*

H. W. DeLong, Sr.] (N.p., 1982), 60–61; 1860 U.S. Census, North Dansville, New York; Willard A. Heaps and Porter W. Heaps, *The Singing Sixties: The Spirit of Civil War Days Drawn from the Music of the Times* (Norman: University of Oklahoma Press, 1960), 259; "Concert by James G. Clark," *Cattaraugus Freeman*, October 14, 1863; "James G. Clark," *Cattaraugus Union*, August 7, 1863.

24. "The Prize Poem," *American Presbyterian*, February 4, 1864: 33; "The Melancholy Death of Sergeant Humiston," *Cattaraugus Freeman*, February 10, 1864.

25. "The Children of the Battle-Field," *American Presbyterian*, April 21, 1864: 125; "Prize Poem," *American Presbyterian*, April 28, 1864, 134.

26. James G. Clark, "The Children of the Battle Field" (Philadelphia: Lee & Walker, 1864); "Children of the Battlefield," *American Presbyterian*, October 6, 1864, 316; Heaps and Heaps, *The Singing Sixties*, 8.

27. "James G. Clark," *Cattaraugus Freeman*, December 8, 1864; Clark, *Poetry and Song*, 41–42; Clark, *Poems and Songs by James Gowdy Clark*, 56–57.

28. "Children of the Battle-Field," *American Presbyterian*, October 6, 1864, 316; "Children of the Battle-Field," *American Presbyterian*, December 15, 1864, 396.

29. W. A. Devon, *War Lyrics* (New York: Devon & Benedict, Publishers, n.d.), 37–39; Anonymous, "Carte de Visite," in John Trusedale, *The Blue Coats, and How They Lived, Fought and Died for the Union* (Philadelphia: National Publishing Co., 1867), 201–202.

30. "From Our Rochester Correspondent," *American Presbyterian*, February 25, 1864, 60.

31. "The Children of the Battle Field," carte-de-visite by Wenderoth, Taylor & Brown, 912–914 Chestnut Street, Philadelphia.

32. "Visit Recalls Wartime Story," *Gettysburg Star and Sentinel*, October 31, 1914; Alice Humiston to Dear Fred, October 28, 1914, courtesy of David Humiston Kelley.

33. Amos Humiston pension file, National Archives.

34. "The Soldier's Children," *New York Times*, May 15, 1865, 2.

35. William Gladstone, "The Children of the Battle Field," *Military Images* 2, no. 5 (March–April 1981): 9.

36. "The Family of Serg't. Humiston," *American Presbyterian*, July 6, 1865, 212.

37. Broadside, "Story," Office of the National Homestead, Philadelphia, n.d.; "Visit Recalls Wartime Story," *Gettysburg Star and Sentinel*, October 31, 1914.

38. Kenneth Kysor, Cattaraugus County Historian, to author, January 15, March 4, 1997; 1865 New York State Census, Town of Portville.

39. "An Affecting Story Spoiled," *Baltimore Clipper*, August 22, 1865, 4.

40. "The Romance of War," *Cattaraugus Freeman*, December 2, 1863; "Returned," *Cattaraugus Union*, August 24, 1865.

41. "An Affecting Story Spoiled," *Gettysburg Compiler*, August 28, 1865; "A Report about Sergt. Humiston Contradicted," *New York Times*, September 3, 1865; "Sergeant Humiston," *Gettysburg Compiler*, September 4, 1865.

CHAPTER 12

The Homestead

IN NOVEMBER 1865 the *American Presbyterian* announced the organization the previous month of the Homestead Association, dedicated to raising funds to establish an asylum for Union soldiers' orphans. The association targeted Sunday schools—"nurseries of patriotism, as well as of piety"—as a main resource. Participating schools would receive cartes de visite of the Humiston children and copies of "The Children of the Battle Field" sheet music to distribute to their pupils. Any Sunday school contributing $25 to the fund would hold one share in the home and be entitled to name one orphan for admission. Shareholding schools would also be entitled to vote for the ultimate location of the orphanage—at Valley Forge of Revolutionary fame or on Cemetery Hill in Gettysburg. The association also appealed to the general public for funds and announced it had already raised $22,000 for the cause. While fund raising progressed, the organizers planned to house orphans on a temporary basis in Philadelphia. The announcement was signed by association president James Pollock, treasurer Peter B. Simons, and secretary J. Francis Bourns.[1]

Dr. Bourns's dream of a soldiers' orphans' home, inspired by the devotion of Amos Humiston, began its transformation to reality with the establishment of the Homestead Association. It was an auspicious start—an idea with much emotional appeal, backed by men of prominence, blessed with a hefty endowment. The money had apparently been raised by the same principals in an earlier effort to found a soldiers' and sailors' home near Philadelphia, meant to house veterans and their families (an effort that seems to have been subsumed by the orphanage drive) augmented by donations from association members, many of whom were men of means, and sales of "Children of the Battle-Field" photographs and sheet music.[2]

The association had been quietly raising funds and supporting approximately thirty orphans in Philadelphia for several months when it formally organized in March 1866 by adopting a constitution and electing officers. James Pollock, the prewar governor of Pennsylvania, declined permanent election as president on account of other obligations, but accepted a directorship. Taking his place at the head of the organization was the Reverend Matthew Simpson, bishop of the Methodist Episcopal church. Eight vice presidents (including Portville lumber magnate John Mersereau) and twenty-eight directors served as the association's governing body. Notable among the latter were Edward McPherson of Gettysburg, former congressman and clerk of the House of Representatives; James A. Garfield of Ohio, former general and future president; Nathaniel P. Banks of Massachusetts, general and congressman; and Jay Cooke, Philadelphia financier extraordinaire.[3]

Seven directors formed an executive committee to keep the closest watch over association matters. All were Philadelphians. Chairman was the Reverend Richard Newton, a doctor of divinity. Peter Simons, a jeweler and president of Philadelphia's Young Men's Christian Association, was treasurer. Dr. Bourns was general secretary, and Abraham Martin, a zealous worker in the Sunday school movement for fifty years, fondly known to devout Philadelphians as "Father Martin," was recording secretary. Rounding out the committee were druggist George W. Fahnestock and Alexander Brown, described in city directories as a "gentleman."[4]

In May 1866, the *Gettysburg Star and Sentinel* announced that "in all probability" the orphanage would be located in Gettysburg, "adding one more feature to the interesting associations connected with our later history." The Sunday school voting had favored Gettysburg over Valley Forge for the site of the orphanage, and the executive committee had recommended to the board of directors the purchase of a property known to Gettysburg residents as the Captain John Myers place, after its long-time owner. Consisting of approximately two acres on the Baltimore Pike, on the northern slope of Cemetery Hill, this property was deemed by the paper "a beautiful location." It certainly was a symbolically fitting site, directly adjacent to the Soldiers' National Cemetery and the grave of the soldier who inspired the drive for the orphanage. The lot featured a garden and orchard, a good water supply, a stable, and a large two-story brick house, built about 1837. Home to the elderly John Myers in 1863, the house was said to have been General Howard's headquarters during the battle. In the field across the pike from the dwelling were lunettes that had protected 11th Corps batteries during the battle. Myers had sold his place in November 1865, and since then the property had changed hands a second time.[5]

Two days after the announcement in the *Star and Sentinel*, on May 10, a meeting of townspeople convened at the Adams County Court House and witnessed the appointment of a local committee to aid the orphanage. Twenty-six prominent Gettysburgians were chosen, divided equally among men and women. Among them were storekeeper John Schick and lawyer Robert McCreary, both of whom had been involved in Christian Commission work after the battle, lawyer David McConaughy, photographer Charles J. Tyson, contractor William C. Stallsmith, Jane Wills, wife of attorney David Wills, and Harriet Harper, wife of *Adams Sentinel and General Advertiser* editor Robert Harper.[6]

The day after its appointment, the committee met in the lecture room of St. James Lutheran Church, across York Street from the lot where Amos Humiston had been found. Temporary officers were selected and subcommittees formed to report their progress to Dr. Bourns and seek donations from Gettysburg citizens. Committee members were assigned to oversee fund raising in four designated wards, and in their first week of work they collected $292.60. On May 14 the *Gettysburg Compiler* reported the purchase of the Myers property for $3,500, and a week later the local executive committee was authorized to conclude negotiations for the property.[7]

While the purchase was being completed, Dr. Bourns issued the first report of the Sunday school fund-raising effort. Schools affiliated with churches in Pennsylvania, New Jersey, Delaware, New York, Kentucky, Illinois, Massachusetts, and Ohio had purchased shares worth more than $4,300. Leading the way with eleven shares each were the Sunday schools of Presbyterian churches in Towanda, Pennsylvania, and Lambertville, New Jersey.[8]

In June the *Adams Sentinel* noted the former Myers home was soon to be enlarged to make it suitable for the orphanage. Committee member William Stallsmith was hired to superintend the work. Throughout the summer and into the fall, work proceeded on the building. The two-floor house was enlarged to three stories by the addition of a mansard roof (an architectural style newly fashionable in Gettysburg that summer), and the red-brick exterior was painted a light color. Costs totaled more than $5,800, considerably higher than the committee's estimate; much of the unforeseen expense was for the large amount of materials used. During the renovation, a group of Stallsmith's workers paused in their work to pose for an unidentified photographer, some of them perched on the cornice in front of the new mansard roof.[9]

In September the *American Presbyterian* published a lengthy article in support of the orphanage, recapitulating the now-familiar story of its inspiration. "The fidelity and affection of the dying sergeant for his own little household," John Mears wrote, "has set in motion a stream of benevolent intentions and efforts designed to embrace many bereaved families in widely different sections of the country." Considering the great good arising out of the Humiston tragedy, the editor declared, "Parental love has secured for the humble soldier his personal share in the gratitude of his countrymen, and has made his name immortal." Mears then revealed that the Humiston family would continue to be connected to the Homestead. Philinda Humiston had accepted a position as the orphanage's housekeeper, he reported, and Frank, Alice, and Fred—"whose photographs are almost as familiar as Lincoln's and Grant's to the people"—would be the first children admitted to the institution. (As it worked out, Philinda's job at the Homestead turned out to be wardrobe mistress.) "Thus," Mears thought, "there is a beautiful Providence running through the history of the Homestead Association, marking the commencement, the location of its building, and the persons of its managers and inmates; a Providence which we earnestly hope and believe will illuminate its future career." Unfortunately, the Homestead was destined to be forsaken by providence, and inklings of future trouble were not long in coming.[10]

A controversy arose when the Philadelphia board of directors insisted on opening the orphanage before work was completed on the building. "This was done in opposition to the wishes of [our local] Committee," observed Robert McCreary, who noted that the Philadelphians "were exceedingly urgent to have the institution opened and forwarded the orphans and teachers in advance of proper arrangements to receive and accommodate them." With the staff and children suddenly on their doorstep, the Gettysburg committee had no choice but to yield to the Philadelphia board's wishes. Volunteers opened their homes to the orphans and worked for days preparing carpets, bedding, and apparel to outfit the new orphanage.[11]

Philinda, Frank, Alice, and Fred arrived at Gettysburg in advance of the other orphans and staff. More than three years after they had lost him, his wife and children were reunited with Amos in Gettysburg. The day of their arrival, they visited his grave in the Soldiers' National Cemetery, and the youngsters covered his headstone with flowers.[12]

While the Humistons settled into temporary accommodations in Gettysburg, poignant scenes were enacted in Philadelphia. A large congregation gathered on a Sunday evening at the German Street Church to bid farewell to bright-eyed, seven-year-old "Willie," whose father was killed at Antietam. After hymns, prayers, and a spirited address by Abraham Martin, the Sunday school children, whose shares were sending Willie to the Homestead, came forward with their parents and other friends to bid the boy goodbye. "The scene was an affecting one," a reporter noted, "and the meeting will long be remembered by the friends of the soldiers and their fatherless children."[13]

On the morning of October 25, 1866, twenty-two soldiers' orphans, ranging in age from five to twelve, assembled at the Pennsylvania Railroad depot in Philadelphia in preparation for their trip to Gettysburg. With them were the new institution's matron, Mrs. M. Tilden, and teacher, Miss Letitia Howe. Each child was comfortably clad and carried an ample basket lunch, the gift of Father Martin. Dr. Bourns and another Philadelphia man were in charge of the children and accompanied them to Gettysburg. "The mothers and friends of the children parted from them with many tears and tender farewells," the *American Presbyterian* reported, "and in some cases with heartbreaking reluctance."[14]

That evening the orphans arrived in Gettysburg and were placed in various homes. Within five days after their arrival in the borough, the children left their temporary quarters and settled in at the Homestead. By the end of October, another half-dozen children had arrived, and Mrs. Tilden, Letitia Howe, and Philinda Humiston were "bringing things into system rapidly" at their new home.[15]

The formal inauguration of the Homestead was held on November 20. A crowd estimated at several thousand people assembled at the town square in Gettysburg at two o'clock that afternoon and formed a procession. The borough was decked out as if for a holiday, with flags flying from public buildings and private homes. A brass band led the way to Cemetery Hill, followed by officers of the Homestead and the day's speakers, clergymen, professors and students of Pennsylvania College and the Lutheran Theological Seminary, court officials, Sunday school groups (which turned out in full force), citizens, and visitors. The procession was several blocks long, and on arriving at the Homestead, it merged with another large crowd already gathered there. Observers noted that visitors from Philadelphia, Baltimore, Washington, and other large cities—many of them women— had traveled to Gettysburg to attend the ceremony.

The audience filled to overflowing the lawn and playground on the south side of the Homestead, while the orphans and speakers occupied the porch running down the side of the building. Frank, Alice, Fred, and the other children were wearing neat uniforms—the girls in light blue merino frocks, black sacks, and hats; the boys in dark blue uniforms with brass buttons, and glazed caps. Dr. Bourns presided over the ceremony. The crowd fell silent as John Mears opened the proceedings with a prayer. The children followed by singing "America." The Reverend Alexander Reed, a member of the Philadelphia board, gave an opening address emphasizing the nation's obligation to its soldiers, particularly its fallen heroes, an obligation that could only partially be met by ample support and care for their orphaned children. A select choir, perched on the makeshift balcony of the porch roof, sang an ode written especially for the occasion by Isabella James of Philadelphia. A Gettysburg committee member, the Reverend Dr. Charles A. Hay of the Lutheran Theological Seminary faculty, spoke next.

He reminded the crowd of Governor Curtin's promises to Pennsylvania regiments to care for the widows and orphans of her fallen soldiers. The Homestead, Hay declared, was one of the fulfillments of that pledge. "Indeed, it goes further," he observed, "and proposes to receive loyal soldiers' orphans from all parts of the Union; the orphans of Southern States, too, if the blood of the patriot flowed in the veins of their fallen fathers." After Hay's address the crowd sang the doxology, received a benediction, and dispersed, to reassemble that evening in Christ Lutheran Church on Chambersburg Street.

A large congregation filled the pews for the nighttime exercises. Staging had been erected at the sides of the church and in front of the pulpit, on which were seated the orphans, the speakers, and distinguished guests. The children, nattily dressed in their new outfits, attracted much attention from the audience; the readily recognizable, rosy-cheeked faces of Frank, Alice, and Fred Humiston drew particular notice. A choir performed several pieces as the crowd settled, and a prayer opened the exercises.

Edward McPherson presided over the evening ceremony. The first speaker he introduced was the Reverend Heber Newton of Philadelphia's St. Paul's Church, who gave an eloquent and emotional description of the inspiration he felt during a visit to the battlefield, the lessons to be learned from the scene of the great conflict, and the duties owed to children orphaned by the war. Newton expressed assurance that everyone who visited the battleground would return to their homes with a resolve to do more than ever for soldiers' orphans. He closed with a strong appeal to the congregation to support the Homestead with their prayers as well as their contributions.

John Mears spoke next and mesmerized the crowd with a spellbinding account of the incident that had inspired the orphanage. As Mears related the familiar story of the death and discovery of Amos Humiston, a reporter for the *Adams Sentinel* found it "thrilling" to be in the presence of Philinda and the children while their tale was told. Mears was, the reporter noted, "warmed up with a subject in which his whole soul seemed to be enlisted." The *American Presbyterian* editor spoke of two prominent ideas inspired by viewing the battlefield: the providence of God and the bravery of man. Both were to be found in the example of Amos Humiston. In the National Cemetery, Mears observed, "The very next grave to that of the sergeant is marked 'Unknown.' And why was not his marked in a similar manner? When his body was found there was no mark whatever by which to identify it. But the deep affection of the father, which still glowed in his dying breast, saved him from sinking into an unknown grave." Mears concluded his stirring address by declaring the orphan children a solemn charge upon the people of Gettysburg, and asked the citizens for their liberality, their sympathy, and their prayers for the institution.

The Reverend J. R. Warner of Gettysburg's Presbyterian Church made the closing address. He displayed the original ambrotype found in Amos's hands and spoke movingly of the dying father's affection. He described General Lee riding through the streets of Gettysburg past the dead and unknown sergeant, and declared to hearty applause that if he had a thousand lives, he would "rather in every one of them have been the dead patriot sergeant, than the living traitor-general." After a choir repeated Isabella James's ode, the entire audience closed the program by joining in singing the doxology. All told, a reporter thought, the day's events were "a fitting sequence to those which have taken place before in commemoration of the great struggle which, on the field in 1863, sealed the fate of the rebellion." For the Humiston family, the ceremonies must have had an emotional impact similar to that of the mass meeting at the Portville Presbyterian Church more than two years before.[16]

From the church the orphans were conveyed through the lamp-lit village to their new home on Cemetery Hill and a new life as inmates of an institution in an unfamiliar town. With the resilience of children, Frank, Alice, and Fred seem to have adopted tolerably well to their new situation. Their mother, however, had difficulties adjusting to life at the Homestead. When an opportunity arose to escape Gettysburg, Philinda immediately grasped it.

Life soon settled into a routine. In addition to Matron Tilden, Teacher Howe, and Wardrobe Mistress Humiston, the Homestead staff included a seamstress, a nurse, a cook, and a laundress. Both adults and children were rather cloistered. Visits from Gettysburg residents were restricted to two hours on Wednesday afternoons (although, curiously, "strangers" were allowed to visit for two hours each weekday afternoon). No visitors were admitted on Saturdays or Sundays. The instruction, household, and sanitary committees of the Gettysburg board paid weekly visits. Expenditures were initially high, with considerable expense going to furnish the various rooms, but were expected to fall as time passed. With a number of applications on file, the Gettysburg committee recommended to the Philadelphia board that the Homestead population be increased to fifty, the capacity of the house. They also urged the addition of more extensive quarters as soon as possible.[17]

A report of the committee on education also suggested expansion. The small, low-ceilinged classroom was poorly ventilated and consequently full of "very impure" air, and the cramped space hindered the teacher's management of her pupils. Nevertheless, the committee praised Letitia Howe for faithfully discharging her duties, maintaining good order, offering thorough instruction, and aiming to advance her pupils. After listening to the children recite their lessons and examining their copybooks, the committee was impressed with their accomplishments. "We think they will have a very favorable comparison, in their progress & order, with any school within our knowledge," it reported.[18]

Christmas 1866 brought a welcome break from the usual routine. In anticipation of the coming holiday, a group of Gettysburg ladies appealed to the citizenry for donations of food, to be left at committeeman Charles Tyson's photography studio. Although donations from the countryside were limited, the women gathered enough turkeys, chickens, butter, eggs, and vegetables to provide a hearty feast for the orphans. That first yuletide in Gettysburg, Frank Humiston received a token of remembrance from Portville, a carte-de-visite album presented to him by Marilla Wheeler.[19]

The season witnessed another noteworthy event at the Homestead: a visit by General Meade. The general regretted that his stop in Gettysburg was so hurried that he was unable to make a proper inspection of the orphanage. "I saw enough, however, to satisfy me that the children placed there are well cared for, and their wants, physical and mental, properly attended to," Meade assured the Reverend Richard Newton in Philadelphia. In delivering a ringing endorsement of the Homestead, Meade tacitly approved of Newton's call for an enlarged building and an increase in funds. An expansion of the orphanage's work was essential, Newton declared, "to render our Institution worthy the title National, and especially to meet in some good measure the touching appeals coming to us from many widowed mothers for their children thus left upon the country's care."[20]

Every week, applications for admission arrived from all parts of the North. The Homestead population grew to about thirty-five orphans by the beginning of 1867, and contributions from Sunday schools continued to be steady. An accounting made near the time of Meade's visit revealed almost two thousand dollars in contributions from Sunday schools across the North, many of them in Michigan.[21] On a regular basis, the Philadelphia board was receiving letters like this one from upstate New York:

To the Managers of the "National Orphan Homestead."

The enclosed sum of money $2.50 (two dollars fifty cents) was contributed by a class of little girls in our Sunday School at their recent semi-annual gathering; and when the usual question was put by the Teacher as to what disposition should be made of their collections for the past 6 months your "Homestead" was decided upon. The amount is small, but the best wishes for your prosperity both from

The Homestead

Teachers & scholars I have no doubt goes with it. May I ask for an acknowledge-
ment of its reception that they may know it has reached its destination.

Yours truly
Miss S. C. Dillingham
Salina
Onondaga Co. N.Y.
Sept 7th 1866[22]

Sales of Humiston photographs continued to provide income for the
Homestead. The inscription on the back of Frederick Gutekunst's retouched portrait of Amos was altered to indicate that the cartes-de-visite
were "sold in aid of the Orphan's Homestead." A carte-de-visite copy of
the famous ambrotype of the children by an unknown photographer was
issued in September 1867, with an out-of-date announcement by Dr.
Bourns that "these copies are sold in the furtherance of the National Sabbath School effort to found in Pennsylvania an Asylum for dependent Orphans of Soldiers; in memorial of our perpetuated Union."[23]
Another photograph produced in 1867, sold to benefit the Homestead,
documented a noteworthy event in its history. The occasion was the first
visit to Gettysburg by a most distinguished visitor: General Ulysses S.
Grant. On the morning of June 21, as Grant and his party set out to tour
the battlefield, they made a special stop at the Homestead to be photographed with the orphans. This visit was most likely arranged by Charles
Tyson, the photographer and orphanage committeeman, perhaps assisted
by committeewoman Jane Wills, who with her husband, David, hosted
Grant during his stay in Gettysburg. Tyson subsequently copyrighted the
two images he produced that morning in the name of the Homestead's
executive committee and sold prints exclusively to benefit the orphanage.
Accompanying Grant were his wartime aide-de-camp, General Horace
Porter; General Samuel W. Crawford, who had commanded a division at
Gettysburg; and Pennsylvania governor John W. Geary, who had also led
a division in the battle. (For the last year of the war, the 154th New York
had belonged to Geary's division, and the governor was perhaps aware of
the connection between the Homestead and one of his old regiments.) As
the party dismounted at the orphanage, Geary went ahead to help the staff
align the children while Tyson readied his camera in a field across the pike
from the building. Philinda had the children nattily turned out—the girls
in matching dresses and bonnets, the boys in military-style suits and caps.
While the girls formed a single line in order of height, the boys formed two
lines, with taller lads in the second rank. With the children arranged, the
four dignitaries posed between the two lines, a few steps in front of the
Homestead's open door, the immense Geary (who towered over his com-

panions even without the tall top hat he wore that day) facing General Grant. As Tyson made his exposures, the camera lens caught some peripheral figures: men and horses to the right and what appears to be several women to the left—perhaps Philinda and her staff associates.[24]

Meeting generals and governors must have been a heady experience for the Humistons. Because of their unique situation, it seems likely that Philinda and the children were singled out for special mention when they were introduced to Grant, Meade, Geary, and the others. It seems equally likely that the victors of Appomattox and Gettysburg had something special to say to the most famous inhabitants of the Homestead during their visits.

Another noteworthy event of 1867, albeit less exciting than the visit of General Grant, was the incorporation of "The National Homestead at Gettysburg" (as it was officially called) by an act of the Pennsylvania legislature, which was approved by Governor Geary on March 22. Among the corporators, in addition to familiar names from the officers and directors of the Philadelphia board, were Generals Meade and Howard, and William Hayward, author of the poem and song "The Unknown Soldier!" Dr. Bourns's brother, James Cuthbertson Burns, another corporator, was soon to take an active role in the day-to-day operations of the Homestead. In addition to the named corporators, anyone could become a member of the Homestead association for an annual contribution of five dollars or a lifetime contribution of fifty dollars.

General Meade's interest in the institution was sincere, and his support was not merely symbolic. When the corporators met in May 1867 to elect a board of directors, the general chaired the meeting. The original board was reelected with but few changes, with Bishop Simpson continuing as president. General Meade was elected a vice president.[25]

Changes in Philadelphia were mirrored by changes in Gettysburg, notably the appointment of a new staff. Gone were Matron Tilden and Teacher Howe; Philinda was the only original staff member to keep her position. The new superintendent of the Homestead was William S. Norton, a Civil War veteran who had served with the 153d New York Infantry in the Red River and Shenandoah Valley campaigns in Louisiana and Virginia, and rose through the ranks from private to first lieutenant. Assisting Norton was his wife, and rounding out the staff were Philinda Humiston, Miss E. Latimer, a Miss Clayton, and James Burns.[26]

Miss Latimer was an avid poet, and in 1867 her poem "The Unknown" was published in Philadelphia. Written for the Homestead, the verses ended with a plea for financial support of the institution. Although unstated, proceeds from sales of the slender, handsomely produced volume undoubtedly went to benefit the orphanage. But "The Unknown" was more than just a solicitation for the Homestead; it was the magnum opus of Humiston poetry. Its verses related Amos's dialogue with Philinda over his decision to enlist, the family's hopes and fears during his absence, his death on the battlefield, his burial and identification. Some of it was purely imaginary (Amos's final thoughts were described), but the sections pertaining to Philinda's experiences can be judged as accurate, considering she and the poet were friends.[27]

A revised version of "The Unknown" and three other of Miss Latimer's poems were published as a book, *Idyls of Gettysburg*, in Philadelphia in 1872. "This volume, thus presented," Miss Latimer wrote in a preface, "is to aid that most beautiful Charity, The National Orphan Homestead at Gettysburg. To this end, the net proceeds through all its editions are made sacred, while this class of orphanage shall claim, as now, protection and support." The final poem in the book, "National Orphan Homestead," described Miss Latimer's "first sight of the Gettysburg battle field, and first night at the Homestead"—a nightmare vision of the battle raging again.

The second version of "The Unknown" offers additional strong indications that Philinda shared intimate recollections with Miss Latimer. In a passage headed "Night watch near Fredericksburg," for example, there are distinct echoes of Amos's 1863 poem "To my wife." Miss Latimer's poem is consequently the closest thing we have to Philinda Humiston's own version of events.[28]

Poetry by Miss Latimer was featured prominently in several holiday commemorations that the Homestead orphans took part in during 1868. In February the public was invited to a reception and open house at the orphanage on Washington's Birthday. Twenty-five-cent tickets were sold in advance at the stores of John Schick, Henry J. Fahnestock, and Alexander D. Buehler (all members of the local Homestead committee) and met with a wide patronage. As the audience gathered on the afternoon of February 22, they found the entrance to the Homestead decorated with an illuminated motto, "God bless our Home," and the school room bedecked with flags, placards, portraits, and evergreen wreaths. There, on an elevated platform, sat sixty orphans. Representing much painstaking labor by Philinda, the thirty-five girls were attired in blue dresses with white sashes, to which were affixed shields bearing the names of states. The twenty-five boys wore shields and miniature flags.

Like the children's costumes and the Homestead's decorations, the program was a patriotic extravaganza. After a Pennsylvania College professor opened the ceremony with a prayer, four of the children recited a poem by Miss Latimer titled "Salutation to the Flag." Major Cleeton of New Haven, Connecticut, the Homestead's New England soliciting agent, read an essay on Washington's boyhood, and Lieutenant Norton read another original poem by Miss Latimer. Then came the centerpiece of the production: a

"Tribute to Washington" in the form of an allegorical tableau, with thirteen of the orphans representing the original states, declaiming poetry and song composed by Miss Latimer. David McConaughy made some remarks, Major Cleeton related his interesting experiences while raising money for the orphanage, and the children closed the program by singing "America." Then the party retired to the yard, where the youngsters enjoyed watching a local Zouave company, colorfully and exotically garbed, go through the evolutions of the drill. The entire event was such a success that it was repeated, virtually without change, on Washington's Birthday a year later.[29]

Spring and summer of 1868 brought commemorations that touched even closer the circumstances of the Homestead's orphans. That year John A. Logan, former Union general and commander of the Grand Army of the Republic, the fledgling Union veterans' organization, declared May 30 to be Memorial Day, a day to decorate the graves of the Union dead with flowers, remember their sacrifice, and be inspired to a greater patriotism by their example. Here was an occasion ideally suited to the participation of the Homestead orphans. On that first Memorial Day in Gettysburg, Frank, Alice, Fred, and the other children led a procession to the Soldiers' National Cemetery, laden with banners representing the various northern states and fragrant bouquets of spring blossoms. After a service including an address and benediction, the orphans decorated the graves, passing from row to row, chanting as they laid flowers on the stones of Amos Humiston and his thousands of silent companions:

> Lightly, lightly, lovingly tread
> O'er the dust of the patriot dead
> Strew the flowers and the triumph wreath
> O'er the brave who sleep beneath.
>
> Lightly, lightly, lovingly rest
> Wreath and flower upon each breast
> Offerings pure and sought with care
> Sacred made by love and prayer.

That evening a ceremony was held in the Homestead school room. Professor Martin Luther Stoever of Pennsylvania College offered a prayer, the children performed some vocal selections under the lead of Lieutenant Norton, and Miss Latimer read an original poem commemorating the sacrifices made in behalf of the republic by its fallen soldiers. So ended a day of bittersweet emotion for the Humistons and the other Homestead residents, a day of solemn communion with their fallen fathers.[30]

Those emotions were wrenched to the surface again a little over a month later. On the evening of July 3, 1868, the Homestead orphans presented an entertainment at Gettysburg's Agricultural Hall to mark the fifth anniversary of the battle. Tickets were offered at twenty-five cents, but a hot night kept people away, and the hall was only about two-thirds full for the performance. The interior was draped with national flags, and "Gettysburg 1863" was spelled out in large gilt letters above the platform on which the orphans and staff were seated. The boys prefaced the program with a military drill, wielding miniature rifles. Chants, prayers, salutes to the flag, poems (including one by the prolific Miss Latimer), songs, and a dress parade by the boys made up the fifteen-act presentation. Lieutenant Norton led the singing and accompanied the orphans on the melodeon, and offered a solo rendition of "Gone to the War." A string band added its music. Alice and a group of girls performed the "Gettysburg Battle Song," and the Humiston boys took part in a salute to the flag and a recollection of "Five Years Ago Today."[31]

Weeks stretched into months and slowly slid into years as time passed at the Homestead. The place took on the familiarity of home to the Humistons: the first-floor dining room, kitchen, parlor, and library; Philinda's room and the nursery on the second floor; the children's beds in the third-story dormitory; the numbered boxes Philinda made for the wardrobe room, where she mended the girls' red plaid flannel winter dresses and brown and white gingham summer checks; the porch running the length of the south side of the building, overlooking the lot where the children played; the cherry trees in the orchard. And Gettysburg scenes replaced Portville sights in the children's memory: the nearby house where Jennie Wade was killed during the battle (becoming the only civilian fatality); the Presbyterian church, where the family worshipped; the stone wall surrounding the Soldiers' National Cemetery, which Frank, Alice, and Fred loved to walk on. Not far from the Homestead playground, at the gate to the national cemetery, stood the small stone house of John McAllister. "Uncle John" was a great favorite with all of the orphans, who enjoyed the little trinkets he made for them, the walks he took with them, and the funny stories he shared with them.[32]

Miss Latimer noted enthusiasm building among the children as Christmas, and an anticipated visit from St. Nicholas, approached in 1868. Two boys from the Homestead, peeking into Gettysburg's express office, excitedly reported that forty boxes were awaiting delivery to the orphanage. The parcels arrived on Christmas Eve and were opened one by one in the school room, with the entire Homestead family present. Boots, sleds, and candy, Miss Latimer reported, "found immediate use." Many of the children received presents from their sponsoring Sunday schools, but those that did not were not forgotten, and were given a penny paper doll or a painted tin toy.

A week later, shouts of "Happy New Year!" rang in the orphanage as 1869 made its debut. Sleet and rain marred outdoor activities, but the children enjoyed a special meal prepared by friends of the Homestead and a special ceremony after evening worship, in which one of the Philadelphia boys was awarded "an elegant military toy" for compiling the most good conduct credits over the past year.[33]

The year was marked by changes. The Nortons departed and were replaced by another couple, Professor Charles E. Hilton—a Bowdoin College graduate and former head of a Philadelphia preparatory school—and his wife, Elizabeth A. Hilton. Miss Latimer assumed the title of vice principal and matron. Philinda Humiston retained the position she had now held under three superintendents. The Homestead was enlarged in the summer by the construction of a new building, a three-story clapboard structure with a mansard roof, erected by William Stallsmith. The addition was positioned south of the brick building and set back from the pike so that the new structure's front porch met the porch running along the side of the older building at a perpendicular angle. The additional space enabled the population of the Homestead to approach and then surpass a hundred orphans.[34]

The institution gained an official voice when it began publication of the *Homestead Journal* in January 1869. Edited by Dr. Bourns and published bimonthly in Philadelphia, the *Journal* included official documents relating to the Homestead, lists of donors, biographical sketches of the orphans, and poetry, including compositions by Bourns and verses inspired by Amos Humiston. In an editorial in the inaugural issue, Dr. Bourns declared that "the instruction and influences under which the children are placed are such as to make the Homestead equal to any institution of the kind in the country."[35]

By the beginning of 1869, 546 Sunday schools, from sixteen different states, had contributed at least $25 each, led by the St. John's Protestant Episcopal Sabbath School of Yonkers, New York, with $300. In a few cases, Sunday schools had received financial support from Grand Army of the Republic posts, enabling three orphans to reside at the Homestead. More than fifty men and women had contributed more than $100 each, granting them the title of "Honorary Life Director," among them the late president, James Buchanan, and a former member of the Homestead board of directors, Jay Cooke. Another seventy or so had paid $50 to become "Life Members," including Dr. Bourns, James Burns, William Hayward, Generals Howard and Meade, David McConaughy, and John A. Roebling of Trenton, New Jersey, the builder of great suspension bridges. The Homestead was in excellent financial health: treasurer Peter Simons reported $17,850.14 on hand as of January 1, 1869.[36]

The Homestead

More than two years old, the Homestead had woven itself deeply into the fabric of the Gettysburg community. Memorial Day ceremonies in 1869 once again featured the orphans in a prominent role, decorating the graves of Union veterans in Evergreen Cemetery in addition to those in the Soldiers' National Cemetery. On July 1 of that year the children were present at the dedication of the Soldiers' National Monument in the national cemetery, and immediately afterward General Meade and Governor Geary paid a visit to the Homestead. In an impromptu ceremony, Meade accepted a handsome silk flag—the gift of some Baltimore supporters—on behalf of the orphanage. After acknowledging the kindness of the donors, the general made a pleasant address to the children, and after the boys offered three hearty cheers for the governor, Geary responded with a few words. A company of Zouaves closed the informal program with three cheers apiece for Meade, Geary, and the Homestead. It was another exciting day for the Humiston children, even though it marked another anniversary of their father's death.[37]

An early issue of the *Homestead Journal* contained an essay by Dr. Bourns entitled "Uncles." "Little folks sometimes have uncles that please them, and try to make them happy," the doctor wrote. "The children at the Homestead have several uncles." As an example he cited Uncle John McAllister, "a great favorite." But Bourns also considered himself to be an avuncular figure to the orphans. "Another uncle is Uncle Frank," he wrote. "But he does not live there, and only sometimes makes a visit. So the children write letters to him when he does not come to see them." One such a letter was printed verbatim, a short missive to Dr. Bourns from Frank Humiston mentioning a visit with Uncle John McAllister ("we had a good deal of fun"), playing with some new boys, and the antics of a little dog the children had adopted as a pet.[38]

The state of the relationship between the Humistons and "Uncle Frank" Bourns during this period is uncertain. Young Frank Humiston's 1869 letter to the doctor sent love to his "Dear Friend," but how Philinda felt toward the man who had controlled her destiny for the previous five years is unknown. Whether she received a salary for her work at the Homestead is also undocumented, but early in 1869 she took belated advantage of an 1866 act of Congress increasing the pensions of widows and orphans. Along with her application she submitted an affidavit, witnessed by Robert McCreary and Jacob A. Kitzmiller of Gettysburg (a Civil War veteran, law student under David Wills, and borough postmaster), declaring that her children were all under the age of sixteen and that she had never remarried, given up support of the children, or permitted them to be adopted. She also submitted affidavits from her sister, Eliza Ensworth Lake (then living in Michigan), and Dr. Thomas Jackson of Portville, both testifying in her support. The increase was granted in April 1869, and Philinda commenced receiving an extra two dollars per month for each of the three children.[39]

Frank, Alice, and Fred Humiston posed for photographs in Gettysburg for the first time since they sat for the celebrated ambrotype in Western New York about five years before. Homestead committeeman Charles Tyson sold his photography business to his employees, William H. Tipton and Robert A. Myers, in 1868; cartes de visite of the children were made under the imprints of both firms. Frank, Alice, and Fred posed individually for the camera on one occasion, Frank in a uniform complete with shoulder straps, sword, and sash, Fred in a more modest uniform. At least five photographs were taken over the years of the children as a trio, all by Tipton & Myers. The photographers chose not to arrange the children in the same order as their famous pose, preferring to position Alice between her two brothers and, in the final Gettysburg portrait, with Alice and Fred standing on either side of Frank, hands resting on their seated brother's shoulders. The Tyson and Tipton & Myers pictures were apparently produced for the private use of the family, but William Tipton, who eventually obtained sole ownership of the business (and kept it until his death in 1929), retained the negatives. Years after the Humistons left Gettysburg, Tipton would copyright an image of the children and offer it for sale.[40]

Tipton & Myers also produced two carte-de-visite portraits of Philinda Humiston. Frank, Alice, and Fred posed for many portraits throughout their lives after their famous first picture, but Philinda seems to have been camera shy. The Tipton & Myers cartes are the only photographs of her known to survive other than a single picture taken during her later years. One of them appears to be a copy of an earlier image, perhaps an ambrotype made as a companion to Amos's only life portrait. The other image depicts Philinda as she appeared during her Homestead years, about the time she made a most momentous decision—one that steered the Humiston family in an entirely new direction.[41]

On Tuesday, October 26, 1869, with about a hundred people in attendance, including all of the orphans and staff members present as witnesses, Philinda Humiston of Gettysburg, Pennsylvania, and Asa Barnes of Becket, Massachusetts, were married at the Homestead by the Reverend William H. Hillis. Following the ceremony the orphanage staff served the bridal party a fine dinner.[42]

If Humiston family lore is correct, it was strictly a marriage of convenience. According to the story, Barnes paid a chance visit to the Homestead, and Philinda promptly forgot him. But when she later received a proposal of marriage in a letter from him, she accepted. She was so dissatisfied with life at the Homestead—and disapproved so much of certain things that happened there—that she agreed to marry a stranger to escape the place. There was, a later generation declared, much family talk about the orphanage that never got into print, and the children as well as their mother were all glad to leave Gettysburg.[43]

It was the third marriage for both bride and groom, and somewhat of a May–December match as well—Asa Barnes was twenty-four years Philinda's senior. Both of his previous marriages had left him a widower (his first wife died after a year of marriage, his second after twenty years). Born in Tolland, Massachusetts, in 1807, he converted to the Methodist Episcopal church as a young man and was licensed as a preacher soon after. Barnes loved the doctrines and usages of the church, and delighted in quoting the gospel. For forty years he served local parishes, retiring from the active ministry about the time he wed Philinda.[44]

The marriage resulted in a temporary breakup of the Humistons. Following a ten-day visit to Nunda, Philinda journeyed to Becket to set up housekeeping with her new husband, while Frank, Alice, and Fred returned to the Homestead to maintain continuity in their schoolwork, particularly to enable Frank to continue his studies of Latin, Greek, and mathematics. When a census taker visited the orphanage in June 1870, he recorded the Humiston children together with eighty-five other orphans, Charles and Elizabeth Hilton as principal and vice principal, respectively, James Burns as steward, and Mary S. Ridgely, Philinda's replacement, as superintendent of sewing. After a separation of two years, mother and children were reunited in Becket in 1871. A probate court appointed Asa Barnes guardian of Frank, Alice, and Fred on May 2 of that year, and the Humistons embarked on a new life in New England.[45]

NOTES

1. *American Presbyterian*, November 30, 1865, 380.

2. "U.S. Soldiers' and Sailors' Home of Pennsylvania," *American Presbyterian*, August 17, 1865, 261.

3. "The National Orphans' Homestead," *American Presbyterian*, March 8, 1866, 73; "The National Orphan Homestead," Edward McPherson Papers, 631KK, Manuscript Division, Library of Congress (hereafter McPherson Papers).

4. "The National Orphan Homestead," McPherson Papers; *McElroy's Philadelphia City Directory for 1866* (Philadelphia: A. McElroy, 1866), 57, 105, 233, 490, 548, 671; "A Veteran," *American Presbyterian*, November 16, 1865, 364; "Gettysburg National Orphans' Homestead," *American Presbyterian*, June 20, 1867, 193.

5. "This Benevolent Institute," *Gettysburg Star and Sentinel*, May 8, 1866; "The Property Owned by Capt. John Myers," *Gettysburg Compiler*, May 14, 1866;

William A. Frassanito, *Early Photography at Gettysburg* (Gettysburg: Thomas Publications, 1995), 137–139.

6. Unsigned minutes of meeting, May 10, 1866, McPherson Papers; "The Soldiers' Orphans Home Gettysburg, Pennsylvania," undated typescript, Gettysburg National Military Park.

7. Unsigned minutes of meeting, May 11, 1866, and C. J. Tyson, secretary pro tempore, "Minutes of the Board of Managers of the Orphans Homestead," May 18, 21, 1866, McPherson Papers; "The Property owned by Capt. John Myers."

8. "The National Orphans' Homestead, at Gettysburg. National Sabbath-school Enterprise," *American Presbyterian*, June 7, 1866, 181.

9. R. G. McCreary, "To the Local Committee of the Orphans Homestead," McPherson Papers; Frassanito, *Early Photography at Gettysburg*, 138; photograph of workmen renovating the Myers house, courtesy of Henry Deeks. According to "The Soldiers' Orphans' Home," *Gettysburg Compiler*, April 15, 1903, a weatherboard wing, formerly part of the barn on the Myers property, was moved adjacent to the house and altered during the renovation of the main building.

10. "The National Orphans' Homestead at Gettysburg," *American Presbyterian*, September 27, 1866, 308; McCreary, "To the Local Committee of the Orphans Homestead."

11. McCreary, "To the Local Committee of the Orphans Homestead."

12. "The Gettysburg Orphans' Homestead," *American Presbyterian*, November 1, 1866, 348; "Story" (Philadelphia: National Homestead, n.d.).

13. "German Church and the National Orphans' Homestead," *American Presbyterian*, October 25, 1866, 340.

14. "The Gettysburg Orphans' Homestead," 348.

15. "Orphans Arrive at the Homestead," *Gettysburg Star and Sentinel*, October 30, 1866; "The Soldiers' Orphans Home," *Adams Sentinel and General Advertiser*, October 30, 1866; McCreary, "To the Local Committee of the Orphans Homestead."

16. "Inauguration of the Soldiers' Orphans Homestead at Gettysburg, November 20, 1866," *Adams Sentinel and General Advertiser*, November 27, 1866; "Inauguration of the National Orphans' Homestead at Gettysburg," *American Presbyterian*, November 29, 1866: 380; "National Gratitude," *Philadelphia Inquirer*, November 21, 1866: 1; Isabella James, "Inauguration Ode," broadside, courtesy of Brown University Library.

17. McCreary, "To the Local Committee of the Orphans Homestead."

18. C. E. Breidenbaugh and Annie Danner, "Report, Committee on Education, March 1, 1867," McPherson Papers.

19. "Soldiers' Orphans," *Adams Sentinel and General Advertiser*, December 4, 1866; "The Orphans," *Adams Sentinel and General Advertiser*, January 1, 1867; inscription on flyleaf of carte-de-visite album, courtesy of David Humiston Kelley (hereafter DHK).

20. "Our Country's Orphans," *Adams Sentinel and General Advertiser*, January 29, 1867; "The Gettysburg Orphans' Homestead," *American Presbyterian*, February 14, 1867, 51.

21. "The Soldier's Orphans' Home," *Adams Sentinel and General Advertiser,* January 29, 1867.

22. McPherson Papers.

23. "Sergt. Amos Humiston, of the 154th N.Y. Vols.," carte de visite by F. Gutekunst, author's collection; "The Children of the Battle Field!" carte de visite, photographer unknown, courtesy of Henry Deeks.

24. "A Desirable Picture," *Gettysburg Star and Sentinel,* June 26, 1867; Frassanito, *Early Photography at Gettysburg,* 135–137; Kathleen Collins, "Photographic Fundraising: Civil War Philanthropy," *History of Photography* 11, no. 3 (July–September 1987): 183–184.

25. *Adams Sentinel and General Advertiser,* April 23, 1867; *Homestead Journal* 1, no. 1 (January 1869): 3–5.

26. "Orphans' Home," *Gettysburg Star and Sentinel,* February 26, 1868; New York State Adjutant General, *Annual Report of the Adjutant General of the State of New York* (Albany: Brandow Printing Company, State Legislative Printers, 1905, Serial No. 39), 1038; Frederick Phisterer, *New York in the War of the Rebellion* (Albany: Weed, Parsons and Company, 1890), 492–493.

27. Miss E. Latimer, *"The Unknown"* (Philadelphia: Bryson & Son, 1867).

28. Miss E. Latimer, *Idyls of Gettysburg* (Philadelphia: George Maclean, 1872).

29. "A Reception," *Gettysburg Star and Sentinel,* February 19, 1868; "Orphans' Home," *Gettysburg Star and Sentinel,* February 26, 1868; "Washington's Birthday at Gettysburg," *Homestead Journal* 1, no. 2 (March 1869): 1–2.

30. "Memorial Day, May 30, 1868, Orphans Participate," *Gettysburg Star and Sentinel,* June 3, 1868; Stuart McConnell, *Glorious Contentment: The Grand Army of the Republic, 1865–1900* (Chapel Hill: University of North Carolina Press, 1992), 183–185.

31. "Soldier's Orphans," *Gettysburg Star and Sentinel,* June 24, 1868; "Orphans' Homestead," *Gettysburg Star and Sentinel,* July 10, 1868.

32. Alice Humiston to Dear Fred [Humiston], October 28, 1914, courtesy of DHK; "Uncles," *Homestead Journal* 1, no. 2 (March 1869): 11; Mary Ruth Collins and Cindy A. Stouffer, *One Soldier's Legacy: The National Homestead at Gettysburg* (Gettysburg: Thomas Publications, 1993), 37.

33. E. Latimer, "The Holidays at the Orphans' Homestead at Gettysburg," *Homestead Journal* 1, no. 1 (January 1869): 1–3; "The Orphans' Homestead," *Sunday-School Times,* January 30, 1869, 55.

34. "Meeting of the Executive Committee," *Homestead Journal* 1, no. 1 (January 1869): 8; "The Institution," *Homestead Journal* 1, no. 2 (March 1869): 6; "Addition to the Homestead," *Gettysburg Star and Sentinel,* May 21, 1869; William A. Frassanito, *The Gettysburg Bicentennial Album* (Gettysburg: Adams County Historical Society, 1987), 62.

35. "Explanatory," *The Homestead Journal* 1, no. 1 (January 1869): 6.

36. "Explanatory," "Life Directors," "Life Members," "Balance in the Treasury," "Shareholding Sabbath Schools," *Homestead Journal* 1, no. 1 (January 1869): 6–8; "The Grand Army," *Homestead Journal* 1, no. 2 (March 1869): 6–7.

37. "Remember the Orphans," *Gettysburg Star and Sentinel*, June 25, 1869; "Flag Presentation," *Gettysburg Star and Sentinel*, July 2, 1869.

38. "Uncles," *Homestead Journal* 1, no. 2 (March 1869): 11–12.

39. "Claim for increase of widow's pension"; affidavit of Philinda B. Humiston, Robert G. McCreary and Jacob A. Kitzmiller, January 6, 1869; affidavit of Eliza Lake, February 15, 1869; affidavit of Thomas S. Jackson, February 19, 1869; notice of increase of pension, April 5, 1869; Amos Humiston pension records, National Archives.

40. Cartes-de-visite of Frank and Alice Humiston by Tyson's Excelsior Photographic Portrait Galleries, of Fred Humiston and all three children by Tipton & Myers, "successors to C. J. Tyson," courtesy of DHK; Gerard A. Patterson, *Debris of Battle: The Wounded of Gettysburg* (Mechanicsburg, Pa.: Stackpole Books, 1997), 194; Frassanito, *Early Photography at Gettysburg*, 29–40.

41. Cartes-de-visite of Philinda Humiston by Tipton & Myers, courtesy of DHK.

42. Marriage certificate, courtesy of DHK; Warren Humiston memoir, August 1870, Vol. 1, p. 268, courtesy of David B. Morgan.

43. Marian Reynolds, "Letter Ties the Centuries," *Olean Times Herald*, April 23, 1962, 18.

44. J. A. Barnes, "Asa Barnes," obituary, unidentified, undated clipping courtesy of DHK.

45. Collins and Stouffer, *One Soldier's Legacy*, 111–113, 125; Warren Humiston memoir, August 1870, Vol. 1, p. 268; Commonwealth of Massachusetts, Berkshire County Probate Court, certificate of guardianship, May 2, 1871, Amos Humiston pension records.

CHAPTER 13

A Tarnished Legacy

HIS WIFE AND children no longer lived there, but the Homestead continued to represent Amos Humiston's legacy—"his sculptured stone," as Miss Latimer called it in the subtitle of her epic poem "The Unknown"—in a most satisfying manner. The orphanage was flourishing when the Humistons left it; a well-run, financially secure, highly regarded facet of the Gettysburg community, sustaining scores of the offspring of the nation's fallen soldiers—which made it all the sadder when, within years after the Humistons departed, dastardly deeds and deceit brought the orphanage to a disgraceful demise.

It was as if when the Humistons left, the soul of the Homestead went with them. For a few years, affairs at the orphanage continued to progress satisfactorily. "We are pleased to see a growing interest in the Homestead on the part of our citizens," a Gettysburg newspaper noted in 1870. "Such an institution is an honor and a blessing to any community." Public examinations of the orphans by their teachers that summer so pleased a crowd of visitors that one of them treated the entire student body to ice cream.[1]

Five years later, in response to a letter from Frank Humiston, Dr. Bourns wrote, "Within a day or two past I have received account of the good health of the Homestead family." But by that time the orphanage was perched on the brink of disaster, and the doctor was a primary cause of its difficulties.[2]

Sunday schools continued to make financial contributions, and children continued to arrive at the orphanage after the Humistons left. As predicted at the Homestead's inauguration, some of the youngsters were the offspring of martyred Southern Unionists. In the summer of 1869, five boys from Rheatown, Tennessee, departed for Gettysburg. One of them was sponsored by his local Sunday school and the others by Philadelphia schools, in a special arrangement worked out by Dr. Bourns. The boys were bid farewell with an elaborate and emotional ceremony at a Rheatown church, during which the story of Amos Humiston was recounted to the intense interest of all.[3]

Professor and Mrs. Hilton left the Homestead late in 1870 to accept positions in the public schools in Washington, D.C. Nothing is known of the background of the new administrator, Mrs. Rosa J. Carmichael, but she was highly regarded by Francis Bourns. "As a teacher and disciplinarian, Mrs. Carmichael has few equals," the doctor wrote, "and she is a most assiduous and faithful worker, laboring often beyond her strength in school and out." Assisting Mrs. Carmichael were steward James Burns (who took charge of the boys outside the classroom), and Miss Lida J. Blair, another successor to Philinda Humiston, who managed the clothing department and instructed the girls in sewing.[4]

Dr. Bourns described a generally healthy institution in a report to the Homestead board of directors in May 1872, reprinted in the Gettysburg press. The population of orphans stood at seventy. The children were in uniformly good health, they were carefully supervised and well educated, and their religious training was scrupulous. They also were involved in a variety of extracurricular work: the girls were engaged in housekeeping, sewing, and knitting, and the boys were working in the garden and handling chores around the buildings. Only one sour note was sounded in the report: the Homestead had a deficit of more than $500. But, Dr. Bourns reported, one of the institution's agents had already raised enough to cover the shortfall.[5]

Twice during the early 1870s, petitions were presented to Congress seeking appropriations for the Homestead. In April 1870 a plea signed by Bishop Simpson, General Meade, George Stuart, and Jay Cooke, among others, sought $75,000 to extend the Homestead buildings and enlarge its operations. The Senate Committee on Military Affairs agreed to report a bill giving the institution $20,000, but it failed to pass. A petition presented in 1872 sought $50,000 for educational purposes at the Homestead. It too was defeated. Without congressional support, the Homestead Association was left to its own devices to sustain itself financially.[6]

Mention of the Homestead virtually disappeared from the pages of Gettysburg newspapers after the publication of Dr. Bourns's May 1872 report. The part played by the children in Memorial Day ceremonies was reported annually, but other stories concerning the orphanage ran on only a couple of occasions in the next few years. A story written by several of the older orphans in January 1873 described the delight of the children when two local men treated them to a surprise sleigh ride. In July 1874, a newspaper notice described some new stereoscopic photographs of the Homestead by

A Tarnished Legacy

William Tipton, including one of the orphans at play on the grounds, and recommended them as "a creditable specimen of art."[7]

Starting in 1873, another organization joined the orphans in the annual Memorial Day processions to Cemetery Hill: Gettysburg's Corporal Skelly Post, No. 9, Grand Army of the Republic. The Skelly Post veterans immediately assumed a major role in the local Decoration Day ceremonies. A member of the post presented the main address at the cemetery during the 1874 observance. Rain washed out the morning exercises in 1875, but the veterans were not to be deterred, and an alternate procession left the Skelly Post room in the evening. The orphans joined the line of march at the Homestead, and the children and the Grand Army men shared the task of strewing flowers.[8]

It was the last Memorial Day ceremony for the Homestead orphans. On May 30, 1876, Rosa Carmichael refused to allow the children to participate, and they forlornly watched the distant exercises from the yard of the orphanage. That pathetic scene symbolized the beginning of the end for the Homestead. Mrs. Carmichael's action might have been taken to spite Skelly Post, because by that time the matron and the veterans were adversaries. Rumors of mistreatment of the orphans by Mrs. Carmichael had been circulating in Gettysburg, and the Grand Army men had taken it upon themselves to launch an investigation. They concluded the matron was prone to "general misconduct and tyranny" and vowed "to remedy this evil." The first result of the GAR probe came twelve days after the holiday, on June 11, when Rosa Carmichael was arrested and charged with cruelty to one of the orphans.[9]

Released on $300 bail, she returned to the orphanage. Skelly Post removed her victim, young George W. Lundon, from the Homestead, placed him in the protective custody of a veteran, and appointed a committee to investigate the charges against Mrs. Carmichael. In August a grand jury indicted her on charges of aggravated assault and battery on Lundon. In the absence of the prosecutor, the case was continued to the court's November term, and Mrs. Carmichael was released on $600 recognizance. That fall she was found guilty on the first count of aggravated assault, not guilty on the second and third counts, and sentenced to pay a fine of $20 plus court costs, whereupon she returned to the Homestead.[10]

Meanwhile, in Philadelphia, a rift separated Francis Bourns and the Homestead board of directors. In August, about the time Rosa Carmichael was indicted, two members of the board—Major David R. B. Nevin, a lawyer who had replaced the Reverend Newton as chairman of the executive committee, and General James Stewart, Jr., an accomplished soldier during the war, now a Philadelphia commission merchant and the city's future chief of police—traveled to Gettysburg to investigate conditions at the Homestead. They discovered that the orphanage was more than $2,000 in debt and that only about thirty children were residents. "We have been forced to the conclusion that the institution has outlived its day of usefulness," they wrote. "Its revenues are small and unreliable, its indebtedness large and daily increasing, its number of pupils *small* and sundry alleged claims against it *large*." This last was an apparent reference to the rumors swirling around Gettysburg about the conduct of Rosa Carmichael. Taking all into consideration, Nevin and Stewart recommended "the closing of the Homestead at once and the transfer of the children to their respective homes, or such charitable institutions as may hereafter be decided by the Board." They also recommended that Robert McCreary be authorized to take charge of the Homestead and settle claims against it.[11]

Although the Nevin and Stewart report made no specific mention of Francis Bourns, the doctor took it as a personal attack. He responded by declaring some of the old board members out—including General Stewart—and replacing them with new members. But that gambit backfired when Bourns's appointees, on learning of the situation, refused to act except in cooperation with the initial board.[12]

On October 19, a board meeting was convened in Philadelphia by Major Nevin. Although invited, Dr. Bourns refused to attend. Eight members were present, including Bishop Simpson and other old board members and at least one of Bourns's new appointees. General Stewart attended on the board's invitation. The report Nevin and Stewart had made in August was read and unanimously approved. Then, on a motion ironically made by the Bourns appointee, the board resolved "to demand of Dr. Bourns the books and papers" belonging to the Homestead.[13]

Six days later, the board met again and resolved to settle claims made against the orphanage by merchant (and former Gettysburg committee member) Henry Fahnestock, baker Baltzer Newport, butcher George B. Stover, and others. (This was a belated action. The creditors had won judgments against the Homestead in court; an execution had been issued in June, another in October, and another was to come in February 1877.) The board also resolved that Robert McCreary be authorized to close the Homestead at once and to transfer the children to new homes, and that all collection of money in support of the institution immediately cease.[14]

Inexplicably, those final steps were not immediately taken, and the situation continued to deteriorate. Rumors about Rosa Carmichael, rife in Gettysburg, readily reached the ear of Captain John M. Vanderslice of Philadelphia when he arrived in the borough to attend Decoration Day ceremonies in 1877. Vanderslice, assistant adjutant general of the Depart-

A Tarnished Legacy

ment of Pennsylvania, GAR, was outraged by what he heard in Gettysburg. On his return to Philadelphia he published an exposé in the *Philadelphia Times* using the alias "G.A.R." A week later, on June 14, the story was reprinted in the *Gettysburg Star and Sentinel*, and at last the public veil of silence regarding conditions at the Homestead was lifted. After years of whispered rumors, the news exploded in the borough like a bombshell.

Vanderslice charged that the Philadelphia board had allowed control of the institution to consolidate solely in the hands of Dr. Bourns. He scoffed at the pretentiousness of the doctor in changing his name from Burns to Bourns. He alleged that the "evil nature" of Rosa Carmichael had driven away the last teacher and that no school had been taught at the Homestead for two years. He reviewed the Nevin and Stewart report, the attempted takeover of the board by Dr. Bourns, and Mrs. Carmichael's criminal record. He alleged that her behavior had worsened since her conviction, "until the abuses in the institution have made it a stench in the nostrils of the community, and the people justly demand that some decided and prompt action shall be taken by the proper authorities." He then cited several chilling examples.

Mrs. Carmichael had a "taskmaster," Vanderslice charged, a brutal boy about nineteen years old, a former Homestead orphan, who "beats and kicks in the most cruel manner little children of tender age, and does it to the apparent delight of the matron and with her certain approval." On the bitter cold Christmas Eve of 1876, Carmichael penned a four- or five-year-old boy in the outhouse, where he remained until midnight, when neighbors—"both of whom had been attracted to the spot by the piteous screams of the little fellow, who was scared almost out of his senses"—interceded and secured his release. On another occasion, the matron forced a little girl to stand atop a desk without moving, "till she had to be lifted down, exhausted and helpless." Girls on the Homestead grounds had been seen wearing boys' clothing.[15]

Orphan Isabella Hunter, who turned seventeen on the day Vanderslice's article ran in Gettysburg, had been "a little bright-eyed girl" when she arrived at the Homestead in 1868. Her mother had died in 1865 and her father, a veteran of a Pennsylvania heavy artillery regiment, succumbed to consumption in 1867. Young Bella was found wandering the streets of Philadelphia, homeless and friendless, and sent to the Homestead under the sponsorship of a Philadelphia Sunday school. Now, Vanderslice charged, Bella Hunter was a "miserable, broken-spirited girl . . . the slave of Mrs. Carmichael." Under the cruel matron's supervision and hounded by Carmichael's heartless teenaged accomplice, Bella was forced to perform the most menial tasks, was locked in her room the rest of the time, and had been beaten and kicked. The whole community knew of the girl's hard fate, Vanderslice alleged, "and yet there were none, it would seem, to intercede for her."[16]

Vanderslice ended his recital of malfeasance by noting Mrs. Carmichael's refusal to allow the orphans to participate in Memorial Day ceremonies for the second consecutive year. The youngsters were instead forced to watch from the Homestead grounds while "happy children" decorated the soldiers' graves. "These are just a few of the abuses and cruelties practiced in this place," Vanderslice declared. "Are they to be allowed to continue?" Was the Homestead to remain a home to the inhuman Rosa Carmichael, and "a summer resort of Dr. Bourns, where he is waited upon by the little inmates, whose fathers sleep in the adjoining cemetery"? Would Major Nevin, General Stewart, and the rest of the board, or the Gettysburg authorities, or the Society for the Prevention of Cruelty to Children, do anything about the situation? Vanderslice asked. "Must it be left to the Grand Army of the Republic to intercede in behalf of the helpless inmates and abolish this nuisance?"[17]

As if Vanderslice's article had not given Gettysburg citizens enough to mull over, the same issue of the *Star and Sentinel* carried several other items relating to the case. It printed a response to Vanderslice's accusations by Rosa Carmichael, originally published in the *Philadelphia Times* the day after "G.A.R.'s" letter appeared in that paper. The matron apparently had been in Philadelphia when Vanderslice's attack occurred; she had called on him and was told, "with an air of no little menace and self-gratulation," that he had still more charges to make public. She would wait to reply in detail until those other charges were made, Mrs. Carmichael declared, but she pronounced Vanderslice's initial accusations "substantially false as they are slanderous, without, however, accusing him with have doing me wilful wrong."[18]

The matron's self-defense was undermined by a story from the *Waynesboro Village Record*, also reprinted in the June 14 *Star and Sentinel*. It told of a youth of about nineteen years of age, missing part of his left arm, clad in filthy clothing, and shod in a pair of low gum overshoes, who had recently passed through Waynesboro. Richard Hutchinson claimed to have run away from the Homestead, where he and his sister, Lizzie, had been residents since 1869. He made some statements to the *Village Record* about the orphanage "which, if correct," the paper noted, "would seem to show that the Home in question is no credit either to Gettysburg or to whomever manages it." One of his stories concerned Lizzie and Bella Hunter. As a punishment for tearing their dresses, Mrs. Carmichael had forced the two girls to wear boys' clothing for more than two months. "If this youth's information is correct, it seems that the Orphans of soldiers can be op-

A Tarnished Legacy

pressed in the Home close by the National Cemetery," the Waynesboro paper editorialized, "—may pine and long for the treatment of civilized life, and apparently [have] none to help or care for them."[19]

The *Star and Sentinel* did not reprint all of these sensational stories without adding its own commentary. In a long article in the same June 14 issue, it acknowledged that "for several weeks there has been more or less excitement in our community in connection with the management of the Soldiers' Orphan Homestead," excitement intensified by the publication of Vanderslice's article in the Philadelphia press. It admitted that the abuses Vanderslice described had been commonly rumored in Gettysburg for some time. It declared the charges should be immediately investigated and, if found to be true, the situation remedied.

Defending its community, the *Star and Sentinel* declared that "the citizens of Gettysburg are in no wise responsible" for the situation at the Homestead. "Although located in our midst, our people have nothing to do with its administration." The board members were Philadelphia residents, as was Dr. Bourns, who seemed to be the sole director of the Homestead's affairs in any case. The visiting committees of Gettysburg ladies had been forced to cease their inspections of the orphanage years ago. "In fact the management of the institution for the last year or two has not had the confidence of our people," stated the paper. "For two years there has been no teaching—or if any—it has been nominal." This and the rumors of mistreatment had been called to the attention of the Philadelphia board repeatedly, to no avail. Other efforts by Gettysburgians on behalf of the children had also been rebuffed. Skelly Post, "interested in the proper care of the orphans of their fallen comrades, have interfered from time to time, only to be treated with contempt and charged with impertinent espionage." Gettysburg was not to blame for the current crisis, in the opinion of the *Star and Sentinel*. "If there has been neglect to inquire into and reform the management of the Homestead," professed the paper, "the fault must be charged to the Phila. Board, and not to the members of Corporal Skelly Post or the citizens of Gettysburg. The general conviction in this community is that the Homestead has outlived its usefulness and that the sooner it is closed the better."

In closing its article, the *Star and Sentinel* reported that Bella Hunter and Lizzie Hutchinson had indeed been punished by being forced to wear male clothing. Several Gettysburg citizens had looked into the matter and had informally brought the two girls before Judge William McClean of the Adams County Court of Common Pleas, who had offered them the opportunity to select guardians and leave the Homestead. Both left, Bella choosing General Stewart as her guardian. But both girls agreed to stay at the Homestead until arrangements could be finalized rather than move to temporary homes in Gettysburg, and Mrs. Carmichael herself took them to Philadelphia and surrendered them to their guardians. As for the runaway Richard Hutchinson, the Gettysburg paper reported that he was none other than Mrs. Carmichael's supposed enforcer.[20]

The circumstances surrounding the Hutchinsons and Bella Hunter soon led to more unpleasant complications. In the meantime, other shocking allegations were bandied over clotheslines and counters in Gettysburg. All sorts of stories were told. Mrs. Carmichael was said to have suspended children by their arms in barrels. She had hidden mistreated victims from the prying eyes of inspectors. Most scandalous of all were tales of a dungeon in the Homestead cellar, a black hole eight feet long, five feet deep, and only four feet high, unlit and unventilated, where she shackled children to the wall. With Gettysburg in a dither over the Homestead scandal, Skelly Post sent a letter to Dr. Bourns and Mrs. Carmichael demanding their resignations and threatening prosecution.[21]

Edward Woodward, an eccentric Gettysburg umbrella mender who liked to speak in rhyme, fired a literary salvo into the charged atmosphere with the publication of a poem as a small broadside. Woodward criticized the punishment of Bella Hunter and Lizzie Hutchinson in his meandering verses, but his strongest censure was for the refusal of Rosa Carmichael—"a modern Borgia"—to allow the orphans to take part in the Memorial Day rites: "They are kept like galley slaves, while strangers decorate their fathers' graves."[22]

The situation regarding Bella Hunter and the Hutchinson siblings sparked a war of words between David McConaughy and Skelly Post that lasted for months and escalated in vituperation. It began when McConaughy sent a letter to Dr. Bourns suggesting the prompt removal of Bella Hunter and Lizzie Hutchinson from the Homestead as incorrigible disciplinary problems. McConaughy's letter, however, was dated June 7—two days after Rosa Carmichael had escorted the two girls to Philadelphia. The lawyer's anachronistic suggestion would have gone unnoticed if Dr. Bourns had not submitted the letter, along with a cover letter of his own, to the editor of the *Waynesboro Village Record*. Trying to sort the matter out, the editor of the *Village Record* decided that if McConaughy's information regarding the two girls came from the notorious Mrs. Carmichael, "it should be received with a wide margin of allowance. It seems to us the Honorable gent's letter looks thin."[23]

Responding to the Waynesboro article, Skelly Post addressed a lengthy notice to the public in the pages of the *Gettysburg Star and Sentinel*, and the fight between the GAR men and David McConaughy was on. The veterans branded the lawyer's letter to Bourns as "the flimsy trick of a pettifogger written to bolster up the reputation of an institution that has become odious for its brutality and mismanagement." They insinuated

A Tarnished Legacy

McConaughy had suggested the girls' punishment to Carmichael and that the lawyer and the matron had removed the girls from the orphanage to avoid prosecution. They defended their own actions in attacking malfeasance at the Homestead and explained the seeming indifference of the Gettysburg citizenry to the situation at the orphanage. The townspeople's support had been eroded by the constant mismanagement of Dr. Bourns and Mrs. Carmichael. When the doctor's "scandalous tongue" caused visits by the local committees to cease, all checks on Rosa Carmichael's behavior had been removed. "She has gone from bad to worse until the institution has become a public disgrace beyond the tolerance of decent people."[24]

McConaughy counterattacked with an equally wordy letter branding his anonymous accuser a mendacious madman, defending his own actions and motives and those of Dr. Bourns and Mrs. Carmichael, and hinting at the motivation for the Skelly Post's attack: McConaughy had defended Carmichael as her attorney during her 1876 trial. The adversaries traded several more bitter letters in the columns of the *Star and Sentinel*, and the exchange grew increasingly personal, with epithets like "prostitute," "scandal-monger," "illiterate mob," and "skunk! skunk!" tossed back and forth with reckless abandon.[25]

By the time the feud petered out in the newspaper's pages, Rosa Carmichael had left the Homestead, and legal proceedings had been instigated against her and Dr. Bourns. Robert McCreary filed a suit against the two in the Adams County Court of Common Pleas on September 3, 1877, complaining of mismanagement, waste of property, and violation of trust and seeking the appointment of a receiver. Judge McClean granted a temporary injunction restraining the defendants from removing any property from the Homestead or in any way interfering with it, and appointed Major Robert Bell of Gettysburg as receiver, with authority to take charge of the Homestead. Bell was a member of Skelly Post. The Grand Army's war against the Homestead's corrupt regime had been won.[26]

Francis Bourns's legal entanglements tightened during the November court session when McCreary filed a motion to amend the bill of complaint, charging the physician with embezzling large sums of money donated to the Homestead and seeking a full accounting of contributions to the orphanage received by him. At the same time notices were served to Bourns and Carmichael ordering them to file their pleas or answer within thirty days, else the bill would be taken *pro confesso* against them. Those documents were sent to David McConaughy, who served as attorney for both defendants. Major Bell petitioned the court to delay a sale of the Homestead property planned by Adams County sheriff Joseph Spangler to settle suits against the institution, arguing that the sale would force the nine remaining orphans to be "turned upon the streets as objects of charity."

Judge McClean agreed and decided to delay the final closing of the institution and sale of the property until a new board of managers in Philadelphia took satisfactory action to see to the well-being of the remaining children. Members of the new board included Gettysburgians Henry Louis Baugher, president of Pennsylvania College, and David McConaughy. (Considering his personal and professional defense of Dr. Bourns and Mrs. Carmichael, the choice of McConaughy as a board member was seemingly a surprising one. On the other hand, McConaughy's closeness to the two beleaguered defendants perhaps eased the final stages of closing down the orphanage.)[27]

The demise of the Homestead coincided with the end of the year. The *Star and Sentinel* of December 21, 1877, noted that the orphanage was "about winding up" and that the nine last orphans were to leave. Five of the children were scattered to various homes, three were sent to the Home of the Friendless in Philadelphia, and one was adopted by Nicholas G. Wilson, Union veteran and superintendent of the Soldiers' National Cemetery.[28]

About a month later, on January 18, 1878, Sheriff Joseph Spangler seized the Homestead property in pursuance of the writs issued by the Court of Common Pleas. Over three days during the following week, the orphanage's household goods were offered for sale, drawing a large crowd of buyers. Thousand of items were sold, from bathtubs to school desks, sewing machines to coal stoves, a cabinet organ to a lawn mower. Bargain hunters picked the place clean and paid a total of about $850 for the jumble of stuff. Only a few children's garments were left at the close of the sale. Skelly Post bought the most unusual item offered: a pair of iron shackles said to have been used by Rosa Carmichael in her punishments. The veterans displayed them in their post rooms as a grim reminder of the cruelties the children of their fallen comrades had endured, and even had them photographed.[29]

On April 17, 1878, Sheriff Spangler sold the Homestead real estate to a Gettysburg trio, including orphanage creditors Henry Fahnestock and George Stover, for $3,100. After an ending as melodramatic and sad as that of its inspiration Amos Humiston, the Homestead was no more.[30]

Rosa Carmichael seems to have disappeared from the public record after her infamous reign in Gettysburg. Dr. Bourns continued his medical practice in Philadelphia until age forced him to retire circa 1885, spending his summers at his Waynesboro homestead and occasionally submitting his poems to newspapers. Around 1897 he was hit by a bicyclist in a Philadelphia street. The injury, coupled with the debilities of old age, kept him hospitalized until he was moved to the state hospital in Norristown, Pennsylvania. He spent his last months there and died of heart disease on December 20, 1899. When his remains arrived in Waynesboro, they were taken directly to the cemetery on Burns Hill and buried after a brief service.[31]

Not a word in his obituary was devoted to the circumstances that had put Francis Bourns in the public eye: the key role he had played in discovering the identity of Gettysburg's unknown soldier, establishing the Homestead, and bringing about its downfall. His own fall from esteemed benefactor to discredited crook was absolute. But Dr. Bourns continued to maintain a connection with the Humistons after the demise of the Homestead, and he even offered some sporadic help in financing Frank's education. Ultimately, however, the family would remember him as a defrauder.

In 1888, a decade after the fall of the Homestead, Bourns composed a poem that was an expression of his anguish. The Humiston family clipped it from a newspaper, and kept it as a reminder of the perplexing man who had made such an impact on their lives. In "Left Alone," Francis Bourns revealed his torment:

> Thou Light above! the powers of darkness come,
>   Environing where thou hast ever shone;
> Hope and perception grope in baffling gloom;
>   Despair's chill terror in my soul I own,
>   And hope-abandoned, now I am alone.[32]

NOTES

1. "The Orphans' Homestead," *Gettysburg Star and Sentinel*, July 8, 1870.

2. John Francis Bourns to Dear Frank, May 19, 1875, courtesy of David Humiston Kelley (hereafter DHK).

3. "Sabbath-School Meeting in Tennessee. Soldiers' Orphans Sent to Gettysburg, Penn'a.," *Sunday-School Times*, August 7, 1869, 377.

4. "Personal," *Gettysburg Star and Sentinel*, December 16, 1870; "National Homestead—Superintendent's Report," *Gettysburg Star and Sentinel*, May 31, 1872.

5. "National Homestead—Superintendent's Report."

6. "Soldiers' Orphans' Homestead," *Gettysburg Star and Sentinel*, April 15, 1870; "Appropriation," *Gettysburg Star and Sentinel*, undated item; "Finding of Soldier's Body with Photograph of Three Children, Prompts Establishment of Soldiers' Orphans' School in Gettysburg," *Waynesboro [Pennsylvania] Record Herald*, July 7, 1941.

7. "Decoration Day, May 30th, 1872," *Gettysburg Star and Sentinel*, June 7, 1872; "The Orphans' Sleighride," *Gettysburg Star and Sentinel*, January 22, 1873; "Decoration Day, May 30, 1873," *Gettysburg Star and Sentinel*, June 4, 1873; "Photographs of Orphans at Homestead," *Gettysburg Star and Sentinel*, July 14, 1874.

8. "Decoration Day, May 30, 1873," *Gettysburg Star and Sentinel*, June 4,

1873; "Decoration Day, May 30, 1874," *Gettysburg Star and Sentinel*, June 2, 1874; "Decoration Day, May 30, 1875," *Gettysburg Star and Sentinel*, June 3, 1875.

9. "Rosa J. Carmichael Arrested," *Gettysburg Star and Sentinel*, June 15, 1876; Mary Ruth Collins and Cindy A. Stouffer, *One Soldier's Legacy* (Gettysburg: Thomas Publications, 1993), 63.

10. "August Court of Quarter Session," *Gettysburg Star and Sentinel*, August 31, 1876; "November Court Term," *Gettysburg Star and Sentinel*, November 16, 1876; Collins and Stouffer, *One Soldier's Legacy*, 63.

11. Minutes, "Meeting of the Directors of the 'Gettysburg National Homestead for Soldiers Orphans'," October 19, 1876, Edward McPherson Papers, 631KK, Manuscript Division, Library of Congress (hereafter McPherson Papers); *Gopsill's Philadelphia City Directory for 1877* (Philadelphia: James Gopsill, 1877): 1093, 1391; "General Stewart Dies; Hero of Civil War," *Philadelphia Public Ledger*, February 25, 1930, clipping in MOLLUS Scrapbook 25, Insignia Record 1139, Civil War Library and Museum of Philadelphia, Pennsylvania.

12. "The National Homestead for Soldiers' Orphans," *Gettysburg Star and Sentinel*, June 14, 1877.

13. Minutes, "Meeting of the Directors of the 'Gettysburg National Homestead for Soldiers Orphans,' " October 19, 1876, McPherson Papers.

14. Minutes, "Meeting of the Board of Directors of the 'Gettysburg National Homestead for Soldiers Orphans,' " October 25, 1876, McPherson Papers; "The Soldiers' Orphans" Home," *Gettysburg Compiler*, April 15, 1903.

15. "Cruelty to Soldiers' Orphans," *Philadelphia Times*, June 7, 1877, 3; "The National Homestead for Soldiers' Orphans," *Gettysburg Star and Sentinel*, June 14, 1877.

16. "Cruelty to Soldiers' Orphans," 3; Collins and Stouffer, *One Soldier's Legacy*, 40–41, 106–107; list of Homestead orphans, 1866 to 1873, courtesy of Allan L. Cox.

17. "Cruelty to Soldiers' Orphans," 3.

18. "The Soldiers' Orphan School," *Philadelphia Times*, June 8, 1877, 3; "Reply of Mrs. Rosa J. Carmichael," *Gettysburg Star and Sentinel*, June 14, 1877.

19. "A Runaway," *Gettysburg Star and Sentinel*, June 14, 1877, reprinting article from the *Waynesboro Village Record* of June 7, 1877; list of Homestead orphans, 1866 to 1873, courtesy of Allan Cox.

20. "The Gettysburg Soldiers' Orphans Homestead," *Gettysburg Star and Sentinel*, June 14, 1877.

21. "The Soldiers' Orphans' Home," *Gettysburg Compiler*, April 15, 1903; Collins and Stouffer, *One Soldier's Legacy*, 62, 64, 95.

22. Edward Woodward, "Poem," broadside; Rev. Stanley Billheimer to Librarian, Gettysburg College, November 28, 1945; both courtesy Gettysburg National Military Park.

23. "Editor of the 'Record'," *Waynesboro Village Record*, June 28, 1877.

24. "To the Public," *Gettysburg Star and Sentinel*, July 18, 1877.

25. "Controversy over Management of Soldiers' Orphans' Homestead," August

A Tarnished Legacy

1, 1887; "Another Tilt at the Windmill," August 8, 1877; "To the Public," August 15, 1877; "To the Public," August 22, 1877; all in the *Gettysburg Star and Sentinel*. The entire Skelly Post-McConaughy correspondence, along with other newspaper articles and documents relating to the Homestead, are reprinted verbatim in Collins and Stouffer, *One Soldier's Legacy*.

26. "Nearing the End," *Gettysburg Star and Sentinel*, September 3, 1877.

27. "Motion to amend bill of complaint," "Notices of rule to file answer," "Notice of claim under exemption law and demand for an appraisement," "Petition for stay of execution," McPherson Papers; "Soldiers' Orphans Home," *Gettysburg Star and Sentinel*, November 30, 1877. A gap in the Adams County Courthouse's appearance docket books from 1877 to 1889 makes it "virtually impossible to locate the action or results" of the litigation. Wanda Y. Walter, Adams County deputy prothonotary, to author, February 12, 1998.

28. "Soldiers' Orphans Home," *Gettysburg Star and Sentinel*, December 21, 1877.

29. Collins and Stouffer, *One Soldier's Legacy*, 89–91.

30. "The Soldiers' Orphans" Home," *Gettysburg Compiler*, April 15, 1903; "Finding of Soldier's Body with Photograph of Three Children."

31. "Burns," obituary in the *Waynesboro Village Record*, December 28, 1899; entry in "Register of Deaths, Montgomery County, Penna.," courtesy of Historical Society of Montgomery County; *The Medical Directory of Philadelphia 1885* (Philadelphia: P. Blakiston, 1885), 179.

32. J. Francis Bourns, "Left Alone," written in Philadelphia, August 1888, for *Episcopal Recorder*, undated clipping courtesy DHK.

CHAPTER 14

The Family's Later Years

PHILINDA TOOK TO calling herself Linda Barnes after her third marriage. When grandchildren came and grew and learned her story, they occasionally delighted in referring to her as Philinda Betsy Ensworth Smith Humiston Barnes, the names revealing a life history. Philinda in turn loved to tell the children her tale—of her childhood trips in New York State, of Amos's whaling voyage and his promise to take her to the Sandwich Islands, of their journey to Michigan, and of the unhappy years in the Homestead. "Mother is flourishing around in fine style," Alice wrote in 1886, when Philinda was fifty-five years old. "Aunt Linda is spry!" declared a Humiston cousin, and so she remained until age and illness crept up on her.[1]

Philinda's marriage to Asa Barnes lasted less than a dozen years before leaving her a widow for a third time. According to family remembrance, it was not a happy union, but details of any discord have died with the generations. On her marriage to Barnes, Philinda's widow's pension terminated. A few months after he was appointed their guardian, Barnes applied as claimant for a pension on behalf of the children, submitting the form with the usual affidavits. Approved in November 1872, the pension was retroactive to Asa and Philinda's October 1869 marriage. It awarded the family eight dollars a month and an additional two dollars per month for each of the three children, to last until they reached sixteen years of age (which Frank had already passed).[2]

At an undetermined date, the family moved east from Becket to Shirley, Massachusetts, and the children enrolled in the Lawrence Academy in nearby Groton. Among Alice's classmates and friends was a West Groton girl, Carrie Relief Tarbell, who Frank took a shine to. On entering the academy, Frank and Fred, who had been christened without them, chose middle names: Franklin Goodwin Humiston (the married name of his aunt, Amos's sister Lois Ann) and Frederick Roy Humiston.[3]

Frank graduated from Lawrence in 1878. In August he was off to Hanover, New Hampshire, and Dartmouth College—the only one of the three children to receive a higher education. "I had hard work to swallow a big lump in my throat," on leaving home, he admitted to Philinda, but he soon settled in to tackle studies of algebra, Greek, and Latin. Frank apparently began considering a career in medicine at Dartmouth, if not before. He witnessed a couple of operations at the medical school and reported that while other spectators felt faint and had to leave the room, he managed to stand the grisly sights. "Think I shall take in all those little circuses just by way of variety," he blithely wrote to a friend.[4]

During Frank's junior year at Dartmouth, on February 12, 1881, Asa Barnes died at Shirley. During his last few years, an obituary noted, Barnes "thought, talked and wrote much about the future home of the Christian." Dying of pneumonia, the retired preacher had a vision of Christ, and his last intelligible utterance was, "Jesus is inviting me to come and live with Him."[5]

On their own again, Philinda, Alice, and Fred moved farther east, to Cambridge, Massachusetts, where they took in boarders. Frank graduated from Dartmouth with the class of 1882, and he took a job teaching school in Southwick, Massachusetts, in 1883. That fall he entered the University of Pennsylvania Medical School in Philadelphia.[6]

He and a roommate, James Crawford, rented an apartment on Locust Street and commenced their studies. "I was obliged to leave one day on account of faintness, while they were performing some surgical butchering," Frank notified Alice in an early letter from Philadelphia. He soon overcame his squeamishness at the dissecting table, however, and was able to write, "I am getting used to slashing and blood and bad sights and so don't mind much about it." He and Jim Crawford even grew blasé. "We have the head-board of the bed decorated with a grinning skull," Frank informed Alice in 1884. "It makes things look so much more cheerful you know."[7]

Living in Philadelphia brought Frank into contact with old friends from the Homestead who had settled in the city, all of them with families of their own now and doing well. One of them, a close friend of Fred in Gettysburg, had named his baby after Fred, and asked Frank for Fred's address and photograph. During a trip to Washington, Frank tried to look up Mr. and Mrs. Hilton, the former Homestead superintendents. He was saddened to learn that Charles Hilton had recently died and sorry to miss Elizabeth Hilton, who was out when he called. He subsequently struck up a correspondence with Mrs. Hilton.[8]

In Philadelphia Frank again met Dr. Bourns. Frank had worked his way through Dartmouth, and at one point he had notified Philinda from Hanover that he was worried he would not have enough money to complete a term. In Philadelphia, however, Frank received some financial assistance from Dr. Bourns. But his letters home reveal that Frank's relationship with the doctor was not without problems.[9]

"I guess the Dr. will come out all straight," Frank wrote in November 1883, in an early letter from Philadelphia. "He made a little advance the other day." In the coming months, Frank occasionally received money from Bourns, but at other times he complained that the doctor "doesnt make much head way." In March 1884 Frank told Alice, "If I am to get through here before I'm forty it is absolutely necessary for me to do something besides depending on the Dr. It is not [a] very safe dependence I'm afraid. he'll have to stir himself pretty lively to keep up to his agreement."[10]

Money was not the only problem Frank had with the doctor. It seems that Bourns continued to concoct schemes to use the Humiston family story for his own purposes. Interestingly, his plans revolved around photographs. "I don't know what he is intending to do with a picture of our old house," Frank wrote to Philinda, Alice, and Fred in 1883. "He has said nothing to me about it." In 1884, when Bourns asked for photographs of the Humistons, Frank gave the doctor a stern rebuff. "I asked the Dr. what he wanted with our pictures," Frank wrote to Alice. ". . . I gave him to understand that any more publicity concerning us would be discountenanced and strongly objected to by us. he doesn't propose writing about us so rest your anxious spirits on that score."[11]

Frank and his roommate received notice they had successfully passed their final examinations in April 1886. "Jim and I are so tickled we can hardly contain ourselves," he informed his family, who joined him in Philadelphia to celebrate his graduation. That fall, Frank married Carrie Tarbell in West Groton on November 3, and the couple settled in a village about twenty-five miles to the northwest, East Jaffrey (today Jaffrey), New Hampshire. Nestled in the hills below Monadnock Mountain, Jaffrey was home to about fifteen hundred souls. Largely a farming community, the village also boasted a handful of small manufacturers and mills powered by the Contoocook River, and a railroad depot.

In a practice spanning a quarter-century, Dr. Franklin G. Humiston became a revered and beloved figure in Jaffrey. He arrived in the village unknown and friendless, and the general opinion of the townspeople was that he had little chance of success. He had an unimposing presence, they thought—but they also saw something in his face and manner that inspired confidence. On his first night in town, he was called to attend an obstetrical case and delivered the first of a thousand babies he would usher into the world. With steady and devoted service to the townspeople, Dr. Humiston "gained a place in their affections perhaps never equaled by any one else in the history of the town," according to a Jaffrey historian.[12]

Jaffrey residents remembered Dr. Humiston's making his own snowshoes out of long boards so he could reach patients during the great blizzard of 1888. They remembered an emergency in 1896 when he made a hurried nighttime horse-and-buggy trip to a distant town with a young girl who had been bitten by a rabid cat, so they could catch a night train to a New York City hospital in time for the necessary treatment. They remembered his kindness to families that were struggling financially; he would compute his bill by estimating the number of his visits, cutting the number in half, multiplying it by his fee, cutting the resulting number in half, and, if the final figure was ten dollars, subtracting eight.[13]

An admired wife and a growing family helped endear Frank to the Jaffrey community. He and Carrie named their firstborn after his sister. Alice Mildred was born in 1887, after a labor and delivery that Frank called his hardest case yet. ("This makes the fourth girl that I have ushered into the world since last Monday morning," he noted.) Ruth Tarbell Humiston arrived in 1889, followed by Helen Ensworth (1891), Frank (1894), John (1897), and Freda (1899). As his family grew, so did Frank's civic involvement. He was a member of several fraternal organizations, including the Order of the Eastern Star, the Knights Templars, and the Masons.[14]

Of the three children, Fred Humiston left the sparsest record. He appears to have been a happy-go-lucky young man, quick to take to the new fad of bicycling, for example, and attending "bicycle dances." "Freddie is about as usual, has been to two swell dances," Alice wrote in 1886, noting that he took a different girl to each event, hired a carriage to convey his dates, and fell to his knees at one of the dances, leaving large spots of wax on his trousers. He was a dandy in a "tall necktie and swell collar," his sister reported, looking "lovely" and "two sweet for anything." He remained a dapper dresser for the rest of his years. His few surviving letters reveal a puckish humor.[15]

By 1896, Philinda, Alice, and Fred had moved from Cambridge to nearby West Somerville. "We have always had ourselves to look out for and not much to do it with," Alice wrote after the move, "but we are now in a fair way to get our own living." Alice was making a fair salary as a stenographer in a Boston real estate firm, and Fred was making a very good salary— good enough for him to start his own family. Fred married Nettie Orne, of West Somerville, on September 17, 1896. Their daughter Doris Orne Humiston was born in 1897; Eleanor Ensworth Humiston arrived in 1906.[16]

The Family's Later Years

Of the grown Humiston children, Fred "had the best business head of the three," his niece Ruth later wrote. He was a traveling salesman out of Boston, and much of his life was spent on railways and roads, living out of his luggage and covering thousands of miles in a few days. His few surviving letters were written on hotel stationery. Perfunctory in describing his travels and encounters with customers, they livened up when Fred described his pastimes on the road—whether observing ice skaters in Ontario or visiting orange groves and watching polo matches in Orlando. "It's good to have some sport to liven up the monotony of the work," he wrote to his niece Alice during a lengthy Canadian trip in 1905. "Think I shall be glad of a lay off by the time I get home."[17]

Like Frank, Fred was a member of several fraternal organizations. During his times at home, he attended meetings of the Masons, the Ancient Order of United Workmen, the Golden Cross, and the West Somerville Civic Association.[18]

At some point after Fred's marriage, Philinda and Alice returned to Cambridge. Alice continued to do office work for various Boston real estate and insurance firms. Philinda had a new sewing machine and kept busy making clothes for her growing horde of grandchildren, "to us the dearest little folks in the world," according to Alice.[19]

Philinda, or "the little Mother," as her children sometimes called her, enjoyed taking occasional long trips by herself. On her return from one such journey in 1883, Frank wrote from Philadelphia, "I can imagine the joy there was . . . the day you got home. I suppose that Alice was completely beside herself and didn't know who she was or where she was. I suppose you were not at all sorry to get back to your little children again were you?" Alice noted in 1896 that Philinda was making an extended sojourn to New York State and planned to visit Candor.[20]

Despite their antipathy to J. Francis Bourns, Philinda and Alice were fond of the doctor's brother, James Burns, and they corresponded with "Jimmie." They were interested to learn from Frank in 1883 that Burns had announced he was getting married in Waynesboro. Philinda and Alice also maintained a correspondence with their Homestead friend Miss Latimer.[21]

Philinda was evidently tolerant of joshing about her status as a thrice-married woman. In 1886 Frank offered some jocular advice to two young women boarding with the family in Cambridge. "Look a little out for the Mother," he wrote. "She is a sly one, has been in the business, caught three [husbands,] is right up to the tricks of the trade. she can beat you all now if she tries." And to his mother he added, "I am surprised to hear that you are on the look out for another man. I thought that you had had an elegant sufficientcy of them. Next, mother, get a bang up good one with no flies on him. they are the kind."[22]

If she had been seeing or seeking a beau, however, it came to naught, and Linda Barnes remained a widow. She was seventy years of age when she filed for a restoration of her pension (which had lapsed on her marriage to Asa Barnes) in 1901. Two years later, she and Alice left Cambridge and moved to Ashburnham, Massachusetts, about midway between their old home in Shirley and Frank's family in Jaffrey. With Fred's help, mother and daughter refurbished and decorated a house, and fitted out a barn. Alice was going to try raising chickens.[23]

After a few years in Ashburnham, in 1906, Alice purchased a farm in North Leominster, Massachusetts, about five miles from Shirley. She called the place Westview. In addition to her chickens, she had two horses, two cows and a calf, and three dogs. "Alie is flying around like a wind mill," Philinda noted a year after the two moved to the new farm, "sawing wood & feeding cats and pigs and doing lots of other chores."[24]

Alice's North Leominster venture met with a setback in the summer of 1909 when she was plagued by chicken thieves, who, undeterred by her dog, stole about 200 of her flock of 450 over a period of several nights. Alice declared, "I am in for a big loss on my chicken raising for the summer," and thought about setting bear traps or using a gun to protect her property. About a month after the thefts, Alice and Philinda visited Frank's family in Jaffrey. "They brought up chickens, butter, fruit, jelly and lots of things," Carrie noted. "They think they'll have to get away from Westview as they can't stand the chicken stealing and the lonesomeness. so they will try to sell I guess as soon as they can conveniently do it." But Alice persevered, and in 1912 she reported she owned about 480 chickens and 50 roosters.[25]

Philinda, Alice, and Fred were all in Jaffrey on November 3, 1912, to attend a surprise celebration arranged by the townspeople to observe Frank and Carrie's twenty-fifth wedding anniversary. A crowd of about five hundred filled Union Hall, and Frank's daughter Alice proudly noted, "All classes, all sorts and conditions of people were there." An orchestra played, a male quartette sang, and the last of a series of speakers presented Frank with a $600 check, raised by contribution in the town. After some modest and humorous remarks by Frank, he and Carrie greeted the guests, and, their daughter observed, "of all that shook hands with him, there were only two he couldn't call by name." Writing a quarter-century later, a townsman who took part declared the Humiston testimonial "has never been equaled in the history of the town." The next day Frank took his daughter Alice for a ride and said to her, "Well, I guess it pays to be decent, doesn't it?"[26]

After the celebration, one of the participants said to Frank, "Doctor, I am glad that Jaffrey has remembered you. I do not believe in waiting till after people are dead, and then showing appreciation by piling flowers on their coffins." After a thoughtful pause Frank replied, "Well, I have had my flowers." Sadly, it turned out he had received them just in time. He was suffering from gallstones; on December 2 he underwent surgery at Eliot Hospital in Boston. He never recovered. Laid low with pericarditis, he remained hospitalized.[27]

The news of her eldest son's illness hit Philinda hard, Alice reported. "Mother asks every day is Frank coming to day and to night she said 'Tomorrow we must get some kind of a conveyance and drive over and bring Frank where I can take care of him.' When I told her the number of miles she was astonished and when I told her you could not walk yet she thought that pretty hard." When Carrie went to Boston to be with her husband, Philinda and Alice went to Jaffrey to stay with the children, and spend an anxious Christmas.[28]

Days later, Philinda lost her oldest child. On December 30, 1912, after undergoing another operation, Franklin G. Humiston died at age fifty-seven. Jaffrey received the news with an outpouring of grief and sympathy. "Ever cheery, kind and gentle," a local newspaper reported, "he was always ready to respond to the call of the sick and distressed, regardless of financial considerations, and of whether the weather was cold or hot, rainy or blustering. . . . Truly, our world is better because Dr. Humiston has lived." Another reporter offered a succinct opinion: "No man more loving and loved than he." His funeral was held January 2, 1913, from the crowded Jaffrey Congregational Church. All the village businesses closed during the service. Frank's Masonic lodge attended in a body, and laid him to rest in Jaffrey's Conant Cemetery.[29]

"Grandma is failing fast since she came home," Alice wrote to her namesake niece after returning with Philinda to Westview after Frank and Carrie's anniversary party. "Poor little mother her day is almost over." Philinda had been a semi-invalid for years, but around the time Frank was hospitalized she became extremely helpless and required constant watchfulness and care from Alice. They were on a visit to Carrie and the children at Jaffrey when Philinda died of a stroke on November 18, 1913. She was eighty-two years old. The family buried her next to Frank in Conant Cemetery. "I'm sorry the last of Grandma's life had to be so hard for the poor little woman," her granddaughter Alice wrote, "but we can know that she is happy now and that if anyone ever earned a crown of eternal life Grandma did." In thinking of her grandmother's life, Ruth Humiston remarked on "how hard it was, and how varied." Remembering Philinda as "quick and alert, her eyes shining, turning off work of all sorts quicker than other folks can think about it," Ruth declared of Philinda, "Oh, I'm proud of that grandmother of mine!"[30]

Frederick Humiston had been in poor health for some time when he died of acute heart disease at his West Somerville home early in the morning of March 10, 1918. He was fifty-nine. "Poor Freddie & poor Auntie," Frank's daughter Alice wrote on receiving the news. "Glad he won't have to suffer anymore." A funeral service was held at the West Somerville Congregational Church on March 12, and Fred was buried the following day in Jaffrey, next to his mother and older brother in Conant Cemetery. Fred's obituary was the only one of the Humistons' to mention that "he was the son Amos Humiston, who was killed in the battle of Gettysburg while fighting with the Union army."[31]

Cast adrift by the deaths of her mother and brothers, Alice Humiston became a nomad, moving from place to place, visiting her sisters-in-law, and—more than once—living with them or her nieces. Sometimes she chose to live close to Jaffrey, but not actually in the village. In the summer of 1915, for example, she was in Dublin, New Hampshire, about ten miles away, involved in some unspecified work. Her North Leominster chicken farm had failed, and in February 1916 she went to Boston to file for bankruptcy. Seven months later she was in Fitzwilliam, New Hampshire, again in close proximity to Jaffrey. From November 1916 to May 1918 Alice worked in various capacities at the Rhode Island State Home and School for Dependent and Neglected Children in Providence. The institution's superintendent described her as a cooperative and capable worker. "In one instance she brought a girls' cottage from one of the worst cottages on the grounds up to a high state of efficiency," he reported.[32]

After brief stays with niece Alice in Washington, D.C., and the Bronx, New York, Alice was with Carrie in Jaffrey in the summer of 1918, when a sensational wartime crime shocked the town. The unsolved murder of Dr. William K. Dean, a gentleman farmer, would leave a bitter legacy in Jaffrey. The county prosecutor and state attorney general suspected the victim's wife, but she was never charged. Some Jaffrey residents were content to bury the Dean case with the doctor and his wife (who died in 1919). But a majority, including the Humistons, believed Dean was murdered because he knew too much about wartime espionage activities in the area. Many townspeople, among them Ruth Humiston, had observed lights blinking nightly from Monadnock and other peaks and suspected they were the coded signals of German spies. Young Frank Humiston had joined a posse to search for the source of the lights, roaming the woods on his pony, armed with a revolver. "The Dean affair has stirred up people so that nothing much outside of that is talked of," Alice wrote within days after the murder. For weeks she and Carrie were consumed by nervous excitement as Jaffrey swarmed with government agents, wireless operators, aviators, soldiers, detectives, and newspaper reporters.[33]

World War I hurt the Humiston family terribly. Frank Humiston was gassed in France and suffered from the effects for the rest of his life. Helen's husband, Roy S. Ellison, contracted influenza in the army and died in 1918. And John Humiston, known in the family as Jack, was killed by a German shell in June 1918, making Carrie Jaffrey's only Gold Star mother. Jaffrey's American Legion Post No. 11 was named in his honor, and a town baseball park was named Humiston Field to jointly commemorate Jack and his father Franklin.[34]

A few months after the Dean murder, Alice took another job working with institutionalized children. From December 1918 to June 1919, she was employed as an assistant cottage matron at the New York State Training School for Girls in Hudson, New York. The superintendent described her as "reliable [and] faithful in the performance of her duties and honorable in her service," an excellent cook and capable teacher of the pupils in her charge.[35]

March 1920 found Alice with Fred's widow, Nettie, in West Somerville. That year she joined her niece Ruth Humiston in Albany, New York, where Ruth was working for the New York State Department of Health. Alice ran the cafeteria for the department's laboratory during her stay in Albany. In 1922 she made an extended trip to Montana, where both her niece Alice Mildred Humiston and Asa Barnes's son Joseph were then living, and filled an entire album with snapshots of the sights. From 1924 to 1929, Alice maintained a home for elderly women in Rochester, New York.[36]

She left Rochester in early October 1929 aboard a westbound train. After five days of travel, she arrived in Los Angeles, where her niece Alice was working in the library of the University of California at Los Angeles. At first the two women shared a Beverly Hills apartment, but niece Alice— sweet, kind, and considerate—was guilt stricken to find that she could not live with her elderly aunt. Although they continued to see each other often, they agreed to live apart, and "Auntie" moved to Glendale. There Alice linked up with other relatives, her first cousin Charles R. Ensworth (son of Philinda's brother George) and his wife, Grace, who assumed some of the obligation of looking out for her. Charlie Ensworth later estimated he helped Alice move from rooming house to rooming house at least ten times.[37]

A couple of weeks after Alice arrived in California, the stock market crashed on Black Tuesday. Although she owned numerous stocks and must have been hit hard by the catastrophe, Alice could not resist the lure of a potential windfall when an opportunity arose to invest in a newly patented invention, a railroad car coupling device dubbed the Cobb Connector. Falling for rumors of multimillion-dollar investments in the contraption by the United States and foreign governments, she poured her own money into the venture and convinced friends and family members to join her. "I don't dare tell you how much you would make," she wrote to her niece Ruth, "but you could take a good vacation. Take a chance."[38]

Waiting to strike it rich, Alice regarded Depression-era California. She loved the exotic trees and flowers, the open-air Japanese markets offering exotic fruits and vegetables, the twinkling lights at nighttime on hillsides, the theaters and movie houses in Hollywood—one on every corner, it seemed—showing the latest talkies in technicolor. She was less fond of the speeding automobiles (and frequent accidents), the numerous beggars, the Salvation Army volunteers, the full poorhouse. She endured the occasional earthquake with equanimity—"They don't seem to affect me much." She took cooking classes, made patchwork quilts with her Mayflower Circle group, did volunteer work at her Congregational church, and worked on her genealogy.[39]

On the morning of December 16, 1933, Alice was sweeping the rugs in her room in a Glendale rooming house and talking with the woman who lived next door when her skirt brushed the open flame of a heater. Her clothes instantly ignited, and the screams of her friend woke a young man who roomed across the hall, a baker who had just fallen asleep after returning from his night shift. He jumped out of bed, ripped up the hallway carpet, and rolled Alice in it until the fire was extinguished. She had second-degree burns on her hands and her legs, which were scorched from ankle to waist. In response to her pleas, her landlady applied butter to the burns. Dr. Riley Russell arrived about an hour and a half later; he dressed the burns and took her to the Glendale Sanitarium and Hospital. For the next two days, she lapsed in and out of consciousness and delirium, with niece Alice and Grace Ensworth at her bedside, young Alice embracing her aunt and holding her hand. About 11 P.M. on December 18, 1933, Alice Eliza Humiston passed away at age seventy-six.[40]

To ship the body to New Hampshire so Alice could be laid to rest beside her mother and brothers was out of the question; the only money she had when she died was ten dollars in her pocketbook, and her jewelry was worth less than twenty-five dollars. The Cobb Connector was found to be a swindle; her stock was worthless. She owed money to various people. Aside from family letters and photographs, her meager possessions were limited to a chair, a chime clock, two suitcases, and an assortment of bedding. Niece Alice had to pay the hospital bill and as much as she could of the funeral expenses, including the price of a plot in Glendale's Grandview

Memorial Park. Auntie Alice was buried there on December 22, a beautiful, warm day. The minister of her church spoke kindly of her, and a soloist sang two of her favorite hymns. A group of Glendale friends joined her relatives at the graveside service. The cemetery was a large, sunny, garden-like place at the foot of the mountains, niece Alice wrote to her family back east. "Someway I felt quite comfortable about leaving her there, everything was so peaceful and quiet."[41]

The Humistons spent their later lives shunning the spotlight of celebrity, which had shined on them so brightly during the Civil War years. Their renown was based on a heartbreaking family tragedy, and they seemed determined to bury the sad episode firmly in the vanished past. It is remarkable, for example, how few mentions of Amos were made in the vast amount of surviving family correspondence.

In the course of her genealogical work, Alice once opened up to a distant relative while comparing family trees. "My own father died in the battle of Gettysburg," she wrote, "and if you will think back you will probably remember under what circumstances as his death was widely known, and in our younger days we were quite celebrated in a way." More typical was her lengthy correspondence with Wallace D. Humiston, minister of the Congregational church and public librarian in Northfield, Connecticut, who had published a Humiston history. Alice and Wallace exchanged letters on genealogical matters for several years; in all that time, she never mentioned her father's story. Then, in an offhand manner, Wallace wrote, "When I was a boy I came across a poem about a Civil War soldier who was killed in battle, named Amos Humiston. . . . Was he your father?" Only then did Alice share the story.[42]

Strangers did not get so far. After Frank died, a Massachusetts man wrote to Carrie, explaining that he remembered the Humiston story from newspaper accounts during the Civil War years and asking for information about the family. Carrie forwarded the letter to Alice. "I guess that you would laugh if you should see the letter which I got in reply," the man later notified Carrie. "It was signed 'One of the Children,' but by which one of them it was written I don't know. It was typewritten, and was mailed in Boston, but it contained nothing to indicate where it was written. It caustically declined to give me any information."[43]

Philinda, Alice, and Fred often visited Frank and his family in Jaffrey, and the entire Humiston clan was well known and liked in the village. But the collective memory of the townspeople never linked the Humistons to the Civil War story, and the family never spoke of it. Their anonymity in that regard ended in a dramatic fashion. One winter night in Jaffrey's Union Hall, a lecturer made a presentation, illustrated with lantern slides, on the Battle of Gettysburg. Suddenly an image of three children was projected onto the screen over the name "Humiston," and the audience instantly recognized the childhood faces of their beloved town doctor and his sister and brother. The lecturer related the familiar story, and Jaffrey at last knew the background of the Humiston family.[44]

At a family gathering in Jaffrey in 1935, Frank and Carrie's children opened a bundle of their aunt Alice's belongings and distributed them. Among the items were Amos's wartime letters to Philinda. The letters were read, commented on, and returned to the quiet recesses of family memory. To an extent, silence served to suppress the story of their ancestors even within the Humiston family. Amos Frank Humiston, great-grandson and only namesake of his celebrated ancestor, reached middle age before he ever heard the story of Amos and Philinda.[45]

While the Humistons modestly and privately preserved their legacy, the world outside kept the memory of Amos alive. But decades passed before the paths of family and public intersected, and the two parties united to honor his memory.

NOTES

1. Calling card inscribed "Mrs. Linda B. Barnes" and various letters signed Linda Barnes, and Alice E. Humiston (hereinafter AEH) to My Dear Little Sister [Carrie Tarbell Humiston], November 14, 1886, courtesy of David Humiston Kelley; Marian Reynolds, "Letter Ties the Centuries," *Olean Times Herald*, April 23, 1962, 18. Unless otherwise noted, all of the letters, diary entries, documents, newspaper clippings, and the like cited in this chapter are courtesy of David Humiston Kelley.

2. Reynolds, "Letter Ties the Centuries"; "Declaration of Minor Children for Navy Pension," August 17, 1872, "Original Pension of Minor Children," November 19, 1872, Amos Humiston pension file, National Archives.

3. Reynolds, "Letter Ties the Centuries"; AEH to Dear Cousin [Henry S. Humiston], August 27, 1896; Calvin W. Lewis to Carrie R. Humiston, June 17, 1914.

4. "History of the Class of '78," manuscript; Franklin G. Humiston (hereafter FGH) to Dear Mother, August 28, 1878; FGH to Messrs. [Fred] Humiston and [Walter Edgar] Tarbell, November 19, 1878; FGH to Dear Friend Ed [Walter Edgar Tarbell], September 24, 1881.

5. "Return of a Death," July 4, 1901, Amos Humiston pension file, National Archives; "Asa Barnes," undated newspaper clipping.

6. FGH to Dear Mother, September 4, 1881; FGH to Sister Mine, January 16, 1883; "Directory of the [Dartmouth College] Class of '82."

7. FGH to Dear Sister, November 4, 1883; FGH to My Dear Sister, November 10, 1883; FGH to Dear Mother, Sister & Brother, November 28, 1883; FGH to My Dear Sister, December 1883; FGH to Dear Folks at Home, December 9, 1883; FGH to Dear Sister, February 3, 1884; FGH to My Dear Sister, March 9, 1884.

The Family's Later Years

8. FGH to Dear Folks at Home, November 18, 1883; FGH to Dear Sister, February 3, 1884; list of Homestead orphans, courtesy of Allan L. Cox.

9. Albert Annett and Alice E. E. Lehtinen, *History of Jaffrey (Middle Monadnock) New Hampshire: An Average Country Town in the Heart of New England* (Published by the Town, 1937), Vol. 1, 640; FGH to Dear Mother, September 4, 1881.

10. FGH to Dear Folks at Home, November 18, 1883; FGH to Dear Mother, Sister & Brother, November 28, 1883; FGH to Dear Folks at Home, December 9, 1883; FGH to Dear Sister, February 3, 1884; FGH to My Dear Sister, March 9, 1884.

11. FGH to Dear Mother, Sister & Brother, November 28, 1883; FGH to Dear Sister, February 3, 1884.

12. FGH to Dear Alice and All the Rest, April 19, 1886; *Hand-book of Jaffrey, N.H.* (East Jaffrey: George H. Duncan, 1898), 3, 9, 22; Annett and Lehtinen, *History of Jaffrey*, Vol. 1, 639–641.

13. Ruth T. Humiston, "Notes on Humiston," manuscript; Annett and Lehtinen, *History of Jaffrey*, Vol. 3, 203; "Deaths. Dr. Franklin G. Humiston," unidentified newspaper clipping.

14. DHK, "Notes on one branch of the HUMISTON family," 1986; FGH to Dear Mother Tarbell, August 28, 1887; organizational dues receipts.

15. FGH to My Dear Sister, December 1883; AEH to My Dear Little Sister [Carrie Tarbell Humiston], November 14, 1883.

16. AEH to My Dear Mr. [Henry S.] Humiston, August 15, 1896; AEH to Dear Cousin [Henry S. Humiston], August 27, 1896; DHK, "Notes on One Branch of the HUMISTON Family."

17. Reynolds, "Letter Ties the Centuries"; Frederick R. Humiston (hereafter FRH) to My Dear Carrie [Humiston], January 20, 1903; FRH to My Dear Alice [M. Humiston, hereafter AMH], November 24, 1905; FRH to My Dear Boys [Frank and John Humiston], February 22, 1907.

18. "Frederick R. Humiston," *Somerville Journal*, March 15, 1918: 7.

19. Philinda Barnes to Dear Frank, September 19, 1889; AEH to Dear Cousin [Henry S. Humiston], August 27, 1896; AEH to My Dear Little Alice [AMH], April 24, 1897; AEH to My Dear Girlies [AMH, Ruth T. and Helen E. Humiston], April 18, 1899; AEH to Dear Alice and Helen [Humiston], August 28, 1900.

20. FGH to Dear Folks at Home, December 9, 1883; AEH to My Dear Cousin [Henry S. Humiston], October 13, 1896.

21. AEH to My Dear Little Sister [Carrie Tarbell Humiston], November 14, 1886; FGH to Dear Mother, Sister & Brother, November 28, 1883; FGH to Dear Folks at Home, December 9, 1883.

22. FGH to the Inhabitants of No 19 Shepard Street, March 28, 1886.

23. "Declaration of a Widow for Restoration of Pension," July 9, 1901, "Widow's Pension," June 12, 1901, Pension Certificate No. 74921, all in Amos Humiston pension file, National Archives; AEH to Dear Carrie [Humiston] & the rest, July 29, 1903.

24. Kate A. Tarbell to Dear Alice [AMH], May 20, 1906; Philinda Barnes to Dear Alie [AMH], October 21, 1907.

25. "Thieves in Leominster," unidentified newspaper clipping; Carrie T. Humiston to Dear Little Helen [Humiston], September 26, 1909; AEH to My Dear Alice [AMH], November 16, 1912.

26. Annett and Lehtinen, *History of Jaffrey*, Vol. 1, 641–642; AMH to Dear Girls, November 5, 1912.

27. Unidentified newspaper clipping; Ruth T. Humiston to Dear Auntie [Alice E. Humiston], November 23, 1912; Franklin G. Humiston death certificate.

28. AEH to My Dear Frank, December 23, 1912; FGH to My Dear Mother, Sister and children, December 24, 1912.

29. "A New Hampshire Physician," *Boston Evening Transcript*, January 1, 1913, 3; "The Funeral of the Late Dr. Franklin G. Humiston," *Peterborough (New Hampshire) Transcript*, January 9, 1913: 2; unidentified newspaper clipping.

30. AEH to My Dear Alice, November 16, 1912; AEH to U.S. Pension Bureau, November 25, 1913, and to Pension Department for Reimbursement, January 20, 1914, both in Amos Humiston pension file, National Archives; AMH to Dear Auntie and Uncle Fred, November 19, 1913; Ruth T. Humiston to Dear Auntie, November 19, 1913.

31. "Frederick H. Humiston," *Somerville Journal*, March 15, 1918, 7; AMH diary, March 15, 16, 1918.

32. AEH to My Dear Alice [AMH], June 12, July 26, 1915; AEH to Dear Alice, February 11, February 12, 1916; Wallace D. Humiston (hereafter WDH) to Dear Miss [Alice E.] Humiston, September 2, 1916; [Superintendent] Lucius A. Whipple to Miss M. W. Williams, August 25, 1919; AMH diary, August 30–September 1, 1917.

33. Bert Ford, *The Dean Murder Mystery* (Pawtucket, R.I.: Privately Printed for the Relatives, 1920); "Witnesses Tell of Code Lights," unidentified newspaper clipping; AEH to my Dear Alice [AMH], August 28, 1918; AEH to Dear Ruth, September 29, 1918.

34. DHK, "Notes . . . on the HUMISTON family," 1986.

35. [Superintendent] Hortense V. Bunce To Whom It May Concern, August 15, 1919.

36. WDH to My dear Miss [Alice E.] Humiston, March 22, 1920; Reynolds, "Letter Ties the Centuries," *Olean Times Herald*; Fred E. Pomeroy, ed., *Bates Men and Women in the Biological World 1901–1947* (Lewiston, Me.: Tufts Brothers, Printers, n.d.), 176; DHK, "Notes on Alice Eliza Humiston," typescript, July 1993; WDH to Dear Cousin Alice [E. Humiston], June 4, 1924; AEH to My Dear Alice [AMH], September 7, 1924; AEH to Dear Helen [Humiston Kelley], April 25, 1927; AEH to Dear Ruthie [Humiston], October 18, 1929.

37. AEH to Dear Ruthie, October 18, 1929; AMH to Dear Mamma and Freda, January 17, 19, 22, 1930; AMH to Dear Mamma and Helen and Freda, Sunday night [late 1933 or early 1934]; "Ancestors and Descendants of Tracy Ensworth and Harriet Williams," typescript.

The Family's Later Years

38. AEH to My Dear Alice (AMH), September 7, 1924; AEH to My Dear Ruth [Humiston], April 8, 1930.

39. AEH to Dear Ruthie, October 18, 1929; AEH to My Dear Freda [Humiston], December 17, 1932; AMH to Dear Mamma and Freda, January 19, 1930; AMH to Dear Mamma and Freda, January 22, 1930.

40. AMH to Dear Ruth, December 16, 1933; AMH to Dear Ruth, December 26, 1933; "Woman Dies from Effect of Burns," *Glendale News Press*, December 19, 1933.

41. AMH to Dear Ruth, December 26, 1933; AMH to Dear Mamma and Helen and Freda, January 21, 1934; AMH to Dear Ruth, January 30, 1934; list of AEH's belongings at death, in AMH, memorandum book. Alice Eliza Humiston is buried in Grave 64, Tier 7, Section K-A.

42. AEH to My Dear Mr. [Henry S.] Humiston, August 15, 1896; WDH to My dear Miss Humiston, August 6, 1920, November 2, 1920.

43. Calvin W. Lewis to Carrie R. Humiston, June 17, 1914.

44. Annett and Lehtinen, *History of Jaffrey*, Vol. 1, 640.

45. AMH diary, August 25, 1935; Amos Frank Humiston interview, December 16, 1997.

CHAPTER 15

Amos Humiston Remembered

POPULAR CULTURE—NEWSPAPERS, magazines, books, photography, poetry and song—spread Amos Humiston's story during the Civil War, and popular culture has propelled virtually all of its postwar interpretation. The passing eras have not diminished the power of the tale to inspire; it has been told and retold frequently. Recent times have seen a notable surge of interest in Amos, particularly in the two communities most closely linked to his story—Portville and Gettysburg—where meaningful commemorations have demonstrated that his memory has not been forgotten.

When the popular and prolific author and editor Frank Moore published a compendium in 1866 titled *Anecdotes, Poetry and Incidents of the War: North and South*, the celebrated Humiston incident was, of course, included. Moore quoted a portion of the familiar "Whose Father Was He?" article, but, oddly enough, he did not include any follow-up relating Amos's subsequent identification.[1]

Perhaps the most influential author to tell the tale was J. Howard Wert, who as a young man was living at his family's Gettysburg farmhouse when the battle occurred. (After the fighting ended, Wert collected a large number of relics from the battlefield. Among them were more than fifty photographs of women and children—wives, sweethearts and offspring, who in some cases probably never learned of their loved one's fate, unlike Amos's family.) In 1886 Wert published one of the early Gettysburg guidebooks—a full-length book and account of the battle—bearing the cumbersome title, *A Complete Hand-book of the Monuments and Indications and Guide to the Positions on the Gettysburg Battle-Field*. Wert closed his chapter on the 11th Corps' fight of July 1, 1863, with a brief account of the Humiston incident, which he headlined, "A Sad Sight." It was a generally accurate and straightforward telling of the tale, and closed by quoting in full James Clark's familiar lyrics to "Children of the Battle Field."[2]

Wert's version of the Humiston incident formed the basis for many subsequent accounts. In another way, Wert's influence on the story has extended to the present day. At some point, he added one of the familiar cartes-de-visite of the Humiston children to his Gettysburg collection, and trimmed it to fit in a matte and case. That image illustrated two recent Gettysburg books and was alluded to as the original ambrotype found in Amos's hands.[3]

The whereabouts of the original ambrotype are unknown. Francis Bourns returned it to Philinda in Portville in 1864, but it has not been located among the extensive effects preserved by the Humiston family. In her 1914 interview for the Gettysburg newspapers, Alice Humiston intimated that Bourns had somehow regained possession of the ambrotype and accused him of keeping it. "He refused to return it, saying that we would receive it at his death. Even then we did not recover it, and although my brothers have made a number of efforts since that to find the picture, they were unsuccessful in the work." Alice was blunter in making the accusation when she wrote an undated note on an envelope containing a carte-de-visite copy of the ambrotype: "The original was never handed over to the rightful owners, who were cheated out of all the profits from the sale of the picture by Dr Francis Bourns who never did a stroke of work after the pictures began to be sold But lived in comfort all his days. He had absolutely nothing until then so my mother was told by a Lady who knew him well. My mother was young or this would not have happened."

What happened to the famous ambrotype of Frank, Alice, and Fred is one of the great remaining mysteries of the Humiston story.[4]

Following Wert's lead, other guidebook authors related the Humiston incident. Luther W. Minnigh, "Gettysburg Battle-Field Guide and Expositor," slightly modified Wert's account for his popular book, *Gettysburg: What They Did Here*, which remained in print from 1892 well into the twentieth century. Although Minnigh promoted his work as profusely illustrated, a picture did not accompany the Humiston account in the early editions. A revised 1924 printing of Minnigh's guidebook was apparently the first edition to include an illustration with the tale, a postwar Tipton & Myers photograph of Frank, Alice, and Fred. One of Minnigh's competitors, Professor J. Warren Gilbert, included a terse version of the Humiston story in an 1898 guidebook. When Gilbert expanded his work in 1922, he reprinted Wert's "A Sad Sight" article, and illustrated it with a Tipton & Myers portrait of the children. Another concise account appeared in a 1932 guidebook by W. C. Storrick, retired superintendent of guides and long-time employee of the Gettysburg National Park Commission. Unlike Wert, Minnigh, and Gilbert, Storrick made no mention of the Homestead in his piece.[5]

Gettysburg guidebooks confirmed the Humiston incident as one of the most popular human interest stories to emerge from the battle, equal to the tales of John Burns, the elderly Gettysburg resident and War of 1812 veteran who shouldered his musket and entered the fray, and Jennie Wade, the only civilian killed in the battle, hit by a stray bullet while making bread. In the section "Reminiscences of Gettysburg in Prose and Poetry" in Minnigh's guidebook, the John Burns story was presented first, the Humiston story second, and Jennie Wade's tale a couple of pages later.[6]

Years ago, Gettysburg guidebooks kept the Humiston story in the public eye. More recently, periodicals and books have spread the word. A list of the various magazines and journals that have carried Humiston accounts includes many of the scholarly and popular publications devoted to the Civil War era, and the dates of publication span decades. The Humiston story made its first known appearance in cyberspace in 1997 when a magazine article was simultaneously posted on the World Wide Web.[7]

Civil War history has not escaped the epidemic commercialism of the late twentieth century. Pages of the half-dozen or so popular magazines devoted to the conflict are filled with advertisements for Civil War prints, plates, credit cards, videotapes, figurines, travel packages, T-shirts, and reproduction weapons and accouterments. Among recent offerings was a set of cards depicting scenes, incidents, and personalities of the war. One of the cards described "Gettysburg's Unknown Father: The Fate of Amos Humiston," with the children's familiar picture on the front and a brief account on the reverse.[8]

Amos's tale has often been retold in newspapers, mainly during the recent commemorations in Portville and Gettysburg. Descendants of Fred Humiston have preserved an older example: a yellowed newspaper clipping, illustrated by a cut of the three children, which concluded with a solemn observation that obviously touched the family: "Such is the price of a nation's glory—death claiming the noblest of her sons, and households filled with lamentations."[9]

Excluding guidebooks, early books about Gettysburg were chiefly tactical studies of the battle, and neglected human interest stories. For the most part, the historians' Civil War was an epic of generals, sweeping campaigns, and complex battles; Amos Humiston, John Burns, and Jennie Wade were absent from their versions of Gettysburg. More recent years have witnessed a trend to humanize history by infusing it with the perspective of common folk—in the case of Civil War studies, the observations and experiences of the enlisted man. Reflecting this historiographical trend, the Humiston story has been often found in recent books about Gettysburg.

To be sure, Humiston accounts were included in earlier books. When the New York Monuments Commission for the Battlefields of Gettysburg and Chattanooga published three massive volumes in 1902 documenting its task in erecting monuments at Gettysburg, an account of the state's role in the battle prefaced the work, and summarized the circumstances of Amos's identification. "This man was a typical American soldier," the author concluded. "In battle, daring and brave; in death, tender and true." When a member of the 134th New York published his reminiscences in 1904, he recalled the Humiston incident and paraphrased the statement from the Monuments Commission book.[10]

Since the Civil War Centennial, books about Gettysburg, popular and scholarly, have often included the story. Versions have ranged from a simple caption under the familiar photograph of the children to fairly complete summaries, presented with varying degrees of accuracy. The Humiston tale has endured as "one of the most endearing stories associated with the battle," as noted Gettysburg historian William A. Frassanito described it. A chronicler of the Soldiers' National Cemetery has described Amos as "perhaps the most noted burial in the cemetery." Amos has even found his way into a biographical encyclopedia of the Civil War, taking a place among generals and statesmen.[11]

Photographic historians have noted the medium's integral role in the story. The Humiston case has been judged the most remarkable of several instances of wartime sales of cartes de visite to raise funds for charitable causes.[12]

Recent writings about Gettysburg have sometimes wandered down peculiar pathways. Several volumes have related stories of ghosts haunting the battlefield. One such book, warning readers that "Hell is for children, too," summarizes the familiar Humiston story and tells of mysterious screams and cries heard in and around the site of the old Homestead. The speculation is that the poor orphans tortured in Rosa Carmichael's infamous dungeon are crying out in torment from beyond the grave (despite the fact that none of them died owing to her misdeeds). To date, no one has reported seeing the specter of poor Amos wandering about Stratton Street, staring at the ambrotype in his bloodstained hand.[13]

Portville did not honor Amos Humiston as an individual soldier until a century after the war. In fact, when rosters of the town's soldiers and sailors were included in histories of Cattaraugus County published in 1879 and 1893, Amos was surprisingly, and inexplicably, omitted from the lists, despite his national renown.[14]

Amos Humiston Remembered

Amos was indirectly honored when Portville dedicated two special memorials to commemorate its soldier and sailor sons during the revival years. The Presbyterian church, site of the memorable meeting when Dr. Bourns visited Portville in January 1864, was struck by lightning and burned to the ground during a summer thunderstorm in 1895. Within months, a new sanctuary rose on the site; gracing the vestibule was a bronze tablet given by Marilla Wheeler in memory of Portville's soldiers, embossed with the names of Amos Humiston and 161 other boys in blue.[15]

On Memorial Day 1909, a towering granite obelisk in Portville's lovely Chestnut Hill Cemetery was dedicated to the memory of the town's Civil War soldiers and sailors. A large crowd gathered for the ceremony. The main address was delivered by the Reverend John Vincent, who was present when Dr. Bourns met the Humistons in 1864 and made a speech at the Presbyterian church meeting on that occasion, nearly a half-century before. (In the years since the war, Vincent had left a lasting mark on educational and cultural history by cofounding the world-famous religious, educational, and recreational colony since known as the Chautauqua Institution.) In his lengthy and inspiring address at the dedication of Portville's Civil War monument, Vincent referred to his acquaintanceship with President Lincoln and General Grant, but whether he recalled his role in the Humiston story is unknown.[16]

With the passing of her last Civil War veterans in the 1920s and 1930s, Cattaraugus County's memories of the war dimmed. They were revived in the early 1960s during the Civil War Centennial. An Olean newspaper ran a series of feature articles on the war, and one of the earliest columns related the Humiston story and reprinted the familiar photograph of the children. People in Cattaraugus County had long since lost track of the Humiston family, and writer Marian Reynolds expressed a hope that history would repeat itself, and the recirculation of the story and the picture would lead to the discovery of Humiston descendants. It eventually did. Two years later, the paper printed a follow-up article, quoting extensively from a letter written by Frank's daughter Ruth Humiston, relating details of the family's several generations.[17]

Portville's town historian during the centennial years, Bea L. Eldridge, did her part to keep Amos's memory alive with the publication of an article in a historical journal. Miss Eldridge appropriately centered her piece on the celebrated January 1864 meeting in her town's Presbyterian church.[18]

The story was told yet again when the Portville Historical and Preservation Society (PHPS) published a town history to mark the nation's bicentennial in 1976. Publicity for the book focused on its telling of the Humiston tale. Ronda S. Pollock, coeditor of the book and PHPS president, was captivated by the Humistons' story and fascinated by their Portville connections. "It's a story of a Portville family's love and loss," she stated, "a tragedy which becomes heartrending when one learns of Amos's devotion to his wife and children."[19]

In 1988, after the 125th anniversary of Amos Humiston's death at Gettysburg, the PHPS planned a special commemoration to honor the town's best-known Civil War hero. The Portville Presbyterian Church was the appropriate setting for the January 15, 1989 service. A narration of the Humiston story was interspersed with musical selections, both instrumental and vocal, including a duet rendition of "Children of the Battle Field," no doubt the first time the song had been performed in Portville in many years. The success of the special service led the PHPS to plan a more expansive event for later in the year.[20]

The Portville Free Library joined with the PHPS to sponsor Amos Humiston Days on July 1 and 2, 1989. Townspeople and visitors let their imaginations carry them back to Civil War days as they strolled among tents pitched by a reenactment group on the library lawn. Inside the library, viewers examined artifacts and memorabilia from the war, displays on Portville's soldiers, and paintings and drawings of Civil War subjects by local high school students. An ecumenical vesper service was held on the evening of July 1 at the town park, but the other events consisted of festive entertainment. A group of cloggers danced to patriotic tunes, sweets and cakes made from Civil War–era recipes were served at a tea party, and an audience relaxed in lawn chairs to enjoy an afternoon concert of period music in the park. A special souvenir was produced for the occasion—an attractive card containing a reproduction of the famous carte de visite and the lyrics to "Children of the Battle Field." But the highlight of Amos Humiston Days was the presence of Amos and Philinda's great-great-granddaughter, Alice N. Humiston of Fulton, New York, and her two children, Timothy and Carissa. It was the first time Humiston descendants were known to have visited Portville since their renowned ancestors left the town in 1866 to move to Gettysburg. A touching moment occurred when three-year-old Carissa posed for photographs next to a student's painting of the Humiston children, displaying the same round-faced innocence as her famous forebears.

Amos Humiston Days reinforced Portville's interest in its Civil War hero, which had been galvanized the year before in the commemoration at the Presbyterian church. Townspeople were consequently ready to do their part when they learned of another plan to memorialize Amos Humiston, in another town central to his story: Gettysburg.[21]

Like the battlefield guidebook writers, popular Gettysburg photographer William H. Tipton perpetuated the memory of Amos Humiston. During his long career, Tipton produced hundreds of photographs of battlefield landscapes, monuments, groups of veterans and other parties, and person- alities. In a catalog of his offerings, Tipton led off his list of portraits with three well-known subjects: John Burns, Jennie Wade, and the Humiston children. The photograph, taken during the children's Gettysburg years, was offered as a stereoscope at fifteen cents and a cabinet card at twenty cents. Pasted on the back of both versions was a label containing Luther Minnigh's version of the story and the "Children of the Battle Field" lyrics. (Tipton's catalog also included two photographs of orphans at the Home- stead.)[22]

Tipton had photographed the Humiston children several times during their residence at the Homestead, and when he learned that "little, dark- eyed Alice" was in Gettysburg in October 1914—for the first time in forty- five years—he made sure to see her. The photographer "knew more about us than I did," Alice informed Fred. Alice's visit "recalls a touching wartime incident remembered by many of the town's older residents," Gettysburg papers reported, "and a story that has since been the subject of divers newspaper articles." The town's press was eager to retell the story, and Alice was interviewed—"much to my disgust," she admitted to Fred. The resulting article, she judged, was "without the emotion . . . practically cor- rect." (According to the reporter, she had told her tale with tearful eyes.) Most of the piece rehashed the story's familiar details, but it also made public for the first time Alice's allegations against Dr. Bourns.

Details of Alice's visit went unreported in the newspapers, but she out- lined them in a letter to Fred. She visited Amos's grave three times and was pleased to find it in good condition, and to learn that the inscriptions on the soldiers' headstones were being freshly blackened. She received special permission from the caretaker to walk atop the cemetery's stone wall, as she and her brothers had done decades before, and she cut some slips of ivy to plant on Philinda's and Frank's graves. She went through the Home- stead, noting changes inside and out. Some things remained the same as she remembered them. Her mother's old room still opened into the nursery, and the numbered boxes Philinda had made still sat in the old wardrobe room. Alice declared of her formerly unhappy home, "It really makes a lovely old place." She heard many horrifying stories, however, regarding the conduct of Rosa Carmichael. "I found that almost everyone I saw had something hard to remember against her," Alice notified Fred. "She must have had a streak of insane ugliness."

She visited the monument to the 154th New York, dedicated in 1890 at the site of Kuhn's brickyard, and urged Fred's family to "take your cameras if any of you ever go." Misinformed as to where her father had been found, Alice explored the area around a postwar warehouse standing at the Stratton Street railroad crossing, a block north of where Amos had actually been discovered. In the warehouse's yard was a pump, and Alice was led to believe that Amos "fell against this pump, shot right above the heart, so that he could hardly have lived long enough to see the picture which he held in his hand." She was further persuaded when an elderly woman told her about seeing Amos and four other blackened dead soldiers buried in the warehouse yard. It was all apocryphal, but Alice was convinced of the story's veracity.

She toured the battlefield's popular tourist destinations and covered the town as well, seeing the sights, calling on acquaintances, and going to the movies. She attended Sunday services at the Presbyterian church, which she and her mother and brothers used to attend during their years at the Homestead. Gettysburg "is still the same old Dutch town," she told Fred, "with Dutch cooking, Dutch women going to market with baskets on their arms, the women with sunbonnets going all over the town." When she visited the house in which Jennie Wade was shot, she was introduced as "a relic of the war." She visited Evergreen Cemetery, where Uncle John McAllister and other old friends were buried. She made inquiries and received some sketchy information about the Schriver and Beitler families. She wore herself out walking around, and felt as if she was a hundred years old.[23]

Alice never returned to Gettysburg after her 1914 stop, and decades passed before Humiston descendants again visited the town. In the meantime, the Humiston story continued to spread via Minnigh's popular guidebook and was resurrected now and then by the local newspapers.[24]

In midcentury, the story reached a new audience—the tourists who stopped in the various commercial attractions lining Steinwehr Avenue and Baltimore Street during visits to Gettysburg. At the Gettysburg Battlefield Diorama and Museum on Steinwehr Avenue, among hundreds of figurines depicting scenes of the battle was a representation of Sergeant Humiston, complete with the picture of his three children clutched in his hand. The display was augmented in 1958 when Fred Humiston's married daughters, Doris Ladd and Eleanor Cox, presented a Mason Otis carte-de-visite copy of Amos's life portrait and the "Children of the Battle Field" sheet music to the grateful manager of the Diorama. In publicizing the gift, the *Gettysburg Times* declared that the sisters had "established a shrine to their grandfather's memory." (During the same visit, Doris and Eleanor made a similar gift to the manager of the Lincoln Room Museum on the town square.)[25]

In recent decades, the two former buildings of the Homestead have housed businesses that perpetuate memories of the orphanage and the Humistons. After the property was sold in 1878, the original brick building was used at various times as a boarding house and private dwelling. In

1957 it was purchased by Cliff Arquette, a comic actor with roots in vaudeville and radio, best known to the public for his frequent television appearances as "Charley Weaver," a lovable if sometimes caustic old codger. Offstage, Arquette was devoted to his hobbies of cooking, woodworking, and the study of American history. He combined the latter two in his Gettysburg venture, when he opened the renovated former orphanage as Cliff Arquette's Soldiers Museum in 1959. The museum featured old prints and miniature wooden soldiers he had carved. Among the displays was one that told the story of Amos Humiston and the Homestead, and depicted a small orphan boy shackled in Rosa Carmichael's dungeon. "You know," Arquette quipped, "when I told this story on *The Jack Paar Show* I received hundreds of letters from little boys all over the United States who wanted the job of being the little boy in the dungeon. However we decided on this little fellow here because he never disobeys and we don't have to feed him."

Although Arquette sold the building to Gettysburg interests in 1966, the expanded operation took the name Charley Weaver's American Museum of the Civil War, and continued to showcase Arquette's handiwork. In 1991 the property again changed hands, and the attraction was renamed the Soldier's National Museum. Over the years the facade of the building at 777 Baltimore Street has been greatly altered, but the old mansard roof constructed in 1866 is still visible behind it.[26]

Next door at 785 Baltimore Street, occupying the 1869 wood frame addition to the orphanage (which has long since been moved to front on the street), is the Homestead Lodging for Tourists. There the tale of Amos Humiston has been kept alive in a personal manner. Members of the Scott family have owned the property since the early 1920s, and two of them in particular have enthusiastically embraced the history of the Homestead. For decades, Ruth Scott Wisler collected stories and photographs of the orphanage and shared her knowledge with the tourists who lodged at the Homestead, among them descendants of former inmates of the institution. She also lectured, wrote, and gave interviews on the topic, and donated her accumulated research to Gettysburg's Adams County Historical Society. In more recent years Mrs. Wisler's niece, Mary Ruth Collins, has perpetuated her aunt's role as caretaker and proprietress of the Homestead and keeper of the place's memory. Visitors to Gettysburg who choose the Homestead over one of the many nearby motels are treated to the tale as told by Mrs. Collins and shown old photographs, "Children of the Battle Field" sheet music, and other memorabilia of distant years.[27]

Realizing the appeal of the story, officials of the Gettysburg National Military Park mounted a special Humiston display at the park's Visitor Center in 1984, where it has since been viewed by many of the 1.7 million yearly visitors to Gettysburg. The exhibit, titled "Were These the Children of the Dead Soldier?" included copies of the first *American Presbyterian* article, the *Frank Leslie's Illustrated* piece, cartes-de-visite of Amos (as civilian and soldier) and the children, a photograph of the Homestead, a copy of the "Children of the Battle Field" sheet music, and a brief summary of the story.[28]

An indirect tribute to Amos Humiston was next to appear on the Gettysburg scene, in a mural at Coster Avenue, the tiny, isolated portion of the Gettysburg National Military Park where the 154th New York's monument stands. I researched and designed it and painted it with Rhode Island artist Johan Bjurman; the eighty-foot mural was dedicated on July 1, 1988, the 125th anniversary of the battle. The painting, mounted on a warehouse wall, depicted the climactic moment of the brickyard fight, when the Union line was sent reeling by the Confederates. Portraits of several members of the 154th New York were included in the mural, among them, of course, Amos Humiston.[29]

The most profound and permanent remembrance of Amos Humiston in Gettysburg had its genesis during a walking tour in June 1991. At the North Stratton Street railroad crossing, Cindy A. Stouffer of Gettysburg heard for the first time the story of Sergeant Humiston and the Homestead. Stouffer was deeply moved and inspired. "I couldn't understand," she recalled, "why no tribute had been paid to this selfless, loving soldier whose story has never been forgotten, and is told over and over again." She immediately contacted a historian and several Gettysburg town officials, including Mayor Francis I. Linn, and received a positive reaction to her proposal of a permanent memorial to Amos Humiston. A committee, chaired by Stouffer, was formed of a dozen enthusiastic Gettysburg area residents, including Mayor Linn and Mary Ruth Collins of the Homestead Lodging. Calling themselves "Humiston's Buddies," they held their first meeting on March 13, 1992. A design for the monument was reviewed, and it was announced that the Gettysburg Fire Department had granted approval to erect the memorial on its new property at 35 North Stratton Street, at the intersection of Race Horse Alley, near the railroad crossing and not far from where Amos was found. (Judge Russell's old lot, the site of Amos's discovery, had long since been occupied by a garage, once operated by baseball Hall of Fame pitcher Edward S. "Gettysburg Eddie" Plank.) By the time the fire department location was secured, Stouffer had contacted Ronda Pollock in Portville and gained the enthusiastic backing of the PHPS for the project. Mayor Linn wrote to his counterpart in Portville, Mayor Frank Aloi, and the two towns worked in partnership to achieve their goal.[30]

In subsequent months, the design for the monument was finalized, publicity promoted the project in Gettysburg and Portville, a dedication date was set, and a third group offered its support. The *Gettysburg Times* and *Olean Times Herald* announced that the Amos Humiston Memorial, consisting of a bronze plaque with a likeness of Amos and his children and an appropriate inscription, affixed to a granite boulder, would be dedicated in July 1993. Approximately $2,500 in donations were sought. In addition to people in Gettysburg and Portville, descendants of members of the 154th New York, who had been gathering at annual reunions in Cattaraugus County to represent and remember their ancestors since 1986, were solicited for contributions.[31]

As the summer of 1993 approached, excitement built in Gettysburg and Cattaraugus County. The fund-raising drive surpassed its goal, and another round of newspaper articles publicized the upcoming dedication. The villages of Portville and Gettysburg "will be linked together forever," one story noted, "when the two communities pay tribute to Sgt. Amos Humiston." Olean's Twin Tier Civil War Round Table presented a donation to the Portville Central School Marching Band for the band's trip to Gettysburg, where it was scheduled to perform during the ceremony, and numerous Portville residents made travel plans of their own.[32]

At 10 A.M. on Saturday, July 3, 1993, a sunny, hot, and humid day in Gettysburg, a large crowd assembled at Coster Avenue. Among them were more than two hundred people from Portville and vicinity, all sporting buttons reading, "Sgt. Humiston, 154th NY Vols. Portville, NY." A group of reenactors conducted a brief ceremony at the monument to the 154th New York. Then, led by the Portville Central School Marching Band, the crowd proceeded south on North Stratton Street to the grounds of the Gettysburg Fire Department, where their numbers were augmented by other visitors and Gettysburg residents.

At the monument site, the Gettysburg Ceremonial Brass Band and the Portville band performed some musical selections, culminating in a rendition of the National Anthem. Master of ceremonies Walter L. Powell, a member of the Humiston memorial committee, welcomed the audience, Mayor Linn welcomed the out-of-towners to Gettysburg, and Mayor Aloi responded with thanks and an expression of Portville's pride on the occasion. After the Reverend Kenneth Foust of the Portville Presbyterian Church offered an invocation, Dr. Powell introduced the Humiston descendants on hand, other special guests, and his fellow committee members. I had the signal honor of delivering the main address, during which I quoted expressions of love from Amos's wartime letters and read the touching poem Amos dedicated to Philinda on March 25, 1863.

After James A. Getty of Gettysburg made a short presentation in the guise of Abraham Lincoln, Dr. Powell led the audience in a stirring rendition of "The Battle Hymn of the Republic." He then introduced a special visitor from Dumfries, Scotland. Stephen Rady had been moved by reading an account of the Humiston story and had written a letter to Gettysburg's postmaster, whereupon he was invited to attend the ceremony by the memorial committee. The kilt-clad Mr. Rady read a poem he had composed titled "The Unknown Soldier," a worthy successor to the nineteenth-century poetry inspired by Amos Humiston:

> A soldier lies in battle, face buried in the mud;
> A picture of his children there painted in his blood.
> Fighting for their freedom he fought until his death;
> He kissed his children's picture as he took his dying breath.
> His side lost this battle, but no side ever wins;
> For when this war is over, another war begins.

The Portville Singers, a duo composed of Dawn Pierce and Nathan Chaffee of Portville, sang a fine rendition of "Children of the Battle Field." Then came the climactic moment of the day: the unveiling of the monument and presentation of floral tributes by a half-dozen Humiston descendants. The Portville band played "America," the Reverend Robert MacAskill of the Gettysburg Presbyterian Church offered a benediction, and the reenactors shot a volley. As the humidity absorbed the last echoes of the gunfire, a bugler played "Taps" to close the ceremony.[33]

And so, in the sweltering heat of a July day 130 years after the battle, the monument began its long vigil, to stand through the ages as a constant reminder of Amos Humiston's devotion and sacrifice. More than 150,000 Americans of the North and South fought at Gettysburg in 1863. Today more than twelve hundred monuments dot the hills, fields and roadsides to commemorate batteries, brigades, divisions, corps, generals, states, and regiments. Only one of them is dedicated to an individual enlisted man: the memorial to Sergeant Amos Humiston. On the greatest battlefield in the United States, his unique monument commemorates a gesture of love.[34]

NOTES

1. Frank Moore, *Anecdotes, Poetry and Incidents of the War: North and South, 1860–1865* (New York: Printed for the subscribers), 321.

2. J. Howard Wert, *A Complete Hand-Book of the Monuments and Indications and Guide to the Positions on the Gettysburg Battle-Field* (Harrisburg: R. M. Sturgeon & Co., Publishers, 1886), 179–180; Champ Clark, *Gettysburg: The Confederate High Tide* (Alexandria, Va.: Time-Life Books, 1985), 148.

3. Clark, *Gettysburg*, 148–149, 151; Editors of Time-Life Books, *Voices of the Civil War: Gettysburg* (Alexandria, Va.: Time-Life Books, 1995), 149; Michael J. Winey to author, May 14, 1997.

Amos Humiston Remembered

4. "Visit Recalls Wartime Story," unidentified newspaper clipping, October 28, 1914 (also published in *[Gettysburg] Star and Sentinel*, October 31, 1914); Alice Humiston, undated note on an envelope, DHK.

5. Luther W. Minnigh, *Gettysburg: What They Did Here* (n.p., 1892), 123, (Gettysburg: N. A. Meligakes, 1924), 144–145, (Gettysburg: Bookmart, 1954), 144–145; J. Warren Gilbert, *Battle of Gettysburg . . . Made Plain* (n.p., n.d.), 24; Gilbert, *The Battle of Gettysburg Made Plain* (n.p., 1898), 48; Gilbert, *The Blue and Gray: A History of the Conflicts During Lee's Invasion and the Battle of Gettysburg* (n.p., 1922), 132; W. C. Storrick, *Gettysburg: The Place, the Battles, the Outcome* (Harrisburg: J. Horace McFarland Company, 1932), 86.

6. Minnigh, *Gettysburg* (1924 edition), 142–147.

7. "Story of a Picture," *Lincoln Herald* 46, no. 3 (October 1994): 46–47; Robert S. Harper, "An Incident in the Present Fratricidal War," *Civil War History* 5, no. 4 (December 1959): 421–424; Art Costigan, "The Children of the Battlefield," *Civil War Book Exchange* 8, no. 1 (October–November 1981): 1; William Gladstone, "The Children of the Battle Field," *Military Images* 2, no. 5 (March–April 1981): 8–9; Mark Dunkelman and Michael Winey, "The Hunt for Sergeant Humiston," *Civil War Times Illustrated* 21, no. 1 (March 1982): 28–31; Ben Fanton, "Thanks to a Cherished Photograph, 'the Unknown Soldier of Gettysburg' Did Not Remain Unknown for Long," *America's Civil War* (July 1994): 18, 20, 24, 78; Mark H. Dunkelman, "Key to a Mystery," *American History* (May–June 1997): 16–20, 58–61; "Memories," *Genealogical Helper* (September–October 1989): 203; Ben Fanton, "One Soldier's Tale," *Buffalo Magazine*, July 4, 1993, 14–15; "Local Civil War Hero," *Tattered Glory* (newsletter of the Twin Tier Civil War Round Table, Olean, New York) 3, no. 10 (October 1993); Dunkelman, "Key to a Mystery," available May–June 1997 on the Internet at http://www.thehistorynet.com.

8. Stephen T. Foster, "Gettysburg's Unknown Father: The Fate of Amos Humiston," card published by Atlas Editions, USA, 1994.

9. Unidentified, undated newspaper clipping, courtesy of Allan L. Cox.

10. William F. Fox, "New York at Gettysburg," in New York Monuments Commission for the Battlefields of Gettysburg and Chattanooga, *Final Report on the Battlefield of Gettysburg* (Albany: J. B. Lyon Company, Printers, 1902), vol. I, 22; William T. Levey, *The Blue and the Gray: A Sketch of Soldier Life in Camp and Field in the Army of the Civil War* (Schenectady: Roy Burton Myers, Publisher, 1904), 24.

11. William A. Frassanito, *Early Photography at Gettysburg* (Gettysburg: Thomas Publications, 1995), 118; Blake A. Magner, "The Gettysburg Soldiers' National Cemetery: Yesterday and Today," *Gettysburg Magazine*, no. 14 (January 1996): 111; Jack McLaughlin, *Gettysburg: The Long Encampment* (New York: Bonanza Books, 1963), 201; Warren W. Hassler, Jr., *Crisis at the Crossroads: The First Day at Gettysburg* (University: University of Alabama Press, 1970), 82; Clark, *Gettysburg*, 151; David G. Martin, *Gettysburg July 1* (Conshohocken, Pa.: Combined Books, 1995), 316–317; Gregory A. Coco, *A Strange and Blighted Land: Gettysburg: The Aftermath of a Battle* (Gettysburg: Thomas Publications, 1995), 308; Editors of Time-Life Books, *Voices of the Civil War: Gettysburg*, 149; Gerard

A. Patterson, *Debris of Battle: The Wounded of Gettysburg* (Mechanicsburg, Pa.: Stackpole Books, 1997), 194, 198; Stewart Sifakis, *Who Was Who in the Civil War* (New York: Facts on File Publications, 1988), 325; James Cole and Roy E. Frampton, *The Gettysburg National Cemetery: A History and Guide* (Hanover, Pa.: Sheridan Press, 1988), 34; Webb Garrison, *Civil War Curiosities: Strange Stories, Oddities, Events, and Coincidences* (Nashville: Rutledge Hill Press, 1994), 204–205; "Death of Cattaraugus County Veteran Creates a National Drama," in Craig F. Senfield, ed., *Civil War Veterans Cemetery Locator*, Vol. I: *Cattaraugus County, New York* (Olean: Twin Tier Civil War Round Table, 1996), inside back cover.

12. William C. Darrah, *The Carte de Visite in Nineteenth Century Photography* (Gettysburg: W. C. Darrah, Publisher, 1981), 84–86; Kathleen Collins, "Photographic Fundraising: Civil War Philanthropy," *History of Photography* 11, no. 3 (July–September 1987): 181–184.

13. Mark Nesbitt, *Ghosts of Gettysburg III: Spirits, Apparitions and Haunted Places of the Battlefield* (Gettysburg: Thomas Publications), 35–38.

14. Franklin Ellis, ed., *History of Cattaraugus County, New York* (Philadelphia: L. H. Everts, 1879), 123, 138–139; William Adams, ed., *Historical Gazetteer and Biographical Memorial of Cattaraugus County, N.Y.* (Syracuse: Lyman, Horton & Co., Limited, 1893), 238–239, 1006.

15. Thomas C. Pollock and Ronda S. Pollock, eds., *A History of the Town of Portville 1805–1920* (Portville: Portville Historical & Preservation Society, 1986), 17, 25–26; Harry C. Holcomb, *Glimpses of Fifty Years* (Portville: N.p., 1931), 74–76.

16. Pollock and Pollock, *A History of the Town of Portville*, 146; Leon H. Vincent, *John Heyl Vincent: A Biographical Sketch* (New York: Macmillan, 1925), 116–119, 126, 132; Ronda S. Pollock to author, September 22, 1997, quoting *Portville Review* of June 4, 1909.

17. Marian Reynolds, "Photo Has Stellar Role in War Tale," *Olean Times Herald*, May 19, 1960, B-1; Marian Reynolds, "Letter Ties the Centuries," *Olean Times Herald*, April 23, 1962, 18.

18. Bea L. Eldridge, "Interesting Details of a Charity Meeting in Portville, New York," *Yesteryears* 4 (December 1960): 19–20.

19. Pollock and Pollock, *A History of the Town of Portville*, 152–154; "Humiston Story Featured in Portville History Book," *Olean Times Herald*, undated clipping; Lisa Nianiatus, "Amos Humiston: 'Portville Hero' Who Touched Nation's Heart," *Olean Times Herald*, February 14, 1989, 3; Ronda Pollock to author, October 19, 1997.

20. Portville Historical and Preservation Society, *Special Program at the First Presbyterian Church*, 50 min., 1989, videocassette.

21. "Amos Humiston Day—July 1, 1989," *Homespun Collage* 4, no. 2 (May 1989): 1, 2; "Weekend to Remember Amos Humiston in Portville," *Independent Olean Press*, June 26, 1989; Eva White, "Civil War in Portville," unidentified, undated newspaper clipping.

22. W. H. Tipton, *Catalogue of Tipton's Photographic Views of the Battlefield of Gettysburg* (Gettysburg: J. E. Wible, 1894), 2, 8, 33.

Amos Humiston Remembered

23. "Visit Recalls Wartime Story," unidentified newspaper clipping, also published in *[Gettysburg] Star and Sentinel*, October 31, 1914; Alice E. Humiston to Dear Fred, October 28, 1914, courtesy of David Humiston Kelley.

24. "Finding of Soldier's Body, with Photograph of Three Children, Prompts Establishment of Soldiers' Orphans' Home in Gettysburg," *Gettysburg Times*, June 19, 1941, 1, 5.

25. Photograph of exhibit, *Gettysburg Times*, March 27, 1958; "Belmont Sisters Establish Shrine to Grandfather at Gettysburg," *Belmont [Mass.] Herald*, April 10, 1958; "Descendants Give Exhibit to Gettysburg Diorama," *Belmont [Mass.] Citizen*, April 11, 1958: 4; Eleanor Cox to Dear Mr. [Curvin] Heiss [manager, Lincoln Room Museum], March 1, 1958; Eleanor Cox to Dear Mr. [Bernard] Murray [manager, Gettysburg Battlefield Diorama and Museum], April 10, 1958.

26. Mary Ruth Collins and Cindy A. Stouffer, *One Soldier's Legacy: The National Homestead at Gettysburg* (Gettysburg: Thomas Publications, 1993), 93–96; Wolfgang Saxon, "Act of Perfection," *New York Times*, September 24, 1974: 44 [obituary of Cliff Arquette]; Frassanito, *Early Photography at Gettysburg*, 135–138; "Soldiers Natl. Museum Makes Donation to Gettysburg Park," *Civil War News* (October 1997); Brenda F. Showers, manager, Gettysburg Tour Center, to Dear Mrs. [Marian] Reynolds, March 27, 1976, courtesy of the Portville Free Library, Portville, New York.

27. Collins and Stouffer, *One Soldier's Legacy*, 3, 82–83, 95–96, inside back cover; Ruth Scott Wisler to Dear Mr. [Michael J.] Winey, September 6, 1972, courtesy of Michael Winey.

28. Kathleen R. Georg, research historian, Gettysburg National Military Park, to author, December 6, 1982; Michael J. Winey to author, May 17, 1984.

29. Mark H. Dunkelman, *The Coster Avenue Mural in Gettysburg* (Providence: Published by the author, 1989); Dorothy S. Bloom, "80-Foot Mural to Be Dedicated," *Gettysburg Times*, June 28, 1988: 3A; Kathryn Jorgensen, "80-Foot Mural Remembers Veterans of 154th New York," *Civil War News* (August 1989).

30. Cindy A. Stouffer to author, May 31, 1997; Collins and Stouffer, *One Soldier's Legacy*, inside back cover; Harris W. Sacks, "Sgt. Humiston Monument Will Be Erected at Gettysburg Fire Hall," *Gettysburg Times*, May 15, 1993, 9A; Cindy Stouffer to author, February 15, March 16, 1992; William Ridinger to author, March 7, March 22, 1992; Francis I. Linn to Dear Mayor [Frank] Aloi, March 17, 1992; William A. Frassanito, *The Gettysburg Bicentennial Album* (Gettysburg: Adams County Historical Society, 1987), 27–28.

31. H. William Sacks, " 'Gettysburg's Unknown Soldier' Salute Set," *Gettysburg Times*, April 30, 1992: 1A, 3A; Kate Day, "A Soldier's Love for His Family Has Been Retold Down the Years," *Olean Times Herald*, July 6, 1992, A-9; "New Memorial in Gettysburg to Remember Sgt. Humiston," *Civil War News* (August 1992): 55; Cindy Stouffer to author, April 22, June 7, 1992; Author to Dear Descendant[s] of the 154th New York Volunteers, July 1, 1992.

32. Sacks, "Sgt. Humiston Monument," 9A; "July 3rd Ceremony to Honor Amos Humiston in Gettysburg," *Civil War Times* (July 1993): 27; "Civil War Panel to Recognize 2 Portville Groups," *Bradford [Pa.] Era*, June 15, 1993: 2; "Round

the Square," *Bradford Era*, June 17, 1993: 3 [quote]; "Portville Band to Participate in Gettysburg Ceremony," *Olean Times Herald*, June 15, 1993, A-8; "Portville Band Gets Boost for Gettysburg Trip," *Olean Times Herald*, June 27, 1993, C-7; "Humiston Dedication in Gettysburg," *Homespun Collage* 8, no. 3 (June 1993); Cindy Stouffer to author, March 28, May 18, 1993; Walter L. Powell to Dear Friends of Amos Humiston, June 11, 1993.

33. Harris W. Sacks, "Humiston Monument Unveiled in Gettysburg," *Gettysburg Times*, July 5, 1993, 1A, 3A; Elin Marcel, "Remembering One Civil War Tragedy," *[Hanover, Pa.] Evening Sun*, July 4, 1993, A-3; Debbie Jakala, "Portville Builds Bridge Through Time to a Neighbor Who Fell at Gettysburg," *Olean Times Herald*, July 10, 1993, A-2; Doug Coy, "Portville Soldier Honored in Gettysburg," *Independent Olean Press*, July 12, 1993; Warren E. Motts, "Dedication of the Humiston Memorial at Gettysburg," *Blue and Gray Magazine* (October 1994): 44; *Amos Humiston Memorial Dedication July 3, 1993 Program*; Stephen Rady, "The Unknown Soldier," manuscript poem, author's collection; Ronda S. Pollock to author, August 30, 1997; videotape of the ceremony.

34. D. Scott Hartwig and Ann Marie Hartwig, *Gettysburg: The Complete Pictorial of Battlefield Monuments* (Gettysburg: Thomas Publications, 1995); Kathleen Georg Harrison, Senior Historian, Gettysburg National Military Park, to author, October 17, 1995.

Appendix: Songs Inspired by Amos Humiston

THE CHILDREN
OF THE BATTLE FIELD.

POETRY & MUSIC — **BY J. G. CLARK.**

AS SUNG BY THE AUTHOR, AT HIS BALLAD ENTERTAINMENTS.

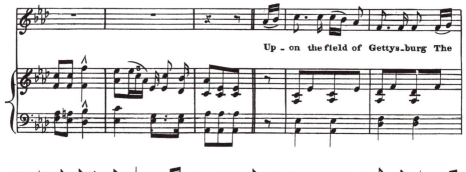

Up - on the field of Gettys - burg The

summer sun was high, When freedom met her haughty foe, Beneath a northern sky; A

9031. 3.

Entered according to Act of Congress A. D. 1864 by Lee & Walker at the Clerk's Office of the Dt. Ct. of the En. Dt. of Pa.

_mong the he_roes of the North, Who swelled her grand ar_ray, And rushed like moun_tain eagles forth From happy homes a _ way. There stood a man of humble fame, A sire of children three, And gazed within a little frame, Their pictured form to see. And blame him not, if in the strife, He breathed a soldier's prayer: O

9031.3.

FATHER, shield the soldier's wife, And for his children care, And for his chil-dren care.

2

Upon the field of Gettysburg
  When morning shone again,
The crimson cloud of battle burst
  In streams of fiery rain;
Our legions quelled the awful flood
  Of shot, and steel, and shell,
While banners, marked with ball and blood,
  Around them rose and fell;
And none more nobly won the name
  Of Champion of the Free,
Than he who pressed the little frame
  That held his children three;
And none were braver in the strife
  Than he who breathed the prayer:
O! FATHER, shield the soldier's wife,
  And for his children care.

3

Upon the Field of Gettysburg
  The full moon slowly rose,
She looked, and saw ten thousand brows
  All pale in death's repose,
And down beside a silver stream,
  From other forms away,
Calm as a warrior in a dream,
  Our fallen comrade lay;
His limbs were cold, his sightless eyes
  Were fixed upon the three
Sweet stars that rose in mem'ry's skies
  To light him o'er death's sea.
Then honored be the soldier's life,
  And hallowed be his prayer,
O! FATHER, shield the soldiers wife,
  And for his children care.

9031.3.

248

THE UNKNOWN SOLDIER!

(Who is he?)

"After the battles of Gettysburg, July, 1st, 2d and 3d, 1863, a Union Soldier was found, in a secluded spot on the field, where, wounded, he had laid himself down to die. In his hands, tightly clasped, was an ambrotype containing the portraits of three small children, and upon this picture his eyes, set in death, rested. The last object upon which the dying father looked was the image of his children, and as he silently gazed upon them, his soul passed away. How touching! How solemn! What pen can describe the emotions of this patriot father as he gazed upon the children, so soon to be made orphans? Wounded and alone, the din of battle still sounding in his ears, he lies down to die. His last thoughts and prayers are for his family. He has finished his work on earth; his last battle has been fought; he has freely given his life to his country; and now, while his life's blood is ebbing, he clasps in his hands the image of his children, and commending them to the God of the fatherless, rests his last lingering look upon them."

When, after the battle, the dead were being buried, this soldier was thus found. The ambrotype was taken from his embrace, and has since been sent to Philadelphia for recognition. Nothing else was found upon his person by which he might be identified. His grave has been marked, however, and if by any means this ambrotype will lead to his recognition, he can be disinterred. This picture is now in the possession of Dr. Bourns, No. 1104 Spring Garden street, Philadelphia, who can be called upon or addressed in reference to it. The children, two boys and a girl, are apparently nine, seven and five years of age; the boys being respectively the oldest and youngest of the three. The youngest boy is sitting in a high chair, and on each side of him are his brother and sister. The oldest boys jacket is made from the same material as his sister's dress. These are the most prominent features of the group. Of what inestimable value will it be to these children, proving, as it does, that the last thoughts of their dying father was for them and them only.

Words by Gen. W. H. Hayward.　　　　　　　　　　　　　　　*Music by Maj. Wilson G. Horner.*

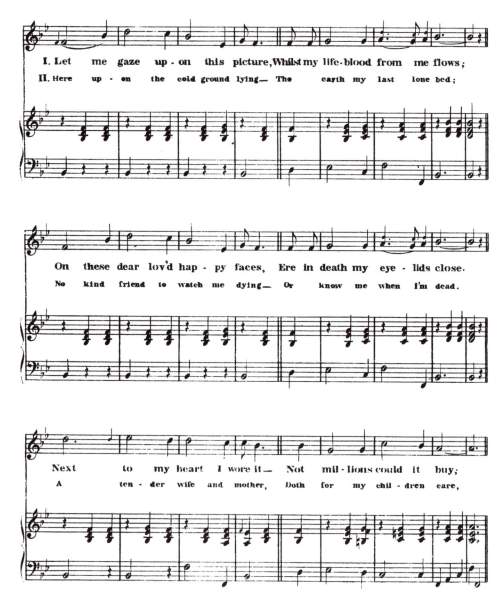

I. Let me gaze up-on this picture, Whilst my life-blood from me flows;
II. Here up-on the cold ground lying— The earth my last lone bed;

On these dear lov'd hap - py faces, Ere in death my eye - lids close.
No kind friend to watch me dying— Or know me when I'm dead.

Next to my heart I wore it— Not mil-lions could it buy;
A ten - der wife and mother, Doth for my chil - dren care,

Let me see my heart's own treasures, And kiss them as I die.
And night-ly bend-ing o'er them, To God breathes forth her prayer.

3

That we all may meet together
　In peace again once more;
That around the happy fire-side
　Kind Heav'n will me restore.
But I feel my pulse grows weaker;
　My eyes— I scarce can see!
Still I recognize the features
　Of my little boy— 'tis he!

4

My darling boys and loving daughter,
　Let none their image tear
From this poor dying, bleeding heart,
　Now offering up this prayer —
Oh, God! protect the mother
　And these my orphans dear;
I die alone— none near me—
　No one to shed a tear.

5

Some stranger hand will find me—
　For me a grave prepare;
On my breast they'll place this picture,
　And say they found it there.
Let *the Flag* be wrapped around me—
　The Stars and Stripes I love!
I die a Union soldier,
　True as the heavens above.

6

The flowers will bloom as sweetly,
　O'er the unknown soldier's grave,
With his heart's loved idols near him,
　And *the Flag* he died to save.
No stone will mark the spot
　Of the stranger 'neath the sod,
Where so peacefully he slumbers,
　Unknown— save to his God.

5932

Bibliographical Note

PRIMARY AND SECONDARY sources are fully cited at first appearance under each chapter in the notes. There are many of them (forty-six newspapers were consulted, for example). Those most essential to telling the Humiston story—and most likely to be of benefit to interested readers—are referred to here.

Invaluable to the study of the Humistons are the papers preserved by David Humiston Kelley, including many family letters spanning several decades. David's 1986 typescript, "Notes on One Branch of the HUMISTON Family," is a helpful outline of family connections. Other useful sources include the state and federal census records for the town of Portville at the Cattaraugus County Memorial and Historical Museum in Little Valley, New York; Amos Humiston's pension records at the National Archives in Washington, D.C.; the biographical sketch in New York (State) Bureau of Military Statistics, *First Annual Report of the Chief of the Bureau of Military Statistics* (n.p., 1864); census records for the towns of Owego and Candor at the Tioga County Historical Society in Owego, New York; Henry B. Pierce and D. Hamilton Hurd, *History of Tioga, Chemung, Tompkins, and Schuyler Counties, New York* (Philadelphia: Everts & Ensign, 1879); and Albert Annett and Alice E. E. Lehtinen, *History of Jaffrey (Middle Monadnock) New Hampshire: An Average Country Town in the Heart of New England* (Jaffrey: Published by the Town, 1937).

Key to understanding the voyage of the *Harrison* is the ship's logbook in the Nicholson Whaling Collection of the Providence (Rhode Island) Public Library. Also useful were the *Harrison*'s whalemen's shipping paper, crew list card files, and protections file cards at the New Bedford (Massachusetts) Free Public Library; and the *Whalemen's Shipping List and Merchants' Transcript* of New Bedford. Two classics, Clifford W. Ashley, *The Yankee Whaler* (New York: Dover, 1991, reprint), and Elmo Paul Hohman, *The American Whaleman: A Study of Life and Labor in the Whaling Industry* (New York: Longmans, Green, 1928), are nicely complemented by two newer studies of the whaleman's life: Briton Cooper Busch, *"Whaling Will Never Do for Me": The American Whaleman in the Nineteenth Century* (Lexington: University Press of Kentucky, 1994), and Margaret S. Creighton, *Rites and Passages: The Experience of American Whaling, 1830–1870* (Cambridge: Cambridge University Press, 1995).

Helpful sources on Portville and Cattaraugus County include William Adams, ed., *Historical Gazetteer and Biographical Memorial of Cattaraugus County, N.Y.* (Syracuse: Lyman, Horton and Co., 1893); Franklin Ellis, ed., *History of Cattaraugus County, New York* (Philadelphia: L. H. Everts, 1879); and Thomas C. Pollock and Ronda S. Pollock, eds., *A History of the Town of Portville, 1805–1920* (Portville, N.Y.: Portville Historical and Preservation Society, 1986).

Amos Humiston's letters, kindly shared with me by Allan L. Cox, reveal the Civil War as Amos experienced it. Helping to round out the picture were the wartime letters of Amos's Company C comrades, Martin V. B. Champlin (courtesy of Richard D. Champlin and Donald K. Ryberg, Jr.); William H. Keyes, Edwin R. Osgood, and James W. Washburn (courtesy of the National Archives); the diaries of Lewis D. Warner (courtesy of John L. Spencer) and Stephen Welch (courtesy of Carolyn Stoltz); and the memoir of Charles W. McKay, "Three Years or During the War, with the Crescent and Star," *National Tribune Scrap Book* (n.p., n.d.). Mark H. Dunkelman and Michael J. Winey, *The Hardtack Regiment: An Illustrated History of the 154th Regiment, New York State Infantry Volunteers* (East Brunswick, N.J.: Fairleigh Dickinson University Press, 1981) is a general history of Amos's regiment; Mark H. Dunkelman and Michael J. Winey, "The Hardtack Regiment in the Brickyard Fight," *Gettysburg Magazine*, no. 8 (January 1993): 17–30, relates the 154th's role at Gettysburg.

Essential for the history of the Homestead are newspapers, in particular the *American Presbyterian*, the *Gettysburg Compiler*, and the *Gettysburg Star and Sentinel* (articles from the latter two are in the orphanage file at the Gettysburg National Military Park Library). The Edward McPherson papers at the Library of Congress in Washington, D.C., contain invaluable Homestead material. Helpful too are issues of *The Homestead Journal, Issued in the Interest of the National Orphans' Homestead, at Gettysburg, Pa.*, and Mary Ruth Collins and Cindy A. Stouffer, *One Soldier's Legacy: The National Homestead at Gettysburg* (Gettysburg: Thomas Publications, 1993).

Acknowledgments

TWO OLD FRIENDS helped put me on the trail of the Humiston story, and so are the first of many to receive my thanks. As teenage neighbors and schoolmates in Amherst, New York, Christopher L. Ford and I shared a deep interest in the Civil War. During the Civil War Centennial, Chris presented me with a copy of Luther W. Minnigh's *Gettysburg: What They Did Here* and thereby introduced me to the Humistons. In more recent years, Chris and his wife, Michelle Wesley, have welcomed me to their Fairfax, Virginia, home during research trips to Washington. Michael J. Winey, curator of Special Collections at the U.S. Army Military History Institute at Carlisle Barracks, Pennsylvania, has been my partner since 1972 in an intensive study of the 154th New York. Our long and productive collaboration has been a valuable learning experience for me. Over the years Mike has shared some rare Humiston materials.

My Humiston research intensified in 1989, and in the years since then, a lengthy list of people has assisted me in matters great and small. Virtually all of them provided help regarding a specific aspect of the Humiston story. In learning about Amos's home town, for example, I was fortunate to have the assistance of Joann K. Lindstrom, director of collections at the Tioga County Historical Society in Owego, New York, who answered many inquiries rapidly and cheerfully. Others in New York State who deserve my thanks include Craig Braack, Allegany County historian, Belmont; Julia A. Chaffee, volunteer, Tioga County Historical Society, Owego; David H. Crowley, town and village historian, Cuba; Ronald J. Fitzgerald, president, Owego-Waverly Abstract Company, Owego; Linda Jacobs, Tioga County Clerk's Office, Owego; Stephen Kratts, Cuba; M. Pat Schaap, Livingston County historian, Geneseo; Marion Springer, Steuben County Clerk's Office, Bath; and Ellsworth Swift, Cuba.

David S. LaSalle of the LaSalle Harness Company in North Scituate, Rhode Island, taught me what I needed to know about Amos's main trade, and shared rare sources with me.

Acknowledgments

My Providence neighbor, Virginia M. Adams, former librarian at the Old Dartmouth Historical Society Whaling Museum in New Bedford, Massachusetts, got me off to a good start in studying Amos's whaling career when she informed me of his service aboard the *Harrison*, told me the whereabouts of the ship's logbook, and suggested some excellent secondary sources. Virginia also kindly read an early draft of the whaling chapters. Philip J. Weimerskirch, special collections librarian at the Providence Public Library, did double duty. In addition to providing many valuable sources from the Nicholson Whaling Collection, including the *Harrison*'s logbook, Phil also supplied me with a number of fine sources from the excellent C. Fiske Harris Collection on the Civil War and Slavery. At the New Bedford Free Public Library I was assisted by Paul Cyr, curator of special collections; and Tina Furtado, archivist. Helping me at The Kendall Whaling Museum in Sharon, Massachusetts, were Stuart M. Frank, director; Michael P. Dyer, assistant curator and librarian; and Louise Dembrowsky, registrar. At the Old Dartmouth Historical Society Whaling Museum in New Bedford, my thanks to Judith M. Downey, librarian; and Laura C. Pereira, library and program assistant. Others who aided my whaling research include Peter J. Blodgett, curator of western historical manuscripts, the Huntington Library, San Marino, California; Charlene Dahlquist, librarian, Lyman House Memorial Museum, Hilo, Hawaii; Kelly Drake, manuscripts assistant, G. W. Blunt White Library, Mystic Seaport Museum, Mystic, Connecticut; Dorothy T. King, librarian, Long Island Collection, East Hampton Library, East Hampton, New York; Scott McCloud, reference librarian, McKinney Library, Albany Institute of History and Art, Albany, New York; Robert R. McKenna, editor, *Nautical World*, New London, Connecticut; Mel E. Smith, librarian, History and Genealogy Unit, Connecticut State Library, Hartford; and Jan Voogd, reference librarian, Phillips Library, Peabody Essex Museum, Salem, Massachusetts.

In Cattaraugus County, New York, I turned—as I have many times in the past—to Kenneth Kysor, Cattaraugus County historian, Little Valley; and Lorna Spencer, curator, Cattaraugus County Memorial and Historical Museum, Little Valley. Both are always helpful and much appreciated. Ronda S. Pollock, president of the Portville Historical and Preservation Society, has always been a ready source of information on her home town and a strong supporter of my various projects, and she and her husband, Thomas C. Pollock, have welcomed me several times for stays at their beautifully restored Portville home.

Since the early 1970s I have contacted more than 550 descendants of members of the 154th New York, who have kindly shared with me more than 1,200 wartime letters and more than a score of diaries written by their ancestors. In this book I have kept the focus tightly on Amos's Company

Acknowledgments

C, and I thank the following descendants of members of the company for sharing materials regarding their ancestors: Richard D. Champlin, Bountiful, Utah; John L. Spencer, Canandaigua, New York; and Carolyn Stoltz, Tonawanda, New York. My appreciation also goes to Donald K. Ryberg, Jr., of Westfield, New York, who has always generously shared his 154th New York finds with me.

In Gettysburg, Pennsylvania, Kathleen Georg Harrison, senior historian at the Gettysburg National Military Park, has been a steady supporter of my work on this and other projects. My sincere thanks go to Cindy A. Stouffer and Mary Ruth Collins for their work to keep the memory of Amos Humiston alive in, respectively, the establishment of his memorial and the operation of the Homestead Lodging. Staying at the Homestead with the Humiston descendants on the weekend of the July 1993 memorial dedication, and having the honor of delivering the main address at the dedication ceremony, was a great pleasure for me. Also in Gettysburg, Charles H. Glatfelter, director of the Adams County Historical Society, aided by Timothy H. Smith, volunteer, answered repeated requests with dispatch. For sharing information and materials, thanks are also due William A. Frassanito, William J. Little, Walter L. Powell, Larry R. Runk, Dean S. Thomas, and Wanda Y. Walter, Adams County deputy prothonotary, all of Gettysburg; and Gregory A. Coco of Bendersville, Pennsylvania.

Much of the Humiston story was disseminated in Philadelphia, and I spent some profitable time there. My thanks to Jennifer Ambrose, visual materials cataloguer, and Jennifer Sanchez, coordinator for rights and reproductions, Library Company of Philadelphia; Kevin Crawford, College of Physicians of Philadelphia Library; Linda Franchini, Microfilm Room, Joseph F. Perry, librarian, Database and Newspaper Center, and Barbara Pilvin, Social Science and History Department, Free Library of Philadelphia; Jim Monday, Union League of Philadelphia; Daniel N. Rolph, reference librarian, Historical Society of Pennsylvania; Kenneth J. Ross, reference librarian, Presbyterian Church Department of History; and Steven J. Wright, curator, and Steve Zerbe, researcher, Civil War Library and Museum.

My thanks to Mary A. Parker of Lexington, Virginia, for summarizing the diaries of J. Francis Bourns and providing his portrait. Also helping with material on the doctor were Todd Andrew Dorsett, Waynesboro, Pennsylvania; Ruth Gembe, Alexander Hamilton Memorial Free Library, Waynesboro; Helen Kuncl, Data Collection, American Medical Association, Chicago, Illinois; Judith A. Meier, librarian, Historical Society of Montgomery County, Norristown, Pennsylvania; and Andrea Struble, Waynesboro Historical Society.

Acknowledgments

I am grateful for the help I received from Washington, D.C.: Sam Daniel, Prints and Photographs Division, and Jeffrey M. Flannery, manuscript reference librarian, at the Library of Congress; and Stuart L. Butler and Michael P. Musick of the Textual Reference Division, National Archives. Thanks too to Fred Pernell, assistant chief for reference, Still Picture Branch, National Archives at College Park, Maryland.

My appreciation to each of the following for help with sundry matters: LeRoy Barnett, archivist, Michigan Historical Center, Lansing; James W. Campbell, librarian and curator of manuscripts, Whitney Library, New Haven Colony Historical Society, New Haven, Connecticut; Patrick J. Cullen, Cattaraugus, New York; Rosemary Cullen, curator, Harris Collection, John Hay Library, Brown University, Providence, Rhode Island; Henry Deeks, Acton, Massachusetts; Jacquelyn Foy, librarian, Gilbert Library, Northfield, Connecticut; Emily B. Geschwindt, reference librarian, Commonwealth Libraries, Harrisburg, Pennsylvania; George E. Humiston, Tampa, Florida; Mark D. Jaeger, Special Collections, Purdue University Library, West Lafayette, Indiana; James Marten, History Department, Marquette University, Milwaukee, Wisconsin; Lorna D. Martinovich, references services manager, Glendale Public Library, Glendale, California; David B. Morgan, Rancho Cucamonga, California; Carolyn M. Picciano, History and Genealogy Unit, Connecticut State Library, Hartford; Tess Riesmeyer, curator of library collections, Litchfield Historical Society, Litchfield, Connecticut; Linda M. Ruel, Rumford, Rhode Island; Michael Russert, Cambridge, New York; and Martha H. Smart, reference assistant, Connecticut Historical Society, Hartford.

It has been a great pleasure to communicate with descendants (or their spouses) of Amos and Philinda Humiston: Darin T. Demagistris, Medford, Massachusetts; Sandra Humiston Hackett, Fulton, New York; Kristin Barr Hood, Old Orchard Beach, Maine; Amos F. Humiston, Orlando, Florida; Alice N. Humiston, Fulton, New York; and Deborah Mnich Humiston, Phoenix, New York.

Special thanks go to two of the Humiston descendants. More than anyone else, Amos and Philinda's great-grandson David Humiston Kelley of Calgary, Alberta, Canada, has preserved and documented the family history. The Humiston story could not have been told without his help. Since we were first in touch in 1990, David has provided me with a massive amount of material, offered steady encouragement, and given the manuscript a close reading. In 1997 he and his wife, Jane, and son, Dennis, welcomed me to their Calgary home, where I slept in a Humiston bed, inspected hundreds of Humiston letters, and looked at scores of Humiston photographs—all preserved by Dave since the closing of the old family

Acknowledgments

homestead in Jaffrey, New Hampshire. Thank you, David, for guiding me into your family's past.

Two serendipitous happenstances led me to another great-grandson of Amos and Philinda, who held the key to this book. At a dinner party given by our mutual friends Dan and Meg Warren of Providence, I met fellow Civil War historian Gardiner H. Shattuck, Jr., of Warwick, Rhode Island. Tuck informed me he was aware of the Humiston story; in fact he had known Amos and Philinda's granddaughter, Eleanor Humiston Cox, when he served as assistant minister at All Saints' Episcopal Church in Belmont, Massachusetts, in the late 1970s. When I phoned the Cox residence in Medford, I reached Allan L. Cox of Watertown, Massachusetts, who told me that his mother, Eleanor (the last surviving grandchild of Amos and Philinda), was in a nursing home, and that he just happened to be on one of his infrequent and brief visits to check on her house. Because of that fortuitous circumstance, I was able to have the pleasure of meeting Eleanor before she passed away, and to discover that the family had preserved Amos's wartime letters to Philinda. Allan very kindly shared the letters with me, and I knew at last I had the makings of a book. Since then, Allan, David, and I have been together on several occasions—in Jaffrey, in Gettysburg, in the Boston area—and I have enjoyed their company very much. In addition to fulfilling my longstanding dream of writing a book about the Humistons, I have had the pleasure of becoming a friend of the family.

My sincere appreciation to Heather R. Staines, history and military studies editor at Praeger, for her advocacy, enthusiasm, and sound advice for the book.

I would be remiss if I did not remember my late parents, Harold and Irene Dunkelman. The stories and artifacts my father passed on to me of his grandfather, Corporal John Langhans of the 154th New York, sparked my interest in the Civil War and led to a lifetime of study. He and my mother were always supportive of my early efforts in Civil War history, writing, and art, and I will always be grateful to them for letting me find my way, and helping me to do so.

Ultimately, the Humiston story is a tale of the love of a husband and father for his wife and children. To express my appreciation of the love and support of my wife, Annette, and son, Karl, as best I can, I dedicate this book to them.

Index

Index

Index

Index

About the Author

MARK H. DUNKELMAN has written and lectured extensively on the 154th New York Volunteer Infantry, Amos Humiston's regiment. He lives in Providence, Rhode Island, with his wife Annette and son Karl.